THE
TWELVE
TISSUE REMEDIES

OF

SHUSSLER

COMPRISING OF

THE THEORY,
THERAPEUTIC APPLICATION,
MATERIA MEDICA & A COMPLETE
REPERTORY OF TISSUE REMEDIES
(Homoeopathically and Bio-Chemically Considered)

By

BOERICKE & DEWEY

Sixth Edition

B. JAIN PUBLISHERS PVT. LTD.
NEW DELHI - 110 055

Reprint Edition: 2003

Price: Rs. 125.00

Published by Kuldeep Jain for

B. Jain Publishers (P) Ltd.

1921, Street No. 10, Chuna Mandi,
Paharganj, New Delhi 110 055 (INDIA)
Phones: 2358 3100, 2358 1300, 2358 0800, 2358 1100
Fax· 011-2358 0471; *Email:* bjain@vsnl.com
Website: www.bjainbooks.com, www.healthharmonybooks.com

Printed in India by
J.J. Offset Printers
522, FIE, Patpar Ganj, Delhi - 110 092

ISBN 81—7021—035—6
BOOK CODE B-2089

PREFACE.

THE steadily increasing demand for this work has exhausted four large editions and necessitated the preparation of a fifth edition. What was intended originally as a mere suggestive guide to the use of a set of valuable remedies has developed by the demands of the profession into a volume comprising the whole of our present therapeutic knowledge of the so-called Twelve Tissue Remedies.

Compilation largely from every available source has to supplement the authors' personal experience and knowledge of these remedies. All the published data have been made use of but thoroughly sifted and critically examined. In its present form, we believe this fifth edition will be found a reliable guide to the use of the Tissue Remedies in disease, not only as far as possible, according to the distinctive theory of Schüssler, as corrected and modified by him up to the time of his death, but especially according to the finer and more discriminating method of Hahnemann.

The clinical evidence of the truth of Schüssler's indications is overwhelming and since his time they have been largely confirmed by homœopathic and eclectic physicians, but the need of thorough systematic provings according to the method of Homœopathy in order to enlarge and precisionize our knowledge of these great medicines is imperative.

Many German editions of Schüssler's *"Abgekürzte Therapie"* have been published since the last edition of this work was issued, the therapeutic development of these remedies has made wonderful strides, and our periodical literature during the past few years has contained many records of cures wrought by them. All this has been incorporated and this work, in its present complete and revised form, is the only adequate presentation of the therapeutic possibilities of the Tissue Remedies existent.

We trust that the same consideration accorded to previous editions will be extended to this by an indulgent profession.

WILLIAM BOERICKE, M. D.,
San Francisco, Cal.
W. A. DEWEY, M. D.,
Ann Arbor, Mich.

July 1, 1914.

Table of Contents.

Preface to First Edition.

THE following treatise on the Twelve Tissue Remedies contains all that Schüssler himself wrote on the subject, and embodies as well the whole published experience of the homœopathic school in their use, besides much original matter from some of our homœopathic practitioners now published for the first time. Our aim has been to give to the profession a complete work on the subject, because we recognize the great value and importance of the Tissue Remedies, and in doing this our work necessarily was one mostly of compilation and arrangement. Every available source from the whole of our journalistic literature and Society proceedings has been made to pay tribute to us; and however imperfect, fragmentary and crude the present work is, we know that it is *complete,* so far as present circumstances will permit.

We believe that the only hope for the future development of these magnificent remedies lies in their study, mainly according to the method of Homœopathy; that they should all be as carefully proved as *Natrum mur.* and *Silicea* already are, and that the results of such provings alone furnish the most accurate indications for their therapeutic uses. Only by careful provings will the permanency of these remedies be secured, and they themselves be preserved from the possible fate of so many newly introduced remedies.

Thorough and systematic proving of drugs on the healthy is the one *true* method for the development of our Materia Medica; but this, from its very excellence, is a thing of slow growth, and the temptation could not be resisted to seek other and shorter methods, always more or less questionable, but sometimes yielding admirable results. The most important of such deviations from the strictly classical method of proving on the healthy was the acceptance of Clinical Symptoms; used cautiously, this source can be of inestimable value, as much of our clinical experience proves.

Why may not the same results follow, by accepting tentatively, and for the time, Schüssler's theories of the respective spheres of actions of his remedies and the indications based thereon, which, to say the least, are bold and often brilliant recommendations for their employment in disease?

Here, in the absence of regular provings of them, we can avail ourselves of this source and enrich our Materia Medica with some remedies that will compare favorably with many polychrests.

Whatever opposition there may be in our ranks to Schüssler's methods, because it is not pure homœopathic practice, we believe would speedily disappear if all critics could join in proving and confirming these valuable remedies, introduced first to American Homœopathy by our own Hering, who surely could not be accused of fathering and furthering anything absolutely mongrel and detrimental to the best interests of our school.

We do not sympathize with the attempt of Schüssler and a few others to look upon the Tissue Remedies as being sufficient for all purposes—provings alone can verify this. For the present, we think, with Dr. J. C. Morgan, that Schüssler throws away a great and necessary complement to his Materia Medica in discarding all organic drugs, as *Bellad., Hyos., Acon.,* etc., which really make the Tissue Remedies more valuable, acting as the opposite blade of the scissors; without these they would often remain incomplete in curative action and might be blamed for the inevitable. We, therefore, have included in our study of the Materia Medica the homœopathic relationship, at present merely suggestive, but a department which, we hope, will be greatly enlarged at some future time.

To those who, by kind encouragement and contributions of clinical cases and observations, have given us valuable assistance in the preparation of the present volume, we desire to express our gratitude and indebtedness, prominent among whom are Prof. Samuel Lilienthal, who kindly placed his valuable library at our disposal; Professors J. C. Morgan, S. Powell Burdick, C. B. Currier, Henry C. Houghton, Wm. E. Leonard, and Drs. Horace F. Ivins, C. E. Fisher, A. P. Davis, I. E. Nicholson, G. H. Martin, and many others whose names are mentioned throughout the work.

WILLIAM BOERICKE, M. D.
W. A. DEWEY, M. D.

San Francisco, Jan. 2, 1888.

Preface to Second Edition.

THE present edition has been thoroughly revised and enlarged by the addition of all the facts relating to the Tissue Remedies that have accumulated for the past two years. In its present state, the book represents the complete presentation of the Biochemical Treatment of Disease by means of the Twelve Tissue Remedies. In order not to increase unnecessarily the bulk of the volume, a number of the clinical cases of the previous edition have been omitted, to make room for new matter and fresh clinical illustrations by the best authorities. The Materia Medica part of the work has been brought up to date by the incorporation of the results of late provings, and we feel indebted especially to Dr. H. C. Allen, of the *Medical Advance*, Hering's *Guiding Symptoms*, and Prof. T. F. Allen's magnificent work, the *Handbook of Materia Medica*, which include much of interest about these remedies. These Tissue Remedies are too precious to be used only on the pathological indications laid down by Schüssler; they all merit careful proving in order to obtain the finer and more distinctive points for their therapeutic application; this has been done with several, and will undoubtedly be carefully done with all. Not until then will the Twelve Tissue Remedies take their rightful position permanently in our Materia Medica, and prove to be polychrests of the highest order.

We trust that this work, in its present revised form, will meet with as favorable reception as was accorded to the first edition.

WILLIAM BOERICKE, M. D.
W. A. DEWEY, M. D.

San Francisco, Jan. 2, 1890.

Preface to Third Edition.

THE generous reception and treatment accorded by the profession to the previous editions of this work rendered the preparation of a new edition a pleasant task. The whole work has practically been rewritten and considerably enlarged. Everything that Dr. Schüssler himself has written up to the publication of his latest, the eighteenth edition of his *"Abgekürzte Therapie"* is included, together with much clinical experience by the homœopathic profession, account of which is scattered throughout our journals and society transactions. The work is thus as complete as it can be at the present time regarding everything pertaining to the Biochemical treatment of disease and its relation to Homœopathy.

Our conception of the true place of the Tissue Remedies has separated us more and more with each new edition from that of their distinguished introducer. While we have abided by his first conception, and endeavor to further their development along the lines of Homœopathy, Schüssler prefers now to look upon the Biochemic method as entirely distinct from Homœopathy, and as an all-sufficient therapeutic procedure and chemical hygiene. Thus, while he relies solely on the chemico-physiological facts and theories as guides for the therapeutic application of his remedies, we, accepting and utilizing all these, add thereto the indications derived from provings—the only legitimate and permanent basis for drug selection in disease. On this account, Dr. Schüssler notwithstanding, we believe that careful provings of these remedies in all potencies should be made by our school. To some extent this has been done since the publication of our second edition, notably of *Kali phos.*, an excellent account of which has been published by Prof. H. C. Allen, M. D., in the *Medical Advance,* the salient features of which are included in our account of that remedy.

In conclusion we wish again to thank the friends who have so kindly and disinterestedly helped the preparation of the present volume by furnishing us with clinical material and observations.

WILLIAM BOERICKE, M. D.
WILLIS A. DEWEY, M. D.

San Francisco, Sept. 1, 1892.

37 - varicose veins — chief remedy calc fluor

38 - cracks in palms of hands — calc fluor

39 - cataracts - calc fluor

39 - tinnitus - calc fluor

40 - cracked appearance of tongue - calc fluor

42 - gouty enlargements of finger joints (spina ventosa) calc fluor

42 - cracking joints, inflammation of knee joint - calc fluor

45 - rapid child bearing - calc phos

46 - night sweats - calc phos

47 - cataracts

PART I.

Introduction to the Theory and General Sketch of the Twelve Tissue Remedies.

HISTORY OF THE TISSUE REMEDIES.

SAMUEL HAHNEMANN, whose genius divined the great importance of the inorganic cell salts as remedial agents of a high order, was the first who began thorough investigation into their pathogenetic effects and therapeutic uses. It was his provings of Lime and Salt and Potash and Silica that prepared the way for the rest of the Tissue Remedies, that showed what vast store-houses of medicinal force these inorganic substances are, although apparently inert in their crude state. He it was who first pointed out how these forces could be unlocked and directed for therapeutic purposes. Later, in 1832, attention was called in a paper published in Stapf's Archiv to the great importance as remedies of all the "essential component parts of the human body," and again, in the same journal, in 1846: "All constituents of the human body principally act on those organs wherein they have a function. All fulfill their functions when they are the cause of symptoms." This from the pen of that remarkable genius in the field of Materia Medica—Constantine Hering.

Later still, we find Grauvogl, in his *Text-Book,* taking some notice of these remarks and amplifying them; but it remained for Dr. Schüssler, of Oldenburg, Germany, to develop these suggestions and make the idea foreshadowed in them the basis of a "new system." In March, 1873, an article, entitled *"An Abridged Homœopathic Therapeutics,"* from his pen, was published in a German Homœopathic journal, in which he says:

"About a year ago I endeavored to discover by experiments on the sick if it were not possible to heal them, provided their diseases were curable at all, with those substances that are the natural, *i. e.,* the physiological function-remedies." Of this no special notice seems to have been taken, until, five months subsequently, Dr. Lorbacher, of Leipzig, came out in the same journal with some critical considerations of it. This was followed by a reply from Schüssler, which ran through seven numbers, giving a more detailed account of this "Abridged System of Homœopathic Therapeutics," the important features of which are incorporated in this work.

The original communication from Schüssler to the German medical journal was translated into English, and published first in the *Medical Investigator,* May, 1873, and soon afterwards in a small work, by Dr. C. Hering, entitled the "Twelve Tissue Remedies," "recommended for investigation" by this great teacher of our school. Several editions were published in rapid succession, from which this historical sketch is mainly derived, and following these appeared the translation of the twelfth German edition, by J. T. O'Connor, M. D., and one by M. Docetti Walker, considerably enlarged by the addition of an appendix popularizing the Biochemic Method. Dr. Schüssler, previous to his death, which occurred early in 1898, published the 25th German edition, in which the application of several of the remedies has been greatly enlarged and considerable new matter added, all of which is incorporated in this work. This edition has been translated into English.

Notwithstanding that Dr. Schüssler denies in the later editions of his work all connection with Homœopathy, and insists that his method is not based upon the homœopathic law of cure, but upon physiologico-chemical processes that take place within the organism, it is nevertheless true that the present wide adoption of the Tissue Remedies in the treatment of disease is the fruit of the seed sown on homœopathic ground as early as 1832, although its development was slow until Schüssler gave it a wonderful impetus by bringing physiological chemistry and physiological and pathological facts to bear on his therapeutic procedure.

THE THEORY OF SCHÜSSLER'S BIOCHEMIC METHOD.

The idea upon which Biochemic Therapeutics is based is the physiological fact that both the structure and vitality of the organs of the body are dependent upon certain necessary quantities and proper apportionment of its in organic constituents. These remain after combustion of the tissues and form the ashes.

The inorganic constituents are, in a very real sense, the material basis of the organs and tissues of the body, and are absolutely essential to their integrity of structure and functional activity. According to Schussler's theory, any disturbance in the molecular motion of these cell salts in living tissues, caused by a deficiency in the requisite amount, constitutes disease,* which can be rectified and the requisite equilibrium re-established by administering the same mineral salts in small quantities. This is supposed to be brought about by virtue of the operation of chemical affinity in the domain of histology; and hence this therapeutic procedure is styled by Schüssler the Biochemic method, and stress is laid on the fact that it is in supposed harmony with well-known facts and laws in physiological chemistry and allied sciences.

---

*Recent experiments, made by Prof. Loeb, seem to prove that the various tissue cells will rapidly disintegrate in the absence of the proper proportion of sodium, potassium and lime salts in the circulating fluid, the normal ratio being 100 molecules of sodium, 2.2 molecules of potassium and 1.5 molecules of lime. Any marked departure from this proportion is followed by a more or less rapid degeneration of protoplasm.

The maintenance of a stable metabolism within the cell is due to the presence of these salts in the proper ratio in the fluid, which surrounds the cell. It is thus a protective process. They maintain a sort of physiologic balance in the liquids surrounding the living cells and any upsetting of this proportional interrelation of the various salts may lead to physiologic disturbance and disease.

THE CONSTITUENTS OF THE HUMAN ORGANISM.

Blood consists of water, sugar, fat, albuminous substances, chloride of sodium, chloride of potash, fluoride of lime, silica, iron, lime, magnesia, soda and potash. The latter are combined with phosphoric, carbonic and sulphuric acids.

The salts of soda predominate in the blood plasma, while those of potash are found especially in the blood corpuscles. Sugar, fat, and the albuminous substances are the so-called organic components of the blood, while the above-named salts and water constitute its inorganic components. Sugar and fat are compounds of carbon, hydrogen and oxygen, while the albuminous substances contain in addition sulphur and nitrogen.

Sulphur, carbon and phosphorus are not present within the organism in a free state, but combined with organic substances.

Sulphur and carbon are found in the albumen, carbon in the carbo-hydrates like sugar, starch and in the products incident to metamorphosis of organic substances. Phosphorus is contained in the lecithins and in the nucleins. The sulphur of the albumen is oxidized by the oxygen of the inspired air, forming sulphuric acid which combines with the bases of the carbonates, forming sulphates and setting free carbonic acid.

TISSUE-BUILDING.

Blood, containing the material for every tissue and cell of the body, furnishes nutriment for every organ, enabling it to perform its individual function; thus it supplies every possible physiological want in the animal economy.

It does this by the transudation of a portion of its plasma into the surrounding tissues through the capillary walls, by which the losses sustained by the cells on account of tissue metamorphosis are made good. According to modern biological views, this pabulum is a material *sui generis,* called irritable matter or protoplasm, and is the only living matter, and is universally diffused throughout the organism, of which it constitutes about one-fifth, the remaining four-fifths being organized and relatively, therefore, dead matter. In its physical character it is nitrogenous, pulpy, structureless, semi-fluid, translucent, homogeneous, similar to that of the ganglionic nerves and to the gray, nervous matter. In this transuded fluid appear fine granules, which unite to form germs, from which, again, cells develop. By the union of these cells are formed the tissues of every kind needed for the upbuilding of the whole organism. Two kinds of substances are needed in this process of tissue-building, and both are found in the blood—namely, the organic and the inorganic constituents. Among the former organic constituents are the sugar, fat and albuminous substances of the blood, serving as the physical basis of the tissues, while the water and salts—namely, potash, lime, silica, iron, magnesium and sodium—are the inorganic substances, which are believed to determine the particular kind of cell to be built up. Other salts may from time to time be found, but the foregoing, however, embrace all which are constantly present. Wherever, then, in the animal organism, new cells are to be generated and formed, there must be present, in sufficient quantity and proper relation, both these organic and inorganic substances. By their presence in the blood, all the organs, viscera and tissues in the body are formed, fixed and made permanent in their functions, and a disturbance here causes disturbed function.

INORGANIC CONSTITUENTS OF CELLS.

The principal inorganic materials of **nerve-cells** are Magnesia phos., Kali phos., Natrum and Ferrum. **Muscle-cells** contain the same, with the addition of Kali mur. **Connective tissue-cells** have for their specific substance Silica, while that of the **elastic tissue-cells** is probably Calcarea fluor. In **bone-cells** we have Calcarea fluor. and Magnesia phos. and a large proportion of Calcarea phos. This latter is found in small quantities in the cells of **muscle, nerve, brain and connective** tissue. **Cartilage** and **mucous cells** have for their specific inorganic material Natrum mur., which is found also in all solid and fluid parts of the body. **Hair** and the **crystalline lens** contain, among other inorganic substances, also Ferrum. The carbonates, *as such,* are, according to Moleschott, without any influence in the process of cell-formation.

FORMATION OF TISSUE CELLS.

The oxygen of the air, upon reaching the tissues through the blood by means of the respiration acts upon the organic substances which are to enter in the formation of new cells. The products of this transformation are the organic materials which form the physical basis of muscle, nerve, connective tissue and mucous substance. None of these substances are present as such in the blood, but are formed within the tissues from the albumen. With them, the inorganic salts form combinations by virtue of chemical affinities, and thus new cells are formed. With the formation of new cells there occurs at the same time a destruction of the old ones, resulting from the action of oxygen on the organic substances forming the basis of these cells. This oxidation has, as a consequence, a breaking down of the cells themselves.

The ultimate results of this combustion of the organic substances are the formation of urea, uric, sulphuric, phosphoric, lactic and carbonic acids, and also water. Some intermediate members of the series, as, for instance, hypoxanthin, acetic and butyric acids, etc., need not be mentioned with this therapeutic method, because, so far as our present knowledge of them extends, they play a very subordinate role. Urea, uric acid and sulphuric acid are the result of the oxidation of the albuminous substances, while phosphoric acid is produced by the oxidation of lecithin contained in the nervous tissue, brain, spinal cord and blood corpuscles. Lactic acid results from the fermentation of milk-sugar, and finally breaks down into carbonic acid and water.

The final products of the oxidation of the organic substances are urea, carbonic acid and water. These, together with the salts set free, leave the tissues, and thereby give place to less fully oxidized organic bodies, which in turn finally undergo the same metamorphosis.

The products of this retrograde tissue change are conveyed through the lymphatics, the connective tissue and the veins, to the gall-bladder, lungs, kidneys, bladder and skin, and are thereby removed from the organism with the excretions, such as the urine, perspiration, fæces, etc.

The importance and dignity of the function of the connective tissue was established after the researches of Virchow and Von Recklinghausen led to a closer study and demonstrated its fertile activity. That which formerly seemed only intended as a filling in or protective covering appears now as the matrix, in which the minute capillaries carry the plasma from the blood to the tissues and return the same to the blood vessels; at the same time it serves as one of the most important breeding places of young cells, which are capable of developing out of the embryonic latent forms to the most differentiated structure of the body.

HEALTH AND DISEASE.

Health may be considered to be the state characterized by normal cell metamorphosis; thus, when by means of digestion of food and drink, recompense is made to the blood for the losses it sustains by furnishing nutritive material to the tissues, this compensation is made in requisite quantities and in proper places, and no disturbance of the motion of the molecules occurs. Under these conditions alone will the building of new cells and the destruction of old ones proceed normally, and the elimination of useless materials be furthered.

Disease is the result of a disturbance of the molecular motion of one of the inorganic tissue salts. The cure consists in the restoration of the equilibrium of the molecular motion by furnishing a minimal dose of the same inorganic substance, since the molecules of the material thus used remedially fill

2

the gap in the chain of molecules of the affected cell or tissue salt.

Virchow says that disease is an altered state of the cell, and hence the normal state of the cell constitutes health. The constitution of the cell is determined by the composition of its nutritive environment exactly as a plant thrives according to the quality of soil around its roots.

In agricultural chemistry we add as fertilizer that element most lacking in the soil. But three essential substances used as fertilizers are required, namely, ammonia, phosphate of lime or potash. The other substances needful for plant nutrition are found in sufficient quantities in the soil. The same law of supplying a lack applies to biochemical remedies; for instance, take the following example:

A child suffering with rickets shows a lack of phosphate of lime in the bones due to a disturbed molecular motion of the molecules of this salt. The quantity of phosphate of lime intended for the bones, but failing to reach its goal, would accumulate within the blood were it not excreted by the urine, for it is the office of the kidneys to maintain the proper composition of the blood, and, therefore, to cast out every foreign substance or surplus supply of any one constituent. Now after the normal molecular motion of the phosphate of lime molecules is again established within the involved nutritive soil by administering small doses of the same salt, the surplus can again enter the general circulation and the cure of the rachitis be brought about.

Every normal cell has the faculty of absorbing or rejecting certain substances. This property is diminished or suspended when the cell has suffered a loss in one of its salts in consequence of any irritation. As soon as this deficiency is made good by a supply of a homogeneous material from the immediate nutritive soil, the equilibrium is re-established. But if the supply is not offered spontaneously, it is to be assumed that the needful salt is lacking in quantity, or, on the other hand, that the diseased cells have suffered a physical alteration besides, which precludes the entrance of the required tissue salt. In such a case the salt must be offered in a more diluted state, that is, a higher trituration or attenuation.

If the altered cells regain their integrity by recovering their loss, they can again perform their normal functions, and bring about the removal by chemical processes of morbid products, exudations, etc. The biochemical therapeutics aids nature in her efforts to cure by supplying the natural remedies lacking in certain parts, that is, the inorganic cell-salts, and in this way corrects abnormal states of physiological chemistry.

The aim of biochemistry is to cover a deficiency directly. All other methods of cure reach this goal indirectly, when they make use of remedial agents heterogeneous to the constituents of the human organism.

DOSE, OR QUANTITY OF TISSUE SALT RE-QUIRED TO RE-ESTABLISH NORMAL CELL EQUILIBRIUM.

Biochemic remedies are administered in minimal doses corresponding in minuteness to the cellular salts in the tissues.

The curative virtue of small doses may be deduced from the following facts:

Throughout nature, atoms and groups of atoms or molecules form the basis of her operations. The growth of animals and plants is the accretion of new atoms or groups of atoms to the existing mass of molecules.

In view of the fact of the action of light, itself imponderable, causing molecule movements in living plants by which carbonic acid is decomposed into carbon and oxygen, and again the action of light on the photographic plate and retina of the eye, it seems impossible of contradiction that infinitely small imponderable particles of matter can act upon the living body. The use of small doses in biochemical treatment is a chemico-physiological necessity. For instance, it is desired to have Glauber's salt reach the blood. It cannot be done by giving it in a concentrated solution. Only the intestinal canal is affected thereby, producing a watery diarrhœa in which the salt is cast out from the organism. But a diluted solution of this salt (Natrum sulph.) will enter the blood and intercellular fluids from the mouth and œsophagus; and by virtue of its hygrometric property will induce passage of an excess of water in the tissues into the venous blood, and an increase of urinary secretion.

Every biochemic remedy must be sufficiently diluted to avoid destroying the function of healthy cells, and to restore disturbed function wherever present.

In the healthy organism, animal or vegetable, the salts are found in solution, corresponding to the third, fourth and fifth decimal dilution of medicines.

The following table of analysis of blood cells in relation to the human organism will show this:

In 1,000 grammes of blood cells the amount of inorganic substances are, according to Bunge's "Text-book of Physiological and Pathological Chemistry," as follows:

Iron	0.998
Kali sulph.	0.132
Kali mur.	3.079
Kali phos.	2.343
Natrum phos.	0.633
Natrum	0.344
Calc. phos.	0.094
Magnes. phos.	0.060

In 1,000 grammes of intercellular fluid (plasma) the proportion of inorganic substances is the following:

Kali sulph.	0.281
Kali mur.	0.359
Natrum mur.	5.545
Natrum phos.	0.271
Natrum	1.532
Calcar. phos.	0.298
Magnes. phos.	0.218
Natrum sulph., Fluor., and Silica, traces.	

Compare with these analyses that of milk. Of this 1 litre or 1,000 grammes, contains

Kali 0.780
Natrum 0.230
Calcarea 0.330
Magnesia 0.060
Iron 0.004
Phosphoric acid 0.470
Chlor. 0.440
Fluor., and Silica, traces.

One litre (a little over a quart) suffices for the daily food of an infant weighing about 6 kilogrammes (13¼ pounds).

Now if 6 centigrammes (3.5 of a grain) of magnesia are sufficient to cover the needful daily supply of magnesia for an infant, how minute must be the dose of magnesia to be given for a neuralgia which is caused by an inconceivably small deficiency of this salt in a minute portion of the nerve tissue.

The mineral contents of one cell are infinitely small. According to the calculations of C. Schmidt, the physiologist, each blood corpuscle contains about one-billionth part of a gramme of Kali mur. This corresponds to the twelfth decimal trituration.

Similarly active in very small doses are some of the remedies used by the old school; for instance, corrosive sublimate, of which Prof. Hugo Schulz says that a solution of 1-600,000 to 1-800,000 brings about quite powerful fermentation, one far above the normal, in a grape sugar solution to which yeast has been added. (See *Berliner Klinische Wochenschrift*, Nov. 4, 1889.)

The inorganic substances which serve plants for nutrition are taken up by them only in minimal quantities. Liebig, in his chemical letters, observes that the strongest manure of earthy phosphates in a coarse powder cannot be compared in its action with a much smaller quantity finely divided, which by its sub-division can be diffused throughout the soil. Each rootlet requires but a small quantity of nourishment where it is in contact with the soil, but for its functional activity and existence it is requisite that this minimum be present just at that spot. The insoluble mineral substances found in the soil must be dissolved by the acid juices of the fibres of the root before they can reach the vegetable organism.

A mineral, when it reaches the human stomach, is acted upon by the muriatic acid contained in the gastric juice. If this is a salt of iron, the chloride will be formed. Now if it is desirable to administer the phosphate of iron for therapeutic purposes, it must be kept out of the stomach. For this purpose a minimal dose is required—the medicine must be diluted to such a degree that its molecules may penetrate the epithelium of the mouth, pharynx, œsophagus and reach the blood through the capillary walls. Those substances that are insoluble in water must be triturated to the sixth decimal potency at least; those soluble in water may penetrate the epithelial cells in lower dilutions.

In some of the mineral waters, the mineral salts are present only *in quantities corresponding to* the 6th and 8th decimal dilutions; thus in the waters of Rilchingen Magnesia phosph. is present only in the 8th, Kali mur. in the 5th and Silica in the 6th dilution.

Dr. Behneke, in his balneological letters, correctly observes that the relative proportion and the degree of concentration in which the salt is present in the mineral water is of great importance. Many of the most famous springs owe their good results to the fact that the curative constituents are present only in greatly diluted states, and that the best results are frequently obtained from doses usually considered very minute.

The adaptability of minimal doses to the end in view is in entire harmony with physiological and chemical facts, as may be seen from the following words of Professor Valentine, the well-known physiologist:

"Nature works everywhere with an infinite number of small magnitudes, which, whether in homogeneous or heterogeneous aggregations, can only be perceived by our relatively obtuse organs of sense when in definite masses. The smallest picture which our eyes perceive proceeds from millions of waves of light; a granule of salt that we are hardly able to taste contains myriads of groups of atoms which no sentient eye will ever view."

This fact is also illustrated by the well-known experiments

of Professors Kirchoff and Bunsen with common salt by taking three milligrammes (less than 1/20 of a grain), which are blown into a room containing 60 cubic metres of air. In a few minutes sodium lines appear in a flame standing at a considerable distance, which can be distinguished by the unaided eye.

Modern science gives numerous illustrations of the power of infinitesimal quantities. We will refer only to very few: one is by that most excellent observer, Darwin. In his work on *Insectivorous Plants* he says: "It is an astonishing fact * * * * that so inconceivably minute a quantity as 1-20,-000,000 of a grain' [a much smaller quantity than the 6th decimal trituration, the usually prescribed strength of the Tissue Remedies] of ammonia phosphate should induce changes in a gland, sufficient to cause a motor impulse to be sent down the whole length of the tentacle, this impulse exciting movements through an angle of about 180°."

Now, although the presence of common salt can be perceived by the nerves of taste, even if the crude salt touch the peripheral ends of these nerves, still in such a crude and undiluted form it is questionable whether the salt can enter and be taken up by the ducts of the neurilemma. For this purpose it seems much more reasonable to suppose that the degree of attenuation attained by the triturations is more appropriate to meet the want of the required molecules of salts.

Atropin, even when diluted more than a million-fold, produces, according to Reuter, dilatation of the pupil in man and the lower warm-blooded animals.

A litre (a little more than a quart) of milk contains about four milligrammes of iron, and a child nourished upon milk only receives therewith less than one milligramme or 1/65 of a grain of iron at a dose. If four milligrammes represent the daily supply of iron contributed to the nourishment and growth of the child (for it is distributed to all the iron-bearing cells of the organism), how small should be the dose, therapeutically considered, of a salt of iron given to allay a molecular disturbance occurring in a small cell territory, such a disturbance, for instance, as determines the hyperæmia of irritation?

The amount of fluorine contained in milk has, as yet, not been quantitatively determined; the amount of it in the organism is much less than that of iron. It may be assumed that the amount of fluorine contained in milk is represented by a tenth of a milligramme; therefore, one milligramme of calcium fluoride, *pro dosi,* if prescribed as a remedy, would be a large dose.

The evolution from the crystalline inorganic to the cellular organic appears to be accomplished by means of refinement of particles and increase of vibratory activity [Hermann Hille, Ph. D.]. Do not the pharmaceutical procedures of Homœopathy do this very thing?

The dose of a remedy prescribed according to chemical therapeutics had better be too small than too large; for if too small a repetition of it will attain the desired end, but if too large it will fail to accomplish the purpose in view.

Large doses of iron, given to cure chlorosis, disorder the stomach, pass off unused with the fæces, and in most cases leave the disease unaffected.

Hydrochloric acid, when diluted a thousand-fold with water, dissolves with ease at the temperature of the body fibrin and gluten, and this solvent powder does not increase, but diminishes, if the proportion of acid in the dilution be increased.—(*Liebig's Chemical Letters.*)

PREPARATION AND DOSE.

The Tissue Remedies are prepared for therapeutic purposes, like all homœopathic remedies, according to the decimal or centesimal scale in trituration or dilution. The crude, chemically pure article is taken and triturated with sugar of milk, one part of the drug to nine parts of sugar of milk, for at least two hours. This gives the first decimal trituration, each grain containing one-tenth of a grain of the cell salt triturated.

One part of this first decimal trituration is then used, and other nine parts of sugar of milk added and again triturated two hours, which gives the second decimal trituration, and is equivalent to the first centesimal trituration, each grain containing one-hundredth of the triturated cell salt. But experience has shown, as may be seen, too, from the illustrations above that even this minute subdivision is too gross for many purposes in the animal economy, and so this triturating and subdividing process has been kept up to the sixth, twelfth and even higher preparations.

SCHÜSSLER'S OWN PROCEDURE.

At first Schüssler began with the sixth centesimal or twelfth decimal trituration; but he, very early in his practice, adopted the sixth decimal preparation as the one most generally useful. Lately the lower triturations of Potassium and Sodium salts, the third decimal, of others the fourth and fifth, have been productive of equally good results. In the last edition of his *"Abgekürzte Therapie"* he says on this point: "In my practice I employ the sixth decimal trituration generally. *Ferrum phos., Silicea* and *Calcarea fluor.* I usually give in the 12th trituration. In acute diseases, a dose consisting of a powder, size of a pea, should be given every hour or two; in chronic diseases 3 or 4 times daily. The powder may be given dry on the tongue, or dissolved in a spoonful of water."

We, ourselves, have had the most satisfactory results from the sixth decimal trituration, rarely going higher, at times lower, and generally we prefer to give the selected remedy in solution by dissolving a good-sized powder in a tumbler, half full of water, and administering teaspoonful doses every hour or two.

These triturations may be moulded into tablets usually of one grain each; the dose being two or three taken dry on tongue or dissolved in water.

If liquid solutions are used, a few drops may be dissolved in water, or pellets or disks may be saturated and given in that way. The latter is especially to be recommended with children.

FREQUENCY OF DOSES.

In acute cases, a dose every hour or two; in severe, painful affections, a dose every ten to fifteen minutes; in chronic affections, one to four doses daily.

In suitable cases the external use of the remedies is indicated and has been found useful. For this purpose the lower triturations may be used.

In determining the dose of a biochemic remedy, the *amount* of the morbid product involved is no important factor. For instance, a very small deficiency of *Natrum mur.* in the cells of the epithelial layer of a serous sac may give rise to a massive serous exudation; and as minute a supply of *Natrum mur.* corresponding to the deficiency may bring about a complete resorption of the exudation.

Guided by the relative quantities of the cell salts, each practitioner can select the proper dose of the indicated biochemic remedy.

One milligramme (1-100 grain = to the 2d decimal trituration) of a substance is estimated to contain 16 trillions of molecules. According to this estimate, the 6th decimal trituration of it would contain about 16 billions; this quantity is more than sufficient to restore disturbed molecular motions to the normal.

It may be urged as an objection that the molecules of a given salt administered as a medicine would unite with their like contained in the blood, and thus render illusory any curative attempt. But this combination cannot take place simply because the carbonic acid present in the blood forms an isolating medium of the salts.

RELATION OF THE BIOCHEMIC TO THE HOMŒOPATHIC TREATMENT.

Often the question has been asked, "Is Schüsslerism Homœopathy?" and it has as often been answered in the affirmative as in the negative. Schüssler himself claimed that it is not in any way related to Homœopathy, claiming for it a separate system of therapeutics.

He claims with others that the Tissue Remedies act by supplying deficiencies. This idea, taken literally, seems erroneous; for example, in a disturbance of the molecules of *Natr. mur.* there is not necessarily a **deficiency** in the amount of *Natr. mur.* in the body, but rather a lack of continuity in the arrangement of the existing molecules in the body. This salt given as a remedy does not supply a lack or deficiency of salt, as the quantity given is usually too infinitesimal for the purpose, and were this the case it might be given in quantity with food and drink with the desired effect. The deficiency that it **does** supply in minimal doses is in the arrangement of the equilibrium of the chain of *Natr. mur.* molecules in the affected tissues as before explained, thus causing them to perform their function properly; for, since the deficit is a molecular one, the supply must also be molecular.

This idea of the action of remedies is not new, as any one who has carefully perused the works of that astute observer, Von Grauvogl, can testify. Many of Schüssler's ideas are foreshadowed in Grauvogl and Hering.

It has always been a matter of dispute as to how our homœopathic remedies act. The question, embracing as it does that of infinitesimal doses, is one of the most interesting for Homœopathy and therapeutics generally.

The following table shows, so far as analyses have been made, that the twelve tissue salts are constituents of many of our well known and proved remedies of the vegetable kingdom:

TABLE.

Ferr. phos.	China, Gelsem., Veratr., Acon., Arnica, Anis. stel., Phytol., Berb. vulg., Rhus, Asaf. (4), Viburn. pr., Secale (.25), Graphites (2.74), Rumex, Ailanthus.
Calc. phos.	China, Viburn. pr., Ail., Phytol., Berb. vulg., Coloc. (27). Graphites.
Natr. phos.	Rheum, Ail., Anis. stel., Hamam.
Kali phos.	Pulsat., Bapt., Rhus, Veratr., Epiphegus, Viburn. pr., Digit., Cimicif., Cactus gr., Stramon., Xanth., Ail., Anis. stel., Hamam., Phytol., Cactus.

Kali mur.	Phytol., Sanguin., Stilling., Pinus c., Asclep., Viburn. pr., Ail., Anis. stel., Hamam., Cimicif.
Natr. mur.	Cedron, Arum tr., Ail., Anis. stel., Hamam., Cimicif., Secale (.50).
Calc. fluor.	Phytol.
Silicea.	Equisetum (nearly 18.2), Cimicif. (4.), Chelidon., Graphites (13.), Secale (15), Lycopodium.
Calc. sulph.	Apocyn., Ail., Asaf. (6.2).
Natr. sulph.	Apocyn., Iris v., Chamom., Chionanthus, Lycop., Bryon., Podoph., Chelid., Nux vom., Anis. stel., Hamam., Cimicif.
Kali sulph.	Pulsat., Hydrast., Myr. cer., Cimicif., Phytol., Viburn. pr., Anis. stel., Hamam.
Magnes. phos.	Viburn. op., Bellad., Lobel., Stramon., Viburn. pr., Ail., Secale (.50), Coloc. (3), Gelsem., Rhus, Graphites.
Natrum mur.	Arum triphyllum.

The figures in the above table indicate the percentage.

This table is a very incomplete one, as analyses have only been made of comparatively few of the remedies of the animal and vegetable kingdoms that we use; and many of these analyses have been made so crudely as only to note the presence of these salts in them, not giving their proportions. To do this accurately would entail much time and expense. Of course, this, to the allopath, is a question of no moment whatever; but to us, as homœopaths, who deal with infinitesimals, such an enormous quantity as 18.2 per cent. of *Silicea* occurring in *Equisetum;* 6 per cent. of potash and sodium salts occurring in *Hamam.;* 4 per cent. of *Silicea* in *Cimicif.;* 3 per cent. of *Magnes. phos.* in *Coloc.,* as well as other inorganic constituents in varying quantities, becomes a matter of vital importance. Could we have an *exact* quantitative and proportionate analysis of any one drug from the animal or vegetable kingdom, we could then dissect its symptoms and tell which belonged to one tissue salt and which to another; and it is highly probable that we, by this means, could easily explain why the symptoms of one drug are so often found under the pathogenesis of another, why one is characteristic in one drug and only generic in another, when, indeed, it may not rightly belong to either, but to an inorganic tissue salt, a constituent of each drug.

Perhaps the drug of which as complete an analysis has been made as of any is *Phytolacca decandra*. After evaporation and incineration, which remove the organic constituents, there remain 8.4 per cent. of the inorganic; of these, 6.8 per cent. are soluble and consist mostly of the salts of potash, while the insoluble remainder, 1.6 per cent., consists of calcium, iron and silica. If we compare the pathogenesis of *Phytol.* with the biochemical application of these salts, we shall see a striking and significant analogy. As the largest quantity of the inorganic salts therein contained is potash, we shall find that more symptoms of *Phytol.* correspond to the *Kalis,* while fewer symptoms correspond to the calcium, iron and silica. The following table illustrates this:

Kali Mur.	Kali Phos.	Kali Sulph.	Calc. Phos.	Calc. Fluor.	Calc. Sulph.	Ferr. Phos.	Silicea
Eustachian tubes obstructed. Watery discharge from the nostrils. Ulcers in the mouth, on tonsils and in throat. Mucus hawked up with difficulty. Diphtheria. Sick-headache. Catarrhal ophthalmia. Stuffy cold in head. Small ulcers in mouth. Inflamed gums. Loss of appetite. Vomiting of clotted blood. Diarrhœa. Bleeding Piles. Constipation. Red deposits in urine, gonorrhœa and gleet. Syphilis, chancres, ulcers. Hard lumps in breast. Gathered breasts. Hoarseness; aphonia. Sputa thick and tough. Finger-joints swollen. Rheumatism worse by motion. Ulcers on legs. Glands swollen and inflamed. Sycosis. Scarlatina with angina.	Irritability. Fearfulness. Melancholic. Gloomy. Urgent desire to urinate. Cancrum oris. Early and profuse menstruation. Vertigo. Face hippocratic. Pains in cancer. Great exhaustion and prostration. Sciatica. Feels tired on awaking. Fœtid, ichorous pus.	Yellow coating on tongue. Cough worse at night. Suffocative feeling. Rheumatic pains shift about. Syphilis. Hoarseness worse toward evening. Chronic rheumatism of joints.	Glands inflamed and swollen. Pains worse at night. Retarded dentition.	Knots, kernels and hardened glands in the female breasts. Fissure of rectum, aching in the lumbar region. Nodes on the legs.	Hastens suppuration. Tinea capitis. Gathered breasts. Boils.	Bones inflamed. Feeling of sand in eyes. Burning sensation. Vomiting of blood and slime. Pain through sternum with cough.	Hastens suppuration. Sweat of toes. Periosteal pains. Ulcers.

Were the analysis quantitatively correct, we should probably find some *Natr. mur.*, as one of the prominent symptoms of *Phytol.* is acrid, watery discharge from the nose, just as it is more than likely that the well known characteristic nasal symptom of *Arum triphyllum*—the acrid, excoriating discharge—may be due to the large amount of *Natrum mur.* this plant contains.

This would explain why we have different sets of symptoms under one homœopathic drug, appearing to antagonize each other—each is produced by a different tissue salt.

This much for the vegetable and animal kingdom, substances that can be reduced by analysis to elementary bodies. In the mineral kingdom the action is somewhat different. Nothing need be said of such remedies as are compounds of sulphur and phosphorus, as they derive their medicinal power by combinations which form tissue salts. The carbonates become transformed into the phosphates; this disposes of such drugs as *Kali carb., Calc. carb., Magnes. carb.,* etc.

There only remain the minerals, such as *Aurum, Platinum, Argentum,* etc. These in a crude state are acknowledged inert, and we triturate them to develop their power. In the crude state they do not appear to be materially changed by any of the organic acids of the body. When we finally divide these they still remain the same, but a new power has been developed in them, a *catalytic* power.

Examples of *catalytic* power are, unfortunately, very few. Of the known ones is the following:

Platinum in mass produces no change—no combination of oxygen and hydrogen—as it will do, as chemistry teaches us, when it is finely divided, without being changed itself.

This is *catalysis,* wherein one body produces changes in another without itself being changed. The wherefore of this action is not known, but it still remains a fact. Catalysis is *contact action,* and by this contact action, mineral drugs act inert in the crude state, by trituration a *contact* action is developed, which causes changes, and when given to the healthy produces *symptoms*.

This rationally explains how inert substances acquire by subdivision (trituration) medicinal properties. This has long been a stumbling-block to many in studying Homœopathy.

Do we not when we *prove a drug*—that is, administer it to the healthy to produce symptoms—and nearly all our homœopathic provings are made, more or less, with the potentized drug, which process also potentizes the inorganic salts therein contained—do we not produce a disturbance in the molecular equilibrium of the tissue salts contained in the drug given? For example: When we give *Phytol.* to prove it, do we not, by virtue of 6.8 per cent. of potash salts it contains, cause a molecular disturbance of these salts, which would not occur were they given in so crude a form as not to be taken up by the ducts of the neurilemma of the nerves of taste, etc.?

This disturbance is only to be corrected when arising from disease by giving *Phytol.* in potency, the potash salts in it being the part which gives it its curative power.

This view by no means takes away the fact that each drug is an entity, to be proved as a whole.

But these very salts in certain proportions are its essential substratum, whose presence is necessary to fix, determine and embody the inner essence of the drug; and it is a question to be decided whether we could obtain the same results by giving the inorganic salt constituents of a drug as by giving the drug itself. It seems to us, were it possible, that the former would be a more elementary Homœopathy, and this an indirect Biochemistry.

But the salts in plants may have acquired vital properties that their corresponding salts in the mineral kingdom do not possess. They are prepared by and in organization, and may thus act peculiarly on animal organization. This thought was suggested by the brilliant Dr. J. J. Garth Wilkinson in a letter to the authors, and he mentioned his use of Silica prepared from the large bamboos in India that seemed especially serviceable in acute rather than in chronic cases.

Schussler, in several of his editions, admits this and says that disturbed molecular motion of inorganic cell salts showing itself as disease is rectified by Biochemistry *directly* by the administration of *homogeneous* substances, whereas it is rectified by Homœopathy *indirectly* by the administration of *heterogeneous* substances.

PART II.

Materia Medica of the Twelve Tissue Remedies.

CALCAREA FLUORICA.

Synonyms.—Calcii Fluoridum. Calcium Fluoride. Calcarea Fluorata.

Common Name.—Fluorspar. Fluoride of Lime.

Chemical Properties.—Formula, $Ca\ F_2$. Specific gravity of crystals, 3.4. It contains 58.21 parts of calcium. It occurs in nature in mineral fluorspar; it is beautifully crystalline, crystallizing in various colors and in cubical or octahedral form. It is practically insoluble in water, but is decomposed by sulphuric acid generating hydrofluoric acid.

Preparation.—Selected pieces of crystal fluorspar are prepared by trituration, according to the methods of homœopathic pharmacy.

Physiologico-chemical Data.—*Calc. fluor.* is found in the surface of the bones and in the enamel of the teeth. It is also a constituent of the elastic fibres and of epidermis. Elastic fibres are found in the skin, in the connective tissue, and in the vascular walls.

A disturbance of the equilibrium of the molecules of *Calc. fluor.* causes a continued dilatation, or chronically relaxed condition, of the implicated fibres. If the elastic fibres of any portion of the vessels of the connective tissue or of the lymphatic system have arrived at such a condition of relaxation, the absorption of a solid exudation in such a part cannot take place. In consequence, induration of the parts sets in. When the elastic fibres of the blood vessels suffer a disturbance of the molecules of *Calc. fluor.*, such pathological enlargements of blood vessels take place, which make their appearance as hæmorrhoidal tumors, varicose and enlarged veins and vascular tumors, indurated glands, post-partum hæmorrhage, uterine displacements and weakening of abdominal walls.

Loss of *Calcarea fluorica* in the system is thus seen to be followed by:

1. A hard, knotty exudation on the surface of a bone.

2. A relaxation of the elastic fibres, hence dilatation of vessels, relaxation and displacements of the uterus, relaxation of the abdominal walls, hence "hanging belly," hæmorrhage of womb; all absence of after-pains.

3. Exudation of Keratin from the cells of the epidermis. (Keratin is contained in the skin, hair and nails.) The exudation dries readily and forms an adhering crust. Frequently found in the palms of the hands, which, through labor, form fissures and cracks.

In regard to the resorption of induration, two possibilities are to be thought of:

(*a*) The elastic fibres near the induration have lost their functional ability on account of the pressure exerted. Molecules of *Calcarea fluor.* administered restore their functional integrity and thus are enabled to throw off the exudation, which will then be absorbed by the lymphatic vessels.

(*b*) By means of the volumetric force of Carbonic acid contained in the blood a part of the Fluorine is split off the fluoride of lime, this combines with nascent Hydrogen, forming Hydrofluoric acid, which gradually dissolves the molecules of the morbid product, and these are taken up by the lymphatics. The part played by the Carbonic acid can be assumed by Sulphuric acid as well. The latter is formed during the oxidation of albuminoids.

In a similar manner, as explained under *b*, it is possible for *Calcarea fluor.* to bring about solution of a laryngeal croupous or diphtheritic exudation.

General Biochemical Action.—Diseases having their seat in the substance forming the surface of bone, enamel of the teeth, and part of all elastic fibres, whether of the skin, the connective tissues, or the walls of the blood vessels, etc. Thus: all ailments which can be traced to relaxed conditions of any of the elastic fibres, including dilatation of the blood vessels, arterial and venous blood-tumors and piles, varicose and enlarged veins, indurated glands of stony hardness. Malnutrition of bones, especially of the teeth. Exostosis after injuries. Pendulous abdomen. Uterine displacements, etc. Indurations.

Guiding Symptoms and Characteristic Indications.

Mental Symptoms.—Great depression, groundless fears of financial ruin. Indecision. Disposition to set a higher value on money than natural to him.

Head and Scalp.—Blood-tumors on the parietal bones of newborn infants, on a rough, bony base. Bruises of the bones of the scalp, with hard, rough, uneven lumps. Hard excrescences on the scalp. Cephal-hæmatoma. Ulcers of the scalp with callous, hard edges. Headache with faintish nausea in afternoon, better in the evening. In a proving by Dr. Sarah N. Smith the following symptom was quite constant: "A sort of creaking, straining and drawing, similar to the noise made by a cornstalk fiddle and greatly interfering with sleep."

Eyes.—Flickering and sparks before the eyes, spots on the cornea, conjunctivitis, styes. Blurred vision after using eyes, eyeballs ache, better closing eyes and pressing lightly. **Cataract.** Enlarged meibomian glands. Cases of partial blindness. Dimness of vision from overstraining the eyes. Tumors of the eyelids. Ulceration of cornea, if edges are hard.

Ears.—Calcareous deposits on the tympani, tinnitus. Mastoid disease when periosteum is affected.

Nose.—Cold in the head, ineffectual desire to sneeze, stuffy cold, dry, coryza, ozæna. Copious, offensive, thick, greenish, lumpy, yellow nasal discharge. Osseous growths. Affections of nasal bones; odor of dead bone disappears after use of the remedy. Adenoid growths in post-nasal space and pharynx. Hypertrophy of Luschka's tonsil and accompanying hypertrophies of mucous membrane in posterior portions of nares, so often found in infancy and childhood.

Face.—Hard swelling on the cheek with pain or toothache, hard swelling on the jawbone, cold sores rather small, hard herpetic sores on lips from cold, not diffused like *Natr. mur.* Caries of malar bone and fangs of teeth, oozing dark, offensive, bloody fluid, swelling of bone on outer surface.

Mouth.—Gumboil with hard swelling on the jaw, stony hard swelling on the jawbone. Cold sores at corners of mouth. Great dryness of mouth. Ulceration of mouth and throat manifesting congenital hereditary syphilis.

Tongue.—Cracked appearance of the tongue with or without pain. Induration of the tongue, hardening after inflammation.

Teeth.—Delayed dentition. Enamel of the teeth rough and deficient. Unnatural looseness of the teeth with or without pain, teeth become loose in their sockets. Malnutrition of the teeth. Toothache with pain if any food touches the tooth. Toothache with a looseness of the teeth.

Throat.—Diphtheria when the affection has gone to the windpipe. Relaxed throat with tickling in the larynx when caused by elongation of the uvula. Uvula relaxed, causing irritation, tickling and cough. Hawking of mucus in the morning. Burning in throat better by warm drinks. Great dryness of throat. Large indurated tonsils after *Baryta*.

Gastric Symptoms.—Vomiting of undigested food. Hiccough from hawking of mucus, weakening and recurring during the day. Flatulence. Cutting pain in liver, better motion.

Abdomen and Stool.—Confined bowels, inability to expel fæces. Fissure of the anus, and intensely sore crack near the lower end of the bowel. Bleeding hæmorrhoids. Itching of anus as from pinworms. Internal or blind piles, frequently with pain in the back, generally far down on the sacrum, and constipation. Piles with pressure of blood to the head. Pain in right hypochrondrium, worse lying on painful side. Much wind in lower bowels. Diarrhœa in gouty subjects.

Urinary Organs.—Copious urine, frequent urging. Urine scanty and high colored, and emits a pungent odor.

Sexual Organs.—Constant dribbling of seminal and prostatic fluid with dwindling of the testes. Indurated and nodular testes. Hydrocele. Displacements of the uterus. Dragging pain in the region of the uterus and thighs, down-bearing of the uterus. Varicose veins of vulva.

To tone up the contractile power of the uterus in cases of flooding. Excessive catamenia with bearing-down pain. Uterine fibroid. Hard nodules in mammæ. Syphilis. Hunterian chancre, for the induration.

Pregnancy.—After-pains if due to weak, feeble contractions. Hard knots in the breast. Given during pregnancy, it favors easy confinement.

Respiratory System.—Tickling in larynx. Dryness and hoarseness. Cough hacking from tickling in larynx, as from a foreign body. Hoarseness after reading aloud. *The chief remedy in true croup.* In asthma when specks or small lumps of yellowish mucus are brought up after much exertion; cough with expectoration of tiny lumps of yellow, tough mucus; with tickling sensation and irritation on lying down, from elongation of the uvula or deep at the back of the throat. Suppressed respiration, epiglottis feels closed or as if breathing through a thick substance.

Circulatory Organs.—Aneurism at an early stage may be reduced or kept in check by this remedy and *Ferr. phos.*, provided that the *iodide of potash* had not been taken. Dilatation, enlargement of the blood vessels; being the chief remedy to restore the contractility of the elastic fibres. Dilatation of the heart with palpitation. Chief remedy for vascular tumors with dilated blood vessels. Varicose ulcerations of the veins; also the chief remedy for varicose or enlarged veins. Enlargement, hypertrophy of the heart.

Neck and Back.—Indurated cervical glands of stony hardness. Small goitres. Backache simulating spinal irritation, with weak, dragging, down-bearing pain. Tired feeling and pain in the lower part of the back (sacrum), with a sensation of fulness or burning pain, and confined bowels. Chronic cases of lumbago; aggravation on beginning to move and amelioration by continued motion. Glenard's disease.

Extremities.—Ganglia or encysted tumors at the back of

the wrist. *Felon* (3x trit.). Gouty enlargements of the joints of the fingers, spina ventosa. Lumbago from strains. Inflammation of knee-joint, chronic synovitis. Cracking in the joints. Phalanges easily dislocated. Suppuration of bones. Osseous tumor on spine or scapula. Swelling of elbow-joint, crepitation, showing want of synovial fluid. Exostoses on fingers. Osseous growths and enlargements of bone with or without caries, particularly of traumatic origin. Spavin of horses. Chronic synovitis.

Nervous Symptoms.—Weakness and fatigue all day, especially in the morning.

Sleep.—Vivid dreams, with sense of impending danger; of new scenes, places, etc.

Febrile Symptoms.—Attacks of fever, lasting a week or more, with thirst; dry, brown tongue.

Skin.—Lesions. Squamous types with a tendency to fissure formation, and the skin is hard and thickened. Vesiculopustular lesions may also be found with associated crusts. [Ralph Bernstein.] Chaps and cracks of the skin. Fissures or *cracks in the palms of the hands* or hard skin with formation of crusts. Fissure of anus. Suppuration with callous, hard edges. Whitlow, gathered finger. Occasional erysipelas. Indolent, fistulous ulcers, secreting thick, yellow pus. Varicose ulcers of long standing have been cured by the remedy. Carbuncles. Indurations. Fibroma. Ichthyosis. Keratosis. Xanthoma.

Eczema due to venous hyperæmia; worse in damp weather, better at night. Squamous eczema, with thickening and cracking of skin. Eczema of anus consequent to hæmorrhoids.

Tissues.—Solidified infiltrations; thus *indurated glands of stony hardness*. Osseous growths, especially in tarsal and carpal articulation. *Knots and kernels and tumors in the female breast.* Bruises on surface of bone, with hard, rough and uneven lumps, as on shin. Dropsy caused by heart disease. Anæmia. Ganglion, cystic tumors, from a strain of the elastic fibres. Elastic fibres relaxed. **Swellings or indurated enlargements,** having their seat in the fasciæ and capsular ligaments of joints or in the tendons. Spina ventosa. Indolent ulcers. Ulceration of bone or enamel, bone injected. Whitlow or felons. Exudation from surface of bones, which quickly harden and assume a nodular ·or jagged form. Suppuration of bones. Caries and necrosis, with burning, boring pains and heat in parts; discharge of thin, acrid, ichorous mucus.

Modalities.—Worse in damp weather and during rest; better by cold fomentations, rubbing and heat.

Homœopathic Data.—*Calc. fluor.* has been proved by J. B. Bell, and the proving is reported in full in *Allen's Encyclopedia,* vol. x, page 398. The most complete data are to be found in the *Guiding Symptoms,* vol. iii. The drug had been very little used, if at all, homœopathically, until Schüssler brought it into prominence.

Administration.—The higher potencies of this drug give the best results, especially in affections of the bones. It can also be used externally in such diseases as fissura ani, bony growths, hæmorrhoids, varicose veins and whitlow. It is applied by dissolving about twenty grains of the desired potency in half a glass of water and applying it on cotton, lint or other media. Schüssler recommended the 12th decimal trituration, but the 3x and 6x have been found very efficient.

Relationship.—*Calcarea fluorica* should be studied in its symptoms of the mind and larynx in connection with its relative *Calc. carb.;* in its sleep symptoms with *Fluoric acid.* In fibroid indurations compare *Calc. jod., Kali jod., Mag. mur.* It corresponds to many symptoms of *Phosphor., Mercur., Ruta, Aurum, Silicea,* etc. Often useful after *Rhus* in lumbago, having the same modalities; after *Silicea* in suppurations; after *Bryonia* and *Calcarea* in arthritis; after *Sticta* and *Ferrum phos.* in synovitis; after *Natrum mur.* in cold sores. Compare: in swelling of skull of infants, *Silicea;* in suppuration of bones, *Calc. phosph., Asafœt., Silicea;* in spavin of horses, *Phosph. acid* and *Silicea.* In anæmia it is useful after *Calcar. phosph.;* in arterio-sclerosis compare the iodides, especially of *Baryta, Calc.* and *Plumbum,* also *Baryta mur.*

Groups for Study.—For indurations : *Calc. fluor., Baryta iod., Calcar. iod., Hecla lava, Asterias, Conium, Phytolacca, Carbo anim., Mercur. prot. iod., Silicea.* For Ozæna : *Cadmium, Calc. phos., Nitric acid, Kali bich., Aurum, Hepar, Antimon. sulph. aur., Aurum mur. natron., Arsenic. iod., Natrum carb., Syphilin.*

CALCAREA PHOSPHORICA.

Synonyms.—Calcii Phosphas Precipitata. Calcis Phosphas. Precipitated Phosphate of Calcium. Calcium Phosphate.

Common Name.—Phosphate of Lime.

Chemical Properties.—Formula $Ca_3 (PO_4)_2$.

Dr. Hering prepared this by dropping dilute phosphoric acid into lime-water as long as a white precipitate was formed. This was washed with distilled water and dried on a water-bath. Insoluble in water or alcohol, soluble in dilute nitric acid and other acids, and. to a certain extent, in carbonic acid water.

Preparation.—The Phosphate of Lime is prepared by trituration, as directed in our Pharmacopœias.

Physiologico-chemical Data.—*Calc. phos.* is absolutely essential to the proper growth and nutrition of the body. This salt is found in the blood-plasma and corpuscles, saliva, gastric juice, bones, connective tissue, teeth, milk, etc. It gives solidity to the bones. *Calc. phos.* has a special chemical affinity for albumen, which forms the organic basis for this salt in the tissue-cells, and is required wherever albumen or albuminous substances are found in the secretions. It also supplies new blood-cells, becoming the first remedy in anæmia and chlorosis. It is of the greatest importance to the soft and growing tissues, promoting cell growth, supplying the first basis for the new tissues, hence is necessary to initiate growth. It is the nutritive salt for the periosteum and through it for bones. Important for the life of the blood, without it there is no coagulation.

General Biochemical Action.—*Calc. phos.* is curative in disease depending upon a disturbed action of the lime-molecules in the body, such as occurs in the tardy formation of callus around the ends of fractured bones, in the unnatural growth and defective nutrition of bone and other textures found in rickets and similar diseased conditions; thus the sphere of action of this remedy includes **all bone diseases** depending on a diseased quality of the blood of a dyscrasic taint, involving also the dermoid tissues with the osseous. When from any cause an insufficient amount of Phosphate of Lime is assimilated for the uses of the animal economy, the vegetative system suffers primarily, causing **defective nutrition,** imperfect cell-growth and consequent decay and destruction of tissue, especially the osseous and glandular systems. It is of use **during dentition, in** convulsions and spasms occurring in weak, scrofulous subjects, stimulating nutrition, etc. Another important feature is its **restorative power** after acute diseases, either directly or preparing the way for other remedies, by stimulating the system to their action, thus becoming an important **intercurrent** remedy. Schüssler, recognizing the origin of the red bloodglobules in the white or embryonic ones, and crediting this drug with nutritive stimulation of the white globules, claims it promotes the formation of red globules indirectly by promoting that of the white globules. Practically, this drug proves itself a real tonic in many cases; in chronic wasting diseases and hectic, when the phosphate is found in excess in the urine, thus corresponding to faulty secondary assimilation and to faulty workings of the excretory organs. In anæmia of young, rapidly growing people; in women weakened by rapid child-bearing; prolonged suckling or excessive menstruation or leucorrhœa; in accompanying diseases with exhaustive discharges, as in chronic bronchitis, tubercular diarrhœa and night-sweats, abscesses and scrofulous sores, through its great power on the secretions, it acts curatively.

In old age, where the regenerative function decreases in the nervous tissue. *Calc. phos.* is well indicated, and we find it useful in senile cutaneous and vaginal itching, as well as during convalescence from severe acute diseases. In tuberculosis pulmonum, with its emaciation, night-sweats, hæmoptysis and other marked physical symptoms, *Calc. phos.* in low potencies holds out great promise to ameliorate the severity of the case; equally great is its benefit in pollutions of young married men (and sexual excitement of women) and onanists. In the osseous expansions of rachitic children, Traeger uses cider internally and externally, and gives at the same time *Calc. phos.* or *Calc. fluor.* This is also his favorite treatment in chlorosis (cider-whey, and three times a day about 10 grains of the second trituration of *Calc. phos.*), and he prefers it by far to the usual iron treatment. In chorea during puberty the salts of lime quiet our patients far better than the remedies usually recommended.

Pains where bones form sutures or symphyses and numb, crawling pains with chilliness, due to anæmic symptoms, worse from wet, tendency to perspiration and glandular enlargement. Sensations mostly in small spots. Phosphatic diathesis. General lack of vital heat and aggravation from wet.

If the molecular motion of *Calc. phos.* is disturbed within the epithelial cells of serous membranes, a sero-albuminous exudation within the sacs takes place. In this way develop hydrops genu, hygroma patellæ, etc. Minute doses of *Calc. phos.* will absorb these exudations.

If the cells of the epidermis have lost *Calc. phos.* albumen will be thrown upon the surface and by drying, form a crust, a desquamation of which can be brought about therapeutically by administering *Calc. phos.* Similar albuminous secretions take place on mucous surfaces, if their epithelium is diseased through loss of *Calc. phos.*

Spasms and pains caused by anæmia are cured by this remedy. These pains are accompanied by formication, sensation of coldness and numbness.

Often serviceable where the symptoms seem to call for Lime or Phosphorus, combining as it does the alterative and nourishing properties of lime and the nutritive and stimulating properties of phosphorus. [Dr. T. M. Strong.]

Guiding Symptoms and Characteristic Indications.

Mental Symptoms.—Impaired memory, mental anxiety with all troubles. Unable to sustained mental effort. Feeble minded children. Children are peevish and fretful, stupid, slow of comprehension. After grief, vexation, disappointment.

Head and Scalp.—Vertigo in old age; headache ameliorated by sudden sneezing, leaving a sense of soreness in the nostrils; a cold feeling in the head; the head feels cold to the touch. Headaches before and during the second dentition; **worse near the region of the sutures,** after mental exertion and from dampness and **change of weather.** Headache with flatulence. Rheumatic headaches, tearing in bones of the skull. Crawling, **as if ice water were on upper part of occiput.** Headache of school-girls who are maturing and are nervous, restless, with diarrhœa, caused by jellies and sour things. Sensation of ice lying on upper part of occiput. **Fontanelles remain open too long, skull is soft and thin.** Chronic hydrocephalus; very large head, bones separated. Craniotabes. Scalp sore, tense, creeping, numbness; itching of scalp in the evening. Scrofulous ulcers on the top of the head. Hydrocephaloid conditions, acute or chronic; also to prevent these conditions. Bald spots on head.

Eyes.—Spasmodic affections of the eyelids if *Magnes. phos.* fails. Amaurosis and cataract. Inflammation of the eyes and excessive dryness during dentition. Photophobia. Cannot use eyes by gaslight. Ulcers on cornea. Opacities following inflammation of the eyes. Scrofulous keratitis. Ophthalmia in scrofulous persons. Congenital amblyopia in children of a rachitic constitution and scrofulous diathesis.

Ears.—Outer ears feel cold. All bones around the ear ache and hurt. Earache with rheumatic complaints, associated with swollen glands in scrofulous children. Chronic catarrh of the ear with throat difficulty at the same time.

Dermatitis of the auditory canal, with serous exudate, almost odorless, whitish epidemic scales and sebaceous matter, moist, soft and pultaceous, lying in the canal; meatus, red, swollen, irritable, itching, hot; ear sensitive to cold and patient has mucous and glandular troubles generally. Stuffed feeling in the ears, with considerable deafness but rarely any tinnitus, inflation easy, causing bubbling rales and immediate improvement in hearing. Aching, tearing pains about the ears, with ulceration around the auricles. Difficult hearing, singing and noises in the ears. For tubal and tympanic catarrhs in children and strumous youths.

When a patient is suffering from a wasting disease, gradually losing flesh, with a thin, offensive discharge from abundant granulations in the drum cavity, I have never known the *phosphate of lime* fail to produce beneficial changes. *Calcarea hypophos.* is preferred as being particularly adapted to the treatment of suppurative inflammation of the middle ear in phthisical subjects. [Rounds.]

Nose.—Point of nose icy-cold. Swollen, ulcerated nose in scrofulous children. Cold in head, with albuminous discharge from the nose, fluent in cold room, stopped in warm air and outdoors. Sneezing and sore nostrils. Chronic colds in anæmic and scrofulous patients. Large pedunculated nasal polypi. Ozæna, with *Calc. fluor.* Nose-bleed in afternoon. Pressure at root of nose with frontal headache or supra-orbital pains on one or both sides, particularly if involvement of the ethmoid or frontal sinus is feared. Mucous membrane pale and relaxed or fungous. Flabby and ulcerated. Mild mucous discharge mixed with crusts and occasionally with blood.

Face.—Face full of pimples, especially with girls. Complexion sallow, dirty, greasy-looking. Cold sweat on face. Faceache; pain in the superior maxillary bone, aggravated at night. Swelling of parotid and submaxillary glands, with earache. Lupus. Freckles.

Mouth.—Disgusting taste in the mouth in the morning. Bitter, with headache. A dislike to open mouth on account of pain from swollen tonsils. Upper lip swollen and painful.

Tongue.—Tongue swollen, numb, stiff, with pimples on it, white, furred. Bitter taste in morning with headache.

Teeth.—Teeth develop slowly; **complaints during teething;** too rapid decay of teeth. Convulsions in teething after

Magnes. phos. Toothache with tearing, boring pain, worse at night. Gums painful and inflamed, or pale gums.

Throat.—External glands painful. Hoarseness day and night. Burning in larynx and back of tongue. **Sore aching in the throat, with much pain in every direction on swallowing.** Constant hemming and hawking when talking. **Chronic enlargement of the tonsils.** Clergyman's sore throat. **Relaxed sore throat.**

Naso-Pharynx.—Roughness of the throat, with difficult deglutition. Sore, aching on swallowing; burning from surrounding parts toward throat. Mucous membrane thickened. Dryness and burning during empty swallowing, and in swallowing first mouthful, aggravated if one has not spoken or swallowed for a short time (*Canth.,* burning on deglutition extending downwards; *Actæa rac.,* empty deglutition, painful). Sore throat, with tickling cough in the evening; worse after going to bed. Kind of contraction in throat, as after much weeping or after running. Sore throat in morning on waking, aggravated right side, low down in back of fauces, ameliorated by swallowing, disappearing during breakfast. If patient catches cold it is associated with dryness and soreness in the throat, the faucial tonsils, pharynx, larynx or bronchi receiving the brunt of the attack (in *Calc. carb.* it is the catarrhal conditions which are aggravated); stitches in the throat and chest; heat in the upper part of chest and arms. On empty deglutition, sensation of having swallowed uvula, and it was adherent to posterior wall, causing choking, only ameliorated by again swallowing; palate relaxed. Fullness of throat, either sensory or due to presence of bloody mucus. Naso-pharyngeal discharge is more tenacious than profuse; patient continually clearing the throat, to rid the larynx of its viscid secretion. Discharge of yellow-white, thick mucus; downward passage of scabs in pharynx.

Pale, flabby hypertrophy of tonsils, with perhaps ulceration in spots or chronic inflammation and hypertrophy of pharyngeal follicles, accompanied by other glandular enlargements in young persons of strumous or lymphatic constitutions. Chronic tonsillitis, with inflammation of middle ear; throat hurts more from swallowing saliva than food or warm drinks. (*Merc. sol.*). The tonsils, if hypertrophied, are smaller than the other *Calcareas,* and offer greater resistance to the probe; the Luschka tonsil similar, both being of a more natural color than *Calc. carb.* [Dr. T. M. Strong.]

Gastric Symptoms.—Heartburn and flatulence. Unusual hunger. Sinking sensation in epigastrium. Pain after eating, with soreness on pressure. The sufferings from the stomach are aggravated by taking even the smallest quantity of food. Dyspepsia with distress in stomach, temporarily relieved by eating and by raising wind. When fasting, pain goes to the spine. Infant wants to nurse all the time, and vomits often and easily. Pain in the stomach with debility. Vomiting after cold water and ice cream. Headache and diarrhœa, worse eating. **Craves bacon, ham, salted or smoked meats. Much flatulence. Abdomen sunken and flabby.** Mesenteric glands enlarged. Colic at every attempt to eat. Marasmus.

Abdomen and Stool.—Soreness and burning, and empty sinking sensation around navel. Colic, with green, slimy undigested diarrhœa with fœtid flatus. **Cholera infantum,** great desire for indigestible things—ham, smoked meat, etc.; abdomen sunken, flabby. Tubercular diarrhœa. **Stool is hot, watery, profuse, offensive, noisy and sputtering.** Useful in summer complaint and marasmus, and in teething children. Diarrhœa aggravated by fruit. Crying spells, caused by soreness and pain around navel, every time the child nurses. Removes disposition to intestinal worms in anæmic and weakly patients (*Natr. phos.*). Gall-stones, to prevent re-formation of new ones. Abdominal herniæ. Chronic oozing hæmorrhoids in anæmic or weakly patients. Fissures of anus. **Fistula in ano, alternating with chest symptoms, or in persons who have pain in all the joints from any change of weather.** Painless fistulæ. Costiveness, hard stool with blood, especially in old people, associated with depression of mind, vertigo, headache and chronic cough. Hernia in anæmic patients. Tabes mesenterica. Offensive pus with stools. Neuralgia ani. Severe pain in lower part of sacrum, coming on after stool and lasting entire day until retiring to bed.

Urinary Organs.—Phosphaturia. Wetting the bed and general debility. Frequent urging to urinate. Cutting pains in the urethra and neck of the bladder. Enuresis in old people and small children, with great debility. Diabetes mellitus where the lungs are implicated. Urine copious with weariness. Bright's disease, for the albumen (alternate with *Kali phos.*). Gravel, calculus, phosphatic deposits, increase of urine, with flocculent sediment. Stone in the bladder, to prevent re-formation of same. Hydrocele.

Sexual Organs.—Sexual desire increased. Painful erections. Gonorrhœal rheumatism worse in every cold change in weather. [*Mendorrhin.*] Chronic gonorrhœa in anæmic subjects, with sharp pain in urethra and prostate gland, itching and soreness. Swelling of testicles and scrotum.

Female Organs.—Weakness and distress in uterine region. **Uterine displacements with rheumatic pains.** Prolapsus uteri with weak, sinking feelings, worse after defæcation. Throbbing in the genitals, with voluptuous feelings, indicated also in tendency to masturbation in scrofulous children. Nymphomania worse before menses. Oophoritis. Violent backache with uterine pains. Soreness in the sacro-iliac synchondroses. Leucorrhœa, as a constitutional tonic, discharge like white of an egg, cream-like, worse in morning, with sexual excitement, patient being disinclined to move about. Amenorrhœa. Menses too early in young girls. Discharge bright red, returning every two weeks, less painful than otherwise. Menstruation during lactation. In adults menses too late and dark, especially in rheumatic subjects, preceded by sexual excitement, accompanied and followed by great weakness, distress and rheumatic pains. Labor-like pains before and during menses; sometimes after stool or micturition; worse from change of weather. Burning in vagina. Hardness of mammæ.

Pregnancy.—Pains, burning and soreness in the mammæ;

4

they feel enlarged. Spoiled milk of mother; it is salty and bluish, and child refuses it. Decline after puerpera and during pregnancy. Prolapsus in debilitated persons (with *Kali phos.*). **After prolonged nursing,** with weak voice, cough and weakness and pain between shoulders. Weariness in all limbs during pregnancy.

Respiratory Symptoms.—Hoarseness and cough day and night. **Involuntary sighing.** Cough with expectoration of yellow albuminous mucus, not watery, worse mornings, with sore, dry throat. Soreness of chest to touch. Sore pain about sternum and clavicle, with contraction of chest and difficult breathing. Frequent hawking to clear the voice. **Chest difficulties associated with fistula in ano.** Chronic cough of consumptives who suffer from coldness of the extremities. Incipient phthisis in anæmic patients. Profuse sweat, especially about the head and neck. Whooping cough, in obstinate cases, or in teething children and weakly constitutions. Suffocative cough in children; better lying down, worse sitting. Suffocative fits in children after nursing, aggravated after crying, face blue, attacks followed by relaxation, frequent, short, difficult breathing. Catarrhs in scrofulous or gouty constitutions with anæmia. Spasm of glottis from retarded dentition.

Circulatory Organs.—Palpitation with anxiety, followed by a trembling weakness, particularly of calves. Non-closure of foramen ovale. Circulation imperfect. Retarded circulation, parts feel numb. Sharp pain around the heart during inspiration.

Neck and Back.—Thin neck in children. Rheumatic pain and stiffness of neck from slightest draught. Backache in the lumbar region in the morning on awaking. Cramp-like pain in neck and around shoulder blades, small of back, region of kidneys, when lifting, or blowing the nose. Soreness around sacro-iliac symphysis. Aching in os coccygis. Potts' disease. Spinal curvature in young girls especially at puberty. Spina bifida. Buttocks and back "asleep."

Extremities.—Sore aching in shoulders and shoulder blades, and along arms; cannot lift arm. Shooting through elbows.

Cramp-like pains in forearms, wrists, fingers, and especially in the thumb. Ulcerative pain in roots of finger nails. Gouty nodosities. **Rheumatism of the joints with cold or numb feeling.** Rheumatism worse from change of weather, getting well in spring and returning in autumn. Numbness of the limbs and coldness or a sensation of ants creeping on the parts affected. *Sensation as if parts were asleep.* Rheumatic gout, worse at night and in bad weather. Aching in all the limbs, with great weakness. Rheumatic pains flying about. Aching soreness of thighs. Pains in knees, worse walking. Lower limbs feel numb. Feet icy cold. Pain in shinbones. Cramp in calves. Ankle joint feels as if dislocated. Gouty pain in toes and ankle joints; they become painful in cold weather. Coxarthrocace, third stage. Bursæ. Chronic synovitis. Swelling of the epipheses. Bow legs in children. Slow in learning to walk. Fistulous ulcer on the foot joints and on the malleoli. Potts' disease. Spinal curvature. Lumbar abscess. Syphilitic periostitis and ulcers.

Nervous Symptoms.—Neuralgias, commencing at night, recurring periodically; deep-seated, as if in the bone; tearing pains, worse from any change of weather, with sensation of **crawling, numbness** and **coldness.** or like electrical shocks. Pain in small spots. Rheumatic paralysis. **Languor,** weariness, especially ascending. Indisposition to work. Trembling of limbs. Great debility after weakening, acute diseases. Convulsions from teething. Spasms of all kinds after *Magnes. phos.* fails. Epilepsy.

Sleep.—Drowsiness, especially in old people, associated with gloomy thoughts. Hard to wake in the morning. Children cry out at night. Constant stretching and yawning.

Febrile Symptoms.—Creeping shivering. Copious **night-sweats in phthisis.** Cold sweat appears on the face and coldness of the body. Chronic intermittent fever in scrofulous children. Cold goes through entire body.

Skin.—Skin dry and cold, wrinkled. Becomes red and itches after a bath. Copper-colored, full of pimples. Pimples on upper part of body. Ulceration of scars. Chafed skin, ex-

coriations. Itchiness of the skin. *Senile itching of the skin.*
Eczema with yellow, white scabs or vesicles in anæmic, scrofulous or gouty constitutions. Freckles are lessened by the use
of this remedy. Herpes, acute or chronic, with itching.
Lupus. Prurigo, pruritus; itching of the skin. Vaginal
pruritus of old women. Albuminous exudations in or on the
skin. Tubercles on the skin. Scrofulous ulceration also of
the bones. Boils form ulcers. Acne rosacea.

Tissues.—Anæmia and chlorosis to supply new blood cells.
Flabby, shrunken, emaciated children. Complexion waxy,
greenish, white. Exostoses, osteophytes, bone diseases.
Condyles swollen. **Rickets. Non-union of fractured bones.**
Spina bifida. **Polypi,** nasal, rectal and uterine. Tabes, phosphatic diathesis. Defective nutrition. Bones thin and brittle.
Dropsical affections. Irregularity in development. Emacia-
tions, accompanying ailments. Leucæmia. Excess of white
corpuscles. Broncocele, goitre, cysts. Tumor albus. Pancreatic diseases. Bursæ. Soreness of tendons and of joints.

Modalities.—The symptoms are generally worse from cold,
motion, **change of weather,** *sensitive to cold,* from getting
wet and dampness generally. Many symptoms are ameliorated
by lying down, rest.

Homœopathic Data.—Proved by C. Hering, collected in
Guiding Symptoms, vol. iii, and *Allen's Encyclopedia.* A
history of the different provings is found in the *Hahnemannian Monthly,* March, 1871, by C. Hering; also a Resume by
him in the *North American Journal of Homœopathy,* vol. xx.

Administration.—The lower triturations, 3x to 6x, are the
potencies usually employed, probably achieving most satisfactory results, although the higher potencies, 30 to 200, have
given brilliant clinical results. Schüssler prescribes the 6x
trituration. Large doses are useless and even injurious. Prolonged administration has produced nephritic colic and passage of small calculi. For the aged, this remedy should not be
given in the lower potencies.

Relationship.—Very similar t *alc. carb.,* but with *Calc.
phos.* the patient, whose comple> on is dirty-white or brown,

is usually emaciated; it corresponds more to the acute affections of the lungs. In general the phosphate prefers the dark complexion, dark eyes and hair, while the carbonate acts best in the light-haired and blue-eyed. It occupies a ground between *Calc. carb.* and *Phosphor.*, supplementing the latter frequently to great advantage. *Calc. phos.* and *Berberis* have both been beneficial in fistula in ano; both have great similarity in chest symptoms, particularly such as follow surgical operations. In anæmic headaches of school girls, follow by *Magnes. phos.* In dental caries, similar to *Fluor. ac., Magnes. phos.* and *Silicea;* in epilepsy, *Ferr. phos., Kali mur., Kali phos.* and *Silicea;* in diabetes, *Kali phos., Natr. phos.;* the latter also is similar in worm affections. Follows *China* in hydrocephaloid and anæmia. Complementary to *Carb. an.* and *Ruta.* In neurasthenia *Calc. hypophos.* may be called for preferably for similar symptoms. In the copious sweats after weakening, acute diseases compare *Psorin.* In acute articular rheumatism, if after *Natr. mur,* and *Kali phos.* there remains a trace of the disease. In lupus, compare *Kali mur.* Buttermilk and koumyss are invaluable foods for the aged, because the lactic acid in them dissolves the *phosphate of lime* and prevents the ossification in tendons, arteries and elsewhere. As a remedy for the aged compare *Baryta.* In anæmia and chlorosis compare also *Natr. mur.*, which has a great affinity with *Calc. phos.*, especially with constipation, palpitation on lying down, earthy complexion. In acne *Calc. picr.* is more frequently useful for boys, the *Calc. phos.* for girls. Dyspepsia temporarily relieved by eating is met by *Calc. phos.*, but the drug for which this symptom is specific is *Anacardium. Chelidon.* has a similar condition. Compare *Helonias* in the mental depression, debility and phosphatic urine. *Silicea,* anæmia of infants, thin and puny, with a tendency to rickets, but with much oily perspiration on the head; also *Ferr., Cupr., Arsenic.,* etc. *Zinc.* is complementary in hydrocephaloid, and *Ruta* in joint affections. In non-union of fractures compare *Symphytum.* In consumption *Calc. phos.* is followed well by *Silicea, Sulph., Tuberc.;* and often indicated after *Phos., Merc., Iod., Ars. iod.*

CALCAREA SULPHURICA.*

Synonyms.—Calcii Sulphas. Calcium Sulphate.

Common Name.—Gypsum. Plaster of Paris.

Chemical Properties.—Formula, $Ca\,SO_4$. It is found in nature as anhydrite, gypsum, alabaster and selenite; also in various waters constituting one source of permanent hardness. Molecular wt. 172. It occurs in flattened prisms (selenite) and in earthy mases (gypsum). It is a fine, white crystalline powder, soluble in 400 parts of cold water, insoluble in alcohol and in dilute nitric and hydrochloric acids. It can be obtained by precipitating a solution of calcium chloride with dilute sulphuric acid.

Preparation.—By trituration, as directed in our *Pharmacopœias.*

Physiologico-chemical Data.—Present only in the bile according to Bunge, and even here not constant. The *Calcarea sulph.* contained in the bile comes from the liver, where it fulfilled the function of destroying wornout, red blood corpuscles, by taking away their water.

Through a deficiency of *Calcar. sulph.* in the liver this destruction of unfit corpuscles is delayed, hence the blood soon contains an oversupply of useless cells. Under normal conditions all useless blood corpuscles disintegrate by means of *Calcar. sulph.* in the liver; their remnants are excreted through biliary action from the circulation by the shortest route. But if a part of these useless corpuscles must be destroyed by oxidation within the circulation, their elimination will thereby be rendered tardy.

Such remnants as are not excreted by way of the liver from the circulation, nor taken up by the lymphatics, reach the

---

*In the last years of Dr. Schüssler's life this remedy was discarded from his list, leaving only *eleven,* instead of twelve tissue remedies. It has been thought best to retain the original number contained in the previous editions of this work, as much clinical evidence in favor of this remedy has been collected. In the later editions of Schüssler's Therapeutics *Natrum phos.* and *Silica* are substituted for this remedy.

mucous membranes and skin, producing there catarrh and eruptions.

General Biochemical Action.—*Calc. sulph.* stands in close relation to suppurations. It cures purulent discharges from the mucous membranes and purulent exudations in serous sacs, as well as tubercular ulcers or abscesses of the intestines, and ulcers of the cornea, etc. It is curative in suppurations at that stage in which matter is discharging or continuing to ooze after the infiltrated places have discharged their contents of pus. All ailments in which the process of discharge continues too long and the suppuration is affecting the epithelial tissues. Acts upon the connective tissue. If there is a deficiency of it in any small part of its domains, suppuration is the result. The presence of **pus with a vent** is the general indication.

Guiding Symptoms and Characteristic Indications.

Mental Symptoms.—Changeable mood. Sudden loss of memory; of consciousness. Absent-minded and irritable. Anxious, better in open air. Discontented, full of fears.

Head and Scalp.—Scaldhead of children, if there be purulent discharge or yellow, purulent crusts. Suppuration, etc., about the scalp. Headache with nausea and with feeling as if eyes were sunken. Headache comes on from becoming cold, but made better by cool air. Pain around whole head, worse forehead. Craniotabes. Vertigo, with deadly nausea, on moving head quickly. Much dandruff. Hair falls out.

Eyes.—Deep-seated abscess of the cornea. Inflammation of the eyes with discharge of thick, yellow matter. Hypopyon; to absorb the effusion of pus in the eye, after *Silicea*. Retinitis. Deep ulcers of the cornea. Ophthalmia, pus thick and yellow. Cornea steamy, pus in anterior chamber; sensation as from a foreign body; has to tie up eye; after injury to the eye from a splinter. Phlyctenular keratitis and phlyctenular conjunctivitis when accompanied by swelling of cervical glands. Hemiopia. Twitching of eyelids. Inflamed canthi.

Ears.—Deafness with discharge of matter from the middle

ear, sometimes mixed with blood, after *Silicea*. Pimples around ear. Sensitive swellings behind ear with tendency to suppuration.

Nose.—Cold in the head, with thick, yellowish, purulent secretion, frequently tinged with blood. Nosebleed. One-sided discharge from nose. Edges of nostrils sore. Yellowish discharge from posterior nares. Dryness of nose, crusts form, itching, obstructed.

Face.—Swelling of the cheek if suppuration threatens. Tender pimples under the beard. Herpetic eruptions on the face. **Pimples and pustules on the face.**

Mouth.—Inside of lips sore. Raw sores on lips. Dry, hot mouth. *Gum-boils.*

Tongue.—Tongue flabby, resembling a layer of dried clay. Sour, soapy, acrid taste. Yellow coating at base. Inflammation of the tongue when suppurating. Clay-colored coating.

Teeth.—Rheumatic toothache. Toothache with inside of gums swollen and sore; swollen cheek. Gums bleed on brushing teeth. Gum-boils, ulcerated teeth.

Throat.—Suppurating sore throat. Last stage of ulcerated sore throat, with discharge of yellow matter. Suppurating stage of tonsilitis when abscess is discharging. Diphtheritis of the soft palate; fauces are much swollen. Quinsy, discharging pus. Choking [*Hepar*].

Gastric Symptoms.—Desire for fruit, tea, claret, and green, sour vegetables. Great thirst and appetite. Nausea, with vertigo. While eating, roof of mouth sore. Burning pain in stomach. Craves stimulants to overcome the tremulous weakness.

Abdomen and Stool.—Purulent diarrhœa, mixed with blood. Dysentery, stools purulent, sanious. Intestinal ulcers with typhus. **Painless abscesses about the anus** in cases of fistula. Pain in region of liver, in right side of pelvis, followed by weakness, nausea and pain in stomach. Diarrhœa after maple sugar and from change of weather, in children worse after eating, painless, involuntary. Itching of rectum, moisture about anus. Prolapsus ani. Costiveness, with hectic fever and difficult breathing. Pus-like, slimy discharge from the bowels.

Urinary and Sexual Organs.—Red urine with hectic fever. Cystitis, chronic state, pus forming. Nephritis. To control the suppuration in cases of bubo alternately with *Silicea.* Gonorrhœa with purulent, sanious discharge. Abscess of the prostate. Chronic suppurating stage of syphilis. Glandular ulceration, etc. Spermatorrhœa. Menses late, long-lasting, with headache, twitchings, great weakness. Extravasation of pus within the pelvic tissues unconfined by any pyogenic membrane. Itching after menses, in vagina, swelling of labia.

Respiratory System.—Cough with purulent and sanious sputa and hectic fever. Asthma with hectic fever. Empyema, pus forming in the lungs or pleural cavities. Purulent, sanious expectoration. Pain across the chest. Pneumonia, third stage. Obstinate hoarseness. Third stage of bronchitis. Empyema after thoracentesis. Consumption. Oppression and soreness of chest Burning and weakness in chest. Purulent sputa. Catarrh, with thick, lumpy, white-yellow or pus-like secretions. Croup after *Kali mur.* In children, severe cough with malaise in the chest, green stools, herpetic eruptions.

Pregnancy.—Mastitis, when matter is discharging, after *Silicea.*

Circulatory Organs.—Pericarditis. suppurative stage. Palpitation at night.

Back and Extremities.—Pain in back and coccyx. Fingers stiff. Carbuncles on the back. Last stage of gathered finger, when the suppuration is continuing and only superficial. Gouty joints. Cramp in calves. Ischias. Acute and chronic rheumatism. Hip-joint disease, for the discharge of pus; this remedy with *Ferr. phos.* and complete rest will cure this disease. Suppurating wounds. **Burning-itching of soles of feet.**

Nervous Symptoms.—Twitchings. Weakness and languor. Neuralgia in aged persons. Craves stimulants to overcome the tremulous weakness.

Sleep.—Sleepy during the day, wakeful at night. Dreamed she had a convulsion from fright. Sleepless from thoughts.

Febrile Symptoms.—Chronic intermittents with evening chill; chill begins in feet. Evening fever with chilliness. Typhus when diarrhœa sets in. Hectic fever, caused by formation of pus, with burning in soles.

Skin.—**Herpetic eruptions** all over. Boils; to reduce and control suppurations. Cuts, wounds, bruises, etc., unhealthy, discharging pus; they do not heal readily. Burns and scalds, second remedy for the purulent stage. Carbuncles discharging pus. Chilblains, suppurating stage. Crusta lactea. Yellow, purulent crusts or discharge. Purulent exudations in or upon the skin. Festers, furuncles, pimples, pustules, scabs. Skin affections with yellowish scabs. Smallpox pustules discharging matter. Purulent sores and suppurations. Ulcers of lower limbs. Many little matterless pimples under the hair, bleeding when scratched.

Tissues.—Diseases of the connective tissue. Abscesses; to shorten the suppurating process and limit the discharge of pus. If given after *Silicea* it will cause the abscess to heal. Serous swellings. Complaints from straining muscles and tendons; lame back. Broken down constitution from drunkenness. Cystic tumors. Third stage of inflammation, with lumpy or bloody discharge. **Mucous discharge** in cough, leucorrhœa, gonorrhœa, etc., **yellow thick and lumpy.** Discharges of matter or sanious pus from the skin or mucous linings. Effusions when pus forms. Lymphatic glands discharging pus. Ulcerations of the glands. Suppurations, articular or anywhere on the body. Excessive granulations, painful, etc. Malignant growths after ulceration has set in.

Modalities.—Aggravation and renewal of the symptoms after working and washing in water; after walking; walking fast; overheated; warmth.

Homœopathic Data.—*Calc. sulph.* was proved by Dr. Clarence Conant. The proving appeared in the *Transactions of the American Institute of Homœopathy,* 1873. It is also to be found in *Allen's Encyclopedia,* vol. ii, page 410. Nothing especially characteristic appears in this proving. In the *Guiding Symptoms,* vol. iii, page 227, is found a complete arrangement of the symptoms of this remedy.

Administration.—This remedy is also useful externally in such affections as felons, ulcers and abscesses. The most common potencies for internal use are the 6x and 12x. Low potencies are most useful in purulent eye troubles.

Homœopathic Relationship.—*Calc. sulph.* resembles *Hepar sulph.*, but acts deeper and more intensely, and is often useful after *Hepar* has ceased to act. It is also useful when *Kali mur.* ceases to act. *Apocynum* contains *Calc. sulph.* Compare *Calend.* in suppurations; *Kali mur.* in milk-crust and other skin affections, swollen cheek, croup, dysentery; *Natr. sulph.* in post-scarlatinal dropsy; *Silicea* in hard or suppurating glands, ulcers of the corneæ, tonsilitis, mastitis, frostbites; *Pyrogen* also has tendency to the formation of abscesses.

In neuralgia it occupies a ground between the very acute pains of *Magnes. phos.* and the paralyzing ones of *Kali phos.* (more in aged persons, if there is a want of regenerative force of the nervous tissue).

In the third stage of inflammation (resolution) after *Kali mur.*, if the discharge is lumpy and bloody; but if yellow or mucous, *Kali sulph.*; if pus-like or bloody pus, *Silicea.* In carbuncles, *Anthracine* is better. *Calc. sulph.* is often useful after *Kali mur.*, when the latter has but partially relieved, also after *Bellad.* and other acute remedies. When well selected remedies act only a short time, *Calcar. sulph.* shares importance with *Sulphur, Tuberculin* and *Psorinum.*

FERRUM PHOSPHORICUM.

Synonyms.—Ferroso-ferric Phosphate. Ferri Phosphas.

Common Name.—Phosphate of Iron.

Chemical Properties.—Formula, $Fe_3(PO_4)_2$. It is prepared by mixing sodium phosphate with sulphate of iron in certain proportions. The resulting precipitate is filtered, washed and dried, and rubbed to a powder, which is bluish-gray from exposure to the air, without odor or taste. Soluble in acids, but insoluble in alcohol or water. It is probably this phosphate which is capable of turning blue, which occurs in the lungs in phthisis in bluish pus and expectorations.

Preparation.—The pure phosphate of iron is prepared by trituration, as directed in the homœopathic *Pharmacopœias*.

Physiologico-chemical Data.—Iron is found in the hæmoglobin or coloring matter of the red blood corpuscles. According to Dalton, it is not found in such considerable quantities in any of the other tissues of the body except in hair. In a man weighing 65 kilogrammes (165 pounds) there would be 2.82 grammes (44 grains) of iron contained in the entire blood of the body. The organic basis of every cell is albumen. Since albumen contains iron, each cell must likewise contain iron. Iron and its salts have the property of attracting oxygen. The iron of the blood corpuscles takes up the oxygen from the inspired air. This is carried to every cell throughout the organism by means of the mutual reaction of *Iron* and *Kali sulph.* A disturbance of the equilibrium of the iron molecules in the muscular fibres causes a relaxation. This, occurring in the muscular coats of the vessels, causes a dilatation and accumulation of blood in the blood vessels—congestion—blood-pressure being increased, the walls rupture, and hæmorrhage results. Again, if the muscular walls of the intestinal villi suffer a relaxation from the disturbed equilibrium of the iron molecules diarrhœa results; when this occurs in the muscular walls of the intestines themselves the peristaltic action of the bowels is weakened and becomes less active. This causes tendency to constipation. Anything causing a relaxation of the muscular walls of a vessel, and consequent hyperæmia, such as an injury, finds its remedy in *Ferr. phos.*, as this remedy in minute doses restores the equilibrium to the iron molecules, thus strengthening the muscular fibres. Through its power of attracting oxygen iron becomes a useful remedy in such diseases of the blood corpuscles as anæmia, chlorosis and leucæmia.

General Biochemical Action.—From the above it is readily seen that *Ferr. phos.* becomes the first remedy in all cases depending on a relaxed condition of muscular tissue, wherever found; also for an abnormal condition of the blood corpuscles themselves.

If a new supply of iron molecules is given to the relaxed muscle cells, caused by the lack of iron, their normal tonicity is restored, the circular fibres of the vessels contract to normal bounds, with equalizing of the circulation and abatement of the fever.

Its field of action, then, is in all ailments of a hyperæmic or congestive nature, with the usual accompaniments of these conditions, such as pain, heat, swelling and redness, quickened pulse and increased circulation; in a word, all **febrile disturbances and inflammations at their onset, especially before exudation commences.** Anæmia, want of red blood, etc. Especially useful in debility of children with failing appetite, becoming dull and listless, loss of weight and strength. *Ferr. phos.* not only improves the strength, but helps to increase the bodily development and regulates the bowels.

This drug is by Schüssler supposed to be no longer indicated when exudation or even suppuration takes place; but if adapted to the individual patient it may still be depended upon. Only when it fails to do any more good should it be relinquished.

In many inflammatory and some eruptive fevers, especially in the young and sensitive, seeming to stand midway between the intensity of *Acon.* and *Bellad.* and the dullness of *Gelsem.*

Iron is the biochemic remedy for:
1. The first stage of all inflammations.
2. Pains that are worse from motion and better from cold.
3. Hæmorrhages caused by hyperæmia.
4. Fresh wounds caused by mechanical injuries.

Guiding Symptoms and Characteristic Indications.

Mental Symptoms.—Indifference to ordinary matters. Loss of courage and hope, better after sleep. Trifles seem like mountains, annoyed at trifles. Hyperæmia of the brain, producing delirium, maniacal mood, mania transitoria. Delirium tremens, very talkative. Dizziness from congestion, consequence of anger. Inability to command the right words or express himself.

Head and Scalp.—Rush of blood to the head. Headache from a gouty predisposition (*Natr. sulph.*). Dull, heavy pain on top, during profuse menses, from cold. Bruising, pressing or stitching pain and **soreness to the touch.** Pain as if a nail were being driven in one side, over the eye. Congestive headaches, hammering pain, worse right side; pressing a cold object against the spot seems to relieve the pain; relieved by nosebleed. Headache with vomiting of undigested food, top of head sensitive to cold air, noise, jar; cannot bear to have the hair touched. Dull right-sided headache from vertex to right supra-orbital region. Ill effects of sun-heat (follow with *Calc. phos.*). It is the chief remedy in headaches of children, throbbing sensation in the head, **red face** and suffused eyes; worse from shaking the head, stooping and motion. Blind headache, sick headache, with vomiting of undigested food; vertigo, with rush of blood to the head. Symptoms of meningitis, with drowsiness and heaviness. First stage of eruptions on the scalp; soreness of scalp; sensitive to cold and touch.

Eyes.—Suffused eyes. Acute hyperæmia of the conjunctiva. Inflammation of the eyes, with acute pain, without secretion of mucus or pus. Acute conjunctivitis. Conjunctivitis, with relaxation of conjunctiva and photophobia. Pain in the eyeball, aggravated by moving the eyes. Retinitis. **Eyes inflamed, red, with burning sensation, sore and red-looking, and retinal congestion. Sensation as if grains of sand were under eyelids.** Encysted tumor of the lids. Stye on lower lid of right eye. Neuralgia along inner orbit and nose.

Ears.—Sensitive to noise. Earache after exposure to cold or wet. Inflammatory earache, with burning or throbbing pain, or sharp, stitching pain. Tension, throbbing and heat in the ears. Noises in the ears arising through blood-pressure, from relaxed condition of the veins not returning the blood properly. **First stage of otitis;** radiating pains, pulsation in the ear; every impulse of the heart is felt there. Quick pulse, should be feeble and compressible, indicating marked debility.

Redness of meatus and hyperæmia of drumhead. Marked congestion of the membrane. Circumscribed, dark, inflammatory appearance. Deafness from inflammatory action, or suppuration when there is cutting pain, tension or throbbing. Tinnitus aurium. A marked tendency of the inflammatory process to be diffused instead of circumscribed; dark, beefy redness of parts, muco-purulent discharge, if any, and a tendency to hæmorrhage; the complete establishment of the discharge is not followed by relief of the pain; paroxysmal and radiating character of the pain. Inflammation of the external ear. Mastoid process swollen and sore. Chronic, nonsuppurative catarrh of the middle ear, with thickening of membrana tympani and probable anchylosis of small bones.

Nose.—First stage of all colds in the head, predisposition to catch cold. Smarting, especially in the right nasal passage, worse on inspiration. Nasal catarrh, with trickling sensations, bloody discharge. Crusts form, discharge excoriating. Congested nasal mucous membranes. Catarrhal fever. **Epistaxis,** especially in children, and a concomitant of other complaints. Nosebleed of bright red blood. "Its indication in beginning of colds or in congestion of the mucous membranes anywhere is similar to *Aconite,* but its period of usefulness is much longer. Unless *Aconite* be given immediately after exposure in my experience it is useless, but the remedial value of *Ferrum phos.* continues for several hours." [R. S. Copeland.]

Face.—A florid complexion, with less nerve tension than that of *Bellad.* Throbbing pain with sweat over head and face. Faceache, with flushing, heat and quickened pulse; worse on moving; with throbbing or pressing pain, flushed face, with accompanying sensation of coldness in the nape of the neck; flushed face when a precursor of recurring headaches. Anæmic, chlorotic face; earthy, pale, sallow. Dark circles under eyes. Cheek sore and hot, when cold applications are grateful. Congestive or inflammatory tic douloureux.

Mouth.—Gums hot and inflamed; redness of the mucous membrane of the mouth.

Tongue.—Furred tongue, or clean and red, with headache. Inflammation of the tongue with dark red swelling.

Teeth.—Toothache with hot cheek, worse with hot, better with cold liquids or food; teething troubles with feverishness; great soreness of tooth to touch or pressure. Teeth feel elongated. Cannot close jaws without pain.

Throat.—Inflammation of the fauces. Redness and pain without exudation. **Ulcerated throat,** to relieve congestion, heat, fever, pain and throbbing. **Sore throat, dry, red, inflamed, with much pain.** Pharyngeal abscess. Red and inflamed tonsils and swollen glands. **First stage of diphtheria** to lessen the fever. Hæmorrhages from pharynx, larynx, trachea and, perhaps, bronchi. Acute catarrhal affections of the Eustachian tubes. Sore throats of singers and those who use the voice daily. Submaxillary glands enlarged.

Gastric Symptoms.—Aversion to meat and milk. Thirst for cold water. Desire for some stimulant, brandy, ale. Greasy eructation. First stage of gastritis, with pain, swelling and tenderness at the pit of the stomach. Dyspepsia with flushed, hot face, epigastrium tender to the touch. Furred tongue, beating and throbbing pain, red, flushed face, **vomiting of undigested food.** Indigestion from relaxed condition of blood vessels of the stomach, pain after taking food and on pressure. Deathly sickness at the stomach. Inflammatory stomach-ache in children from chill, with loose evacuations. **Vomiting of bright-red blood.** Flatulence bringing back the taste of the food eaten, loss of appetite, distaste for milk. After eating, nausea and vomiting of food; vomited matters are sometimes very sour; cannot take acids, herrings, meat, or coffee and cakes. Persistent vomiting of food. Vomits sometimes before breakfast.

Abdomen and Stool.—First stage of all gastric and enteric fevers; the chilly stage, also in the first stage of cholera and of peritonitis. Constipation with heat in the lower bowel, associated with prolapse and hæmorrhoids and aversion to meat diet. Diarrhœa. Cholera infantum, with red face, full, soft pulse; stools watery, even bloody, after checked perspiration. Stool watery, contains mucus and blood; urging, but no tenesmus. Diarrhœa from a relaxed state of the intestinal villi, not

taking up the usual amount of moisture. **Stools undigested.**
Diarrhœa caused by a chill. Dysentery (alternately with *Kali
mur.*). **Hæmorrhoids,** inflamed or bleeding, bright-red blood
with a tendency to coagulate, before any induration occurs.
Disposition to prolapsus recti. Inflamed and incarcerated herniæ. Intestinal and thread-worms.

Urinary Organs.—Frequent desire to urinate; urine spurts
out with every cough. Hæmaturia. First stage of cystitis
with heat, pain or feverishness. Diabetes when there is a
quickened pulse or when there exists pain, tension, throbbing
or heat or congestion in any part of the system. **Incontinence
of urine from weakness of the sphincter.** Diurnal enuresis
depending on irritation of the neck of the bladder. Ischuria;
suppression of the urine with heat, especially in little children.
Any inflammatory pain in the kidneys. Bright's disease with
febrile disturbances. Irritation at the neck of the bladder
and prostate. Symptoms are worse the longer the patient
stands and better after urinating. Polyuria simplex, excessive secretion of urine.

Sexual Organs.—Varicocele with pain in testicles. Bubo
with heat, throbbing or feverishness. First stage of orchitis
or of epididymitis and gonorrhœa. Seminal emissions. *Ferrum phos.* has a close relationship with conditions of irritability of the womb, associated with trouble in the bladder,
and also with the lining membrane of the womb. Menstrual
colic with flushing of the face and quickened pulse, vomiting
of undigested food, sometimes tasting acid. First stage of
metritis to remove fever, pain and heat. Excessive congestion
at the monthly periods, blood bright red. Menses every three
weeks; profuse, with pressure in abdomen and small of the
back and pain on top of the head. Bearing-down sensations
and constant, dull ovarian pains. Dysmenorrhœa with frequent urging to urinate. Congestive dysmenorrhœa pains before, and during first days of flow. Vaginismus; vaginitis,
vagina dry and hot, pain in the vagina on coition or examination. Spasm of the vagina on account of the increased sensitiveness and dryness.

.5

Pregnancy and Labor.—First stage of mastitis. Morning sickness of pregnancy, with vomiting of food as taken, with or without taste. After pains and as a preventive of the fever of lactation.

Respiratory Symptoms.—Acute, febrile or initiatory stage of all inflammatory affections of the respiratory tract. Rhinitis, laryngitis, trachitis, bronchitis, pneumonia, pleurisy and pleuro-pneumonia. **Bronchitis of young children.** Phthisis florida. Expectoration scanty, blood-streaked, chest sore, bruised. It is the chief and first remedy for the stitches in the side, catch in the breath, dyspnœa and cough, and should be continued until free perspiration is established. Congestion of the lungs with debility and oppression. Hæmoptysis after a concussion or fall, with short, oppressed breathing and high fever. In bronchial affections with heat and burning soreness, no expectoration. In chronic bronchitis when a fresh aggravation sets in. Short, painful, tickling cough from an irritation or tickling in the windpipe. Spasmodic cough with involuntary emission of urine. Hard, dry cough with soreness of the lungs. Cough with rattling of mucus in chest, worse at night. Croup, for the febrile symptoms. Whooping cough with vomiting of food; **loss of voice, hoarseness,** huskiness after singing or exertion of speaking, soreness, irritation and pain in the larynx.

Circulatory Organs.—First or congestive stage of carditis, pericarditis, endocarditis and arteritis. In aneurism, to establish normal circulation and remove complications arising from excessive action of the heart. Dilatation of the heart or of the blood vessels, telangiectasi and nævi. Palpitation of the heart, pulse, rapid and quick. Varicose veins. Phlebitis and lymphangitis, first stage. Pulse full, round, not rope-like.

Back and Extremities.—Stiff neck from cold. Pains in the back, loins and over kidneys. Also in knees and ankles, shooting pains. Rheumatic pains worse on motion; movement sets up and increases the pain. Rheumatism felt only during motion and better from warmth. **Articular rheumatism,** especially of the shoulder; pains extend to the upper part of the chest, attack one joint after another; muscular or sub-acute rheumatism. Lameness, stiffness from cold. Rheumatic pain in right wrist and in shoulder. Inflamed fingers, first stage of whitlow. Hip-joint disease for pain, throbbing, inflammation and heat of the soft parts. Strains of ligaments and tendons, tenalgia crepitans, creaking in the sinews at the back of the hand. Crick in the back (*Calc. sulph.*). Hands swollen and painful. Palms of hands are hot.

Nervous Symptoms.—Malaise, weariness, great prostration, debility of children, with no organic lesion. Feeling of indolence. Feels the need of a stimulant. Rheumatic paralysis. Nervousness at night. Convulsions with fever in teething children. Epilepsy, with blood rushing to the head. Congestive and inflammatory neuralgias from cold.

Sleep.—Sleeplessness from a hyperæmic condition of the brain. Restless at night. Anxious dreams; drowsiness in the afternoon.

Febrile Symptoms.—All catarrhal and inflammatory fevers during the chilly or initiatory stage, rigors, heat, quickened pulse and pain. Rheumatic, gastric, enteric and typhoid fevers during the chilly stage, heat and feverishness at the beginning of any disease or ailment. Intermittent fever with vomiting of food. Simple cases of scarlet fever. First stage of typhus. Chill every day at 1 P. M. High fever, quick pulse and increased temperature; copious night-sweats; dry heat of palms, face, throat and chest.

Skin.—Hyperæmia; from mechanical injuries, fresh wounds, not yet suppurating. Capillary congestion, with burning of the skin, more exercise and warmth. Abscesses, boils, carbuncles and **felons**; at the commencement of these affections this remedy reduces heat, blood-accumulation, pain and throbbing. Chicken-pox, **erysipelas** and erysipelatous inflammations of the skin, for the fever and pain. Suppurative processes on the skin with febrile symptoms. Measles, **scarlet fever** and small-pox. Pimples, acne, for the pain and heat and congestion. Ulcers with febrile accompaniments. Nævus.

Tissues.—*Anæmia, blood-poverty,* want of red blood.

Leucæmia. **Hyperæmia,** from relaxation of muscular fibres of blood vessels. **Pre-exudative stage of inflammation.** Hæmorrhages from any part of the body; blood bright red, with a tendency to coagulate rapidly. **Epistaxis,** especially in children. Mechanical injuries, results of kicks, blows, falls and cuts, for the inflammatory symptoms. Bone diseases when the soft parts are red, inflamed and painful. Dropsy from loss of blood and draining of the system. Varicose veins in young persons. Fractures, especially if soft parts are wounded. First stage of ostitis. Sprains externally as well as internally. Glandular ulceration. Wounds of the soft parts, with inflammatory symptoms. To be given in true chlorosis after *Calc. phos.*

Modalities.—All the pains of this remedy are aggravated by motion, excitement, warmth, and are relieved by cold and slow motion. Acts brilliantly in old people.

Homœopathic Data.—*Ferr. phos.* was proved by J. C. Morgan, M. D., in 1876. The symptomatology is to be found in *Allen's Encyclopædia,* vol. x, and in the *Cyclopædia of Drug Pathogenesis,* vol. ii. The wide and extensive usefulness of this drug is entirely owing to its introduction by Schussler. The provings up to the present time do not give a sufficient basis for the broad clinical applications that have been made of it according to the indications of Schüssler, although the provings, so far as they have gone, support these.

Administration.—Triturations and dilutions from the 6x to the 12x are recommended by Schüssler, although for anæmia much lower preparations have been used, as the 1x or 2x. Competent and trustworthy observers have found it advisable not to use this remedy below the 12x at night, as it is exceedingly liable to cause sleeplessness. Its external application is also recommended by Schüssler in such diseases as sprains, wounds, hæmorrhages, hæmorrhoids, etc. Cures with the 200th potency are reported in catarrh, summer complaint, gonorrhœa, etc. Dr. Morgan (the prover) used the 30th potency in water in scarlatina.

Relationship.—Corresponding as it does to the first stage of inflammation without exudation, its nearest analogue is *Acon.* *Rumex* contains a large amount of organic iron and is similar in respiratory and digestive symptoms. It stands midway between *Acon.* and *Gels.* Schüssler expresses himself as follows in regard to the use of *Acon.* for similar indications: "In the cases in which the vegetable remedy *Acon.* is used for irritation—hyperæmia—the basis of the first stage of all inflammations—the practice is indirect biochemistry. Regarding the way and the mode in which *Acon.* can bring about a cure, there are two **possibilities** to be thought of. Either the *Acon.* molecules, which have reached the seat of the disease, serve as a temporary substitute for iron molecules, which have ceased to perform their function, but only until the functional disturbance has been repaired by means of the vital circulation, or the *Acon.* molecules cause at once the introduction of new iron molecules into the diseased tissue, and are themselves ejected as foreign bodies as soon as the integrity of the latter has been restored—a fate which naturally also would be shared by those *Acon.* molecules which might have served as substitutes. Each of these possibilities would rest on **indirect** biochemistry. The healing of the irritation—hyperæmia—however, by means of *Ferr. phos.* is a **direct** biochemic procedure." (*Walker's Ed. of Schüssler's Diphth.*)

Aconite has a more bounding pulse and the characteristic restlessness and anxiety; *Gelsem.* a more soft, flowing pulse and more drowsiness and dulness.

In anæmic conditions compare also *China,* with which it has many symptoms in common. It is interesting to note that the tree from which *China* is obtained is always found in a ferruginous locality.

In its action upon the respiratory organs it clearly stands between **iron** and **phosphorus.** Like *Ferr.,* it is indicated in congestion of the respiratory organs, even when there is considerable fever. Especially notice that the oppression and dyspnœa, both of which are extremely marked in *Ferr.* and *Phosphor.,* are duplicated in this compound and afford good indications for its use; so, in a general way, symptoms of oppression like *Phosphor.* should be treated by this drug. (Allen, *Handbook.*)

Ferr. phos. corresponds in many points also to *Bryon., Bellad.* and *Arnica,* and to *Hepar* and *Mercur.,* especially in acute inflammation of middle ear. In the debility, loss of strength and vitality of children, it is the remedy if the flesh be firm, complexion delicate, hair light and curly; but *Sulphur* takes its place in dark-complexioned children, with flabby muscles, long and lank hair and moist skin. In the rheumatic affections of the aged, when the muscles are stiff and weakened, with a disposition to painful cramps. compare *Strych. phos.* California Zinfandel wine, a pure claret, the product of the vine growing in a volcanic, virgin soil, strongly impregnated with iron, possesses virtues in cases of anæmic tendency, probably due to the iron soil on which it grows. After *Ferr. phos.* is frequently indicated *Kali mur.* Especially in diphtheria, pneumonia, croup, etc., etc., often, also, *Kali sulph.*

In chlorosis, follow or precede *Calc. phos.*

In hæmorrhoids, *Calc. fluor.*

In diabetes, *Natr. sulph.*

In broncho-pneumonia, *Tart. emet.*

In ear affections, catarrhal deafness, *Calendula* and *Hydrastis.*

In headaches, *Natrum phos.* often follows well.

KALI MURIATICUM.

Synonyms.—Potassium Chloride. Kali Chloratum. Kali Chloridum. Potassii Chloridum.

Common Names.—Chloride of Potash or Chloride of Potassium. (N. B.—This drug must not be confounded with Kali Chloricum, whose synonyms are Potassium Chlorate, Potassæ Chloras and Potassii Chloras, whose common name is Chlorate of Potash, and whose formula is $K\ Cl\ O_3$. This has been proved, and the authors of the *"Guiding Symptoms"* have deemed them sufficiently similar to Schüssler's *Kali mur.* to incorporate them in their work. See Vol. VI., *"Guiding Symptoms."*)

Chemical Properties.—Formula, K Cl. Occurs in nature in mineral carnallite. It may be prepared by neutralizing pure aqueous hydrochloric acid with pure potassium carbonate or hydrate. It crystallizes in cubes, occasionally in octahedrons. The crystals are colorless or white, melt at a low red heat and volatilize at a high temperature without decomposition. It is soluble in three parts of cold and two of boiling water, and is insoluble in strong alcohol.

Preparation.—The pure chloride is prepared by trituration according to homœopathic pharmacy rules.

Physiologico-chemical Data.—This salt, according to Schüssler, stands in a chemical relation to fibrin; disturbances in its molecular action cause fibrinous exudations. Without the presence of this salt no new brain-cell formation would take place. This salt is found in the blood corpuscles, **muscles,** nerve and brain-cells, as well as in the inter-cellular fluids. In its physiological character it is closely related to the sodium chloride, many of the properties of which it shares. It is found in the blood in greater quantity than any other inorganic salt except its close relative Sodium chloride. The relation being as follows: *Kali mur.,* 4 parts in 1,000; *Natrum mur.,* 5½ parts in 1,000. If the cells of the epidermis, in consequence of any irritation, lose molecules of *Kali mur.,* fibrin in the form of a white or whitish-gray exudation, is thrown off. This, in drying, becomes a mealy eruption. If the irritation extends to the tissues beneath the epidermis, both fibrin and serum will exude, and the involved part of the skin will be pushed up in the form of blisters. This is exactly what takes place in small-pox, cow-pox, vaccine disease. Similar processes can take place within and amongst epithelial cells. If the integrity of the affected tissue is again restored by the administration of *Kali mur.* molecules, then a reabsorption or throwing off of the exudation occurs. Either result is attained probably by the production of hydrochloric acid formed by one part of chlorine from the K Cl with hydrogen. The action of this hydrochloric acid consists in dissolving the fibrin in the formative (nascent) state.

General Action.—*Kali mur.* corresponds to the second stage of inflammations of serous membranes when the exudation is of a plastic or fibrinous character. If leucocytes remain after the absorption of the fibrin of a plastic exudation, *Natrum phosph.* is serviceable. *Kali mur.* answers to croupous or diphtheritic exudations, and hence is useful in such diseases as diphtheria, dysentery, croup, croupous pneumonia, **fibrinous exudations in the interstitial connective tissues,** lymphatic enlargements, infiltrated inflammations, cutaneous eruptions from bad vaccine virus, etc. The principal general characteristic symptoms are **a white or gray coating at the base of the tongue, white or gray exudations, glandular swellings, discharges or expectorations of a thick, white, fibrinous slime or phlegm** from any mucous surface, or flourlike scaling of the skin, torpor of the liver, etc.

Kali mur. is one of the most useful and positive of all our remedies in the hands of the aurist—chiefly suited to the second or later stages of catarrhal states.

Guiding Symptoms and Characteristic Indications.

Mental Symptoms.—Patient imagines he must starve.

Head and Scalp.—Headache with vomiting, hawking up of white, milk-like mucus. Sick headache with white-coated tongue, or vomiting of white phlegm, arising from a sluggish liver, want of appetite, etc. In meningitis as a second remedy. Crusta lactea. Dandruff.

Eyes.—Discharge of white mucus from the eyes, or yellow, greenish matter and yellow, purulent scabs. Specks of matter on the lids. Superficial, flat ulcer of the eye arising from a vesicle. Blisters on cornea. Feeling of sand in the eyes. Iritis. Cataract, after *Calc. fluor.* Ulcers of asthenic type, tedious cases, redness not excessive, dirty-white, yellow, discharge moderate. Onyx and hypopyon. Trachoma. Parenchymatous keratitis. Retinitis when exudation sets in.

Ears.—Chronic catarrhal conditions of the middle ear. Deafness or earache from congestion and swelling of the middle ear or Eustachian tubes, with swelling of the glands, or cracking noises on blowing the nose or swallowing. Deafness due to throat troubles, white tongue, etc. Deafness from swelling of external ear. Moist exfoliation of epithelial layer of the tympanic membrane. Granular conditions of external meatus and membrana tympani. Excessive granulations. Proliferous form of middle ear inflammation, stuffy sensation, deafness and naso-pharyngeal obstruction. **Closed Eustachian tubes.** "When Politzer bag fails to open tubes, after a few doses of *Kali muriaticum* they may be inflated easily." (R. S. Copeland.) Retracted membrana tympani. Walls of external meatus atrophied. Seems to act more on right Eustachian tube. Glands about the ear swollen. **Snapping and noises in the ear.**

Nose.—Catarrh, phlegm white, thick. Stuffy cold in the head, whitish-gray tongue. Dry coryza. Vault of pharynx covered with adherent crusts. Nosebleed in the afternoon. (Holbrook.)

Face.—Cheeks swollen and painful. Faceache from swelling of face or gums.

Mouth.—Aphthæ, thrush, white ulcers in the mouths of little children or nursing mothers. Canker, excoriation and rawness of the mouth. Swollen glands about jaw and neck.

Tongue.—For the swelling in inflammation of the tongue. Coating of tongue **grayish-white, dryish or slimy.** Mapped tongue.

Teeth.—Gumboil before matter forms. Toothache with swelling of the gums and cheeks.

Throat.—The sole remedy **in most cases of diphtheria,** with *Ferr. phos.* Gargle also with same. Mumps, swelling of the parotid glands. Pharyngitis, throat swollen, spots or pustules appear with gray or whitish exudation (follicular). Adenoids are frequently cured by it. Hawks up offensive, cheesy, small lumps. Pain on swallowing. Syphilitic sore throat. Second remedy in tonsilitis as soon as swelling appears. Tonsils inflamed, enlarged so much can hardly breathe. Grayish patches or spots in throat. White deposits. Tonsils spotted gray or white. Adherent crusts in vault of pharynx.

A proving of the 6x trituration is reported in the *Homœo-pathic Recorder,* 1900. The drug caused a bad sore throat, pain on swallowing even water, tonsils inflamed, throat filled with tough, stringy mucus, ankle joints puffy. Prover was perfectly well until he commenced to take the *Kali mur.*

Gastric Symptoms.—Want of appetite. Biliousness with gray or white tongue. Dyspepsia and indigestion, with a whitish-gray tongue, sick feeling after taking fat, pain and heavy feeling on the right side under the shoulder. Fatty or rich food causes indigestion. Indigestion with vomiting of white, opaque mucus; water gathers in the mouth. Gastritis when caused by taking too hot drinks. Pain in the stomach, with constipation, vomiting of thick, white phlegm, or dark, clotted, viscid blood. Bitter taste with obstinate constipation. Jaundice with these symptoms. (Holbrook.)

Abdomen and Stool.—Jaundice if caused by a chill result-ing in catarrh of the duodenum, stools light in color. Sluggish action or complete torpidity of the liver, pain in right side, pale yellow evacuations, constipation and furred tongue. Typhoid or enteric fever, looseness of bowels, flocculent evacuations. Abdominal tenderness and swelling. Typhus, with constipation. Small white thread worms, causing itch-ing at the anus (*Natr. phos.*). Flatulence, abdominal swelling, etc. Second stage of peritonitis, typhlitis and perityphlitis (see clinical case under typhlitis). **Constipation,** light-colored stools denoting want of bile, sluggish action of liver, or oc-curing in consequence of some primary disturbance, espe-cially where fat and pastry disagree. **Diarrhœa,** after fatty food, and in typhoid fever, with pale yellow, ochre or clay-colored stools, white or slimy stools. **Dysentery,** purging, with slimy stools. **Hæmorrhoids,** bleeding piles, blood dark and thick, fibrinous, clotted.

Urinary and Sexual Organs.—Acute cases of inflamma-tion of the bladder, in the second stage, when swelling has set in and discharge is thick, white mucus. Chief remedy in chronic cystitis. Inflammatory affections of the kidneys. Dark colored urine, deposit of uric acid. The principal remedy in gonorrhœa and orchitis, resulting from a suppression of the same. In bubo for the soft swelling, and in soft chancres it is also the chief remedy (3x). Chronic stage of syphilis with characteristic pathological conditions. Gleet combined with eczema, visible or latent. Menstruation too late or suppresed, checked or too early, excessive discharge, dark clotted or tough, black blood, like tar. Amenorrhœa, menses suppressed. Periods too frequent. Leucorrhœa, discharge of milky-white mucus, thick, non-irritating, bland. Ulceration of the os and cervix uteri, with the characteristic discharge of thick, white, bland secretions. Chronic congestion of the uterus, hypertrophy, second stage (see *Calc. fluor.*).

Pregnancy.—Morning sickness with vomiting of white phlegm. Puerperal fever, chief remedy. Mastitis, gathered breast, to control the swelling.

Respiratory Symptoms.—Loss of voice, hoarseness from cold, tongue white. Asthma with gastric derangements, mucus white and hard to cough up. Bronchial asthma, second stage of bronchitis, when thick, white phlegm forms. Cough in phthisis, thick, white, milky sputa. Loud, noisy stomach cough; cough short, acute and spasmodic, like whooping cough, expectoration thick and white. Protruded appearance of eyes, white tongue, croupy, hard cough, harsh and barking. In croup the principal remedy for the exudation. Pneumonia, second stage, white, viscid expectoration. Pleurisy, second stage, with plastic exudations and adhesions. Wheezing rales, or rattling sounds of air passing through thick, tenacious mucus in the bronchi, difficult to cough up; hard cough. Child grasps at throat during a coughing spell.

Circulatory Organs.—Embolism, blood in a condition favoring formation of clots, which act as plugs. Second stage of pericarditis, plastic exudation, adhesions, etc. Palpitation from excessive flow of blood to the heart in hypertrophic conditions.

Back and Extremities.—Glands of neck swollen. Rheumatic fever, exudation and swelling around the joints. Acute articular rheumatism. Rheumatic gouty pains, if worse on motion and if tongue be coated white. Rheumatic pains felt only during motion or increased by it (*Ferr. phos.*). Nightly rheumatic pains worse from warmth of bed; lightning-like from small of back to feet; must get out of bed and sit up. Hands get stiff while writing. Chronic rheumatism and swelling, when all movements cause pain. Chronic swelling of the legs and feet, painless, itching violently. Second stage of hip-joint disease. Ulcers on extremities, fibrinous discharges, bunions. Tenalgia crepitans, creaking of the tendons on the back of the hand. Chilblains on hands or feet or any part.

Nervous Symptoms.—The specific or chief remedy in epilepsy, especially if occurring with or after suppression of eczema or other eruptions. Should be persisted in for some time. Tabes dorsalis.

Sleep.—Startled at the least noise. Somnolence. Restless sleep.

Febrile Symptoms.—Congestions and inflammations, second stage of any organ or part of the body. The second remedy in gastric, enteric or typhoid fever. In puerperal fever, the chief remedy for the exudation; also in rheumatic fever. In scarlet fever, with *Ferr. phos.,* suffices to cure most cass. Typhus fever, for the constipation. Intermittent fever, with characteristic accompaniments of this drug. Scarlet fever, as preventive. Catarrhal fever, great chilliness, tne least cold air chills him through, has to sit close to the fire to keep warm and is chilly. Better covered up in bed. (Holbrook.)

Skin.—Abscess, boils, carbuncles, etc., in the second stage, when interstitial exudation takes place, and to cause swelling to disappear before matter forms. Acne, erythema, eczema and other eruptions on the skin, with vesicles containing thick, white contents. Albuminoid eczema, or other skin disease, arising after vaccination with bad vaccine lymph. Eczema from suppressed or deranged uterine functions. Dry, flour-like scales on the skin. Obstinate eczema, crusta lactea, scurfy eruption on the head and face of little children. Its use in obstinate eczemas has been repeatedly verified. Burns of all degrees (externally also), blisters, etc. The 3x dissolved in water will frequently instantly relieve the pain of severe burns. Bunions, chilblains, eruptions connected with stomach or menstrual derangement. Erysipelas vesiculosa, the principal remedy. Herpes, shingles, lupus, measles, hoarse cough and glandular swellings, also for after-effects. Pimples on the face, neck, etc. Smallpox, principal remedy; controls formation of pustules. Ulcers with whitish, flour-like coating, or fibrinous, white discharge. Sycosis, primary remedy. Ingrowing toenail. Warts on hands.

Tissues.—Anæmia, as an intercurrent if skin affections be present. Hæmorrhages, dark, black, clotted, or tough blood. Effects of blows, cuts and bruises, for the swelling. Dropsy, arising from heart, liver or kidney disease, from obstruction of the bile-ducts, from weakness of the heart with palpitation. Whitish liquid is drawn off; white mucous sediment in the urine and white tongue. Fibrinous and lymph exudations in the interstitial connective tissues not becoming absorbed. **Chief remedy in glandular swellings, follicular infiltrations.** Proud flesh, exuberant granulations. Scrofulous enlargement of the glands. Scurvy, hard infiltrations. Second remedy in sprains, strumous conditions. Bad effects of vaccination. Syphilis.

Modalities.—All the stomach and abdominal symptoms of this drug are worse after taking **fatty food, pastry, or any rich food.** The rheumatic and other pains are increased and aggravated by **motion.** "It is a *sluggish* remedy for *sluggish* symptoms and *sluggish* constitutions, being anti-scrofulous, anti-sycotic and anti-syphilitic." (Saunders.)

Homœopathic Data.—Hering's *Guiding Symptoms,* Vol. VI, contains a complete resumé of symptoms of this drug, but unfortunately they are mixed up with symptoms of *Kali chloricum* with no distinguishing sign, rendering the collection of symptoms less valuable for purposes of study than would be the case had they been kept separate.

Administration.—Triturations and dilutions. Schüssler's

preference is for the 6x or 12x, though latterly he has given lower potencies. In diphtheria he recommends a gargle of the 3x, 10 or 15 grains in a tumbler of water. Its external application is also recommended in burns, boils, carbuncles, skin affections, warts, etc., to be applied on lint dressings.

Relationship.—Corresponding as it does to the second stage of all inflammatory troubles, immediately upon appearance of exudation, its nearest concordants are *Bryon.*, *Mercur.*, *Apis*, *Thuja*, *Spongia*, *Iodine*, *Pulsat.*, *Rhus* and *Sulphur.*

Analyses of the following drugs show them to contain *Kali mur.* in quite considerable quantities (homœopathically considered) : *Phytol.*, *Sanguin.*, *Stilling.*, *Pinus Can.*, *Asclep.*, *Ailanth.*, *Anis. stell.*, *Hamam*, *Virg.*, *Cimicif.*, *Berber.* Most of these possess many symptoms in common with *Kali mur.* When full chemical analyses shall have been made of the various drugs, vegetable and animal, we shall be able to compare the symptoms of each drug with those of its component parts. Compare in Eustachian tube troubles *Merc. dulc.* In syphilis follow with *Kali sulph.* and *Silicea.* In lupus, *Calc. phos.*

In Schüssler's Therapeutics *Kali mur.* assumes a role much like *Sulphur* in pure Homœopathy, as a deep-acting remedy with eradicating tendencies, useful as an intercurrent, and to prepare the way for other indicated remedies. *Kali mur.* is frequently followed by *Calc. sulph.*, which latter **completes** the action of the former. *Kali mur.* follows *Ferr. phos.*, when the true lymph-exudation of ripening interstitial inflammation sets in. It also supercedes *Natr. mur.* when the deeper layers of epithelium, adjoining the connective tissue basement, are involved, and even suffer exfoliation, causing a white-coated tongue and an opaque-whitish secretion. (Morgan.)

Kali mur. may be compared with the chlorate, *Kali chlor.*, the most poisonous of all the potash salts, a violent irritant of the whole gastro-intestinal mucous membrane, producing gangrenous ulceration. Compare in aphthæ, dysentery, epithelioma and nephritis. See Allen's *Handbook.*

KALI PHOSPHORICUM.

Synonyms.—Potassium Phosphate. Potassii Phosphas.

Common Name.—Phosphate of Potash.

Chemical Properties.—Formula, $K_2 H P O_4$. Prepared by mixing aqueous phosphoric acid with a sufficient quantity of potash, hydrate or carbonate, until the reaction is slightly alkaline, and evaporating. It crystallizes with difficulty. It is very deliquescent; it is freely soluble in water and insoluble in alcohol.

Preparation.—It is prepared by trituration, as directed by the rules of homœopathic pharmacy.

Physiologico-chemical Data.—*Kali phos.* is a constituent of all animal fluids and tissues, notably of the brain, nerves, muscles and blood-cells. All tissue-forming substances retain it with the greatest obstinacy, all nutritious fluids contain it, hence we may well conclude that it is indispensable to the formation of tissues. We know also that the oxidation processes, the change of gases in the respiration and other chemical transformations in the blood, as well as the saponifying of the fat and its further oxidation, are brought about by the presence of the alkalies, and chiefly by the presence of *Kali phos.* This alkaline reaction is essential to a large number of vital processes taking place in the interior, and is present, without exception, in all the animal fluids which are actually contained in the circulating system, or in the closed cavities of the body. (Dalton.) It is found that the nerves retain their vital properties for a long time and very completely in a solution of this salt. **By the diminution** of the excretion of *Kali phos.* in the urine, conditions are produced within the organism which may present many-sided resistance to the typhus-decomposing element, as well as to the extension of the typhus process. (Grauvogl.) *Kali phos.* is an antiseptic and hinders the decay of tissues. Adynamia and decay are the **characteristic** states of *Kali phos.*

The most important discovery of Liebig, that phosphate of

potash is predominant in the serum of the muscles and chloride of sodium in the circulating blood, we have often made great use of, particularly with regard to preferring the one or the other nourishment. (Hering.) A disturbance of the *Kali phos.* molecules has for its results:

1. In the mental sphere such conditions as bashfulness, anxiety, fear, tearfulness, suspicion, homesickness, weakness of memory, depression, etc.

2. In the vaso-motor nerves: Pulse at first small and frequent, later retardation.

3. In sensory nerves: Pain with paralytic sensation.

4. In motor nerves: Muscular and nerve prostration to paralysis.

5. Trophic fibres of sympathetic nerve: Retardation of nutrition to complete cessation within a circumscribed cellular domain, hence softening and degeneration of involved nerves.

General Action.—Conditions arising from **want of nerve power,** as prostration, exertion, loss of mental vigor, depression. According to the observations of the provers by Dr. Royal, the most prominent, persistent sensation, was prostration. This was referred to the mind, nerves and muscles. *Kali phos.* acts upon the brain and nerve cells, upon the corpuscles of the blood affecting the nutrition, causing irritation, slight inflammation and a certain degree of degeneration. In general, a sluggish condition of mind, which will act if aroused; also an exhausted mental condition after mental exertion or great strain. It corresponds to the hosts of conditions known as **neurasthenia,** in which field it has won its greatest laurels. An intense odor from all the emanations of the body is an accompaniment very frequently. It is a restorative in muscular debility following acute diseases, myalgia and wasting of muscular tissue, all dependent upon impaired innervation. Atrophic condition in old people. In cases from rapid decomposition of the blood corpuscles and muscle juice, such as hæmorrhages of a septic nature, scorbutus, stomatitis, gangrenous angina, phagedænic chancre, offensive, carrion-like diarrhœa, adynamic or typhoid conditions, etc.

Guiding Symptoms and Characteristic Indications.

Mental Symptoms.—Anxiety, **nervous dread** without any special cause, gloomy moods, fancies, looks on the dark side of everything, dark forebodings. Great despondency about business and pecuniary affairs. Indisposition to mix with people. Disinclined to converse. **Brain-fag from overwork. Depressed spirits, general irritability,** or great impatience. **Loss of memory,** omits letters or words in writing, uses wrong words, confusion of ideas. Dread of and oversensitiveness to noise. Dulness, want of energy, the slightest labor seems a heavy task. Undecided, captious, changeable. Rambling talk while wide awake (*Natr. mur.*). Effects of fright. After-effects of grief. Hallucinations and illusions of senses. Homesickness, haunted by visions of the past and longing after them. **Hysteria** from sudden emotions, fits of laughter and crying, false impressions. Insanity, mania and other mental derangements. Profound hypochondria and melancholia. Puerperal mania. Sighing depression. Shyness, excessive blushing from emotional sensitiveness. Stupor and low delirium. Whining and fretful disposition. Hysterical yawning. Delirium tremens, fear, sleeplessness, restlessness and suspicion, rambling talk. Grasping at imaginary objects. Mental aberrations. Softening of the brain, early stage, starting on being touched. Mental symptoms in children: Cross and ill tempered, fretful, frightened, screaming, whining. Night terrors. Shyness and excessive blushing. Somnambulism. Very nervous, starts at the slightest sound. Talks while asleep. Wants to be carried while awake from room to room. Wakes easily. (Holbrook.) Dr. George Royal in his provings finds irritability, nervousness, depression, drowsiness, inability to remember and restlessness prominent mental symptoms.

Head and Scalp.—Vertigo on rising, from lying, on standing up, from sitting and when looking upward. Vertigo and giddiness from nervous exhaustion and weakness. Dull pain in frontal region, worse in close room. Head feels dull and tired. **Cerebral anæmia.** Concussion of the brain. Asthenic conditions. Headaches, nervous, sensitive to noise, confusion. Headache of students and those worn out by fatigue. Headaches are relieved by gentle motion. Pains and weight in the **back of the head**, and across the eyes, **better while eating,** with feeling of weariness and exhaustion, inability for thought and characteristic mental symptoms. Headache with weary, empty, gone feeling at stomach. Menstrual headache with hunger. Neuralgic headache, humming in the ears, with feeling of inability to remain up, yet better under cheerful excitement; tearful mood, better when eating. Water on the brain. Itching of scalp. Back of head sore as if hair was pulled. Severe pain in the left mastoid; worse on motion and in open air.

Eyes.—Weakness of sight, loss of perceptive power, after diphtheria, from exhaustion. Excited, staring appearance of the eyes. Strabismus or loss of accommodation after diphtheria. Dropping of eyelids. Inco-ordination of ocular muscles and loss of accommodation for near objects. Sensation of sand or sticks in the eyes. Soreness of eyeballs—sore around edges of lids and burn as though full of smoke. Eyelids twitch, sight blurred. Black spots before the eyes.

Ears.—Deafness from want of nervous perception, with weakness and exhaustion of the nerves. Noises in the ears from nervous exhaustion, on falling asleep. Discharges of foul, offensive, ichorous pus from the ears. Ulceration of membrana tympani and middle ear suppurations; when discharges are foul, ichorous, **offensive,** fœtid or sanious. Atrophic conditions in old people, tendency of the tissues to shrivel up and become scaly. Humming and buzzing in the ears (*Magnes. phos.*). Itching in the auditory canal. Hearing supersensitive, cannot bear any noise.

Nose.—Epistaxis in weak, delicate constitutions, predisposition to same. Ozæna, offensive yellow crusts, ulcers. Thick **yellow discharge.** Sneezes from slightest exposure. Yellow crusts blown from nose followed by epistaxis. Thick mucus hawked from posterior nares.

Face.—Livid and sunken, with hollow eyes. Red, hot, burning face and forehead; at other times pale and yellow.

Neuralgic faceache, with great exhaustion after the attack. Right-sided neuralgia, relieved by cold applications. Neuralgic stitches from upper teeth to left ear. Pain in maxillary bones, better from eating, speaking and touch. Loss of power in facial muscles, causing contortions. Itching of face under beard; pimples. Facial paralysis from working in the water.

Mouth.—Hydroa on lips. Pimples and sore crusts on lips. Peeling of skin. Stomatitis; breath offensive, fœtid. Gums spongy and receding. Noma, cancrum oris; ashy-gray ulcers. Offensive odor from mouth. Saliva profuse, thick and salty.

Tongue.—Excessively dry in the morning. Feels as if it would cleave to the roof of the mouth. Tongue white, slimy, brownish like French mustard. Inflammation of the tongue when excessive dryness occurs or exhaustion sets in; edges of tongue red and sore.

Teeth.—Predisposition to bleeding of the gums; red seam on the gums. Severe pain in decayed or filled teeth. Toothache alternates with frontal headache. Toothache of highly nervous, delicate or pale, emotional persons, with easily-bleeding gums; they have a bright red seam or line on them. Nervous chattering of the teeth. Speech slow and inarticulate. Gums spongy and receding. Teeth feel sore. Grinding of teeth.

Throat.—Tonsils large and sore, with white, solid deposits like diptheritic membrane. Throat very dry; desire to swallow all the time. Hoarseness and loss of voice. Salty mucus raised from throat. Gangrenous sore throat. Croup, last stage, syncope and nervous prostration. After-effects of diphtheria. Weakness of sight, nasal speech and paralysis of any part. Malignant gangrenous conditions, prostrations, etc. Paralysis of the vocal cords.

Gastric Symptoms.—Gastric ulcer, because this is a disturbance of the trophic nerves. Excessive hungry feeling soon after taking food. A nervous "gone sensation" at the pit of stomach. Gaseous eructations. Gastritis when treatment has been delayed with asthenic conditions. Indigestion with nervous depression. Stomachache from fright or excitement. Very thirsty. Nausea and vomiting of sour, bitter food and of blood. Empty, gnawing sensation relieved by eating. Belching of gas tasting bitter and sour. Constant pain at epigastrium in a small spot. Deep green or blue vomiting from brain troubles.

Abdomen.—Weakness in the left side under the heart. Splenic troubles, flatulence with distress about the heart, of left side of stomach. Abdomen swells, dry tongue, etc. Typhoid fever, debility and other characteristic symptoms of this drug. Abdomen distended with gas. Bearing down pains. Colic in hypogastrium with ineffectual urging to stool; better bending double. Collapse, livid, bluish countenance and low pulse.

Stool and Anus.—Diarrhœa; painless, watery, from fright or other depressing causes, with great prostration; stools putrid, like rice water, bloody, carrion-like odor. Putrid and typhoid dysentery. Watery stool with imperative call, followed by tenesmus. Cholera symptoms. **Noisy, offensive flatus.** Profuse, painless, offensive and imperative stool while eating, followed by unsatisfied urging. Rectum burns and feels sore after movements, prolapsed. Bowels constipated. Stools dark brown, streaked with yellowish-green mucus. Paretic condition of rectum and colon. Hæmorrhoids, sore, painful and itching.

Sexual Organs.—Intense sexual desire; priapism in the morning. Impotence and painful emissions at night, without erection. Sexual instinct depressed, much of the time entirely dormant. Utter prostration and weak vision after coitus. Phagedænic chancres. Balanitis. **Female:** Menses premature and profuse in nervous subjects. Irregular, scanty, almost black, offensive odor. **Amenorrhœa with depression of spirits, lassitude, and general nervous debility.** Dull headache with menses, very tired and sleepy, legs ache, stitching all through pelvis and womb. Pain in left side and ovaries. Intense pain across the sacrum. Leucorrhœa, yellowish, blistering, **orange-colored,** scalding, acrid. **Intense sexual desire** after menses. Menstrual ːc in pale, lachrymose, nervous females. **Hysteria,** seɪ ˌtion of a ball rising in throat. **Nervousness.**

Urinary Organs.—Enuresis in larger children. Paretic conditions of bladder. Incontinence of urine from nervous debility. Frequent urination or passing of much water, frequent scalding. Bleeding from the urethra. Incontinence from paralysis of the sphincter of the bladder. Cystitis in asthenic conditions with prostration. Bright's disease of the kidneys. Diabetes with nervous weakness, voracious appetite, etc. Gonorrhœa with discharge of blood. Urine quite yellow like saffron. Itching in urethra. Cutting pain in bladder and urethra.

Pregnancy.—Threatened miscarriage in nervous subjects. **Puerperal mania, childbed fever.** Feeble and ineffectual labor pains, spurious labor-pains, tedious labor from constitutional weakness. Mastitis when the pus is brownish, dirty-looking, offensive odor, adynamic condition.

Respiratory Symptoms.—Asthma from the least food. Asthma (large doses and often repeated, 3x), depressed condition of nervous system. Loss of voice from paralysis of vocal cords. Hay asthma. Hoarseness with exhausted feeling from over-exertion of the voice, if rheumatic or nervous. Cough from irritation in the trachea, which feels sore. Expectoration thick, yellow, salty, fœtid. Chest very sore. Whooping cough in the highly nervous, with great exhaustion. Acute œdema of lungs, spasmodic cough with frothy, serous masses being brought up in excess and threatening suffocation. Shortness of breath when going up-stairs, or on any exertion. Croup, last stage, extreme weakness, pale or livid countenance.

Circulatory Organs.—Feeling of faintness in nervous people, or dizziness from weak action of the heart. Faintness from fright, fatigue, etc. Intermittent action of the heart, with nervous sensitiveness, from emotions, grief or care, with **palpitation.** Functional disturbances of the heart with weak, anxious, nervous state. Palpitation from slightest mental emotion or from walking up-stairs. Pulse intermittent, irregular, or below normal. Palpitation after rheumatic fever, with exhaustion. Anæmia, blood poor, palpitation with sleeplessness and restlessness. Sluggish circulation.

Back and Extremities.—Spinal anæmia. Idiopathic softening of the spinal cord, patient has trouble in guiding himself; loss of power of movement, he stumbles and trips easily. **Paralytic or rheumatic lameness,** with stiffness after rest, yet becoming better by gentle motion. Pain in back and extremities, relieved by motion, aching between scapulæ. Finger tips as if asleep. **Itching of palms and soles.** Itching of legs at night with numbness and weakness. Burning of feet—fidgety feeling in feet. Pains worse on rising from a sitting posture and by violent exertion. Bruised and painful feelings in parts affected, also discoloration. Acute and chronic rheur atism, pains disappear on moving about, severe in the morning after rest and on first rising from a sitting position, parts feel stiff. Exertion and fatigue aggravate. Stiffness, paralytic tendency. Pain in the hips. Paralyzing, drawing pain in sole of foot. Chilblains on the toes. Muscular weakness after severe illness.

Nervous Symptoms.—The great nervous tissue salt. **Neuralgic pains occurring in any organ, with depression, failure of strength, sensitiveness to noise and light, improved during pleasant excitement, and by gentle motion, but most felt when quiet or alone.** Sciatica. Dragging pain down back of thigh to knee, torpor, stiffness, great restlessness and pain, nervous exhaustion, etc. **Nervousness** without any reasonable cause; patient sheds tears and makes "mountains out of molehills." **Paralysis of any part of the body,** partial, paraplegia, hemiplegia, facial, or of the bladder, upper lid, etc. Paralysis usually comes on suddenly. Atrophic paralysis. Locomotor paralysis, loss of motor force, or stimulating power. Creeping paralysis in which the progress is slow, and tendency to wasting of the body, with loss of sense of touch, facial paralysis. Epilepsy, sunken countenance, coldness and palpitation after the attack. Attacks come from a fright. Hysteria, attacks from sudden emotion, feeling of a ball rising in the throat, nervous, restless, fidgety feeling. Trembling sensation. General debility, with nervousness and irritability. Bodily pains felt too acutely. Easily startled. Fears burglars. Neurasthenia, especially from sexual excess, characterized by severe spinal irritation. Nervousness due to sexual excitement with aching in sacrum, sleeplessness, aching in occiput and back, frequent micturition, despondency. [Dr. J. C. Nottingham.] **Paroxysms of pain, with subsequent exhaustion.** Infantile paralysis. **Spinal anæmia** from exhausting diseases, with laming pain, worse while at rest, but manifest on beginning to move.

Sleep.—Sleeplessness, after worry or excitement from nervous causes. Somnambulism, walking in sleep in children. Yawning, stretching and weariness, with sensation of emptiness at pit of stomach. Hysterical yawning. Constant dreaming of fire, robbers, of falling, ghosts, etc. Night terrors of children. Awakening from sound sleep screaming with fright. Lascivious dreams. No desire to rise in the morning. Twitching of muscles, on falling asleep.

Febrile Symptoms.—Intermittent fever; fœtid, debilitating, profuse perspiration. Typhus, malignant, putrid, camp, nervous or brain fevers. The chief remedy in typhoid, gastric and enteric fevers with brown, dry tongue, petechiæ, sleeplessness, stupor, delirium, etc. All typhoid and malignant symptoms are met by this drug. High temperature. Scarlet fever, putrid conditions of the throat, exhaustion, stupor, etc. Excessive and exhausting perspiration with fœtid odor. Perspiration while eating, with weakness at stomach. Hay fever; for nervous irritability.

Skin.—Eczema if oversensitiveness and nervousness accompany it. Felons, abscess and carbuncle when the matter becomes fœtid. Pemphigus malignus, blisters and blebs over the body, watery contents, skin wrinkled and withered-looking. Greasy scabs with offensive smell. **Alopecia areata.** Irritating secretions on skin. **Itching of the inside of hands and feet** where the skin is thickest. **Itching of the skin with** crawling sensation; gentle friction agreeable, excess causes soreness and chafing. Smallpox, putrid conditions. Chilblains on the toes, hands or ears, tingling and itching pain. Malignant pustule.

Tissues.—Anæmic conditions. Losing flesh all the time.

Atrophy, wasting diseases with putrid stools. Hæmorrhages. Blood dark, thin and not coagulating, putrid. General debility and exhaustion. Persons who suffer from suppressed sexual instinct or too much indulgence. Serous, ichorous, sanious, foul and offensive exudations, corroding, chafing exudations. **Gangrenous conditions.** Mortification in the early stages. Cancer; for the pains, offensive discharges and discolorations. Rickets with putrid discharges from the bowels. Scurvy with gangrenous conditions. **Septic hæmorrhages.** Suppurations with dirty, foul, ichorous, offensive discharge of pus. Leucæmia lienalis, typhus, putrid states. Atrophic condition in old people, tissues dry, scaly, lack of vitality. Discharges have a carrion-like odor.

Modalities.—According to Dr. Royal's careful provings, the general modalities are **better** from rest, nourishment and heat; **worse** from excitement, worry and both mental and physical exertion. Many symptoms of this remedy are aggravated by noise, by rising from a sitting posture, by exertion and continued exercise and after rest. **Cold air aggravates all pains.** The characteristic ameliorations are gentle motion, **eating,** under excitement and company; worse when alone. Pains and itching worse 2 to 5 A. M.

Homœopathic Data.—The remedy has been proved by the Provers' Union of Chicago, under the direction of Dr. H. C. Allen, the salient features of which are included in the above symptomatology. Later, Prof. Royal at the University of Iowa made provings, the report of which is published in the Transactions of the Institute for 1907. The salient points are included in above symptomatology. Another so-called proving has been made for Dr. B. Fincke, in a very sensitive young woman, with the c. m. potency held between the fingers! We must confess that we have not read the account of this heroic proving, as we could not conscientiously incorporate it in our treatise. However, any one interested in this curiosity can find a report of it in the Proceedings of I. H. A. Transactions, and also in *The Medical Advance,* March, 1892, in which number   Dr. Allen's arrangement of his proving can be found. A carefully prepared differential diagnosis of the phosphates from the imperfect materials, then in hand by the late Dr. Samuel Lilienthal, can be found in the Tranactions of the American Institute of Homœopathy for 1890. The drug merits more extended, careful provings with all potencies.

Administration.—The lower potencies seem to work best; thus the 2x or 3x in asthma is recommended by Schüssler. However, the higher, 6x and 12x, and high potencies have all been employed with success.

Relationship.—Probably the nearest analogues are *Rhus tox.* and *Phosph.*, with which it has many symptoms in common. The nervous symptoms of *Pulsat.* seem to depend on the amount of *Kali phos.* present. The peculiar mental state of *Pulsat.* is also found under this remedy. *Phytol.* also has many symptoms in common with *Kali phos.* Compare the sciatica. *Ignat.*, too, probably contains *Kali phos.*, as the hysterical symptoms are nearly identical. *Kali phos.* in its actions as a nerve sedative is related to *Ignat., Coffea, Hyoscy., Chamom.* In menstrual headaches compare *Zinc., Cimicif., Gelsem. Cyclamen, etc.* In bladder troubles *Kali phos.* often finds a complementary remedy in *Magnes. phos.*, the latter corresponding more to the spasmodic affections, while *Kali phos.* more to the paralytic symptoms. In incipient paralysis of the brain, when nephritic irritation accompanies, compare *Zinc. phos.* In hæmorrhages, bright or dark red, thin, watery, not clotted, follow *Kali phos.* by *Natr. mur.*, also *Nitr. ac.* After weakening diseases, the French variety of mushrooms, which contain large quantities of *Kali phos.*, restore the muscles more quickly than anything else. In its disordered mental conditions compare *Cyclam.*, which frequently corrects the abnormal, dreamlike, mental state of the insane. Compare *Kali mur.* in puerperal fever. In post-diphtheritic complaints compare *Lachesis, Caust.* In the gangrenous conditions compare *Kali chlor.*

Groups for study with *Kali phos.*:

1. Nervous system, *Cimicif., Hyos., Stramon., Zinc., Silicea, Ignat., Anacard., Conium, Staphisag.*

2.   Blood degeneration, *Baptis., Mur. acid, Laches., Crotalus, Kreosote, Arsenic., Carbo, China.*

KALI SULPHURICUM.

Synonyms.—Potassium Sulphate. Kali Sulphas. Potassæ Sulphas.

Common Name.—Sulphate of Potash.

Chemical Properties.—Formula, $K\ SO_4$. Occurs native in lavas, etc. Crystallizes in short, permanent, colorless four- and six-sided prisms. It is soluble in ten parts of cold and three parts of boiling water. It is insoluble in alcohol. It has a sharp, bitter, saline taste.

Preparation.—Pure sulphate of potash is prepared by trituration, as directed under the rules of homœopathic pharmacy.

Physiologico-chemical Data.—This remedy, according to Schüssler, is the function remedy of the epidermis and of the epithelium. A deficiency of this cell salt causes a yellow, slimy deposit on the tongue, slimy, thin, or decidedly yellow or greenish discharge and secretions of watery matter from any of the mucous surfaces, and epithelial or epidermal desquamation. The yellowness is probably due to retrograde metamorphosis—fatty degeneration of inflammatory products and of effete epithelium, etc.

The sulphates in nature and the oxide of iron serve as oxygen carriers. If sulphate and iron oxide come in contact simultaneously with an organic substance in a state of decay they give off their oxygen, and sulphate of iron is formed thereby; this may again be decomposed by the oxygen of the air, forming sulphuric acid and iron oxide, which, under favorable conditions, become again carriers of oxygen. Similar processes may occur in the human organism. Therefore, of the sulphates, *Kali sulph.* probably plays an important role, because it is found in the cells and in the intercellular fluids, muscles, nerves, epithelium and in the blood corpuscles. It is the carrier of oxygen. The oxygen taken up by the iron contained in the blood corpuscles is carried to every cell of the organism by the reciprocal action of *Kali sulph.* and iron. Every cell requires for its growth and development the vitalizing influence of oxygen. But its continued action oxidizes the organic basis of the cells. Hence, they disintegrate into their constituent elements. A deficiency of *Kali sulph.* may, according to location and extent, occasion the following symptoms: Feeling of heaviness and weariness, vertigo, chilliness, palpitation, fear, melancholy, toothache, headache, pains in the limbs, which intermit and change location. These pains are worse in closed rooms, warmth and towards evening, and better in fresh, open air, that is rich in oxygen.

Epidermis and epithelial cells poorly fed with oxygen loosen and desquamate freely. If oxygen is brought to the suffering parts by means of *Kali sulph.* the formation of new cells is thereby furthered, and these hasten, by their activity, to promote the desquamation of the old ones.

General Action.—It is applicable to the third stage of inflammation or to its stage of retrogression, the sulphates being characteristic products of the oxidation of tissue and the potassium having its special sphere in the solids, and the resulting salt becomes a prominent constituent of their ashes, whence we can infer its homœopathicity to the same stage. Ailments accompanied by profuse desquamation of epidermis. Yellow mucous discharges. Rise in temperature at night producing an evening aggravation. Another characteristic indication is amelioration in the cool, open air. Diseases caused by a retrocession of eruptions. To produce perspiration if *Ferr. phos.* fails.

Guiding Symptoms and Characteristic Indications.

Mental Symptoms.—Fear of falling. *Very irritable.* Anxiety in evening. Mental exertion aggravates. Always in a hurry. *Timid.*

Head and Scalp.—Vertigo, especially on looking and rising. Headache, which grows worse in a warm room and in the evening, and is better in the cool or open air. Falling out of the hair, bald spots. Rheumatic headaches, beginning in the evening and in a heated atmosphere; worse moving head from side to side or backward. Copious scaling of scalp, moist and sticky. Dandruff and scaldhead.

Eyes.—Cataract, opacity of the crystalline lens. Yellow crusts on the eyelids, **yellowish** or greenish, purulent discharge from the eyes. Conjunctivitis, ophthalmia neonatorum. Abscess of the cornea. Hypopyon.

Ears.—Deafness from congestion of the tympanic cavity, or with catarrh and swelling of Eustachian lining. Worse in a heated room, with a yellow, slimy coating on the tongue. Earache, with discharge of watery or **yellow** matter. Secretion of **thin, bright-yellow,** or greenish fluid after inflammation. (**Thick,** pus-like discharge, *Calc. sulph.*) Pain under the ear, sharp, cutting pain, tension, stitches and piercing below the mastoid process. Stinking otorrhœa. Polypoid excrescence closes the meatus.

Nose.—Colds with yellow, slimy expectorations, or discharge of watery matter. Patient feels generally worse in the evening or in a heated room. Decidedly yellow or yellowish-green discharges from the nose. After *Ferr. phos.* in colds, if the latter does not produce free perspiration and the skin remains dry. Old catarrh with yellowish, viscous secretion. Nose obstructed, together with yellowish discharge from the nares. Smell lost. Ozæna. Itching of nose.

Face.—Faceache aggravated in a heated room and in the evening, improved in cool or open air. Pallid face. Face red, features distorted. Epithelioma.

Mouth.—Lower lip swollen. Dryness and desquamation of the lower lip, peels off in large flakes; burning heat in the mouth.

Tongue.—Coating yellow and slimy, sometimes with whitish edge. Insipid, pappy taste. Lips, tongue and gums white. Taste lost.

Teeth.—Toothache worse in warmth and evening, better in cool, open air. Chronic painfulness of the gums.

Throat.—Dryness and **constriction.** Hawking of mucus. Tonsils swollen. Difficult swallowing. Engorgement of the naso-pharyngeal mucous membrane, especially after operation for adenoids, shown in mouth breathing, snoring, etc.

Gastric Symptoms.—Burning heat in stomach; burning thirst, nausea and vomiting. Chronic catarrh of the stomach, with yellow, slimy, coated tongue. Indigestion with sensation of pressure as of a load and fullness at the pit of the stomach, painful, and water gathers in the mouth. Sensation of faintness in the stomach. Colicky pains in stomach, when *Magnes. phos.* fails. Deep-seated pain in stomach. Gastric fever with a rise of temperature in the evening and fall in the morning. Thirstlessness. Dread of hot drinks. Jaundice from gastro-duodenal catarrh.

Abdomen and Stool.—Yellow, slimy, watery, purulent diarrhœa, with characteristic tongue. Pains resembling colic. Abdomen feels cold to touch. Pains similar to flatulent colic, caused by great heat, from excitement and sudden coldness of the part following. Gas escaping from the bowels has a sulphurous odor. Purging and severe colic. Habitual constipation. Pain in rectum and anus during stool. Internal and external hæmorrhoids, with characteristic tongue and secretions. Typhoid and enteric fevers, with rise of temperature at night and fall in the morning. Tympanitic abdomen, cramp and every indication of approaching peritonitis. Abdomen very tense and cold. **Violent itching of anus,** stitching and tenesmus. Symptoms of cholera. Black, thin, offensive stools. Post-scarlatinal nephritis.

Sexual Organs.—Gonorrhœa, slimy, yellow or greenish discharge. Balanitis, gleet. Orchitis, after suppressed gonorrhœa. Leucorrhœa, discharge of yellow, greenish, slimy or watery secretions. Menstruation too late and too scanty, with a feeling of weight and fulness in the abdomen, and headache, yellow-coated tongue. Syphilis with characteristic evening aggravation. Metrorrhagia, bearing down in pelvis. Burning in genitals.

Urinary Organs.—Chronic cystitis. Urination painful, frequent at night; dribbling. Albuminuria; copious viscid deposit.

Respiratory Organs.—Bronchial asthma with yellow expectoration, worse in the warm season or in a hot atmosphere. Bronchitis, expectoration distinctly yellow, or greenish, slimy, or watery and profuse. Cough worse in the evening with heat. Pneumonia. Coarse rales but cannot cough up much mucus, sputa consists of watery matter. Mucus slips back and is generally swallowed; hard, hoarse cough like croup. Weary feeling in the pharynx. **Great rattling in the chest, rattling of mucus with cough.** Third stage of catarrhal cough, with free, yellowish expectoration. Croupy hoarseness, speaking is fatiguing, hoarseness from cold. Whooping cough with yellow, slimy expectoration. Pneumonia with wheezing; yellow, loose, rattling phlegm is coughed up, or watery matter. Suffocative feeling in a hot atmosphere. Desire for cool air.

Circulatory Organs.—Pulse quick with throbbing, boring pain over crest of ilium. Pulse scarcely perceptible. *Pulsation* all over the body.

Back and Extremities.—Neuralgic or rheumatic pains in the back, nape of the neck or in the limbs, periodical, worse in the evening or in a warm room, and decidedly better in a cool atmosphere. Rheumatic pains in the joints or any part of the body, when of a **shifting, wandering, flitting nature,** settling in one place, then another, with characteristic modalities. Fungoid inflammation of the joints. Cramps in upper and lower extremities. Scaly eruptions mostly on arms, better from hot water.

Nervous Symptoms.—Neuralgic pains in different parts of the body, with tendency to shift in locality. Chorea.

Sleep.—Very vivid dreams. Night-mare. Restless sleep, wakes early and frequently.

Febrile Symptoms.—Temperature rises in the evening until midnight, then falls again. It assists in promoting perspiration, hence it should be given frequently, and warm coverings at the same time should be applied. Intermittent fever with yellow, slimy, coated tongue. Fevers from blood poisoning, gastric, enteric and typhoid fevers, scarlet fever, stage of desquamation, cold sweat.

Skin Lesions.—Vesico-pustular and papular. There is a greenish-yellow exudate with the formation of a thin crust which is quite loosely attached, but the condition may resolve itself into the squamous type and then the crusts become dry and give off an abundance of scales. (Bernstein.) Skin inactive (give in hot drinks while in bed, wrapped in blankets). Epithelial cancer, with discharge of thin, yellow, serous matter. Eczema, when the discharge is yellow or greenish, watery, or when suddenly suppressed. Sudden retrocession of the rash, from a chill or other causes, in any eruptive disease—measles, scarlet fever, eczema, etc., when the skin is harsh and dry. Blistering erysipelas; to favor falling off of scabs. Burning, itching, papular eruption. Diseased condition of the nails, interrupted growth, etc. (*Silicea*). Skin scales freely on a sticky base. Sores on the skin with yellow, watery secretion; surrounding skin peels off. Effects of ivy poison, nettlerash. In smallpox to promote falling off of crusts and formation of healthy skin. Scaly tetter in the palms. Chafing of children. Old tetters. Tuberculous ulcers with a continuous oozing of yellow pus and lymph.

Tissues.—The grand characteristics are the **evening aggravation** and the **amelioration in the cool air. Great aggravation in a heated room**; also the characteristic secretion from mucous membranes, yellow, sticky, slimy.

Homœopathic Data.—No regular proving, but a brief collection of symptoms derived from very large doses, old school sources, is found in *Allen's Encyclopædia*, vols. v and x, and vol. vi, *Guiding Symptoms*. They are included in the above.

Administration.—Schüssler recommends the 12x and 6x, these giving the best results. In febrile conditions it must be given frequently. It is recommended externally in dandruff and diseases of the scalp. Often completes a cure commenced by *Kali mur.*

Relationship.—The nearest analogue to *Kali sulph.* appears to be *Pulsat.* It is interesting to compare these two remedies, as they have many symptoms in common. Thus both have:

Aggravation of symptoms in a warm room. Amelioration in the cool and open air. Discharges from mucous membranes are yellow, purulent in character; sometimes yellowish-green. Coating of tongue yellow and slimy. Pressure and feeling of fulness in stomach. Gonorrhœa with yellow or yellowish-green, bland discharge. Yellow mucous expectoration from the lungs on coughing. Hoarseness from a simple cold. Pains in the limbs, worse at night and from warmth; better in cool, open air. Palpitation of the heart. Migratory or shifting and wandering rheumatic pains. A chemical analysis of *Pulsat.* shows that one of its constituents is *Kali sulph.*, another is *Kali phos.* and another is *Calc. phos.* Its mucous symptoms probably are due to the presence of *Kali sulph.*, and its mental and nervous symptoms to *Kali phos.;* but, of course, this is pure hypothesis, and only suggested for further study and observation. *Kali sulph.* often follows with advantage *Kali mur.* Compatible remedies in itching and redness of skin: *Acetic acid, Arsen., Calc. carb., Dolichos, Hepar, Puls., Rhus, Sepia, Silicea, Sulphur, Urtica.*

Compare *Natr. mur.* in deafness, pain in stomach, coarse rales and profuse exudations, but these are more watery in *Natr. mur.*

MAGNESIA PHOSPHORICA.

Synonyms.—Magnesium Phosphoricum.

Common Name.—Phosphate of Magnesia.

Chemical Properties.—Formula, $Mg\ HPO_4$, $7H_2O$. It is made by mixing phosphate of soda with sulphate of magnesia. The crystals resulting are six-sided, needle-like. They have a cooling, sweetish taste. They are sparingly soluble in water; 322 parts dissolving one part after standing a long time. Boiling decomposes it. It exists in the grains of cereals, and can be detected in considerable quantity in beer.

Preparation.—The salt is triturated according to the rules of homœopathic pharmacy.

Physiologico-chemical Data.—It is an earthy constituent of muscles, nerves, bone, brain, (grey substance much more) spine, sperma (especially rich in *Magnes. phos.*), teeth and blood corpuscles. A disturbance of its molecular motion causes cramps, pains and paralysis. Schüssler says that the action of *Magnes. phos.* is the reverse of that of iron. By functional disturbance of the molecules of the latter the muscular fibres relax; through the functional disturbances of the magnesium molecules they contract; hence it is the remedy for cramps, convulsions and other nervous phenomena.

General Action.—Diseases having their seat in the nerve-fibre cells or in the terminal bulbs of the nerves, in the muscles or in the muscular tissue itself, are cured by this remedy. It corresponds to pains of all kinds with the exception of burning pains; it is especially related to cramping pains. Pains which are darting, spasmodic in character, boring, lightning-like, accompanied by a constrictive feeling. They are often changing in locality, and are **relieved by warmth and pressure.** It is purely **antispasmodic,** and hence is curative in cramps, spasms of the glottis, tetanus, epilepsy, spasmodic retention of the urine, paralysis agitans, etc. It is **best** adapted to lean, thin, emaciated persons of a highly nervous organization, and prefers light complexion and the right side of the body. Cold in general favors its action exceedingly, whereas heat and pressure interfere with it. Hence the patient is relieved by these. Attacks are often attended with great prostration and sometimes with profuse sweat. The *Magnes. phos.* patient is languid, tired, exhausted, unable to sit up, whether he is suffering from acute or chronic affections.

Guiding Symptoms and General Characteristics.

Mental Symptoms.—Illusions of the senses, forgetful, dulness and inability to think clearly, indisposition to mental effort. Sobbing with lamenting. Laments all the time about the pain, with hiccoughing. Talking to herself constantly or sitting still in moody silence. Carries things from place to place. Provings give indisposition for mental or physical exertion.

Head and Scalp.—Brain troubles of children, with uncon-

7

sciousness and convulsive symptoms. Headache, pains shooting, darting, stabbing, shifting, intermittent, spasmodic, paroxysmal and neuralgic, **always relieved by the application
of warmth.** Nervous headaches with sparks before the eyes.
Very acute pains in the head, more in young and strong persons, constant while attending school or **after mental labor,**
or from any injurious stimulus. Pain on top and back of
head extending down the spine, most severe between the
shoulders. Headache from occiput, spreading over whole head
with nausea and **chilliness.** Scalp feels rough; much dandruff; pustules. The Iowa provings show pains in the head;
in all cases but one, they were left sided, worse quick motion of
the head by stooping and jarring. Some relief from pressure
but most frequently from **walking in open air.** Vertigo was
present in most cases. Three provers had sensations as if
contents of head were sloshing around or parts of brain changing places.

Eyes.—Vision affected, sees colors before the eyes (chromatopsia), sparks, eyes sensitive to light, photophobia, diplopia,
pupils contracted, dulness of vision from involvement of the
optic nerve or retina. Dark spots float before the eyes.
Nystagmus, spasmodic squinting, ptosis or drooping of the
eyelids. Twitching of eyelids. **Orbital and supraorbital
neuralgias, worse on the right side and relieved by warmth**
applied externally, and exquisitely sensitive to touch. Increased lachrymation with the pain. Itching of lids. "Retinitis
Pigmentosa" (R. S. C.). Eyes tire easily; can only read a
few lines. Lids heavy as if pressed by weight.

Ears.—Weakness of the auditory nerve-fibres causing deafness. Otalgia purely nervous in character, better from heat.
Neuralgic pain worse behind right ear, made worse by going
into cold air and **washing face and neck in cold water.** "A
remedy to be thought of in all forms of internal ear disease."
(Copeland).

Nose.—Loss or perversion of the sense of smell, even without catarrhal troubles. Alternate stoppage and profuse gushing discharge. Smarting and rawness, worse left side. Cold
in head, alternately dry and loose.

Face.—Neuralgia, supra- and infra-orbital. Prosopalgia, lightning-like pains, intermittent, always better from warmth; worse on touch, pressure, cold and on right side, at 2 P. M. and in bed. Neuralgic pains of right side from infra-orbital foramen to incisor tooth, gradually radiating over the entire right side of face, worse by touch, opening the mouth, cold air and when body gets cold. From washing or standing in cold water. From exposure to a strong north wind. Dr. Berridge cured a case having "Shooting pain from right upper jaw to forehead and ear" with this remedy.

Mouth.—Convulsive twitchings of the angles of mouth. Sensation of painful contraction at articulation of lower jaw, with backward jerking. Spasmodic stammering. Trismus; lock-jaw. Mouth dry with sticky saliva, cracks at the corners of the lips.

Tongue.—Generally clean with pain in stomach; coated white, with diarrhœa; bright red, with rawness in mouth, left side sore, smarting like canker-sore, making eating painful as if scalded.

Teeth.—Very sensitive to touch or cold air. Cannot brush teeth with cold water. Toothache worse after going to bed, changes place rapidly; worse from cold things, cold washing; **better by heat and hot liquids** (if cold, *Ferr. phos., Bry., Coff.*). **Severe pains in decayed or filled teeth.** Ulceration of teeth with swelling of glands of face, throat and neck **and swelling** of tongue. **Complaints of teething children. Spasms** without febrile symptoms.

Throat.—Goitre. Soreness and stiffness, especially right side; parts seem puffy, **with chilliness** and aching all over; swallowing painful with pain in back of head. Must swallow. Dropping from posterior nares, with sneezing and rough throat. Spasm of the glottis. Spasmodic constriction of the throat on attempting to swallow liquids, with choking sensation. One prover hawked up a fibrinous cast of the pharynx.

Gastric Symptoms.—Sensitive to acids and averse to coffee. Craves sugar. Hiccough with retching day and night. Obstinate singultus, causing long lasting soreness. Regurgitation of food. Burning, tasteless eructations, better drinking hot water. Heartburn. Gastralgia, with clean tongue, relieved by warmth and bending double. Pain worse from touch at epigastrium and renewed by drinking cold water. Spasms or cramps in the stomach, pain as if a band were tightly laced around the body. Flatulent distention of stomach with constrictive pain. Flatulent dyspepsia. Nausea and vomiting.

Abdomen.—Enteralgia. Flatulent colic forcing patient to bend double, relieved by rubbing, warmth, pressure, accompanied with belching of gas which gives no relief. Incarcerated flatulence; rumbling and belching. **Flatulent colic of children and the newborn.** Abdominal pains cause great restlessness, radiate from navel, and are worse from stretching the body out, often accompanied by a watery diarrhœa. Cannot lie on back stretched out, has to lie bent over. **Bloated, full sensation in abdomen; must loosen clothing, walk about** and constantly pass flatus. Provers showed colic-like, cramping pains, coming on before stool, persisting after stool with relief from pressure.

Stool.—Diarrhœa, watery, with vomiting and cramps in calves; with chilliness and pain in stomach. Stools expelled with force. Dysentery, with cramp-like pains, spasmodic retention of urine; cutting, lightning-like pains in hæmorrhoids, so severe as to cause fainting; most severe in rectum and abdomen. Pains in rectum with every stool. Pain with prolonged spasm of abdominal muscles. Constipation of infants, with spasmodic pain at every attempt at stool, indicated by sharp, shrill cry; much gas and rumbling and flatulent colic. Constipation was the rule in the provers. Stools dry, hard and dark brown, passed with difficulty.

Urinary and Sexual Organs.—Constant urging to urinate when standing or walking. Spasm of the bladder; child passes large quantities of urine; spasmodic urinary complaints; spasmodic retention; spasm of the neck of the bladder; painful urging. Nocturnal enuresis from nervous irritation. Vesical neuralgia after the use of catheter. Deficiency or excess of phosphates. Gravel. Sexual desire increased.

Female.—Menstrual colic; pain precedes flow; intermittent, worse on right side, great relief from heat. Ovarian neuralgia, worse on right side. Vaginismus. Ovaritis. **Membranous dysmenorrhœa.** (Has cured a number of cases.) Menses too early, with dark, fibrinous, stringy flow. Swelling of external parts. Severe cramping pains over entire pelvis, sharp pains in both ovaries and small of back, could feel womb contract and force out blood. Prompt relief from application of heat. Flow dark, clotted, intermittent.

Pregnancy.—Spasmodic labor pains, with cramps in the legs, crampy pains, excessive expulsive efforts. Puerperal convulsions (intercurrent). Relaxes contracted uterus. Retained placenta.

Respiratory System.—Asthma when flatulence is troublesome. Spasmodic closure of the windpipe, with sudden, shrill voice, constriction of the chest. Persistent semi-chronic cough of a pseudo-catarrhal, nervous character. True spasmodic cough, coming on in paroxysms without expectoration; convulsive fits of nervous cough ending in a whoop; whooping cough, spasmodic cough at night, with difficulty in lying down. Darting pains in the chest, more on right side, which radiate from pain in bowels. Oppression of chest, shortness of breath. Constriction of chest and throat, with spasmodic, dry, tickling cough. Respiratory muscles appear weak. Chest seems to collapse during expiration. Chest pains worse from motion.

Circulatory Organs.—Angina pectoris, neuralgic spasms (better given in hot water); nervous palpitation of the heart when spasmodic. Heart action easily excited. Palpitation relieved by lying on left side. Apex beat visible through clothing.

Neck and Back.—Sore pain in lower part of back, in neck and small of back. Acute, boring, darting, neuralgic pains in any part of the back. Shifting pains; intercostal neuralgia. Dorsal spine very painful and sensitive to touch.

Extremities.—Darting pains in shoulders and arms, worse in right. Joints painful. Involuntary shaking of the hands.

Paralysis agitans. Tingling sensations. Neuralgia in lower limbs, at night, mostly with spasmodic muscular contractions; legs ache after getting in bed. Sensation in limbs like a shock of electricity, followed by muscular soreness. Cramps in calves. Sciatica with excruciating, spasmodic pains. Violent pains in acute rheumatism of the joints (as intercurrent during rheumatic fever). Deficiency in locomotive power. Feet very tender. Pains aggravated by the slightest touch.

Nervous Symptoms.—Nutrition and function remedy for the nerve tissues. **Languid, tired, exhausted,** unable to sit up. Alcoholism. Nightly neuralgias, with spasmodic muscular contractions. Spasms from idiopathic affections of motor nervous tissues. Twitchings all over body during waking hours. Lightning-like pains. Convulsions with stiffness of the limbs or of the body, fingers clenched, thumbs drawn in. Singultus. **Chorea,** involuntary movements and contortions of the limbs. Epilepsy resulting from vicious habits, spasms, stiffness of limbs, clenched fists and teeth. Paralysis agitans, trembling of hands, limbs, or shaking of head. Paralysis of nerve fibres. Writer's cramp. Piano or violin player's cramp. Tetanic spasms, lock-jaw (rub it into the gums). Convulsive sobbing. The provings at the Iowa College show that the drug profoundly affects the nerve centres causing a lowering of nerve tonic.

Sleep.—Spasmodic yawning. Insomnia from exhaustion or lack of brain nutrition. Drowsiness. Sleep disturbed by troublesome dreams, by pain in occiput and back of neck.

Febrile Symptoms.—Intermittent fever with cramps in the calves. **Chilliness** after dinner, in evening, about 7 P. M. **Chills run up and down the back with shivering;** are followed by a suffocating sensation. Severe chills about 9 A. M. Bilious fever. Profuse sweat.

Skin.—Burning and stinging pain in bunions and corns. Barber's itch; herpetic eruptions with white scales. Boils. Rash like insect bites; worse about knees, ankles and elbows.

Tissues.—Spasms and neuralgias. Nervous asthma. Spasm of glottis. Chorea. Tetanus. Bad effects from injurious stimulants.

Modalities.—All the pains of this remedy are characteristically worse on the right side, from cold, cold air, draught of air, cold washing and from touch. They are always relieved by warmth, heat, pressure, bending double, and friction. In the Iowa proving the left side seemed to be more frequently involved than the right. Open air relieved vertigo and head symptoms.

Homœopathic Data.—Since its introduction by Schüssler this magnificent remedy has been proved by Drs. W. P. Wesselhœft, J. A. Gann and other members of the I. H. A., by which the main indications of Schüssler were verified and others added, thus giving us a polychrest of the highest order. All the provings have been arranged systematically by Dr. H. C. Allen, and published in the *Medical Advance,* December, 1889. The foregoing symptomatology contains all that seemed to us reliable and worthy of preservation. A resumé of its symptoms is also given in Hering's *Guiding Symptoms,* vol. vii. In 1906 *Magnesia phosphorica* was proved by eight students of the Homœopathic Department of Iowa State University, and the more striking features of the proving have been here incorporated.

Administration.—Schüssler recommends the 6x trituration, and adds that it acts best when given in hot water. Many practitioners have verified this valuable hint, and found also that in case of failure with this preparation, the lower potencies, such as the first and second, would cure. In colic, Dr. J. C. Morgan advises the 30x in water, and frequent doses. But in view of the really surprising and apparently wholly trustworthy results obtained by the provers with the high and highest potencies, we would recommend these should the lower fail.

Relationship.—*Magnes. phos.* has won its greatest laurels in the treatment of nervous affections, neuralgias especially. Here, in a general way, it finds another tissue remedy with which it shares the honors. This is *Kali phos.,* which is more truly the nutritive brain remedy, and clinically corresponds more to paretic affections, while *Magnes. phos.* does more to spasmodic affections.   The general modality differs, too, *Kali phos.* having amelioration by cold applications.   In studying the action of this drug, we find the most striking resemblance in the colic and other neuralgic symptoms with *Colocynth.;* and it certainly is a suggestive and interesting fact that *Colocynth.* contains 3 per cent. of *Magnes. phos.*   The flatulent colic reminds also of *Dioscorea.*   Another near relative is *Gelsem.*   The provings of both show a close correspondence in the mixture of spasmodic and paretic symptoms, hence their successful employment in hysteria, hypochondriasis and spinal irritation.   The chill up and down the back is common to both.   Naturally enough come into this physiological group *Ignat.* and *Nux mosch.,* which compare especially in the flatulent symptoms of both and the spasmodic of *Ignat.*   In spasms *Magnes. phos.* is like *Bellad.,* and follows it frequently, should it fail and the patient present the dilated pupils, staring eyes and starting at slightest noise.   In strabismus, if caused by worms, compare *Natrum phos.;* in watery secretions, diarrhœa, etc., *Natrum mur.;* in epilepsy, *Kali mur., Calc. phos.,* and *Silicea;* affections of the right side of the body, *Bellad., Bryon., Chelid., Kali carb., Lycop., Podoph.*   The violent pains remind of *Bellad., Stramon.;* the shifting rapidly changing of *Puls., Kali sulph., Lac can.;* the squeezing, constricting sensation of *Cactus, Calc., Iod.* and *Sulph.*   The menstrual and labor-pains resemble *Viburn.,* also *Pulsat.,* but, unlike this, are better by heat.   *Cimicif.* has much similarity here, but its pains are more steady, those of *Magnes. phos.* more spasmodic. Again, the pains of *Magnes. phos.* seem to be more in the deeper structures—ovaries, fundus; those of *Cimicif.* more in the ligamentous (A. P. Davis).   In membranous dysmenorrhœa remember *Borax* and *Acetic acid* and *Viburn. op.*   Among plants containing *Magnes. phos.* may be mentioned *Lobelia, Symphytum, Stramon.* and *Viburn.,* which probably explains the presence of similar symptoms.   In the nightly neuralgic pains relieved by heat compare also *Ars.;* and its action on the nervous system generally compare *Zinc.*

   Antidotes.—*Bellad., Gelsem., Lachesis.*

NATRUM MURIATICUM.

Synonyms.—Sodium Chloride. Chloruretum Sodicum. Natrum Chloratum Purum. Sodii Chloridum. Chloride of Sodium.

Common Names.—Common Salt. Table Salt.

Chemical Properties.—Formula, Na Cl. It occurs abundantly in nature, nearly everywhere. It crystallizes from aqueous solutions in colorless, transparent, anhydrous cubes; it is soluble in three parts of cold water, scarcely more in boiling. It is insoluble in absolute alcohol. Its watery solutions dissolve several bodies insoluble in water, *e. g., Calc. phos.*, etc. One gramme of salt contains Chlorin 0.6 and Natrum 0.4.

Preparation.—One part by weight of pure chloride of sodium is dissolved in nine parts by weight of distilled water. Amount of drug power, one-tenth. Dilutions and triturations should be prepared according to Hahnemann's methods.

Physiologico-chemical Data.—Prof. Loeb's experiments prove that the various tissue cells will rapidly disintegrate in the absence of the proper proportion of sodium, potassium and brine salts in the circulating fluid, the normal ratio being 100 molecules of sodium, 2.2 molecules of potassium, and 1.5 molecules of lime. Any marked departure from this proportion is followed by a more or less rapid degeneration of protoplasm. While the cell structure contains none of the salts, their presence in the proper ratio in the fluid which surrounds the cell results in a protective action on the cell membrane. This protective process he calls "tanning," and to it he ascribes the maintenance of a stable metabolism within the cell. It seems that the chief factor in maintaining this protoplasmic equilibrium is the antagonistic action between the lime salt and the sodium and potassium.

Whether, in the absence of the lime, the others act as a direct poison, or the deficiency of lime weakens the protection of the cell and so allows a direct attack on the protoplasm by some other toxin, or whether the absence of this tanning process on the cell wall permits of an unstable diffusion of fluids in the cell, has not yet been determined.

Common salt is more widely distributed in nature than any other substance except water. This salt is a constituent of every liquid and solid part of the body. It is the most important of the chemical substances found in the blood plasma, here being present in the proportion of about 0.7 per cent. From the simple constitution, and from the fact that the body cells readily take up Sodium chloride, whereas they do not so readily take up other salts, the phosphates, sulphates, etc., salt is the great regulator of osmotic tension in the organism, and performs by this means one of its chief functions, viz., keeping the blood serum at a uniform specific gravity. The whole quantity of salt in the human body is approximately eleven ounces, and if more than sufficient to counterbalance the daily waste is introduced into the system, it is at once excreted by the kidneys. (T. G. Stonham.)

This function of salt to regulate the degree of moisture within the cells is accomplished by virtue of its property of attracting water, which is imbibed as drink or in the food, and reaching the blood through the epithelial cells of the mucous membrane, whence it may finally reach the various cells, giving them the needful degree of moisture. Every cell contains soda, combining with nascent chlorine, which is formed by the splitting up of the chloride of sodium contained in the intercellular fluids. This chloride of sodium within the cell thus produced has the property of attracting water; in consequence of which the cell enlarges and is divided. Only in this way does division of cells for purposes of cell multiplication take place.

If no chloride of sodium is formed within the cells, the water destined to supply their moisture is retained in the intercellular fluids, and a **hydræmia** results. The patient then shows a watery, **bloated** appearance, is **languid, drowsy, lachrymose, chilly,** especially along the spine and extremities, inclined to watery exudations, salivation, etc. He craves salt. Although a plentiful supply of salt may be offered in the food, the diseased condition is not removed, simply because the cells cannot take up the particles of salt unless offered in a very dilute solution.

An oversupply of salt within the intercellular fluids often occasions a salty taste, due to the irritation of the **glossophar-yngeal** and **lingual** nerves. Such a condition also causes acridity of secretions of mucous membranes or of open wounds.

Chloride of sodium contained in the healthy epithelial cells of serous membranes regulates the osmosis of water from the arterial blood to the several serous sacs. A disturbance of the functions of these salt molecules is followed by a watery exudation within the sacs. By the therapeutic application of small doses of *Natrum mur.* the cells are enabled to reabsorb the exudation.

A disturbance of the molecular motion of this salt in the epithelium of the tear glands, or in the salivary glands is followed by lachrymation or ptyalism.

If the dental branch of the fifth nerve is irritated, and the disturbance reaches the lachrymal glands, which is done by means of the secretory fibres of the sympathetic, and which results in a disturbance of the function of the molecules of salt in these cells, we have a toothache accompanied by a profuse flow of saliva.

The epithelial cells of the intestinal mucous membrane transfer, by means of their salt, the water taken with the food into the blood contained in the branches of the portal vein. A disturbance of their function through any irritation results in a reverse flow. Serum enters the intestinal canal, and a watery diarrhœa results in consequence. And if the irritation reaches the mucous cells of the intestines, a watery, mucous diarrhœa results. The mucin of the mucous cells appears on the surface as a glairy, transparent mucus. The normal secretion of mucus is decreased if the mucous cells contain too little salt and mucin.

It is the sodium chloride particularly which regulates the

quantity of water entering into the composition of the blood corpuscles, thereby preserving their form and consistence; and it seems to perform an analogous office with regard to the other semi-solids of the body. (Dalton.)

Salt is excreted again through the urine, sweat, and especially tears. It is found mostly in the fluid parts of the body, while *Kali mur.* more in the formed tissues.

The *Natr. mur.* molecules contained in the epithelial cells of the peptic glands become split up by the mild action of the carbonic acid of the blood, its chlorine is separated, and the free soda unites with the carbonic acid, and this combination reaches the blood while the chlorine, united to the hydrogen and dissolved in water, reaches the stomach as hydrochloric acid. If on account of the want of salt in the epithelial cells of the peptic glands no HCl can be formed, there arises an increase of the exudated alkaline mucus from the superficial epithelium of the mucous membrane of the stomach. Diluted hydrochloric acid, given in order to reduce the secretion of the superficial epithelial cell to the proper quantity, is but a palliative procedure; a rational cure must be effected by restoring the disturbed motion of the NaCl molecules which are found in the nourishing fluid of the epithelial cells of the peptic glands by means of administering homogeneous molecules.

This is also the function remedy of mucin, which is contained in the epithelial cells of all mucous membranes. It cures catarrh of such when its characteristic exudation is present; just as the hydrochloric acid formed in the epithelial cells of the peptic glands reduces the increased alkaline mucous exudation of the superficial epithelium to the right quantity, so can the hydrochloric acid that is formed by splitting up of the chloride of sodium within the mucin of all mucous membranes limit the secretion of the mucus in the formative (nascent) stage.

It is a fact that hydrochloric acid is obtained from salt (*Natr. mur.*), not only by means of carbonic acid acting upon the salt in a mass, but a similar result is obtained by the action of water. In the former the carbonic acid unites with the sodium which has lost its chlorine, and this combination reaches the blood; in the other case, sodium hydroxyd results, which dissolves the mucin and increases the secretion of mucus. This explains the origin of catarrh in damp atmospheres.

In consequence of a marked disturbance of the function of salt, blood serum may transude into the stomach and vomiting of a watery secretion (waterbrash) will result. If salt is lacking in a portion of cells (**below**) the epidermis, their proper amount of water cannot be received, and the epidermis rises in blisters, with clear, watery contents. Similar blisters, from corresponding disturbances, may arise on the conjunctiva.

In consequence of a disturbed function of salt we may find at the same time, though in different places, secretions either increased or decreased. For instance, a gastric catarrh with vomiting of water or mucus may exist, together with a constipation, caused by a lessened secretion of mucus in the colon. Excessive salt taking causes profound nutritive changes, dropsies and œdemas, alteration in the blood causing a condition of anæmia and leucocytosis, retention of effete materials giving gouty symptoms.

Among the main effects of undue salt-eating we find:

1) A thickening and partial paralysis of the vocal cords and an almost continual sore throat. Fluent coryza.

2) A pale and waxy color, with dryness of the cuticle, which yet perspires too freely upon exertion. Sallow appearance.

3) Constipation or chronic diarrhœa.

4) Abnormal appetite. Incessant thirst.

5) Plethora and corpulence.

6) Retarded endosmosis and exosmosis.

7) Thinning of the blood, slow circulation and lowered temperature. Constant feeling of coldness, especially down the back.

8) Dandruff, cutaneous affections, deposits and abscesses. Irritating, papular rash.

General Action.—*Natr. mur.* promotes the activity of tissue change and increases the excretion of urea, hence its use in chronic scrofulous ailments affecting the glands, bowels and skin. It acts upon the blood, lymphatic system, the mucous lining of the digestive tract and upon liver and spleen. It causes a deterioration of the blood and other vital fluids, partaking of a scorbutic nature, giving rise to inflammation, going on to ulceration and producing distinct dyscrasiæ. It also produces, and hence cures, cachexia like that resulting from ague plus quinine. **Malnutrition and emaciation. Great emaciation, even while eating enormously.** [Hawkes.] **Anæmia,** leucæmia, hydræmia, chlorosis and scorbutus. The atom of common salt is the basement on which the blood-globule is built up, and this fact assigns place and function to this cell-salt. Hence its use in these nutritive defects with their profound blood poverty. A serous discharge is the leader to this drug. It causes pains in any part of the body when they are accompanied by salivation, increased lachrymation, or by vomiting of water or mucus. Mucous membranes everywhere are affected, producing sponginess and swelling with venous hyperæmia, bleeding and increased mucous secretion; hence, catarrhs of all mucous membranes, with secretions of **transparent, watery, coarse, frothy mucus.** Vesicles with watery contents, which burst and leave a thin scurf. Watery vomiting, increased aqueousness of any part of the body, hydrocephalus, etc. **The tongue has a clean, shiny appearance, or bubbles of frothy saliva extend along its sides, or is broad, pallid, puffy, with a pasty coat.** Diminished secretions of any part of the body, salty taste.

Dr. Leon Rosenbusch, of Lemburg, reports a most favorable experience in the use of *Natr. mur.* by subcutaneous injections in cases marked by danger of failing circulation. The following is a resumé by the author of the indications for injection and the amounts to be used:

1. Sudden collapse (five to eight drams of a six per cent. solution).

2. Paresis of the heart muscles from any acute disease (five to eight drams at once, and then one to two drams daily).

3. Acute gastro-enteritis, great weakness after severe vomiting and diarrhœa (eight to twenty ounces of a tepid solution of six per thousand).

4. Hæmorrhage from lungs, stomach or bowels (five drams, then one and a half drams daily).

5. Heart-failure in consequence of chronic disease and cachectic conditions (one and a half drams daily for several days).

The balneological uses of salt as salt water baths, rubs, etc., are especially useful in chronic rheumatism, scrofulous conditions and to free the system from effects of inflammatory internal diseases. Be careful in the use of these measures in cardiac diseases, as insomnia and nervousness is apt to follow.

Salt might be taken by the ounce daily and yet the affected tissue-cells will suffer from a "molecular deficiency" thereof, so that there will occur a suspension of their functions whereby the *serous* and *watery* fluids of the cells and intercellular spaces are no longer equally distributed throughout the organism, thus leading to a watery or *serous exudation,* containing a large amount of unabsorbed *Sodium chloride* and other salts in solution.

If, however, *Sodium chloride* be subjected to the proper "trituration-process," by which means its molecules are rendered infinitely more active through the *unlocking* of a hitherto *latent* force within them, the starved and shrunken blood- and tissue-cells will once again absorb their wonted quantum of serum and so be enabled to continue their division and subdivision into new cells, whilst in the intercellular spaces of that marvellous labyrinthine network, the *connective-tissue,* the watery fluid or serum will be once more so equally distributed throughout, that its *deficiency* (leading to *dryness*) in one part and *excess* (leading to *exudation*) in another will result in complete, normal, fluidic equilibrium.

The importance of this cell-salt cannot be too highly estimated, for it is one of the chiefest of "antidotes," seeing that whenever it or any of the other cell-salts are thrown out of the blood, etc., owing to some irritating drug or other cause, the watery fluids of the body are abnormally called into play, and as *Natrum muriaticum* is the regulator of the distribution of such fluids, a *molecular* or *dynamized* dose thereof will set matters right so far as the fluidic disturbance is concerned. [C. S. Saunders, L. R. C. P.]

Guiding Symptoms and Characteristic Indications.

Mental Symptoms.—Hopeless feeling about the future. Dejection of spirits, **consolation aggravates**; fluttering of the heart follows. **Depression with tendency to dwell on disagreeable and depressing subjects.** Past injuries are called to mind and dwelt upon. **Readiness to shed tears.** Delirium with starting, wandering delirium with frothy appearance of the tongue. **Hypochondriacal mood,** with constipation. Excitement, excessively frolicsome, with inclination to dance and sing; angry irritability with passionate outbursts. Delirium tremens; most cases will be cured by this remedy. **Melancholia at puberty. Brain-fag.** Memory weak. All intellectual labor fatigues.

Head and Scalp.—Headaches mainly in forehead and temples and semi-lateral; congestive type, worse in morning, relieved by sleep, often associated with the menstrual period. Dull, heavy headache, with profusion of tears, drowsiness and unrefreshing sleep. Head nods forward involuntarily from weakness of muscles of neck. Headaches with constipation, from torpor and dryness of a portion of the intestinal mucous tract, when the tongue is clean or covered with bubbles of frothy saliva. Headache with vomiting of transparent phlegm or water, also sick headache with this symptom (*Calc. phos.*). Hemicrania, loss of consciousness and twitching of limbs. **Hammering headache, generally worse in the morning.** Headache of school girls during menses, with burning on the vertex. This is the chief remedy in sunstroke. Engorged venous sinuses with tendency to extravasation, temporary cerebral congestion. **Itching eruption on margin of hair at the nape of neck** with glutinous moisture. Dandruff, white scales on scalp sometimes co-existing with watery secretions from the mouth, nose or eyes. Falling off of hair.

Eyes.—Dimsightedness. Blisters on the cornea, white spots on same. Useful for involvement of the vitreous humor. Gauze before the eyes, letters run together when reading. Headache with eye-strain. **Sunstroke.** Frontal sinus inflammation. Scrofulous ulcers of the cornea with photophobia. Especially in scrofulous or tubercular patients. Discharge of clear mucus from the eyes, or flow of tears with obstruction of tear duct, worse after use of nitrate of silver. Great dryness of lids with pricking, itching and burning; margins red. Conjunctivitis with white mucous secretion and acrid lachrymation. Granulated eyelids with or without secretion of tears. Tarsi much thickened and red. Useful in **blepharitis,** the thick and inflamed lids smart and burn, with acrid lachrymation. Lachrymation with eruption of small vesicles causing scalding of the parts. For **muscular asthenopia** we have no better remedy. Neuralgic pains in the eyes, periodical, with flow of tears and reddened conjunctiva. Ciliary neuralgia coming and going with the sun. Stricture of lachrymal ducts. Opacity of the crystalline lens.

Ears.—Deafness from swelling of the tympanic cavity, with characteristic tongue. Catarrh of tympanic cavity and Eustachian tube (*Kali sulph.*). Roaring in ears. Purulent discharges from ears. **Cracking when chewing.** Itching and burning in the ear, stitches in the ear.

Nose.—Old nasal and pharyngeal catarrhs with loss of smell and taste. Colds causing vesicular eruptions with watery contents, which burst and leave thin scurfs or crusts. Scabs in the nose. Influenza, hay fever. Chronic catarrhs of bloodless patients, mucus having a salty taste. Coryza with clear, watery discharge or alternating with dry coryza, with loss of smell and taste, posterior nares feel dry. Much sneezing. Epistaxis from stooping and from coughing. General morning aggravation of catarrhs. Redness of nose with pimples, vesicles and painful nodules. Nose on one side numb. Cold commencing with sneezing, and fluent colds are cured by *Natrum mur.* 30. Nose sore with sensation of great dryness

8

and feeling of obstruction and discharge like clear white of eggs. May be on one side only.

Face.—Sallow complexion, leaden. Faceache with constipation, with characteristic tongue or vomiting of clear water. Periodical neuralgia after quinine, with lachrymation. Greasy appearance of skin. Sweating while eating. Sycosis, whiskers fall out, with much itching, vesicles with watery contents. Pustular eruption on forehead.

Mouth.—Copious salivation with salt taste. Blisters like pearls around the mouth, humid sores in the commissures. Thrush with salivation. Cracks in lips, burning and painful. Relaxed uvula. Follicular catarrh of pharynx. Lips swollen. Eruptions on chin.

Tongue.—Coating slimy, clear and watery, sero-mucous, and when small bubbles of frothy saliva cover the sides. Loss of taste. Vesicles on the tip of the tongue. Mapped tongue. Tongue numb; stiff. Children are slow in learning to talk. Sensation of a hair on tongue. Dryness of tongue and mouth, more a sensation.

Teeth.—Sensitive, easily bleeding, ulcerated gums. Toothache with involuntary flow of tears or salivation. Looseness of teeth. Ranula, chronic inflammation of the salivary glands. Teething with dribbling saliva. Gumboils with throbbing and boring pains.

Throat.—Neck emaciated. Diphtheria, if the face be puffy and pale, with drowsiness, watery stools, flow of saliva, or vomiting of water. Post-diphtheritic paralysis when food goes the wrong way and only liquids can be swallowed. Sore throat with transparent mucus covering the tonsils. Relaxed uvula, chronic sore throat, with feeling of **plug or lump,** and great dryness of the **throat.** Sensation extending up the Eustachian tube as if ears were plugged. Glazed dry appearance of throat. Constriction and stitches in throat. Follicular pharyngitis, especially in smokers and after *Nitrate of silver* treatment. Swelling of sub-maxillary glands, lips, cervical glands and tonsils. Goitre with watery secretions (chief remedy, *Calc. phos.*). Mumps with salivation and frequent coughing of mucus, tasting salty. Uvula elongated. Inflammation of uvula. Offensive breath.

Gastric Symptoms.—Hiccough. Indigestion with vomiting of clear, frothy water or stringy saliva, or with pain and salivation. Offensive breath. Stomachache with above symptoms. Heaviness and fulness. **Waterbrash,** water coming up into the throat, not acid. Pressure and distention of the stomach, with longing for **salt** food. Longing for salty and bitter things. **Violent thirst** for large quantities. **Ravenous hunger.** Heartburn after eating. Sour taste. **Aversion to bread.** Loss of desire for smoking. Jaundice with drowsiness. Feeling of great weakness and sinking at stomach. Red spots on pit of stomach.

Abdomen and Stool.—Constipation when arising, from want of moisture; dryness of the mucous linings with watery secretions; in other parts, watery vomiting, watery eyes, salivation, etc. Pain in region of liver and spleen. Hæmorrhoidal constipation. Constipation accompanied with much weakness of the intestines. Great torpor but without pain. Dry **stool** producing fissure, burning pain in the rectum. Stinging hæmorrhoids. Herpetic eruption around anus. **Torn, bleeding, smarting feeling after stool, which is hard, difficult and crumbling, with stitches in the rectum.** Proctalgia. Pain in abdominal ring. Diarrhœa with watery, frothy stool. Diarrhœa alternating with constipation. Excoriating watery diarrhœa, involuntary, knows not whether flatus or fæces escape. Great weakness of abdominal muscles and viscera.

Urinary and Sexual Organs.—Polyuria, especially if accompanied with waterbrash and with much emaciation. Hæmaturia from scurvy; cutting and burning after urination. Cannot pass urine in presence of others. Must wait before urine will start. Aching in testicles. Violent itching on scrotum. Loss of hair from pubes. Spermatic cord and testicles painful, swollen and infiltrated. Catarrh of bladder with characteristic discharge. Involuntary urination while walking, coughing, etc. Gonorrhœa with scalding. Chronic gonorrhœa, transparent, watery slime, intensely itching; urethra painfully sore to pressure; cutting in urethra after urination. Chronic syphilis, serous exudation, loss of hair from pubes. Seminal emissions followed by chilliness and lassitude with increased sexual desire. Scrotal œdema. Impotence. Discharge of prostatic fluid. FEMALE. Abundant leucorrhœa of transparent, white, thick mucus or unnatural dryness of vagina with smarting and burning rendering coition painful. Burning and soreness of vagina after urinating. Incontinence of urine. Menstruation, discharge thin, watery, bloody; delayed menstruation, with headache. Pruritus vulvæ. Terrible sadness during menses. Leucorrhœa watery. Copious catamenia with slimy, corroding leucorrhœa; watery, smarting discharges, after or between periods. Scalding, irritating discharges, causing itching and falling off of hair on the pubes. Before menses sad and melancholic; during and after menses, headache. Prolapsus, must sit down to prevent it. Great dryness of the vagina. Chlorosis, dirty look to the skin with palpitation, delaying catamenia. **Uterine troubles relieved by lying on back, on a pillow.** Pressing and pushing towards genitals in the morning.

Pregnancy.—Morning sickness with vomiting of frothy, watery phlegm. Loss of hair during childbirth or lactation. Mammary glands waste.

Respiratory System.—Acute inflammation of the windpipe, with clear, frothy, watery phlegm, loose and rattling, sometimes raised with difficulty. Dry, short cough day and night from irritation at pit of stomach. Bronchitis with cough from tickling behind sternum; cough causes bursting headache, involuntary micturition, pain in abdominal ring and spermatic cord, lachrymation and palpitation and stitches in chest. Chronic bronchial catarrh, "winter cough," cough with bursting headache, tears stream down the cheeks, and involuntary urination. Asthma with profuse watery mucus. Whooping cough with same conditions. Inflammation of the lungs with much rattling phlegm, serous and frothy, coughed up with difficulty. Pleurisy when serous exudation has taken place. Œdema of the lungs with characteristic expectoration. Hoarseness, pain, dyspnœa.

Circulatory Organs.—Pain in region of heart's apex. Worse any movement and deep inspiration. Pulse rapid and intermittent, worse lying on left side, felt all over the body, especially in the epigastrium, in hyperæmic and scorbutic conditions. Fluttering motion of the heart. Sense of constriction. Palpitation with anxiety and sadness, in anæmic conditions. Hypertrophy of the heart, must lie down frequently, has cold hands and numb extremities.

Back and Extremities.—Emaciated neck in children. Backache relieved by lying on something hard, spine and extremities oversensitive. Feeling of coldness in the back. Periodical attacks of gout. Great weakness and weariness. Chronic rheumatism of the joints. Joints crack; rheumatic, gouty pains, involuntary jerking of legs, fidgets or jerkings during sleep. Stiffness and arthritic swellings, ankles weak. Pain in small of back on rising up. Blistering festers on the fingers, containing watery fluid. Hangnails. Skin of hands, especially about nails, dry and cracked. Warts in palms of hands. Pain in hip. Coxalgia. Sciatica—painful contraction of hamstrings. Involuntary jerkings of legs. Weakness in knees and calves. Cracking of joints on motion. Synovitis, herpes in bend of knees. Urticaria about joints. Cracks between toes. Frequent falling asleep of the legs and feet, with weakness of ankle joints.

Nervous Symptoms.—Marked weakness and relaxation of the muscular system; always tired and disinclined for any exertion. Sensation of numbness in suffering parts. Paretic weakness in various muscular groups of the trunk and limbs. Spine oversensitive to touch or pressure. Spinal irritation. Restlessness and twitching of muscles. Paralytic pain in small of back. Paralysis. Neuralgic pains, especially biliary and infra-orbital, recurring at certain times, with flow of saliva or tears. Shootings along the nerve-fibre with watery eruptions. Chorea. Hysterical debility, worse in the morning. Hysterical spasms and debility. Takes cold easily. Easily fatigued. Singultus (*Magnes. phos.*). Epilepsy when frothing at the mouth occurs.

Sleep.—Excessive sleep if traced to an excess of moisture in the brain. The natural amount of sleep is unrefreshing, and he feels tired in the morning on waking. Constant and excessive desire to sleep. Dreams of robbers in the house. Frequent starting during sleep. Sleep very restless and setting in late. Insomnia, with unusual general animation.

Febrile Symptoms.—*Natrum mur.* is a chilly remedy. Different portions of the body feel cold, spine, stomach, hands, feet, etc. Chilly and thirsty at same time. Scarlet fever with drowsiness, twitching or vomiting of watery fluids. Profuse perspiration, also night-sweats. Often the second remedy in rheumatic fever with chilliness and characteristic symptoms. Hay fever with watery discharges from the eyes and nose. Typhus fever when stupor and sleepiness are great. **Intermittent fever after abuse of quinine, living in damp regions,** or newly turned ground. Chill from morning till noon, about 10 A. M., preceded by intense itching, heat with increased headache and thirst, sweat sour and weakening, much backache and throbbing headache, great languor, emaciation, sallow complexion and fever-blisters on the lips. Typhoid or malignant symptoms when such accompaniments as twitchings, drowsiness and watery vomiting occur.

Skin.—All affections with watery blisters or vesicles and thin whitish scales. Greasy, oily, especially on hairy parts where the sweat glands are most numerous or hair becomes dry and falls out. Chronic skin diseases, urticarious and miliary eruptions. Eczema, fine scales or eruptions with watery contents. Herpetic eruptions occurring in the course of a disease, blisters, blebs and watery vesicles on the skin. Herpes in bend of knee and elbow. Colorless, watery vesicles forming into thin scabs or crusts which fall off and readily form again. Intertrigo, soreness of the skin in children, with watery symptoms. Warts on the palms of the hands. White scales on the scalp, intertrigo between thighs and scrotum, with acrid and excoriating discharge. Pemphigus, watery blebs. Shingles or herpes zoster with characteristic symptoms. Herpes circinatus Rupia, blisters, not pustular eruptions.

Sycosis if watery symptoms correspond, beard falls out, dandruff. **Effects of insect-bites.** Nettlerash, itching violently, **appears after bodily exertion,** tetter in bends of joints. Oozing of an acrid substance. It is usually the second remedy in herpes zoster. Eczema from eating too much salt. Fungus hæmatodes. Eczema of eyebrows, behind ears, margin of hairy scalp, on forehead or nape, bend of joints. Nails dry, cracked. Warts in palms of hands. Nettlerash in intermittent fever. Hangnails.

Tissues.—Anasarca, accumulation of serum in the areolar tissues. Dropsy or dropsical swelling, puffiness of the tissues. Serous or watery exudations, serous secretions. Anæmic condition, blood thin and watery; chlorotic conditions; chlorosis. It is the chief remedy (in conjunction with *Calc. phos.*) for *anæmia* and *chlorosis,* as it has been found that iron is present in the blood-albumen of most anæmic persons in quite sufficient quantity; but it is the faulty action of the NaCl, whereby cell-multiplication is arrested, and of the *Calc. phos.,* whereby the young cells cannot be "organized" and so prepared for the process of "ferruginizing" in the spleen, that is the true cause of anæmia and chlorosis, so that the usual method of "drugging" with so-called "iron tonics" is not only useless and even harmful, but actually leads to the very thing for which it is given to correct, viz., an actual deficiency of iron in the blood due to the *irritation* of constantly repeated doses of *crude* iron preparations. Diabetes, Grave's disease, Bright's disease, round worms. Anæmia due to abuse of salt; emaciation pallor with dirty, flaccid, torpid skin; hydræmic, adynamic conditions, varices. Basedow's disease. Addison's disease. Dryness of mucous membranes, going on to erosion. **Emaciation while living well;** emaciation especially of the neck. Cachexia from ague plus quinine. Chronic swelling of lymphatic and sebaceous glands. Gout. Acts upon cartilage, mucous follicles and glands, salivary and mesenteric glands. Catarrhs of all mucous surfaces. All exudations and secretions are transparent, slimy, like boiled starch. The lesions often attack the nails and deform them; the hair of the scalp is often affected by the pustular or scaling type which causes a loss of hair. Associated conditions may be gastric or urinary with emaciation, weakness, headache and mental confusion [Bernstein].

Modalities.—Generally worse in the morning, periodically; at the seaside and in cold weather. Backache is relieved by lying on something hard. Complaints after urinating; after abuse of nitrate of silver; from quinine.

Homœopathic Data.—This drug was first proved by Hahnemann, and appears in vol. iv of the *Chronic Diseases*. It was also re-proved by the Austrian Society of Provers, and the pathogenetic effects recorded by Hahnemann and therapeutic results obtained by the use of the 30th potency brilliantly verified. Its pathogenesis is found complete in the *Chronic Diseases*, but excellent resumés, together with added clinical experience since that publication, can be found in Hering's *Guiding Symptoms*, vol. vii, and Allen's *Handbook of Materia Medica*. An interesting and suggestive little book on *Natrum muriaticum* as a test of the doctrine of *"Drug Dynamization,"* by Dr. Jas. C. Burnett, is also worthy of special mention.

Administration.—Schüssler recommends the 6th potency. The general experience of the homœopathic school seems to be in favor of the higher potencies; thus H. C. Allen, M. D., says it will cure more quickly in the attenuations above the 30th than below. Schüssler recommends also its external application in such diseases as the stings of insects, likewise as a gargle or spray in catarrhal affections.

Relationship.—Compare *Kali sulph.* and *Kali mur.* in catarrhs of the Eustachian tubes and tympanum. In gastric and intestinal conditions compare *Natr. sulph.* In headache of young girls during menses compare *Calc. phos.* and *Ferr. phos.* Headache during catamenia, *Kali sulph.* when metrorrhagic symptoms preponderate. When the menses are scanty, *Natr. mur.* In bites of insects *Ledum* comes nearest, but *Ferr. phos.* and *Kali phos.* have also been successfully employed. *Natr. mur.* has as a close analogue *Lycop.*, which will often be needed to supplement its action. *Natr. mur.*

regulates moisture exudation from the circulation, especially when from the arterial system, while *Natr. sulph.* is more indicated when from the venous system. Complementary drugs: *Apis* and *Arg. nit. Natr. mur.* often precedes *Sepia* and *Sulph.* in chronic diseases. For the excessive use of salt in food give *Phosph.* and *Spirit nitri dulc.* drop doses, also *Natrum mur.* 30 which seems to give to the system the power of disposing of the excess even without altering the habit greatly. For the bad effects of sea-bathing *Ars.* For the bad results of cauterization of any mucous surface with nitrate of silver *Natrum* is the antidote. For dryness of mucous membranes compare *Graphite, Alumina, Bryonia.* In ranula, *Ambra.*

NATRUM PHOSPHORICUM.

Synonyms.—Sodium Phosphate. Natri Phosphas. Phosphas Natricus. Sodæ Phosphas. Sodii Phosphas.

Common Name.—Phosphate of Soda.

Chemical Properties.—Formula, Na_2HPO_4, $12H_2O$. Sp. gravity, 1.55. It is prepared by neutralizing orthophosphoric acid with carbonate of sodium, and is also made from bone-ash. It crystallizes in large, transparent, monoclinic prisms containing twelve molecules of water of crystallization. It has a mild, cooling, saline taste. It is soluble in two parts of hot and in six of cold water. It is insoluble in alcohol. Solutions are slightly alkaline.

Preparation.—The pure phosphate of soda is triturated as directed under homœopathic pharmacy rules. (Should be kept well corked.)

Physiologico-chemical Data.—This salt is found in the blood, in the proportion of 0.3-0.5 : 1000, in muscles, nerve and brain-cells, as well as in the intercellular fluids. Through the presence of this salt, lactic acid is decomposed into carbonic acid and water. It absorbs the carbonic acid, taking up two moleclues for every molecule of itself, and carries it to the lungs, where the oxygen of the air sets the carbonic acid free in exchange for oxygen, which latter is taken up by the iron contained in the blood corpuscles. *Natrum phos.* is the remedy for conditions arising from excess of lactic acid. It prevents inspissation of the bile and mucus with crystallization of cholesterin in the gall duct and will thus remove the cause of many cases of jaundice, hepatic colic, bilious headache and imperfect assimilation of fats from lack of bile. It is useful in podagra, gout, as well as in acute and chronic articular rheumatism, being thus a remedy for the so-called acid diathesis.

The role of this salt in the normal economy, according to Moleschott and Schussler, largely consists in the catalysis of lactic acid in the blood, thus purifying that fluid organ from this effete product of muscular function, which transforms stored glycogen into the acid. The liver is the prime and master laboratory of the animal body. It is essential to both the nitrogenous and the hydro-carbonaceous transformations, to the renewal and the depuration of the blood, to the production of glycogen and grape sugar from starchy and saccharine food, and to the higher oxidation of uric acid, and other effete tissue principles, into urea, ready for elimination by the kidney, and by bile-formation contributes to the intestinal work. When inert, this organ falls short of this extensive function; when overactive, it exceeds it, and overproductions appear with symptomatic effects. These functions are principally due to cell-action. There are two classes of functional or parenchymatous cells; the biliary, spread out as epithelium in the capillary branches of the ducts, in intimate relation with the vessels of the liver and likewise with the remaining set of functional cells—viz.: those of the hepatic acini, also lying in intimate relation to the blood vessels and to the biliary capillaries, with their glandular epithelium. This double duty belongs to the large cells of the acini—viz.: the formation of glycogen and the formation of uric acid. In addition, the old red blood-globules are here in the liver, but in the portal system of veins, now become capillary in the acini, are finally disintegrated, and the new-formed globules perfected. All of these varied functions, separate as they are, undoubtedly assist each other, furnishing necessary chemical exchanges, etc. The glycogen is believed to be mainly carried away in the blood-current, to be stored in the muscular tissues, furnishing motor energy thereto, and being chemically split into two parts of lactic acid. This acid aids in later vital functions of the body, and is at last transformed into carbonic acid and water, while circulating in the blood. This transformation takes place through the presence in the blood of phosphate of soda—*Natr. phos.*—and by a catalytic action of this salt. Any deficiency in this prevents this chemical change, and the lactic acid remains as such. An acid state of the system now prevails; rheumatism, dyspepsia, intestinal troubles, etc., ensue. According to Schüssler, by the administration of molecular doses of this drug, this catalytic action is at once restored—the acid state ceases, and the rheumatic and other symptoms subside.

Uric acid is kept soluble in the blood by the presence of the phosphate of soda and the natural temperature of the blood. Whenever there is a deficiency of this salt, uric acid is combined with the soda, forming the urate of soda, an insoluble salt and deposited near the points producing gout and acute inflammatory rheumatism. During an attack of acute gout, we find that the excretion of uric acid is diminished in proportion to the amount of the deposit of urate of soda around the points.

Natrum phosph. serves to emulsify fatty acids; it is therefore a remedy for all dyspeptic conditions traceable to fats, or such as are aggravated by their use. Besides combining with these acids the phosphate of soda appropriates molecules of albumen, which acts bio-chemically like an acid.

The white blood corpuscles, leucocytes or lymph corpuscles carry molecules of fat and peptones, which latter are modified albuminoids, from the intestinal walls to the blood and thence to the tissues. They do this by virtue of their active movements. From the walls of the intestinal tract the passage of the leucocytes, now laden with peptones, is a direct one, while those carrying the fat molecules reach the goal by an indirect way—namely, through the thoracic duct. Finally they reach the tissues through the walls of the capillaries. Here, after the peptones are retransformed into albuminoids, they are deposited and become material for the growth of young cells which are formed by division.

If the progress of the leucocytes carrying the fat molecules is stopped in their course through the lymphatic glands, skin, bones or lungs, phlegmonous and glandular inflammations, and swellings take place as well as tubercular conditions of these organs and tissues.

Since these stagnated leucocytes contain albumen and fat, their fatty degeneration is rendered possible. So long as this has not actually taken place, *Natrum phosph.* possesses the power to free the leucocytes and thereby again enabling them to carry on their specific function. This it does by its two properties—that of emulsifying fats even if but a trace of a fatty acid is present and its capacity to take up peptonic molecules.

General Action.—Diseases of infants suffering from excess of lactic acid, resulting from overfeeding with milk and sugar. Ailments with excess of acidity. Thin, moist coating on the tongue. The soft palate also has a yellowish, creamy look. Sour eructations, sour vomiting, greenish diarrhœa, pains, spasms, and fever with acid symptoms, etc. Acts also upon the bones and glands, lungs and abdominal organs. The knowledge of its sphere of action has been much enlarged by Schüssler in recent years. It is the principal remedy in scrofulous glands. tuberculosis, etc. Small doses of *Natrum phos.* given subcutaneously have been found to antidote the desire for Morphine and thus break the habit.

Guiding Symptoms and Characteristic Indications.

Mental.—Anxious and apprehensive fear as if something would happen. Dull and without ambition. Imagines on waking at night that pieces of furniture are persons; that he hears footsteps in next room. Nervous, irritable, vexed at trifles. Forgetful. Great mental prostration.

Head and Scalp.—Headaches on crown of head; on awaking in the morning, with creamy appearance at the back part of the palate, and yellow, moist tongue. Severe pain in the head as if the skull were too full, frontal or occipital, with nausea or some slimy vomiting. Intense pressure and heat on the top of the head as if it would open. Giddiness, vertigo with gastric derangements. Sickening headaches, ejection of sour froth.

Eyes.—Discharge of golden-yellow, creamy matter from the eyes. Ophthalmia, discharge of yellow, creamy matter, the lids are glued together in the morning. Hypopyon. Burning lachrymation. See sparks before eyes. Squinting caused by intestinal irritation as from worms. Granular conjunctivitis, when granulations look like small blisters. Scrofulous ophthalmia. Pain over eyes. Dim sight, as if a veil were over eyes.

Ears.—Ears sore, externally, burn and itch. One ear red, hot, frequently itchy, accompanied by gastric derangements and acidity. Roaring in ears.

Nose.—Picking at the nose, associated with acidity of the stomach and worms. Pricking in the nares. Offensive odor before nose. Itching of nose. Catarrh with thick, yellow purulent discharge. Tension over root of nose.

Face.—Red and blotched face, yet not feverish, with acidity, etc., white about nose or mouth. Facial neuralgia; shooting, stitching pain. Soreness of right lower jaw. Paleness or bluish, florid appearance of face, sour risings, etc.

Mouth.—Yellow, creamy coating at the back part of the roof of the mouth. Acid taste in the mouth. Coppery taste.

Tongue.—The great keynote for this remedy is the moist, creamy or golden-yellow coating at the back part of the tongue. Blisters and sensation of hairs on tip of tongue. Difficult speech.

Teeth.—Grinding of the teeth in children during sleep.

Throat.—The same moist, creamy or golden-yellow coating found at the base of the tongue is also found on the soft palate, tonsils and uvula. Inflammation of any part of the throat with this accompaniment calls for *Natr. phos.* It is also usually accompanied by an acid condition of the stomach. Diphtheritic throat, falsely so called. Sensation of a lump in the throat, worse swallowing liquids. Dropping of thick, yellow mucus from posterior nares, worse at night. Naso-pharyngeal catarrh.

Gastric Symptoms.—Acidity, sour risings due to excess of lactic acid. Gastric abrasions and ulcerations. Pain after food, in one spot. Vomiting of sour fluids or of a dark sub-stance like coffee-grounds, sour risings, loss of appetite. Dys-pepsia with characteristic eructations and tongue, sour taste in the mouth. Pain sometimes comes on two hours after taking food. Nausea and vomiting of acid fluids and curdled masses (not food). Waterbrash with acidity. Flatulence with sour risings. Colic in children with symptoms of acidity, such as green, sour-smelling stools, vomiting of curdled milk, etc. Stomachache from presence of worms. Empty, gone feeling in stomach, with feeling of weight above the ensiform carti-lage. Imperfect assimilation of fats from lack of bile.

Abdomen and Stool.—Habitual constipation with occa-sional attacks of diarrhœa in young children. Sclerosis of liver. Acts upon the glandular organs of the intestinal tract. Diarrhœa caused by excess of acidity, stools sour-smelling, green, jelly-like masses of mucus, painful, straining, coagu-lated casein, scanty and frequent. Sudden urging, difficulty in retaining stool. Pain through right groin. Intestinal, long or thread-worms, with characteristic symptoms of acidity or picking of the nose, occasional squinting, pain in the bowels, restless sleep, etc. Itching at the anus from worms, especially at night when warm in bed (injections of same). White or green stools, with diarrhœa and sometimes with jaundice, due to deficiency of bile. Flatulent colic. Obstinate constipation. Itching, sore and raw anus.

Urinary and Sexual Organs.—Hepatic form of diabetes. Constant urging, flow intermits, requires straining. Incon-tinence of urine in children with acidity. Urine dark red with arthritis. Frequent micturition. Atony of bladder. Sem-inal emissions without dreams. Semen thin, watery. Sexual desire gone or increased with erections. Drawing in testicles and spermatic cord. Menses too early, pale, with afternoon headache over eyes, worse after menses, with sensation in knees, as if cords were shortened. Weakness and distress in the uterine region. Prolapse, with weak sinking feeling after stool. Uterine displacement with rheumatic pains. Sterility with acid secretions from the vagina. Leucorrhœa, discharge creamy or honey-colored or acid and watery. Sour-smelling discharges from the uterus. Excitement with sleeplessness before menses.

Pregnancy.—Morning sickness with vomiting of sour masses of fluids.

Respiratory Symptoms.—A useful intercurrent in catarrhal troubles associated with acidity. Phthisis florida in young subjects, with hereditary tendency to sigh, especially during menses. Consumption. Soreness of intercostal muscles and lower sternum. Pains in chest, worse from pressure and deep breathing.

Circulatory Organs.—Trembling about the heart. Pains about the base of heart, relieving pain in limbs, and great toe. Palpitation, feels pulse in different parts of body. Sensation as though shot were rolling through arteries.

Back and Extremities.—Crick in neck. Swelling of glands of neck. **Goitre.** Weak feeling in back and limbs. Cold extremities. Legs give way while walking. Gait unsteady. Spinal anæmia, paralytic weakness of lower extremities. Inside thighs draw. Sore hamstrings. Pain in knees, ankles and shins, in hollow and ball of foot. Synovial crepitation. Arms tired. Contraction of extensor muscles on back of arm. Aching wrists. Crampy pain in hands while writing. Sore feeling in joints. Rheumatic arthritis, especially of joints of fingers, pains suddenly go to the heart.

Nervous Symptoms.—Irritation of the intestines by worms, sometimes causes squinting and twitching of the facial muscles. Nervousness, from mental exertion and sexual excess. Tired feeling, with goneness of stomach, crick in neck, trembling and palpitation. Heaviness, as if paralyzed. Prostration.

Sleep.—Sleep restless with worm troubles, very drowsy, falls asleep while sitting. Sleepless from itching. Wakes easily. Sexual dreams.

Febrile Symptoms.—Intermittent fever with vomiting of acid, sour masses. Acid, exceedingly sour-smelling perspiration. Feet icy-cold during the day, burn at night. Flashes of heat and headache every afternoon.

Skin.—Chafing of the skin. Eczema with symptoms of acidity, secretion creamy, honey-colored. Yellow, jaundiced. Erythema. "Rose rash," golden-yellow scabs. Secretions yellow, like honey, and cause soreness of skin. Crusta lactea. Hives, itching all over body, like insect bites. Much itching at ankle joints with eczematous eruption.

Tissues.—Exudations and secretions yellow, honey-colored. Leucæmia. Swelling of lymphatic glands before hardening. Marasmus of children. Jaundice. Use 1x trit. In bone diseases, to favor deposit of phosphate of lime. Scrofula; its specific action upon glands tends to dissolve the morbidly formed products. Leucocytosis. Rheumatic arthritis. Marked anæmia.

Modalities.—Some of the pains of this remedy were aggravated during a thunderstorm; during menstruation many symptoms have an afternoon and evening aggravation. Aversion to open air.

Homœopathic Data.—Proved under supervision of Dr. E. A. Farrington. The record of the proving is found in Allen's *Encyclopædia,* vol. x, first published in *Hahnemannian Monthly,* vol. xii. An excellent symptomatology of the drug is found in Allen's *Handbook* and Hering's *Guiding Symptoms,* vol. viii.

Administration.—Schüssler recommends the 6x, either in trituration or in dilution. The 4x seems to be the proper potency to use in view of the fact of the relative proportion of this salt in the blood according to Dr. Quesse. It may also be used as an injection in worm troubles. Dr. Morgan prefers infrequent doses of the 30th potency. The higher and highest potencies have also been employed with success.

Relationship.—As a remedy for scrofulosis with similar "acid" symptoms compare *Calc. carb.* In gastric catarrhal affections it is to be compared with *Calcar., Kali carb., Nux, Coccul., Carbo, Carbol. ac.* As a remedial agent for children, for whom *Natr. phos.* is pre-eminently the remedy, where these acid conditions of stomach and bowels are frequent, compare *Rheum,* where the whole body, but especially the stool of the little patient, smells sour. It is interesting to note the association of the peculiar *Natr. phos.* gastric symptoms, so frequently verified clinically, and the symptoms of gout developed in the provings. Remembering the peculiar gouty dyspepsia, we may have in *Natr. phos.* a most useful remedy. Compare here *Colchic., Benz. ac., Guaiac., Lycop., Sulphur.* In itching all over, compare *Dolichos, Urtica, Sulphur,* etc.

NATRUM SULPHURICUM.

Synonyms.—Sodium Sulphate. Sodæ Sulphas. Sodii Sulphas.

Common Name.—Glauber's Salt. Sulphate of Soda.

Chemical Properties.—Formula, Na_2SO_4, $10H_2O$. It occurs rather abundantly in nature: sea water, saline springs, Russian salt lakes, etc. It is prepared by the action of sulphuric acid on common salt and purified by recrystallization. It forms large, colorless, transparent, oblique, rhombic or six-sided prisms, having a cooling, bitter saline taste. They effloresce in warm air at 30° C. They melt in their own water of crystallization, melting also freely at 33° C.; above or below that temperature the solubility decreases.

Preparation.—The pure sulphate of sodium is triturated as directed in the *Homœopathic Pharmacopœias.*

Physiologico-chemical Data.—The sulphuric acid formed by the oxidation of the albuminoids would destroy the tissues were it united in its nascent state with carbonates, by which the carbonic acid is set free. This salt does not appear in the cells, only in the intercellular fluids. It aids and regulates the excretion of superfluous water—*e. g.,* that which arises from

:9

the decomposition of lactic acid with the phosphate of sodium, œdemas, etc. Disturbance of the molecular motion of this salt prevents the elimination of such water from the tissues as is produced by oxidation of organic substances.

The action of *Natrum sulph.* is opposite to that of *Natrum mur.* Both have the property to attract water, but for opposite purposes. *Natrum mur.* attracts the water which is to be used in the organism, while *Natrum sulph.* attracts the water due to retrograde metamorphosis and secures its elimination from the organism.

Natrum mur. furthers the division of cells for purposes of increase. *Natrum sulph.* takes away water from worn-out leucocytes, and thereby accomplishes their disintegration. It is, therefore, the remedy for leucæmia. It irritates epithelial cells and nerves, as will be seen in the following facts:

In consequence of the induced activity by the *Natrum sulph.* of the epithelial cells lining the uriniferous tubes, superfluous water, holding in solution or suspension products of metamorphosis, is sent to the kidneys. This leaves the organism by way of the ureter and bladder as urine.

Natrum sulph., by stimulating the epithelial cells of the bile ducts, pancreas and intestinal canal, furthers the normal secretion of these organs. It also has the function to stimulate the nerves of these parts.

If the sensory nerves of the bladder are not stimulated by *Natrum sulph.* the impulse to urinate is not reported to consciousness and involuntary urination—enuresis—results. If the motor nerves of the detrusor are not irritated, suppression of urine results.

In consequence of an irregular action of *Natrum sulph.* on the nerves supplying the gall apparatus, we may have an increase or diminution of that secretion.

If a diabetes mellitus is caused by a lessened secretion of pancreatic fluid, *Natrum sulph.* may be the remedy required.

If the motor nerves of the colon are not influenced sufficiently by *Natrum sulph.* constipation and flatulent colic result.

If in consequence of disturbed molecular motion of *Natrum*

sulph. the elimination of superfluous water from the intercellular spaces is rendered tardy; hydræmia results.

The hydræmia and the functional disturbances within the gall secreting apparatus are the conditions for the development of the following diseases:

Intermittent and bilious fevers, influenza, vomiting of bile, bilious diarrhœa, œdema, œdematous erysipelas, vesicular eruptions, filled with yellow serum; moist eczema, herpes, sycotic growths, catarrhs, with yellowish-green or green secretions.

Natrum sulph. corresponds to the hydrogenoid constitution of Grauvogl, flabby, watery, hydræmic.

Persons suffering from hydræmia are worse in damp weather, near water, in close, damp dwellings, cellars, etc., and are better under opposite conditions.

General Action.—Like other alkaline sulphates, an active cathartic. It excites the secretion of the intestines and stimulates the activity of the intestinal glands, liver and pancreas. In addition, however, it exhibits a marked similarity to the uric acid diathesis in general, and is certainly a valuable remedy in combating numerous phases of that polymorphous malady. (T. F. Allen.) Gastric bilious conditions, accumulation of water in the areolar tissues, yellow, watery secretions on the skin, or yellowish scales forming an eruption of vesicles. Excessive secretion of bile, liver affections, gravel, sand in the urine, diabetes, gout, figwarts, etc. The chief characteristic is a **dirty greenish-gray or greenish-brown coating on the root of the tongue and aggravation from lying on the left side.** *Natr. sulph.* combines in a measure the wonderful effects of *Natr. mur.* and of *Sulphur* in the Western climate as an active malarial agent. Its complaints are those that are brought on by living in damp houses, basements and cellars. Complaints are worse in wet weather, correspond to the hydrogenoid constitution and sycotic dyscrasia, constitutional conditions in children that result in chest catarrhs and asthmatic complaints. The morbid alterations caused by *Natr. sulph.* begin to be observable near the end of the ileum and in the lower part of the colon. In the latter the follicles appear swollen, with a bright red margin of capillaries; the mucous membrane between is either pale or shows inconsiderable dentritic injections. In the lower part of the ileum the mucous membrane shows a saturated bright red coloring, mostly equal. It is the chief ingredient in the Carlsbad water, so largely used for its action on the liver; also contained in the cold springs of the Isle of Wight, of Pullna, Marienbad and Franzensbad.

Sulphate of Sodium as a Hæmostatic. Reverdin, in a paper read before the French Surgical Association, advocates the employment of the sulphate of sodium as a hæmostatic. He has employed it a number of times successfully; it is used in small doses (10 centigrams—gr. 1½) every hour, in dangerous capillary hæmorrhage either of spontaneous or traumatic origin. As an example, after the removal of a subcutaneous benign tumor there followed a hæmorrhage which resisted all treatment for eight weeks. The same was true of other cases of traumatic origin, and also in cases of menorrhagia.

This remedy was used by Kussmaul, and is apparently popular in the North of Germany in cases of hæmophilia.

By experimental and clinical observation the author determined that this drug should be given by the mouth only, as it is ineffectual when used in subcutaneous injections.

Its continued use has expelled tape worm. Chorea with constipation was treated by Rademacher with a 6 per cent. solution. Dose, a glass during the day, until three or four stools set in.

Guiding Symptoms and Characteristic Indications.

Mental Symptoms.—Suicidal tendency, **must exercise restraint,** attended with wildness and irritability followed by sleepless nights, irritability due to biliousness; delirium. Music, especially melancholic strains, aggravates symptoms; worse in morning. Disheartened. **Mental troubles arising from a fall or other injuries to the head.**

Head and Scalp.—Violent pulsating headache, worse on top of head. Vertigo, dizziness from gastric derangements, excess of bile, with bilious coating on tongue, or bitter taste in the mouth. Sick headache with bilious diarrhœa, or vomiting of bile, bitter taste, colicky pain. Headache with giddiness. Occipital headache. Ill effects of falls on and injuries to the head, and mental troubles arising therefrom. Congestion of blood to head. Violent pains at base of brain, as if crushed in a vise or something gnawing there. Delirium. Burning in top of head. Brain feels as if loose. Scalp sensitive; hair is painful on combing it.

Eyes.—Yellowness of the conjunctivæ. Large, blister-like granulations with burning lachrymation; burning of the edges of the lids. Chronic conjunctivitis, with granular lids, green pus, terrible photophobia. Agglutination of lids in morning with photophobia. Maculæ on cornea.

Ears.—Earache, as if something were forcing its way out, worse in damp weather. Ringing in ears as of bells. Lightning-like stitches through ears.

Nose.—Nosebleed during menses. Ozæna syphilitica, worse every change from dry to wet weather. Stuffing up of nose. Great dryness and burning in nose. Itching of wings of nose. Pus becomes green on exposure to light. Nasal catarrh; hawks up salty mucus.

Face.—Sallow or jaundiced with biliousness. Pain in the zygoma. Vesicles and pimples on face.

Mouth.—Bitter taste in the mouth, full of slime, **thick and tenacious, white,** must hawk up constantly from œsophagus, trachea and stomach. "It wells up from the stomach, always foul and slimy." Burning in mouth. Bad taste in mouth and always full of slime. Vesicular eruptions around the mouth and chin. Roof of mouth sore to touch. Palate very sensitive; better on taking cold things.

Tongue.—Dirty, brownish-green coating or grayish-green. Palate very sensitive, better taking cold things. Taste bitter; slimy tongue. Burning blisters on the tip; red tongue.

Teeth.—Toothache better by tobacco smoke and cool air, also better holding cold water in mouth (*Coffea*). Gums burn. Blisters on gums.

Throat.—In diphtheria when green vomiting occurs as an

intercurrent. Sore throat, feeling of a lump on swallowing; throat dry. Ulcerated sore throat. Pharyngeal catarrh, profuse, thick, tenacious, white mucus. Hawking of salt mucus in morning.

Gastric Symptoms.—Thirst every evening. Stomach feels distended and heavy; constant nausea. Vomiting of bile with bitter, sour taste, giddiness and headache. Vomiting of salty, greenish water. Biliousness, excess of bile, vomiting of bitter fluids, greenish-brown or greenish-gray tongue. Bilious colic with the above symptoms and dark stools. Cannot digest starchy food. Jaundice arising from vexation. Green evacuations, sallow skin, yellow eyeballs. Lead colic (given often and low, 1x, 2x). Sour rising, heartburn and flatulency. Wind colic, worse in the sigmoid flexure; worse before breakfast when the stomach is empty. Aching and cutting pains in region of liver. Liver engorged, **worse lying on left side.** Pain in left hypochondriac region often accompanied by a cough with purulent expectoration. Stomach feels distended. Sensitive to clothing over hypochondria. **Gall stones.**

Abdomen and Stool.—Great flatulence with cutting pains in abdomen and congestion of the liver. Cannot bear tight clothing around the waist. Tympanites in bilious fevers. **Flatulent colic,** often beginning in right groin and spreading over the whole abdomen. Heat in the lower bowels with green bilious discharges. Diarrhœa, stools dark, bilious or of green bile. Hereditary looseness of bowels in old women. Itching of anus. Irritable liver, sometimes after excessive study or mental work. Soreness of the liver to touch, to jars, with sharp, stitching pains in it. Typhlitis. Loose morning stools, particularly after a spell of wet weather. Wart-like eruptions on anus and between thighs, sycosis.

Urinary and Sexual Organs.—Urine loaded with bile. Chief remedy in diabetes. Chronic nephritis, urethral discharge, yellowish-green. Lithic deposits in the urine, brick dust-like coloring matter in the water, often associated with gout. Burning during micturition. Gravel, sandy deposit in the urine. Polyuria simplex, excessive secretions of urine, especially if diabetic. Preputial and scrotal œdema. **Enlarged** prostate; pus and mucus with the urine. Condylomata, soft, fleshy excrescences of syphilitic origin, with greenish discharges. Itching of genitals. Chronic gonorrhœa. **Gonorrhœa and sycosis.** Gonorrhœa suppressed. Female genitals inflamed, swollen and covered with vesicles; nosebleed before menses. Menses are profuse, acrid and corrosive, with colic and constipation, or morning diarrhœa and chilliness. Leucorrhœa, acrid, corrosive; parts inflamed.

Pregnancy.—Vomiting in pregnancy with bitter taste. Phlegmasia, alba dolens. Herpetic vulvitis.

Respiratory Symptoms.—Hoarseness. **Asthma,** worse every change to damp weather. **Humid asthma,** rattling of mucus. Asthma developing from general bronchial catarrh. Sensation of all-goneness in chest. Cough with thick, ropy, greenish, pus-like expectoration; soreness of chest, which is better by pressure, hence patient holds his chest while coughing. Piercing pains, especially in left chest. Dyspnœa during damp weather. Bronchial catarrh, cough worse in early morning (*Kali carb.*).

Circulatory Organs.—Pressure and anxiety in heart region, must go into open air for relief.

Back and Extremities.—Bruised pain in small of back and sacrum. Soreness up and down the spine and neck. **Spinal meningitis,** very important remedy, with drawing back of the neck and spasms in the back. Swelling and suppuration of axillary glands. Panaritium. Stitches in the left hip, trembling of the hands, languor and œdema of the feet. Paronychia. Inflammation and suppuration around roots of nails. Tingling ulcerative pain under nails. Itching of toes. Sciatica when getting up from sitting or turning in bed; no relief in any position. Pains from hips to knees. Rheumatic pains in the limbs if gastric symptoms correspond. Cracking of joints. Locomotor ataxia. Podagra, gout in the feet, acute and chronic cases. Burning in soles and extends to knees. Arthritis.

Nervous Symptoms.—Prostration; tired, weary feeling,

especially about the knees. Restless desire to move. Exhaustion with colic. Chorea with retarded stools. Trembling of the whole body. Twitching of hands and feet during sleep. Hands tremble on writing.

Sleep.—Drowsiness, often the precursor of jaundice, with bilious symptoms, worse in the forenoon and when reading. Heavy, anxious dreams, awakes at night with attack of asthma. Much dreaming soon after falling asleep, starting as if in a fright. Is awakened by flatulent pain.

Febrile Symptoms.—Ague, intermittent fever in all its stages, bilious vomiting. Remittent bilious fever, yellow fever, assuming form of severe bilious remittent fever, greenish-yellow vomit, brown or black. Internal coldness. Chill with icy coldness towards evening. Hot feeling on top of the head. Sweat without thirst. "Soreness in the hepatic region, shifting flatus and tendency to diarrhœa." (J. W. Ward, M. D.)

Skin.—Tendency to warts around eyes, scalp, face, chest, anus, etc. Chafing of the skin in children with bilious symptoms. Eczema. Vesicles, eruptions containing yellow, watery secretions. Fingers swollen and stiff. Palms of hands raw and sore, and exude a watery fluid. Erysipelas, smooth, red, shiny, tingling or painful swelling of the skin. Pemphigus, watery vesicles or blebs over the body, wheals, containing a yellow, watery secretion. Ringworm. Yellow scales after the breaking of vesicles or blisters on the skin. Moist skin affections with bilious symptoms. Œdematous inflammations of the skin. Jaundiced skin, itching while undressing. Sycotic excrescences. Fistulous abscesses of years' standing, discharging, watery pus, surrounded by a broad, bluish line, burrowing.

Tissues.—Regulates water capacity of venous system. Œdema, smooth swelling. Infiltration. Simple dropsy invading the areolar tissues of the body. Sections which are yellow, watery, etc. Sycosis and leucæmia. **Hydrogenoid constitution.** Consumption. Pyæmia. Sciatica.

Modalities.—Always worse in damp, wet weather, feels best in warm and dry weather and in open air. Symptoms such as arise from living in damp houses, basements and cellars, worse from water in any form. Complaints from eating plants that grow near water, fish, etc. Pains make him change position often (*Rhus*). **General aggravation from lying on the left side.**

Homœopathic Data.—Proved first by Schretter in 1832, and by Nenning. The best arrangement of symptoms appeared in Hering's *Materia Medica,* transferred with some additions to *Allen's Encyclopædia.* But the credit of greatly enlarging our philosophical conception and therapeutic application of this drug belongs to Grauvogl, who showed the correspondence of this drug to the so-called hydrogenoid constitution and chronic effects of gonorrhœal infection. His observations have been repeatedly verified.

Administration.—In lead colic low, 1x and 2x, and often. Schüssler recommends the 6x trituration. Grauvogl used mainly the 2x to 6x potency, while the 30 and 200 have been used by Hering and others.

Relationship.—*Natr. sulph.* has many symptoms in common both with the *Natrums* and *Sulphur.* In the eye symptoms compare *Graphit.,* which also has the extreme aggravation from light in chronic eye affections. In the cough *Bryon.* corresponds to *Natr. sulph.,* in the all-gone sensation in chest, soreness and need of steadying the chest, hence relief by pressure; but *Natr. sulph.* has much more the muco-purulent, thick, ropy, yellowish-green expectoration, hence in later stages, *Bryon.* more to the earlier, when cough is more irritable, with much rawness, constriction, burning and sensation of tearing in chest. In asthma compare also *Silicea* as a radical remedy. In gonorrhœa *Natr. sulph.* competes with *Thuja* and *Mercur.* It is painless with *Natr. sulph.,* and the discharge keeps up a yellowish-green, thick discharge. Complementary to *Thuja* for deep-seated sycotic constitutional affections, or where a sycotic condition is engrafted on a hydrogenoid base. In polyuria, *Ferrum phosph., Phosph. acid* precede it. Compare *Stillingia* in hip disease.

SILICEA.

Synonyms.—Silica. Silicea Tera. Silex. Decarbonized white pebble. Acidium Silicicum. The proper name is Silicic Oxide.

Common Names.—Pure Flint or Quartz. Silicious Earth.

Chemical Properties.—Formula, SiO_2. Prepared by fusing silica and carbonate of sodium; dissolving residue filtered and precipitated by hydrochloric acid. It is a white powder, having neither taste nor smell.

Preparation.—Pure *Silicea* is triturated according to the rules of the homœpathic pharmacopœias. Dr. P. Wilde uses preferably the silicate of soda known as "liquid glass," which is freely soluble in water. (See "Administration.") Dr. J. J. Garth Wilkinson preferred the *Silica* obtained from the Bamboo. Found it better in acute conditions.

Physiologico-chemical Data.—Although this inorganic salt is found very abundantly throughout the vegetable kingdom, especially in grasses, grain, palms, etc., it is found comparatively little in the animal kingdom, notably so in the higher orders, the vertebræ. Traces of *Silicea,* however, are found in the ashes of blood, bile or urine, and larger quantities (7 per cent.) in the white of egg, and even more in the ashes of the epidermis, hair and nails. It is also found in the connective tissue, especially embryonic, and hence its action on the spinal cord, brain and nerves must be referred to the investing membrane, the connective tissue, of the nerve-fibres. Disturbance of the function of the *Silicea* molecules causes a turgescence of the cells of the connective tissues involved. This swelling may remain stationary for a time, then disappear or occasion suppuration. Prof. Schultz, of Griefswald University, found this salt also in the lens, in pus and in ovarian cysts.

General Action.—*Silicea* acts more upon the organic substances of the body, involving prominently bones, joints, glands, skin and mucous surfaces, producing malnutrition and corresponding to the scrofulous diathesis. Its action is deep and long-lasting. It is especially suited to imperfectly nourished constitutions, owing to deficient assimilation.

It is the remedy for ailments attended *with pus-formation,* and is closely related to all fistulous burrowings. Wherever pus is formed in an inflamed part of connective tissue or skin, *Silicea* may be used. Deeply-seated scrofulous cachexia and some forms of septic infections (vaccine) find in it a valuable general remedy. Like *Calc. sulph., Silicea* corresponds to the process of suppuration, with the following distinguishing features: *Silicea* ripens abscess, since it **promotes suppuration.** *Calc. sulph.,* by **restraining the suppurative process,** heals suppurating wounds. As long as infiltration, **which can only disappear by suppuration,** lasts, *Silicea* is the remedy, and should be continued until all the infiltrated parts have disappeared. If then the wound fails to heal, give *Calc. sulph.* Ailments affecting the periosteum. Deep-seated suppurations, pus thick and yellow; also in certain reflex affections connected with the nerves. After suppuration has ceased to be active, but the process lingers and the pus forms chronic deposits, small or large, fistulous or otherwise; also, where the general organism is both irritable and weak, and the nervous system is easily aroused to exhausting agitation (as Dunham says, it is contraindicated by general nerve torpor), this is a specific remedy. In localized exhaustion, when the symptoms resemble paralysis—*e. g.,* rectal distention, dilated and irritable heart, great general debility, as after lying-in—it should always be thought of. In general hyperæsthesia and exaggerated reflexes.

Silicea has also the power to reabsorb a bloody or sero-albuminous exudate, existing within the tissues by means of the lymphatics. Here it often follows *Calc. phos.*

Silicea cures chronic gouty rheumatic affections by means of its stimulating effects of the involved connective tissue cells, compelling these to throw off the accumulated urates through the lymphatics.

Silicea can restore suppressed foot-sweats, and in this way be an indirect remedy for diseases resulting from suppression of foot-sweat, for instance: Amblyopia, cataract, paralysis, etc.

If the cells of any part of the connective tissue show a lack of *Silicea* molecules, they atrophy in consequence. The central and peripheral nervous system are definitely affected by *Silicea,* as seen in the languor, sleepiness, anxious dreams, nervous irritability, depression, headaches, trembling and paretic symptoms.

Guiding Symptoms and Characteristic Indications.

Mental Symptoms.—Thought difficult, attention difficult to fix, can be aroused but tires easily, stronger mentally than physically; **he has grit.** Desponding, peevish, disgust of life. **Oversensitive** to noise, etc., and with anxiety. Great irritability. A peculiar mental abstraction, marked by a propensity to toy by the hour with pins and needles. Brain-fag, school girls become confused during recitations because they cannot concentrate their thoughts; want to think but are unable to do so.

Head and Scalp.—Vertigo, patient inclines to fall forward or to the left. Labyrinthine vertigo. Headaches with vertigo, with small nodules on scalp, from hunger, from abdominal irritation, from overstudy, from nervous exhaustion. Headache is throbbing, beating, pressing asunder and coldness of head, with constant need for wrapping it up. **Headache from nape to vertex, more on right side, aggravated by noise, exertion, light, study, and relieved by warmth.** Pressive headache from above downward, with intermittent itching of vulva. Cerebral apoplexy, preceded by deep-seated stitches in the right parietal region and dull, heavy, crampy pains in arms. Scalp very sensitive and sore; itching. Painful pustules. Suppurating wounds. Sweat on head of children, like to keep the head wrapped up warm; large, open fontanelles. Offensive eruption on occiput. Hair falls out. Cephalæmatoma. Nodules on scalp.

Eyes.—A remedy of great importance in diseases of the lachrymal apparatus, especially the lachrymal sac. Lachrymal fistula. **Styes.** Blepharitis. Tarsal tumor. Boils and cystic tumors around eyes and lids. Pustular keratitis. Ulcers of cornea, especially the small round variety with a tendency to perforate; also the sloughing ulcer with sticking pains. (*Hepar.*) Cataract. Amblyopia after suppressed foot-sweat or eruptions. Affections appearing in the angles of the eye. Corneal scars and opacities after small-pox. Ciliary neuralgia, especially over right eye. Pressure and soreness in the orbits. Muscæ volitantes. Letters run together when reading or writing. Caries of the orbit.

Ears.—Sensitive to loud sound. Roaring in ears. Inflammation of middle ear, especially chronic suppuration. Inflammatory swelling of external meatus. Dulness of hearing with swelling and catarrh of the Eustachian tubes and tympanic cavity. Otitis suppurativa. Otorrhœa curdy and ichorous, with caries of the mastoid cells. Inflammation of ear after bathing. Deafness, ears open at times with a loud report.

Nose.—Tip of nose red. Itching of nostrils. **Sneezing;** coryza, nasal catarrh. Ozæna, with fœtid offensive discharge when the affection is seated in the submucous connective tissues or in the periosteum. Chronic coryza with swelling of the mucous membrane, dryness, excoriation, with crusts and loss of smell. Caries of the nasal bones from syphilis or scrofulosis. Intolerable itching of the tip of the nose. Inveterate ulceration producing acrid, corroding discharge. Herpetic eruption around nostrils and lips.

Face.—Faceache with small lumps or nodules on the face. Induration of cellular tissue of the face following gumboil. Sycosis menti, acne and lupus. Skin of face cracks. Caries and necrosis of the jaw. Tumors on the lips. Pale, earthy complexion.

Mouth.—Suppuration of the salivary glands. Mouth gangrenous, with perforating ulcer of the palate. Chronic pharyngitis with constipation. Ulceration of the corners of the mouth.

Tongue.—Induration of the tongue; ulcer on the tongue; sensation of a hair on tongue.

Teeth.—Gums painful on slight pressure, teeth loose. Very violent toothache at night, when neither heat nor cold gives relief, and when caused by chilling of feet. Toothache when the pain is deep-seated in the periosteum, or fibrous membrane covers the root of the teeth and an abscess forms (fistula dentalis). Difficult dentition; gums sensitive and blistered; gumboils.

Throat.—Enlarged thyroid gland. Tonsillitis when the suppurating gland will not heal. Periodical quinsy. Paralysis of the velum pendulum palati.

Gastric Symptoms.—Child vomits as soon as it nurses. Intolerance of alcoholic stimulants. Induration of the pylorus. Chronic dyspepsia with acid eructations, with heartburn and chilliness; vomiting in the A. M. Disgust for meat and for warm food. Extreme hunger.

Abdomen and Stomach.—Large abdomen in children. Enlarged inguinal glands. Constipation associated with spinal affections, due to semi-paralysis of the rectum; particularly if stools recede after having been partly expelled, due to irritable sphincter ani. Hepatic abscess with induration. Infantile diarrhœa, cadaverous-smelling, after vaccination, with much sour perspiration about head, with hard, hot, distended abdomen. Diarrhœa, cadaverous odor. Stools yellow, watery, mushy. Shifting of flatulence. Intensely painful hæmorrhoids. Worm colic. Fissura ani and fistulo in ano. Meteorism.

Urinary and Sexual Organs.—Suppuration of kidneys, urine loaded with pus and mucus. Chronic catarrh of bladder with pus and blood. Prostatitis. Red sandy deposit, uric acid. Enuresis from worms or in chorea. Chronic syphilis with suppurations and indurations. Chronic gonorrhœa, with thick, fœtid, purulent discharge. Sexual erethism, with persistent sexual thoughts, often nocturnal emissions, also with paralytic disease. Impotence. Weakness after coition, easily exhausted. Itching and much sweating about scrotum. Hydrocele. Seminal emissions. Menses are associated with icy coldness over whole body and constipation and fœtid footsweat. Menses early, but scanty; rarely profuse. Burning and itching of pudenda. Nymphomania. Leucorrhœa acrid, profuse, itching. Menses during lactation. Bloody discharge between periods. Hydrosalpinx and pyosalpinx with copious watery discharge. Serous cysts of vagina. Sterility. Abscess of labia, with tendency to fistulous openings. Metrorrhagia due to standing in cold water.

Pregnancy.—Breasts very hard and painful, as if gathering. Inflammation of the breasts, mastitis, to control the formation of the pus, and to absorb the remaining induration. Scirrhus. Nipples crack and ulcerate easily, fistulous ulcers of the mammæ, hard lumps in the mammæ threatening suppuration. Soreness and lameness of feet from instep to sole during pregnancy.

Respiratory Symptoms.—Pneumonia, stage of suppuration. Empyema. Suppurative, rattling, loose, copious expectoration of thick, yellow-green pus, accompanied with hectic fever; profuse night-sweats and great debility. Chronic bronchitis and phthisis. Cough of sickly children with nightsweats. Hoarseness, irritative cough, with feeling of a hair on tongue, provoked by tickling in throat and suprasternal fossa, by cold drinks; worse at night when lying down. Sputa abundant, thick, pus-like, with weakness and deep-seated pain in chest. Phthisical abscess of lungs. Cough and sore throat, with expectoration of little granules smelling bad.

Circulatory Organs.—Palpitation after violent motion or when sitting quietly. Chronic heart disease.

Back and Extremities.—Soreness between shoulders. Spinal curvature, rachitis, **spinal irritation.** Coccyx hurts after riding. Carbuncles along the spine. Spina bifida. Psoas abscess. Hip-joint disease, to prevent or control suppuration. Suppurating wounds of the extremities discharging thick, yellow matter, and the suppuration is deep-seated. **Whitlow, felon,** sensation in tips of fingers as if suppurating, assisting and controlling formation of pus and stimulating growth of new nails. Potts' disease. Proud flesh and caries; old ulcers with burning and lancinating pains. Chronic synovitis of the

knee, with great swelling and anchylosis. Pain in bones, especially shin bones; not worse by pressure. Trembling of hands.
Caries of bone, with fistulous openings, discharging thin pus
and bony fragments. In-growing toe-nails. Habitual fœtid
perspiration of the feet, smelling horribly, suppression causes
other ailments. Offensive sweat in the axillæ. Nails crippled
and brittle, with white spots. In-growing toe-nails. Pains
through foot from ankle to sole. Weak ankles. Feel in-
sufferably tender. Nervous affections following injuries to
spine. Tonic spasm of the hand when writing. Arms and
hands feel heavy and paralyzed. Pain in shoulder and arm at
night, relieved by warm wrappings. Limbs and feet very tired
and as if paralyzed. Knees give out. Joints pain, especially
hips and knees and shoulders. Begins when sitting. Painful
tonic spasm in the feet and toes during a long walk. Diseases brought on by exposure of back to draught of air.

Nervous Symptoms.—Epilepsy occurring at night, the aura
begins in the solar plexus. Pain in various parts of the body,
as if ulcerating. Irritability and sensitiveness of the spine,
with numerous reflex pains. Spasmodic closure of the sphincters. Hysteria and obstinate neuralgia. Suffering parts feel
cold, are sensitive to dampness. Weakness with desire to lie
down. Trembling of limbs and paretic symptoms. Tabes
dorsalis. Spasms from slight provocation. Exhaustion with
erethism.

Sleep.—Sleeplessness from orgasm of blood. Palpitation,
rapid pulse, heat. Talking in sleep. Jerking of limbs during sleep. Bad dreams.

Febrile Symptoms.—Hectic fever during long suppurative
processes. Chilliness all day, on movement, want of animal
heat. Sensitive to cold air. Heat in afternoon and all night
with burning in feet. Sweat at night, with loss of appetite
and prostration. Copious sweat about the head. Offensive
sweat of feet.

Skin.—Skin very sensitive; itching, burning, papules, nodules, ulcers, boils, carbuncles, felons and malignant pustules.
Chilblains. Crusta lactea with an offensive oozing. Eczema

squamosum. Acne. Pustules are extremely painful. Great tendency to boils in any part of the body. Abscesses and carbuncles and subsequent indurations. Ulcers, with proud flesh, putrid, acrid ichor, edges elevated and bluish, fistulous ulcers, and around nails. **Skin heals with difficulty and suppurates easily.** Scrofulous eruptions. Rhagades. Deep-seated, phlegmonous erysipelas. Bursa. Glandular swellings. Variola, suppurative form. Impure vaccination. **Lepra,** especially for the nasal ulceration, nodes and coppery spots. Promotes expulsion of foreign bodies from the tissues, sphincters, etc.

Tissues.—Fungi, easily bleeding abscess with fistulous openings, inflammatory swelling, ulceration and necrosis of bone. Rachitis. Cellular suppuration with slow course and subsequent induration. Malignant and gangrenous inflammations. Enlarged suppurating glands, especially cervical glands. Neglected cases of injury if suppuration threatens. Discharges and excretions offensive. Dropsy. Suppurations of the sebaceous glands, scrofulous diathesis. Enchondroma. Tumor albus.

Modalities.—Symptoms are always worse at night and during full moon. **Amelioration by heat and warm room and in the summer.** Headache relieved by wrapping the head up warm. Abdominal pains, cough, rheumatic pains all relieved by warmth. Worse in the open air, **cold air** and in winter, worse from suppressed foot-sweat or chilling the feet or from cold. Worse before storm. Worse from nerve stimuli. Worse in the morning. All his troubles are made worse by cold.

Homœopathic Data.—This drug was proved by Hahnemann. The first record of it appeared in the *Chronic Diseases,* vol. iii, in 1828.

Administration.—Schüssler recommends the 6x and the 12x potencies, but in the homœopathic school the most brilliant results have followed the use of the higher attenuations (see Clinical Cases, Part III). Its external application is also recommended by Schüssler and others, in carbuncles, ulcers, ulceration of womb, abscess, ozæna as a spray, etc. Massive

10

and repeated doses are indicated in scrofulous, glandular swellings without suppurations. But where there is actual suppuration or even a tendency thereto, high potencies (30th) help in chronic cases, one dose daily, or even less often, in subacute cases, morning and evening—in acute cases from two to three hours. An effective method of using *Silicea* locally is to make a strong decoction of hay. This contains a large percentage of *Silicea*. The silicate of soda should be given in free solution. Percy Wilde, M. D., who introduced this valuable preparation of *Silicea,* gives three to four drops three times daily, and each dose is given in one-third of a tumbler of water, or, better still, in milk. The effect of the remedy must be watched, as it is apt to cause active changes in the tumor within forty-eight hours (see Tumors, Part III).

Relationship.—In suppuration compare *Calcarea sulph.,* the difference being that *Silicea* promotes suppuration and brings the process to maturity, whereas *Calc. sulph.* heals the process by checking it and promoting the healthy granulation. For results from impure vaccination we have, besides *Silicea* and *Thuja, Kali mur.,* which, according to Schüssler, is the one remedy necessary. The *Silicea* headache is similar to *Spigel., Paris, Picric acid, Coccul., Gelsem.* and *Sanguin.* In fistula lachrymalis compare *Natr. mur.* and *Petrol.* In whitlow and ingrowing toe-nail, when *Silicea* fails *Graphit.* often succeeds. In caries and periostitis compare *Asaf., Graphit., Conium, Platina mur.* In tabes compare *Alumina, Ruta. Silicea* is a chronic *Pulsat.,* it corresponds to the chronic form of such diseases as *Pulsat.* cures when acute. *Pulsat.* grows on sandy bottom, and probably contains *Silica* as one of its constituents. In bone diseases it resembles closely *Mercur.,* but it should not be given after *Mercur.,* as it may much complicate the case.

In Moleschott's *Kreislauf des Lebens,* he says that the ashes of *Equiset. hyem.* consist nearly wholly of *Silicea.* The cures of bladder troubles reported by *Equiset.* are probably due to the *Silica* it contains. The mineral springs of Bareges, in the Pyrenees, contain an unusually large amount of *Silicea* in a soluble form, and this spa has been singled out by empirical experience as most valuable in the class of cases for which *Silicea* is homœopathically indicated. (Percy Wilde, M. D.)

In labyrinthine vertigo comparę *Natr. salicy.* In ulceration around the nails, *Psorinum* is invaluable. Allied remedies: *Fluoric acid, Picric acid, Hypericum, Ruta, Mercur.,* etc.

PART III.

Therapeutical Application of the Twelve Tissue Remedies.

ABSCESS.

Ferrum phos.—This is the first remedy to be given in all cases of boils, carbuncles, felons, or any suppurative process, where there are present fever, heat, throbbing pain and congestion in the parts. If given early, this remedy will often abort suppuration.

Kali mur.—Is indicated in the second stage of boils, carbuncles, felons, abscess, etc., where there is swelling, but as yet no pus formation; especially is it indicated in abscesses of the breast, with the above characteristics. It may be given in carbuncles, boils, and other suppurative processes to abort swelling before matter forms. It may also be used as a lotion, applied externally on lint.

Natrum sulph.—Fistulous abscesses of years' standing, discharging watery pus, surrounded by a broad bluish border. Burrowing abscesses. A single dose of the 3d trituration gives everything a favorable turn; the abscesses collapse, the fistulous canals dry up. Paronychia, inflammation or suppuration around roots of nails.

Silicea.—When suppuration appears this remedy should be exhibited at once. It greatly assists the suppurative process, causing the tumor rapidly to ripen, and often to break spontaneously. It is to follow *Kali mur.* in those cases where pus has commenced to form, as in mammary abscess, especially if *Kali mur.* has failed to abort the suppuration. After the abscess breaks or is opened, this remedy should be continued as long as infiltration remains. *Silicea* is also useful in blind boils. In whitlow *Silicea* assists and controls the formation of pus and stimulates the growth of new nails. The use of *Silicea* in all cases of commencing whitlow cannot be over-estimated. A dose every two hours will usually cure the felon in twenty-four hours. (A. P. Davis, M. D.)

Calcarea sulph.—This remedy follows *Silicea* well in suppurative processes, when, notwithstanding the absence of infiltration, the suppuration continues, owing to the torpidity of the affected tissues. It is useful in boils, gathered breasts, whitlow or felon, when they are discharging. It will abort felons and furuncles in the 12x. (W. E. L.) The presence of pus with a vent is an indication for its use. The distinguishing features between this remedy and *Silicea,* in abscesses, are these: *Silicea* ripens abscesses, since it promotes suppuration; *Calcarea sulph.* heals suppurating wounds, since it restrains the suppurative process. It lacks the fœtor of *Silicea.* This remedy is similar to *Hepar sulph.,* but it acts more deeply and intensely. **Painful abscess about anus.** A most useful remedy in **gumboils.**

Kali phos.—This remedy is indicated in abscesses, carbuncles, felons and other suppurative processes when there are adynamic symptoms and the suppurative process becomes unhealthy. The pus is ichorous, bloody, offensive and dirty-looking. In mastitis when the pus is brownish, dirty and foul.

Calcarea fluor.—When the suppurative process affects the bone, or where there are hard, callous edges to the wound, then this remedy will be found effective. In felons a lotion on lint externally has been found to do good. "It is an invaluable remedy in pelvic abscess proceeding from caries of some bone." (Southwick.) "In old cases of fistulous sinuses of the mammæ I have found this remedy especially valuable." (J. W. Ward, M. D.)

CLINICAL CASES.

Patient had taken a slight cold which settled in the gums and the hard and soft palate, and a gumboil began to develop just back of the upper incisors. Gave *Ferrum phos.* with some relief, but the boil seemed determined to suppurate. It continued to swell and grew very painful. After reading an article on *Calc. sulph.* wherein the writer stated, "for gumboils of the teeth it is the only remedy I ever use," I concluded to try it, and accordingly took the 3x in five grain doses, three or four times a day for two days. There was immediate improvement; pain grew less, and, under occasional doses of *Calc. sulph.* the boil absorbed and disappeared. (M. F. R.)

A lady, Mrs. B., suffering from swelling of the leg below the knee, had been attended some months by her doctor, who had poulticed it, and had opened it with a lancet; but there was no discharge. She was unable to walk. It was then painted with iodine without effect; then bandaged to reduce the excessively hard swelling, and cold water poured over it thrice a day. Some parts were blue-looking on removing the bandage. It felt cold and very hard, and looked as if ready to burst; almost twice its usual size. Warm fomentations and *Kali mur.,* taken internally and applied externally, cured the leg in three weeks. (From Schüssler.)

Lilly, aged 6, daughter of the above lady, had an ulcerated tooth with a well developed gumboil as an accessory. Gumboil would not go away, and wishing to see what the Tissue Salts would do for it I gave her a box containing about 125 tablets of *Calc. sulph.* 3x. They should have lasted her ten days or more, but they were sweet and, childlike, she could not resist and so the box full was gone in three days. And so also was the gumboil and ulcerated tooth. (M. F. R.)

In August, 1877, a young man, who had suffered from sciatica some years ago, and had been in the habit of having subcutaneous injections of morphia, developed a boil on the seat. This discharged freely, and would not heal. When, at last, it seemed to be healed and was comparatively well, the patient took cold. Suppuration began again, and this time the discharge was excessive. His mother became alarmed, as he was very weak and had no appetite. His sleep was disturbed, and he felt a constant thirst. I prescribed *Silicea*—a dose every morning on an empty stomach. After one week the mother was able to furnish the very favorable report: "The discharge of matter has been reduced so much that at one time it seemed gone altogether. The great thirst had left him, and his appetite has returned; his sleep is sound, and the shivery, chilly feeling he had has completely gone." *Silicea* has here furnished a brilliant demonstration of its power over suppuration, with its characteristic accompanying symptoms. (Dr. Goullon, Jr.)

A dressmaker, in her busiest season, to her dismay, got a felon on the right thumb. *Ferrum phos.*[12] in water, every three hours, promptly relieved and she supposed cured it. She used it vigorously, and within three days it reappeared with greatly increased pain and hard swelling. *Kali mur.*[12] finished the cure at once, a single drop of pus appearing beneath the cuticle and escaped when snipped with the scissors. (J. C. Morgan, M. D.)

An old gentleman came into my office with tenonitis of the second phalanges. The whole hand was full of thick, yellow pus; had been sore for three months; sleep was a stranger to him; he had been poulticed, lanced and morphined, until the physicians (allopathic) had decided to remove the finger—in fact he came to town for that purpose. His physician being out of the city he came into my office to have me look at it. I told him to let the finger remain on the hand; that although the flexors were all rotten —eaten off—and the periosteum inflamed, yet the finger could be cured. I injected Eucalyptus into the orifice, and it permeated the whole finger and up into the hand. After cleaning the sores I wrapped it up comfortably tight and put him on *Silicea*⁶, a dose every three hours; nothing else was given him; the Eucalyptus dressing was continued every day, and in four weeks the finger was restored to its natural size and shape; but the flexors being all destroyed he could not flex the fingers. The *Silicea*, however, restored all the connective tissue-elements, and the man was well satisfied with the cure. (A. P. Davis, M. D.)

Silicea has proved an excellent remedy. Within the last month I was able to cure a young lady, æt. 16; I did not see her myself. The mother came to me and told me her daughter had been suffering for the past few months from her right foot. The medical men treating her declared that the foot must be amputated. It was fearfully swollen; the discharge of matter was excessive. Her leg was almost bent to a right angle at the knee-joint, and could absolutely not be stretched out. I advised her to give up all internal as well as external remedies, and prescribed *Silicea,* to be taken once daily. Three months later the patient came herself, walking without any assistance. The foot was almost completely healed, with only a slight discharge of matter. Thus I succeeded in a case of discharge of matter from the ear, which had been treated for a long time ineffectually, and caused the patient severe pain day and night. This case was also cured with *Silicea*. (From Schüssler.)

ADDISON'S DISEASE.

Natrum mur.—When nutrition is greatly impaired, tension and heat in the region of the kidneys; earthy complexion, brown spots upon the back of the hands, excessive mental and physical prostration; trembling of legs, dim vision, want of appetite, nausea, vomiting, loathing of meat, constipation. Aversion to motion and labor; frequent yawning and stretching; cold extremities, depression of mind with irritability; vertigo on rising or on trying to walk.

AMENORRHŒA.

Suppression of the Menses.

Kali mur.—Sluggish liver; white coated tongue, and glandular inactivity.

Kali phos.—Suppression of flow with depressed spirits, lassitude and debility, where chest difficulties appear as a result of suppression. Constant dull headache, cross and irritable, fidgety and cannot control herself.

Kali sulph.—Scanty or suppressed menses, with weight and fulness of abdomen.

Natrum mur.—In young girls, when the menses do not appear, or when scanty and at long intervals.

Calcarea phos.—Amenorrhœa in anæmic patients.

CLINICAL CASES.

1. Case of a young girl whose menses had not appeared for several months, and who began to have chest difficulties as a consequence thereof. *Kali phos.*[30], dose night and morning. The menses soon reappeared, and in four weeks she had no more chest pains.

2. A girl, æt. 22, who always had scanty menses, which, during the past year, had completely ceased, and caused head and eye troubles, received, May 12, 1887, *Kali phos.*, six powders. After using it six days the menses reappeared with violent headache and lasted seven days, and her other troubles gradually disappeared. (Monatsblätter.)

Dr. George Royal reports a case of amenorrhœa with the following symptoms, cured with *Kali phos.* 3x: "Constant dull headache, drowsy all day, cross and snappish, cries easily, so fidgety she could not control herself."

ANÆMIA.

Calcarea phos.—This remedy acts by supplying new blood-cells. Pains and cramps dependent on anæmic conditions. Waxy appearance of the skin due to anæmia. Chlorosis, complexion waxy, greenish-white, with constant headache and ringing in ears. Schüssler gives this remedy alone for chlorosis.

"A fine constitutional remedy in old cases of cerebral anæmia where nutrition is manifestly defective." (Arndt.)

"Pernicious anæmia, vertigo when getting up or on rising from sitting; eyes misty; epistaxis, point of the nose cold; pale face, sallow, yellowish, earthy; cold sweat on the face; body cold; foul taste and smell; tongue white, furred at the root most in the morning; nausea and vomiturition; empty, sinking sensation at the epigastrium; watery looseness of the bowels, with urging after stools day or night; urine with flocculent sediment; menorrhagia, blood either bright-red or too dark, palpitation with anxiety, followed by trembling weakness, particularly of the calves, weariness and the greatest weakness." (Arndt.)

This remedy is also useful in leucæmia, or excess of white corpuscles in the blood after exhaustive diseases.

Ferrum phos.—Follows *Calcarea phos.* as soon as improvement of the general health sets in. There is a want of red blood in the system. This remedy, by its power of attracting oxygen, colors the new blood-cells red and enriches them after they have been supplied by *Calcarea phos.* Schüssler in a recent letter says: "Iron, which enters into the formation of young blood-cells, is never absent in the blood-stream of chlorotics. Therefore I have lately abandoned iron, which I recommended in the first editions of my Therapeutics for chlorosis and other anæmic conditions."

Kali mur.—This remedy may have to be given in anæmia, as a secondary remedy or intercurrent, if such symptoms as eczema or eruptions of the skin coexist.

Kali phos.—Cerebral anæmia, anæmic conditions of the brain causing undue nervousness. Poverty of the blood from influences which continually depress the mind and nervous system. This remedy also cures the leucæmia, which is induced by long-continued disorders. "Spinal anæmia, from exhausting diseases, such as diphtheria, reflex paraplegia, with aching pains aggravated by rest, but most manifest on beginning to move about." (Arndt.)

Natrum mur.—In anæmic conditions, where the blood is thin and watery; in chlorotic conditions, with an almost habitual feeling of coldness in the back; chlorosis in young girls, with dead, dirty skin, frequent palpitation, oppression and anxiety in the chest, morning cough, easily fatigued and prostrated, with the characteristic tongue, etc.; malarious cachexia, from ague and *Quinine,* sallow complexion or very pale, pressure and distention of the stomach, constipation with contraction of the anus, terrible sadness.

Natrum phos.—Spinal anæmia, paralytic weakness of the lower extremities, with general prostration, heaviness and sensation of fatigue, especially after a short walk or ascending steps; legs give way, so as to be unable to progress farther.

Natrum sulph.—Hydræmia, sycosis, hydrogenoid constitution of the body, depending upon dampness of weather or dwelling in damp houses; sycosis and hydræmia. (Lilienthal.)

Silicea.—Leucorrhœa instead of menses; attack of momentary blindness or obscuration of vision. Anæmia in infants, thin, delicate and puny, with tendency to rickets.

CLINICAL CASES.

Dr. S. Powell Burdick furnished us with two cases of anæmia, both in young ladies, æt, 19 and 21. Both presented the following characteristic symptoms: Pale, anæmic countenance, great exhaustion, depression of spirits, violent attacks of frontal headache extending to the occiput. The youngest had suffered from this condition for six or seven years, and received treatment from several physicians, homœopathic and allopathic, receiving from the latter large quantites of iron, without any benefit whatever. The eldest had also been anæmic for several days. All their symptoms were promptly relieved, the color returning even to rosy cheeks; the ears, which were formerly pale and almost translucent, became reddish and natural in color. The remedies employed were first *Calcarea phos.*[12], for ten days or two weeks, followed by *Ferrum phos.*[12], for two weeks, then returning to the *Calcarea phos.* again. About six months sufficed to cure permanently in each case.

Young lady, æt. 17, became anæmic and chlorotic, after long continuance at school, becoming so debilitated that she could attend no longer, had no appetite, and desired only to lie about the house, having no ambition to go anywhere or do anything. Her study made her head ache, and she had to give it up entirely; her menses were irregular, absent for months, then a flow varying in quantity. I gave her *Calcarea phos.*[6], as principal remedy, giving also, at times, *Ferrum phos.,* as well. After a few months she became well enough to resume her studies, and could walk anywhere she desired to go, and her color improved. (C. T. M.)

Natrum mur.—W. Rawley, reports a case of anæmia due to the abuse of salt. The patient was emaciated, with general pallor; weakness; sensibility exalted; the menstrual flow never properly established. Bowels inclined to constipation. Has been in the habit of using salt to excess. In treating the case the use was restricted and one dose of *Nat. mur.* 200 given, which was followed by general improvement, the menstrual flow assuming its regular condition and strength, and general health being restored.

ANEURISM.

Calcarea fluor.—This disease at an early stage may be kept in check or reduced with the use of this, the chief remedy, in alternation with *Ferrum phos.,* provided that the iodide of potash has not been taken.

Ferrum phos.—This remedy should be used early to establish normal circulation and remove those complications due to excessive action of the heart; can also be alternated with the preceding with good effect. In small aneurisms with a great deal of throbbing.

ANGINA PECTORIS.

Magnesia phos.—This remedy may be given for the neuralgic spasms of this disease. It should be given in hot water. Neuralgic constrictive pains in chest. It is also a remedy for "false" angina. Dr. Wallace McGeorge has used it successfully in relieving the violence of the paroxysms and in shortening their duration. Its action seems to be prompt.

Ferrum phos.—If accompanied by flushed face, burning or diffused heat, this remedy may be alternated with the preceding.

Kali phos.—If the heart's action be weak or intermittent and if there be tendency to fainting this remedy should be used alternately with *Magnesia phos.*

APHONIA.
See also Hoarseness.

Ferrum phos.—Huskiness after singing or speaking in singers or public speakers, with soreness in the larynx.

ARTHRITIS.

Ferrum phos.—At the commencement this remedy should be given in repeated doses when there are febrile symptoms present, and later on in the disease it may be given as an intercurrent. The joints are painful on moving, motion sets up and increases the pain. Tenalgia crepitans.

Kali mur.—In acute arthritis, for the swelling or when the tongue is coated white. It may be alternated with *Ferrum phos.* Movement aggravates the pains. It is useful especially after *Ferrum phos.* Tenalgia crepitans.

Natrum mur.—Chronic arthritis, joints crack (if tongue and other symptoms correspond, acts probably by increasing the eliminations of the urate of sodium). Synovitis, gout, sore hamstrings (verified).

Natrum mur.—Acute gout (after *Ferr. phos.*). Chronic gout, profuse, sour-smelling sweat. Rheumatic arthritis, especially of finger joints. Urine dark red. Pains go suddenly to heart; sore hamstrings. It seems to have also a marked effect in hot painful swellings of the knee joint.

Magnesia phos.—Useful as an intercurrent remedy for the pains (violent). The keynote is excruciating pains, spasmodic in character.

Kali sulph.—In rheumatic arthritis where the pains shift from one joint to another, aggravated by heat. Shifting and wandering rheumatic pains in the joints. Fungoid arthritis Tumor albus, white swelling.

Silicea.—Suppuration of the joints.

Calcarea sulph.—Suppurative process in the joints.

Natrum sulph.—In acute cases (attacks) of gout. This remedy should be alternated with *Ferrum phos.* In chronic gout it alone suffices. Gout in the feet, acute and chronic. Rheumatic arthritis, especially in joints of fingers, pains suddenly go to heart, urine dark-red.

Calcarea phos.—Rheumatic gout worse at night and in bad weather. Hygroma patellæ. Hydrops genu.

Calcarea fluor.—Gouty enlargements of the finger-joints.

CLINICAL CASES.

Rheumatic pains in joints of the feet, aggravated by motions; *Bryon.* and *Kali iod.* having failed, *Ferrum phos.*, 10th dil., cured.—*Pop. Zeitschrift*, Berlin, 1886.

A shoemaker of Berlin was taken ill after catching cold. There was fever with violent pain in the right shoulder. The first visit I paid was on the third day after he had been taken ill; temperature high, pulse full and quick, thirst and loss of appetite. The right shoulder was very red and sensitive to the touch. He was not able to lie in his bed, as the pressure of the pillows was unbearable. He was lying on the sofa, supported with cushions, so that the shoulder should be free from pressure. I gave my patient *Ferrum phos.*, as much as would cover a sixpenny piece. This was dissolved in a large glass of water, and a teaspoonful of the solution given every hour. Improvement was felt even after a few hours. During the night the patient was able to sleep and on the following day the fever abated; in three days he was able to move the arm pretty freely. In a few days longer he was entirely well. (Sulzer.—From Schüssler.)

ARTHRITIS.—Hot swelling of the knee joint in an anæmic girl was promptly cured in two days with *Natrum phos.* 6x. This and another case very similar in which a like result was obtained is reported in the *Homœopathic World,* Sept. 1908, by Dr. Macnish.

ASTHMA.

Kali phos.—Nervous asthma. In large and oft-repeated doses is the chief remedy for the breathing and depressed condition of the nervous system. Hay asthma and hay fever. Asthma from the least food.

Kali mur.—With gastric derangements. Tongue coated whitish or greenish, furred, and mucus white, and hard to cough up; when this occurs with depression of breathing, alternate with *Kali phos.* Cardiac asthma with sensation as if heart and lungs were constricted.

Natrum mur.—Asthma with profuse frothy mucus. In alternation with *Kali phos.;* also when the tears stream down the face whenever he coughs. Spasmodic jerking with each inspiration.

Calcarea phos.—Bronchial asthma intercurrently, secretion clear and tough. Child gets a suffocative attack on being lifted up from the cradle.

Calcarea fluor.—When specks or small lumps are brought up after much exertion. In alternation with *Kali phos.* These lumps being of yellowish mucus. Oppressed respiration. Epiglottis feels closed, or as if breathing through a thick substance.

Magnesia phos.—In asthma where flatulence is troublesome. Spasmodic nervous asthma. With paroxysmal dry tickling cough and difficulty in lying down.

Kali sulph.—Asthma, bronchial, with yellow expectoration, worse in the warm season or in hot atmosphere. Much rattling mucus. In asthma, when the patient's attacks come on after taking food, and his color becomes bad, or when there is rapid emaciation, or sunken eyes, Dr. Rapp recommends the *Kali* preparations. (Schüssler.)

Natrum phos.—Asthma with thick yellow expectoration.

Natrum sulph.—Very important as a remedy for the sycotic taint, of which asthma is often a manifestation. Attacks, especially in the morning about 4 or 5 o'clock, with cough and raising of glairy slime, expectoration greenish and copious, and vomiting after eating; always worse in damp. rainy weather, from living in basements or cellars. Asthma from digestive disturbances. Loose evacuations on rising in morning. Asthma in children. Asthmatic breathing in young people from a general bronchial catarrh, always worse from every change to damp weather.

Silicea.—Breathing so difficult that the eyes protrude from their sockets; doors and windows must be opened, always during a thunderstorm. As a constitutional remedy with *Natrum sulph.* for eradication of the disease. **Asthma on a cachectic base.**

CLINICAL CASES.

A gentleman in whom attacks of asthma were frequently lasting ten days, with much labored breathing, can hardly talk, thick yellow expectoration with much rattling on chest—*Kali sulph.* 3x relieved at once. (M. E. Douglass, M. D.)

Female, married, æt. 36, asthma, attack violent, greenish, purulent expectoration, a loose evacuation immediately on rising for past two days; *Natrum sulph.*¹⁰⁰ every two hours. Was enabled to lie down that night, respiration and cough much improved and expectoration easier. Next day practically well.

Female, married, æt. 42, subject to attacks for years; expectoration greenish and remarkably copious; *Natrum sulph.* every three hours. Improvement began after a few doses, expectoration becoming paler and less abundant, has felt better since than for years, and one noteworthy fact is that the expectoration stopped in a few doses, whereas under remedies given in previous attacks it had continued for weeks, thus indicating that the *Natrum sulph.* had gotten at the root of the evil. (Wm. J. Guernsey, M. D.)

Dr. O. H. Hall, of Zumbrota, Minn., reports a remarkable case of asthma having passed "through the hands of all the physicians of whom he had ever heard," cured by *Kali phos.* 2x. Eighteen months had passed at time of writing without an attack.—*Minn. Med. Monthly*, Nov., 1886.

Mr. C. has for years had attacks of asthmatic breathing, so marked as to herald his approach at some distance, and coming on after any unusual exertion. He is a tall, strong man, with no family history of lung trouble, albeit rather narrow-chested. Examination of the lungs during a period of remission disclosed no lesion or abnormal sounds, except coarse râles along the larger bronchi. In April, 1887, an especially severe attack, brought on by severe physical exertion, "the worst spell" he has ever had, was promptly relieved by *Natrum sulph.* [200], and occasional doses since have caused the attacks to disappear almost entirely for the first time in many summers. (Wm. E. Leonard, M. D.)

Mrs. E., a lady under my care the past year for chronic bronchitis and other troubles, was seized, on July 9th, with her third annual attack of hay fever—rose cold, or hay asthma, as you please—having contracted the same in Florida. She had formerly been entirely prostrated and forced to bed by these seizures, and dreads them much. Her husband came to me in the evening, a few hours after the sneezing and harsh breathing began, and begged of me to check it if possible. I learned from him that she could not lie down; her breathing was aggravated upon the least motion and accompanied by arching out between the scapulæ. No other point could be elicited that would lead to the more ordinary medicines; indeed, all these had been tried by other physicians in former attacks. I had found *Natrum mur.* to relieve her troubles greatly, and so gave *Natrum sulph.* [200], with strong promise of relief. Nor were we disappointed; she fell asleep in an hour or so after beginning her half-hour doses, and in a few days all signs of asthma were gone. On July 18th no signs of asthmatic breathing could be heard over her lungs, whereas her former attacks had made her wholly miserable for weeks. (Wm. E. Leonard, M. D.)

ATROPHY.

Marasmus.

Calcarea phos.—Scrofulous diseases of children affecting the bones (*Calc. fluor.*). General debility from mal-assimilation of food; delayed dentition. Watery diarrhœa, with flatulence. Abdomen flabby and shrunken. Complexion sallow and child has an old and anxious look.

Kali phos.—Wasting disease when putrid-smelling stools occur. Atrophy of bones.

Natrum mur.—Rapid emaciation of the throat and neck of children; irritability; the children are very slow to learn to talk. Chilliness, earthy complexion and constipation.

Natrum phos.—Marasmus of children who are bottle fed. Abdomen swollen; liver large. Colic after eating. Stools contain undigested food.

Natrum sulph.—Inherited sycotic constitution; bloated abdomen, with much rumbling of wind; stools watery, yellow, gushing, worse on commencing to move in the morning.

Silicea.—**Body wasted while the head is exceedingly large.** Child perspires easily, is nervous and irritable; face emaciated, decrepit looking. **Aversion to the mother's milk;** vomited if taken. Stools offensive and watery. Great prostration upon any change of weather.

CLINICAL CASES.

"Calcarea phos. in non-assimilation of food."

Miss R., aged 5 years, has been very frail all her life, and does not appear to be long for this world. She is very anæmic and has a dirty looking face. Has always been fretful at times and very nervous. Very sensitive and cannot stand any punishment without being sick for a few days. She has no hair and during early life could not hold up her head. Her eyes are sensitive to light. She complains of a bad taste in the mouth and I noticed retarded dentition and chronic enlargement of the tonsils. She had pain in the stomach after eating, and the food seems to lie like a lump in it, and would not eat much because it always caused distress. She had suffered much with costiveness.

Urine highly colored and frequent urging to urinate. Had more or less pain in the limbs and felt restless and wanted to be moving all the time when she felt better. She had a constant leucorrhœa, which was very offensive. She got tired and exhausted very easily and could not stand cold weather. Her bones were very small and weak and could have been easily broken. The child was ordered bathed on going to bed three times a week, and plenty of fresh air. I considered her case nearly a complete picture of *Calcarea phos.* I gave her two cones of the 3x tablets every two hours. It is needless to say that she improved from the first dose almost. Her general condition has remained permanently improved and it certainly is a great victory for the remedy. (O. A. Palmer, M. D.)

BACKACHE.

Silicea.—Spasmodic drawing in back compelling to lie still. Constant aching in centre of spine.

Ferrum phos.—Pains in the back and loins and over kidney. Rheumatic pains felt only on moving. Is almost a specific sometimes.

Kali mur.—Useful after *Ferrum phos.,* if the latter fails to relieve.

Kali phos.—Pains which are laming. The parts affected

feel powerless, gentle movement gradually lessening the pain and stiffness, yet too much exertion increasing the pain (such as walking too far). This kind of pain is always worse after rising from a sitting posture and at the commencement of motion.

Calcarea phos.—Pains with a feeling of numbness, coldness, or with a creeping sensation; worse in the night and during rest. Can also be given alternately with *Ferrum phos.* After exhausting disease. Backache in the lumbar region in the morning when awakening.

Kali sulph.—Pains which are worse in warm rooms and in the evening, better in the open air (cool). Shifting and changing about.

Magnesia phos.—Pains vivid, shooting, boring, intermittent, shifting and neuralgic; relieved by warmth.

Calcarea fluor.—Backache simulating spinal irritation. Tired feeling and pains in the lower part of the back, with a sensation of fulness and burning pain, and confined bowels. Lumbago aggravated on beginning to move, but improved after continuous motion.

Natrum mur.—Pains in small of back relieved by lying on something hard, with characteristic tongue, bubbles of frothy saliva. Pain after prolonged stooping, as if bruised. Weak back, worse in the morning. Spine very sensitive. Neck stiff and emaciated. Great weakness and weariness.

Natrum sulph.—Pain in the back, as if ulcerating, all night; can lie only on the right side. Soreness up and down spine and neck.

Natrum phos.—Pains across loins on awaking in morning.

BITES OF INSECTS.

Natrum mur.—Cures rapidly. Moisten the painful spot and apply thereto *Natrum mur.*, 6th trituration, rubbing it in. Pain ceases at once. (Schüssler.)

11

BONES, DISEASES OF.

Calcarea phos.—Useful to aid the process of repair in fractures. When the bones are weak and soft, caused by soft sponginess, due to want of phosphate of lime molecules. Rachitis, bowlegs in children. Also, for ulceration of bone and wasting of skull-bones. Fistulous ulcers on the ankles; edges callous, ichor putrid Pains along sutures and symphyses of bone.

Ferrum phos.—In bone diseases, when the soft parts are red, hot and painful, inflamed. Ostitis, periostitis. Hip joint disease.

Kali mur.—Second stage of ostitis.

Kali phos.—Atrophy of bones with foul diarrhœa.

Silicea.—Indicated in nearly all diseases of bones. Fistulous openings, discharge offensive. Parts around hard, swollen, bluish-red; fibrous parts of joints, especially of the knee, inflamed. Ulceration of bone, periosteal ulceration. All excretions offensive, pus, stool, sweat, etc. Hip joint disease.

Silicea is oftener indicated and has cured more cases of caries and necrosis than any other remedy. It is a deeply penetrating remedy, and, while closely resembling *Mercur.* in its sphere of action, care must be taken not to administer it after *Mercur.*, as it may much complicate the case. It is more suitable for chronic cases, or after the first stage is past. (Gilchrist.) No other drug so hastens the elimination of the dead bony particles to the largest piece of sequestrum so necessary to the cure of scrofulous diseases of the bones. In many forms of caries, necrosis and in enchondroma of the bones, Grauvogl recommends, as a popular and very effective remedy, hay-baths. Their efficacy depends on the presence of *Silicea*, which has been found as a chemical constituent in a state of solution in hay-baths—three drams of hay containing about one-half grain of *Silicea*. Hence the usefulness of this local measure in diseases of the bone is apparent.

Calcarea sulph.—Ulceration of bone. Craniotabes.

Calcarea fluor.—Hard, rough, corrugated elevations on the surface of the bones. Useful in cephal-hæmatoma (so-called blood-tumor), on the parietal bones of new born infants. Bruises of bones. Exostoses after injuries. Diseases of bones; caries leading to formation of pelvic abscesses. Affections of the nasal bones, causing bad odor to disappear. Nodes and hard bone swellings. Caries in consequence of syphilis or abuse of mercury. Spina ventosa, osteo-sarcoma. Malnutrition of bones, especially the teeth. Osseous growths, especially in the carpal and tarsal articulations. Suppuration of bones. Dental caries, caries of alveolar processes with loosening of teeth.

Magnesia phos.—Spina ventosa alternately with *Calc. fluor.*

Natrum sulph.—Sycosis. Pain in bones, cracking of joints, knees stiff.

CLINICAL CASES.

NON-UNION OF A BROKEN RADIUS AND ULNA.—Mr. D., aged 23 years, who was an anæmic and frail man, received the injury several months before I saw him, and when the splints were removed the soreness was gone, but no union of the bones. The parts were cut down upon, the ends freshened, brought together and supported, and *Calcarea phos.* given three or four times daily, with a very fine result. (O. A. Palmer, M. D.)

ENCHONDROMA INDICIS.—A maiden lady of 60 had a shiny swelling on her left index finger, which had been there for eighteen months. The lump was hard and painful, and of about the size of a small split walnut, but rather flatter. Patient was very nervous and depressed. *Calcarea fluor.* 3x, six grains four times a day. After two weeks the cartilaginous nature had clearly left, and swelling became softer and smaller and disappeared entirely within three months. No change was made in diet or place of abode. (J. C. Burnett, M. D.)

Injury to the tibia of some years' standing; a painful growth appeared on the seat of the injury. This was diagnosed as an osteo-sarcoma by a prominent surgeon, who advised an operation. *Calcarea fluor.*, relieved the pain and reduced the growth. (L. A. Bell, M. D., *Hahnemannian Monthly*, April, 1887.)

Dr. Hansen, of Copenhagen, reports in the *Allg. Hom. Zeit.*, 1886, p. 44, a case of caries of the tibia of three years' standing; fistulous openings led down to the bone, through which splinters of dead bone were being discharged constantly, the secretion therefrom being thick and yellow, accompanied by boring nightly pains. *Calcarea fluor.*[6] cured completely in five months.

ENCHONDROMA CURED BY SILICEA. (From Grauvogl's Text-book.) Boy, æt. 14, metacarpal bones of ring and index and middle fingers and thumb of right hand were swollen to such a degree that oval, hard, knobby masses of uniform surface were formed; joints obliterated and immovable for the past six months. These parts were, at various points, divested of their skin by ulcerated surfaces, under which the bones gave a rough sound to the probe, and places were found here and there which could easily be penetrated, and others again which offered resistance. The boy had no appetite, and was kept at work by a potter, carrying clay. Great pain in the suffering parts, drowsiness during the day, lassitude and depression. According to the doctrines of surgery, there was no other help but disarticulation at the wrist, with a loss of the right hand, since only the little finger and its metacarpal bone seemed free from the disease. *Silicea*⁶, five drops every two hours. In eight days the superficial ulcers began to cicatrize and the tuberous formations had manifestly decreased in extent. After fourteen days more the joints were already movable, though the mobility was very much restricted. After another fortnight all the concomitant symptoms which had been present disappeared, appetite returned, boy was lively and of good cheer, and discharged cured.

A child, æt. 3, had disease of the bone of the forefinger of the left hand, midway between the knuckle and next joint. There was a slight whitish discharge from a minute opening, and the flesh was much swollen and discolored at the place, causing the finger to present a very unpleasant appearance. A physician had, after treating it unsuccessfully, advised amputation of the finger, but the family, not desiring this result of the trouble, decided to try other remedies. Gave her *Silicea*⁶, in solution, which produced improvement at once, and in a few weeks cured the disease in the bone, and the finger resumed its natural appearance, except a slight scar. (C. T. M.)

Dr. C. F. Nichols reports a number of cases of osseous growths cured and benefited by *Calcarea fluor.*[12] (*Organon*, 1880.)

SLOW UNION OF FRACTURE.—Man, æt. 60, had a fracture of the shaft of the femur. It remained movable, in spite of great care, after two months. *Calcarea phos.*[12] was given, at first every night; later every second night. At once the fracture grew firm and was soon well. This is certainly better than instrumental interference. Eighteen months later, the same femur sustained another fracture in its lower portion. The drug was given in like manner as before, but from the beginning. It was well in two months. (J. C. Morgan, M. D.)

In the case of a poor orphan girl, æt. 14, *Silicea* saved her from having her foot amputated. She had been under treatment a long time for bone disease. Her medical man saw no alternative, as the evil only grew worse, but to make arrangements with the infirmary surgeon to have it taken off. This was agreed on, six days before removing her. Her friends were greatly distressed and applied for new remedies. *Silicea*, a dose every hour, was steadily taken, and lotion on lint externally applied. On the fifth day the ankle-bone and surrounding tissues presented such a healthy appearance that all cause for amputation was removed. She continued the treatment for a short time longer, and her case was pronounced perfectly cured. (M. D. W., from Schüssler.)

BRAIN.

See also Meningitis.

Ferrum phos.—First stages of inflammatory troubles.

Kali phos.—Softening of the brain, early state; if with hydrocephalus, give also *Calcarea phos.* Softening as a result of the inflammation, insidious in its approach. Concussion of brain. Putrid stools. Sleeplessness and stupor.

Magnesia phos.—When convulsive symptoms are present. Troubles of sight remaining after cerebral concussion.

Calcarea phos.—Hydrocephalic conditions. Chronic hydrocephalus. Fontanelles remain too long open. Craniotabes.

Calcarea fluor.—Cephal-hæmatoma.

Natrum sulph.—After injuries to the head. Mental troubles following. Intense pain in occipital region.

CLINICAL CASES.

J. C. Morgan, in the *Transactions Pennsylvania Homœopathic Medical Society*, 1882, p. 12, reports some cases of brain troubles in children in which convulsive symptoms were prominent, benefited and cured by *Magnesia phos.*[50]

The following is from an elderly gentleman, Mr. J. M., who had suffered from a prolonged attack of acute and subacute inflammation of the brain. He recovered slowly, but symptoms of softening of the brain set in. He was anxious to give the new remedies a trial. His speech was affected; he seemed to lose momentary consciousness, could not hurry, though he saw himself in great danger of being run over, or stop walking when dangerously close to the quay, and could not be trusted out alone: "I think it is time I were again informing you that I still continue to improve; indeed, I have little to complain of except occasionally—only occasionally—a feeling of mental stupor, the best remedy for which I have found to be *Kali phos.*, which you recommended to me." (M. D. W., from Schüssler.)

BRAIN-FAG.

Calcarea phos.—Nervous prostration, with depression of spirits; profuse night-sweats; pale, wan and emaciated countenance; loss of virile power; habitual coldness and venous congestion of the extremities from debility, sleeplessness and loss of appetite; numb sensations.

Silicea.—Confusion, difficulty of fixing attention. Yielding and anxious mood. Reading and writing fatigue, cannot bear to think. Sense of great debility, but patient can arouse himself, has grit, but soon tires and is compelled to rest. Brain-fag in school girls, become confused during recitations, because they cannot concentrate their thoughts. Want to think, but are unable to do so.

Kali phos.—To restore lost nervous energy. Covers the whole field of neurasthenia. Dull heavy aching in occiput, drowsy and restless, foul breath from tongue.

Natrum mur.—With sleeplessness, gloomy forebodings, exhaustion after talking, embarrassment of the brain.

Magnesia phos.—In many cases of neurasthenia where there are characteristics of neuralgic pains, trembling and general weakness, it is the chief remedy.

CLINICAL CASES.

In treating a number of cases of this trouble, the "Tissue Remedies" have been of the greatest service and the most rapid in their curative action. Cases which have been treated with various other methods and then changed on to the Tissue Remedies soon show the marked change for the better and take on a more rapid improvement. The great variety of causes and the different styles and conditions in which you first find the patients preclude any set rule in treatment, but the prime and all important condition to establish is proper nourishment to every part and tissue, and then to apply by the use of tissue remedies the most necessary demands. In order to supply the proper nourishment it may be necessary for the patient to have change of surroundings, happy occupation, change of air, scenery and food and then to build up with the Tissue Remedies the tissues or forces that have been overtaxed, overworked or under nourished and more or less exhausted. A regular method should be established—regular exercise, regular meals, regular sleep and regular evacuations of the bowels and bladder. These are important. Usually *Kali phos.* is a good remedy to start with, it gets the mind in good condition, and aided by *Calc. phos., Ferrum phos.* or *Natr. phos.*, dependent on condition, soon begins the improvement. Then follow with the *Calc. sulph.* as soon as the *Phos.* has built up the nerve cells, and the *Sulph.* is needed to finish up the work which may take from three months to two years or more, but can be done as positively with these remedies and the proper application of hygiene as it is possible to cure any disease in the domain of curative measures. (F. D. Bittinger, M. D., Dayton, Ohio.)

The following two cases are taken from my note book at a dispensary:

January 23, 1893, Mrs. J———, aged nineteen, twitching of eyelids, worse at 5 P. M. every day, after lamp is lighted. Eyes water with the twitching. Has dread of an accident until a shudder passes over the body; is then relieved of the nervousness. Feels weak, is often dizzy. In walking on the street steers for gutter, either to right or left. Despondent, had chorea when twelve years old, lasting two years. At seventeen had sense of dread at intervals for some months.

Prescribed *Kali phosphoricum* 4x, one grain tablet, four times daily. Jan. 30th mental state and dizziness improved. Remedy repeated. Did not return.

June 4th I went to her home and she told me that the twitching, dread and difficulty in walking passed away during the second week of treatment and had not returned. She was also relieved of the dizziness but has some now, due, she thinks, to pregnancy.

March 30th, Jas. C———, aged twelve, pain in right leg, right arm and back. Drops things, especially if startled. Difficult speech, irritable, restless, constipated, sleep poor. Been nervous since seven years of age, at which time he was kicked in the back. After treatment for two years he was much better. Salt water bath down spine had benefited him. Last attack one month ago.

Kali phosphoricum 4x was prescribed, and he was kept on that remedy with continued improvement.

May 4th, reported better every way, except occasional inability to hold things in right hand; worse in the morning, gets better about noon.

May 11th, holds things with less difficulty, can write with more ease, always at his best at noon.

June 8th, has none of the above symptoms; the spine was bathed with salt water at first, but that measure was discontinued over five weeks ago. (*T. C. Wiggins.*)

A Japanese laborer complained that he could not see after 4 p. m. He could see large objects, as a tree or a man, but could not tell whether he was hoeing out sugar cane or weeds. Learning that he did not notice such a condition on Sundays or holidays, I concluded that fatigue was the cause of his trouble, and put him on *Kali phosphoricum* 6x, with most gratifying improvement in two or three days. Soon he ceased to call. (*T. C. Wiggins.*)

Mr. S———, over sixty years of age, having been under heavy financial strain for months, was suddenly stricken the afternoon of August 14, 1893. He became unconscious in a store, where he had gone for help. I saw him the next day and he was evidently on the verge of prostration. I advised him to give up business and go away for at least a month. He could only leave the city for the rest of the week but that, with *Kali phosphoricum* 6x, helped him to go on with his business, till he could go away for a longer stay, which was some weeks later. He said, "The medicine braced me up wonderfully."

The patient came to California with a modest fortune, which he has lost in unfortunate speculations—a common occurrence.   Anxiety, business cares and overwork had been telling upon him for months.   Finally, about three months ago, while on the local train going home, he suddenly experienced a peculiar cerebral sensation, and became unconscious, but in a few minutes recovered, and asked the conductor to assist him from the train when he arrived at the station, and had the presence of mind to remember a bundle, which lay on the seat at his side, but was still dizzy and confused.   After arriving at home, he experienced a severe spasmodic pain in the cardiac region, which was accompanied by faintness, shortness of breath, and coldness of the extremities.   This lasted several hours, and continued thereafter to return for two weeks or more, without improvement, sometimes several times a day, at irregular intervals.   This finally was attended by more or less mental weakness at times; and, as his physician informed him that he was suffering from an organic affection of the brain, the result of apoplexy, he became very despondent.

After three or four weeks he improved somewhat, but, in performing some trivial manual labor about his home, he experienced a relapse; and, as his physician insisted that his days were few, he concluded to try an eclectic physician, as he employed one in the East formerly as his family adviser.

When the patient came, in company with his wife, we found the case an unpromising one.   He was past sixty years of age, of careworn appearance, despondent, and presenting marked evidence of nervous exhaustion.   There was no paralysis, however, and no evidence of any loss of motor or sensory function, and upon making the effort we found he could call into use all his reasoning faculties.   He complained of sleepless nights from lancinating pains in the left chest and left side of the face.

The prescription was *Kali phos.* 3x, to restore lost nervous energy, and *Magnesia phos.* for the spasmodic pains.   Add five grains to a tumbler half full of water, each agent to be dissolved in a separate glass, and alternating give a teaspoonful every hour during the day, and until bedtime.   In about a week the patient returned for more medicine, and marked improvement was observable.   The careworn, despondent appearance of countenance had more of an expression of comfort and hope.   He said he was better; had felt but one spasmodic attack since beginning the medicine, and could now go about and do light chores without becoming exhausted, and slept well all night.   In another week his wife reported him as well as ever.—Editor *California Medical Journal.*

BRONCHITIS AND BRONCHIAL CATARRH.

Ferrum phos.—Takes the place of *Acon.* in the acute inflammatory stage, or in chronic bronchitis when a fresh aggravation sets in.   It should be given in alternation with the remedy indicated by the expectoration.   Any inflammatory irritation of the bronchi, accompanied with dyspnœa, heat, or burning soreness. Breathing short, oppressed and hurried. **Capillary bronchitis of young children.** Acute, short, spasmodic and very painful cough.

Kali mur.—In the second stage, when thick white phlegm forms, fibrinous in character.

Kali sulph.—When the expectoration is distinctly yellow, watery and profuse, or where it is greenish, slimy and watery. In the stage of resolution.

Natrum mur.—Acute inflammation of the windpipe, with frothy and clear watery phlegm, loose and rattling, sometimes coughed up with difficulty. Chronic bronchitis, bronchial catarrh, "winter cough," with any of the above symptoms. Clear, watery, starch-like sputa. Secretion causes soreness and excoriation. Chronic forms, when sputum is transparent, viscid, weak voice, fluttering of heart. Patient is worse near the seashore.

Calcarea phos.—In anæmic persons where expectoration is albuminous, like the white of an egg.

Calcarea sulph.—Where expectoration is yellow, or yellowish green, or mixed with blood, stage of resolution. Third stage of bronchitis. Ordinary catarrhal colds and in cases similar to those benefited by *Hepar sulph.*

Natrum sulph.—Where exudation causes soreness and chafing. Patient must hold his chest on coughing. Asthmatic spells worse towards morning. Worse in cold, damp, rainy weather.

Silicea.—Cough worse from cold and better from warm drinks. Pus-like expectoration, falls to bottom of vessel containing water and spreads out like sediment. Bronchial affections of rachitic children. Laryngeal morning cough.

CLINICAL CASES.

Numerous cases of bronchitis, broncho-pneumonia and allied affections of the chest, especially in children, have been treated successfully with *Ferrum phos.*, followed by or in alternation with *Kali mur.* Sometimes *Bryon.* has been found an excellent alternating remedy for *Ferrum phos.*, no other treatment having been found necessary.

BURNS.

Kali mur.—Burns of the first degree, also those of the second. Blisters form, also scalds from boiling water. Can be applied externally. White or grayish exudation over wound.

Calcarea sulph.—Burns when suppurating.

Natrum phos.—Burns with suppuration; also externally.

Natrum mur.—When blister has been formed.

CLINICAL CASES.

Dr. J. T. Frawley, of Cleveland, O., uses *Ferrum phos.* 2x as a powder to dust over burns in which there is much heat and redness.

CATARRHAL TROUBLES.

Ferrum phos.—First stage of cold in the head, with circulatory disturbances, catarrhal fever, congestion of nasal mucous membranes. Smarting in nasal passages, worse inspiration; excellent for a predisposition to take cold, alternately with *Calcarea phos.* "*Ferrum phos.* 3x in pharyngeal catarrh, with characteristic white, frothy expectoration, has never disappointed me." (W. R. King.) "For incipient colds it is worth its weight in gold." (Dr. J. P. Lambert.) Small bleeding ulcers in the nose will be frequently cured by this remedy.

Kali mur.—Catarrh when there is white phlegm, thick, not transparent. Dry coryza. Stuffy cold in the head, with a whitish-gray tongue. Adherent crusts in the vault of the pharynx. "I use it often with profit in the purulent stage of acute nasal catarrh. *Kali mur.* has proved to me the most satisfactory remedy in acute inflammations of the naso-pharynx in which there is a decided burning dryness. The appearance is that of redness with marked thickening, almost as though the mucous membrane were solidly infiltrated." (Ivins.) Hawking of mucus from posterior nares. Syphilitic ozæna. Chronic rhinitis and catarrh with closure of the Eustachian tubes, secretions are thick and tenacious, may be opaque, white or yellowish green scabs may form in vault of pharynx.

Calcarea fluor.—Catarrh with expectoration of yellowish, small lumps. Dry coryza. Stuffy cold in the head (alternately with *Kali mur.*), with ineffectual desire to sneeze. Ozæna. Osseous growths and diseases of nasal bones, with offensive odor of dead bone.

Natrum mur.—Catarrhs and colds with watery, transparent, frothy discharges. Chronic catarrhs of bloodless patients. The mucus has sometimes a salty taste. Cold causing vesicular eruptions with watery contents, which burst and leave thin crusts or scabs. Coryza, "running cold," with watery, clear, frothy discharge, worse on going into the cold and on exertion. Influenza. Epistaxis from stooping and from coughing. Posterior nares dry. Loss of sense of smell. Dr. Geo. Herring finds the 1 trit. almost infallible for stopping a cold commencing with sneezing. We have done the same thing frequently with the 30th. Sneezing worse undressing at night and in morning. Fever blisters. Frontal sinus inflammation.

Kali sulph.—Yellow, slimy secretions, or expectorations of watery matter, are conditions calling for this remedy. Patient feels generally worse in the evening or in a heated room. Yellow or yellowish discharge from the nose. Colds with dry skin when perspiration does not set in freely under use of *Ferrum phos.* Engorgement of the nasal-pharyngeal mucous membrane, snoring, mouth-breathing, etc.

Calcarea phos.—Chronic catarrhs and colds in adynamic persons (as an intercurrent remedy). Colds in the head with an albuminous discharge from nose. Sneezing and sore nostrils. Dr. L. A. Bull says: "I frequently began the treatment of chronic catarrhal conditions of the air-passages with *Calcarea phos.* I find that it has quite a decided tonic action, and influences the conditions of the membranes for good. In many places it quite takes place of the *Cinchona* preparations." Large pedunculated nasal polypi. Point of nose icy-cold. Swollen, ulcerated in scrofulous children. Adenoids in the naso-pharynx.

Calcarea sulph.—Cold in the head, with thick, yellow,

opaque, purulent secretions, frequently tinged with blood. It clears up the condition of the mucous glands. Nosebleed.

Natrum phos.—As an intercurrent, when gastric symptoms appear, such as acid risings and yellow base of tongue. Picking at nose. Naso-pharyngeal catarrh, with thick, yellow mucus, especially in the scrofulous ozæna. Offensive odor before nose.

Natrum sulph.—Nosebleed during menses. Ozæna syphilitica, worse every change from dry to wet weather. Catarrhs of mucous membranes in general, characterized by a tendency to profuse secretion of greenish mucus. This is the tissue remedy for *la grippe,* since the disease is caused by an excess of water in the cellular fluids.

Kali phos.—Ozæna, foul, offensive discharge from nose, foul breath, and where secondary nervous troubles arise. Epistaxis and predisposition to same. Yellow crusts blown from nose. Thick, yellow discharge; sneezes from slightest exposure. Thick mucus hawked from posterior nares.

Magnesia phos.—Loss or perversion of sense of smell. Alternate dry and loose coryza. Gushing flow from nostrils.

Silicea.—Ozæna, with offensive discharge from nose, when the affection is seated in the submucous connective tissue or periosteum. (Syringe also with a solution of the same remedy.) Painful, chronic dryness of the nose, or inveterate ulceration, producing acrid, corroding discharge; herpetic eruption around nostrils and lips. Itching of tip of nose.

CLINICAL CASES.

Dr. H. Goullon (*Pop. Zeitschrift*) praises *Natrum phos.* in chronic postnasal catarrh, giving as indications the golden-yellow exudation and yellow tongue, etc., and relates a case cured by *Natrum phos.*[1] after *Kali bich.* had failed, as well as everything else, and the patient had become hypochondriacal.

Case of thick, yellow, offensive ozæna, alternating with watery discharge; has been affected with it for eighteen months; has lost taste and smell; left nostril worse. Catamenia occur every three weeks. Takes cold very easily. Stillborn child three years ago. Gave three doses of *Kali sulph.*[12] in water, to be taken once a week. In one month reported catarrh entirely well; has regained much of the lost senses of smell and taste. (W. P. Wesselhœft, M. D.)

Miss D., a dressmaker, aged twenty-six, of medium size, had a large nasal polypus in the right nostril. The right nasal bone pressed far out of line and obstructed the right lachrymal duct, which was very disfiguring. From this condition, in which she had been unable to breathe through the nostrils for more than four years, she was cured and the nasal bone returned to its place, with breathing ability restored to order in six months by *Natrum mur.* m., one dose a week, and *Saccharum lactis* powders between. (Dr. W. L. Morgan.)

Dr. Breuer, of Munich, reports a case of suppressed foot-sweat, resulting in protracted bronchial catarrh, cured by *Calcarea sulph.* and *Silicea.—A. H. Z.*, 1883.

Case of gentleman, light-complexioned. About once a week a thick, dark brown semi-fluid accumulation of pus formed in the left upper nostril; on being blown out it emitted a terrible stench. About a month previous a piece of carious bone was taken from the antrum highmori, through an upper left alveolus, from which a tooth had been drawn four years previous. The probe entered the antrum freely. *Calcarea, Silicea* and several other remedies proved inefficacious. Three weeks after having taken two doses of *Kali sulph.*⁰ in water, morning and evening, a tablespoonful for four days, nothing more remained of the discharge, and the alveolus closed so that no probe entered. (W. P. Wesselhœft, M. D.)

NATRUM MURIATICUM.—Dr. Louis A. Bull records a case of atrophic rhinopharyngitis in which the skin was "colorless, dry, fishy in appearance and profusely dotted with comedones, large and small." He was reminded, he says, of Boussingault's experiments in withholding salt from animals, and opined that here was a case in which chloride of sodium was not properly assimilated. He used it locally in ten grains to the ounce solution, and internally in dynamized form, with most satisfactory results.—*Hom. Recorder.*

NATRUM MURIATICUM FOR FRONTAL SINUS INFLAMMATION.—One afternoon, some eight years ago, a lady called with her husband to see how urgent was the necessity of having her left frontal sinus operated. She had been told by another specialist that a delay of even twenty-four hours was dangerous. The history she gave of the trouble was in substance as follows:

Five years before she had an acute suppurative inflammation, which, after some weeks of careful treatment, subsided, leaving only a slight tenderness. There were occasional exacerbations of the pain, but no evidence of suppuration. The attack of pain she had lasted for a week or ten days and showed no signs of abating. There was no redness nor swelling, but the entire area was very tender to the touch. Transillumination was uncertain. There was no discharge, but the nasal membranes were intumescent. I could see no immediate necessity for an operation; in fact, I saw no special indication for an operation at all, and so informed them. Medical treatment was recommended, and the advice was accepted. *Natrum muriaticum* was prescribed in the thirtieth potency, with the result that in one week not a trace of the trouble remained, and in the eight years that have elapsed there has been no recurrence.

Case 2.—Several months ago a young lady called, giving a history of incessant pain, quite severe in character, over the left frontal sinus; there had not been a moment's relief in six years. There was, at times, redness, and occasionally swelling of the eyelid in the morning. Transillumination showed dullness, the argyrol tampon bleached out completely in a few minutes; the region was exquisitely sensitive to pressure; a thick mucopurulent discharge filled the nasal cavity. *Natrum muriaticum* 12x gave entire relief of the pain in twenty-four hours. Argyrol tampons were applied three times a week for several weeks, with distinct benefit. Following *Natrum muriaticum, Kali sulphuricum* 12x was given. At the last visit she reported having discharge only in the morning and that as bland in character.

CHICKEN POX.

Ferrum phos.—This remedy alone, or alternately with the remedy indicated by the eruption, such as *Kali mur., Calcarea sulph., Natrum sulph.* or *Silicea.*

CHOLERA.

Ferrum phos.—In the first stage, for the vascular disturbances, alternating with *Kali phos.* Cholera infantum, discharges frequent, watery, even bloody; child is greatly reduced, falls into stupor, red face, dilated pupils, rolling of head and soft, full-flowing pulse, cholera from checked perspiration.

Kali phos.—When the stools have the appearance of rice-water. Collapse, livid, blue countenance and low pulse.

Kali sulph.—Cramps and other symptoms of cholera.

Magnesia phos.—Choleraic cramps. First stage. Watery diarrhœa with vomiting and cramps in calves.

Natrum sulph.—Is, according to Schüssler, the remedy for cholera and cholerine.

Calcarea phos.—Cholera infantum. Green diarrhœa in scrofulous children, slimy, watery, undigested and offensive. Thin body, child looks like an old woman.

CLINICAL CASE.

Old man attacked with severe vomiting and diarrhœa, cramps in calves and rice-water discharges. *Kali phos.* cured. (Schüssler.)

CHOREA.

Calcarea phos.—In scrofulous children. Chorea during puberty in either boys or girls who are deficiently developed.

Magnesia phos.—This is the chief remedy. Involuntary movements and contortions of the limbs, with mute, appealing looks for sympathy. It is especially a remedy in local choreas, such as occupation spasms, writer's cramps, piano and violin players' spasms, etc. Follow or alternate with *Calcarea phos.*

Silicea.—When due to the presence of worms, spasms, sleep disturbed by frightful dreams, distorted eyes, pale face, canine hunger, irritation of nostrils, constipation, great thirst, œdema of face and extremities.

Natrum mur.—Suitable for chronic cases, after fright or suppression of eruptions on the face, paroxysms of jumping regardless of obstructions, twitchings on the right side, worse at full moon, especially in malarial, anæmic and chlorotic states, with thirst and fever.

Natrum phos.—If due to worms, or if acid symptoms are present. (See *Silicea.*)

CLINICAL CASES.

Cases of chorea; face and upper part of body affected; lateral and downward jerking of the mouth, snapping of eyelids, sudden forward motion of head, and other irregular movements. Better during sleep; aggravated at stool and by emotions, *Ignat.* failed. *Magnesia phos.*[3] for three months produced gratifying results, but did not fully cure. Acting on Dr. Schüssler's advice, *Calcarea phos.* 6x was given alternately with *Magnesia phos.*, the former once daily, the latter twice. In one month the child was cured. (D. B. Whittier, M. D.)

Choreic patient talking to herself constantly, or sitting still in moody silence, or carrying things from one place to another and then back again. *Magnesia phos.*[12] cured. (Dr. Sager.)

H. S., æt. 7. Chorea for two years, caused by fright; pale, delicate, anæmic, drinks much water, feverish, white tongue, sore mouth. *Natrum mur.*[200] cured permanently. (C. P. Hart, M. D.)

CHOREA CURED BY MAGNESIA PHOS.—By Dr. John H. Clarke.—Gertrude S——, æt. 6, was admitted to the London Homœopathic Hospital, on March 30th, 1887. She had suffered from well-marked chorea during the preceding eight months, and the usual remedies for such conditions had been administered to her as an out-patient during the previous two months with but small success. No definite cause was to be made out. The child did not suffer from worms, and there was no history of a fright. On admission she twitched all over during her waking hours, but was quiet during sleep. She walked fairly well and could feed herself, but her speech was exceedingly defective. The heart's action was accelerated, but no abnormal sound was to be distinguished. Subsequently, however, a soft, presystolic, blowing sound was at times audible, as if the muscular fibres of the heart participated in the general spasms. The pupils were symmetrically dilated. *Magnesia phos.* was prescribed—two grains of the sixth decimal trituration, three times daily. The improvement which followed was slow, but abundantly manifest. The general twitching became less; the articulation improved, the child took nourishment freely; slept well at night, and lost the scared expression so characteristic of the complaint. By May 17th no vestige of the chorea remained. On being directed to stand up, close the eyes, and hold the arms extended, she did so without difficulty. Subjected to the difficult test of walking blindfolded, she came through triumphantly. Lastly her powers of speech had so much improved that, whereas on her admission the meaning of her utterances was a matter of pure conjecture, by this date her remarks were quite intelligible. Thus within seven weeks this obstinate case of a very troublesome disease yielded completely to *Magnesia phos.*—one of Schüssler's so-called "tissue remedies." No other medicine was given.—*Hom. World,* July, 1887.

COLIC.

Magnesia phos.—Flatulent colic of children, with drawing up of legs. Colic forcing the patient to bend double; eased by friction, warmth and belching of gas. Colic in umbilical region. Muscular contractions. Remittent colic, crampy pain. "Colic of newborn infants. I use it in almost every case with absolute, invariable, prompt and complete success; 30th potency." (J. C. Morgan, M. D.) Colicky babies when they cry half the time; no interference with nutrition. Gall-stone colic.

Natrum phos.—Colic of children, with symptoms of acidity, such as green, sour-smelling stools, vomiting of curdled milk, etc.

Ferrum phos.—Colic at menstrual periods, with heat, flushing of the face and quickened pulse.

Natrum sulph.—Flatulent colic starting in right groin. Bilious colic, with bitter taste in the mouth and grayish or brownish-green coating at the root of the tongue. In lead colic this remedy should be given frequently in the 1x or 2x trituration. Pain in abdomen and small of back as if bruised. Much flatulence. Incarceration of flatus. Flatulent complaints after confinement, with constipation.

Kali sulph.—Pains resembling colic. Abdomen feels cold to touch; sometimes caused by great heat, from excitement and sudden coldness; shortly after, gas escaping smells like sulphur; if *Magnesia phos.* fail.

Kali phos.—Colic in hypogastrium, with ineffectual urging to stool; better bending double. Abdomen distended with gas.

Natrum mur.—"In cases of bilious colic presenting the belching of *Carbo veg.* and the pains of *Diosc.* and *Coloc.* I have found *Natrum mur.* to do excellent service." (C. E. Fisher.)

CLINICAL CASES.

Woman, æt. 50, suffered for two years from gastralgia and enteralgia, attacks lasting several days; at each attack vomiting of a fluid as sour as vinegar. Two allopaths had treated her in vain, diagnosing the affection as cancer of the stomach and wandering kidney. My diagnosis was oversecretion of lactic acid. *Natrum phos.* Improvement set in in two days, and in a few weeks was entirely cured. (Schüssler.)

Case of lady with bilious colic. Was sent for in the night, and for particular reasons did not go. I, however, sent what I thought would relieve her. Early in the morning her husband was again at my office, saying she was no better, but suffering terribly. I gave him a different remedy, to be administered until I could get there. About half past nine I arrived at the house, and found her still suffering excruciating pains. Ascertaining she had vomited bile, and had a very bitter taste in her mouth all the time, I administered a powder of *Natrum sulph.* in a little water. In about two minutes after taking it she said she was considerably relieved for the first time since eleven o'clock in the night. In about five minutes she had a free movement from the bowels, and she continued to improve, and was up and about the next morning.

One of the hard-working clergy of the metropolis was for several years subject to very frequent and very severe attacks of colic, always running on to inflammatory character, violent vomiting, great tenderness of abdomen, restlessness, anxiety, misery. These attacks generally lasted from three days to one week. More than a year ago it was ascertained that the *pain generally commenced in the right groin* and thence spread over the whole abdomen. *Natrum sulph.* was given, the attack yielded immediately, and though he has had several threatenings, he has had no colic since.—Hering's *Materia Medica.*

CONCUSSION OF THE BRAIN.

Kali phos.—Asthenic conditions, dilated pupils, depression of function of the brain-cells resulting from concussion.

Ferrum phos.—Febrile disturbances depending thereon.

Magnesia phos.—When optical illusions accompany.

Calcarea phos.—As an intercurrent sometimes, and with numb sensations.

Natrum sulph.—Chronic effects of falls and blows on head.

CONSTIPATION.

NOTE.—No purging need be resorted to. Constipation occurs frequently in consequence of some primary disturbance. Look for the symptoms of this. The proper remedy will make the bowels move. (Schüssler.)

Kali mur.—Constipation accompanied by a white-coated tongue, also when fat and pastry disagree. Excellent in long standing cases. Torpid liver, light-colored stools through want of bile from sluggish liver.

Kali phos.—Stools dark brown, streaked with yellowish-green mucus. Paretic condition of rectum and colon.

Natrum mur.—Torn, bleeding, smarting feeling after stool. Constipation with much intestinal weakness, and when arising from want of moisture. Dryness of the mucous linings of the bowels, with watery secretions in the other parts; watery vomiting, watery eyes, excess of saliva in the mouth or on the tongue. Drowsiness and waterbrash. Stools are hard, dry and difficult to pass. Accompanied by headache. Hæmorrhoidal constipation. Proctalgia. Pain in abdominal rings. "Constipation of fleshy people, especially those with weak hearts." (Frawley.)

Calcarea phos.—Costive, hard stool with blood, especially in old people, associated with mer   depression, vertigo and headache.

Calcarea fluor.—Inability to expel the fæces.

Natrum phos.—Obstinate constipation. Habitual constipation with occasional attacks of diarrhœa in young children. This remedy is an admirable laxative when administered with the food of infants. Dose, 5 to 10 grains three times daily for a six-months' old child.

Natrum sulph.—Hard, knotty stools streaked with blood, preceded and accompanied by smarting at the anus; difficult expulsion of soft stool; emission of fœtid flatus in large quantities. (Strong.)

Ferrum phos.—Constipation with heat in the lower bowel, caused by atony of muscular fibres of intestines. *"Ferrum phos.* is indicated in obstinate constipation with prolapsus ani and piles, associated with anæmia; face pale, readily flushing, cold hands and feet, palpitation, persistent chilliness, flatulence and fulness of epigastrium, with great aversion to meat diet." (Donaldson.)

Silicea.—Rectum seems to have lost the power of expulsion. Fæces recede after having been partly expelled. Soreness, stitches and shooting pain in anus. Constipation associated with chronic scrofulous and suppurative diseases. Constipation of poorly nourished children with pale, earthy face. Copious perspiration around head, accompanying paralytic diseases.

CLINICAL CASES.

Mrs. H., æt. 26, mother of three children; constipation since birth of last child, three months ago. Cathartics had failed. The stools were hard and dry, were partially expelled with much straining, and then receded into the rectum. *Silicea*[30] cured in four doses, taken night and morning. (I. P. Johnson.)

Dr. Gross, the pupil of Hahnemann, relates a very remarkable case of chronic constipation cured with *Natrum mur.*[30]. The patient, a boy, æt. 11, born of scrofulous parents, has an idiotic brother; patient himself mute and almost an idiot. The poor creature suffered with constipation from birth. Would go three to four weeks without stool. After a course of *Natrum mur.*[30] the constipation was entirely cured. (Full report of the case found in Strong's *Constipation*, p. 72.)

Obstinate constipation, of many years' duration, cured in a few days by *Sod. Chlor.* By C. Stirling Saunder L. R. C. P., Lond.

Mr. ———, aged 25, came to the writer at the end of January last suffering with symptoms of constipation, so obstinate as to have necessitated the habitual use of artificial aperients and laxatives almost daily for many years. He was given the sixth trituration potency of *Sod. Chlor.*, nothing else whatever, and *in a few days' time his bowels were perfectly regular,* but continued the treatment for six weeks, since which he has been able to entirely dispense with even this.

COUGH.

Ferrum phos.—Acute, painful, short, tickling cough. Short, sore, tickling cough from irritation of the windpipe. Short, dry, spasmodic cough, with feeling of soreness in the lungs, no expectoration. Cough hard and dry, with soreness from cold. Cough, with rattling of mucus in chest, worse at night.

Kali mur.—Loud, noisy stomach-cough, with grayish-white tongue. Short, acute and spasmodic, like whooping-cough, requires this remedy. Noisy cough accompanied by wheezing rales, with protruded appearance of the eyes and white or gray-coated tongue. Croupy, hard cough. Child grasps at throat during coughing spell. Persistent, croupy-like hoarseness. Cough with thick, milky-white, gluey, albuminoid phlegm. Cough in consumption with thick, milky-white, tenacious expectoration. White-coated tongue.

Kali phos.—Cough from irritation in the trachea, which feels sore. Expectoration thick, yellow, salty, and fœtid, chest sore.

Kali sulph.—Cough with yellow expectoration or watery matter. Worse in a heated room or in the evening. Mucus slips back and is generally swallowed, suggesting *Causticum;* hard, hoarse cough like croup, weary feeling in the pharynx. The cough is more rattling and the expectoration is more difficult than in *Pulsatilla.* (Linnell.)

Magnesia phos.—True spasmodic cough coming on in fits, paroxysms; without expectoration, spasmodic cough at night, with difficulty upon lying down. Whooping cough. Patients refer the spasm to the pit of the throat. The lungs are sore from the strain of coughing. In dry cough in nervous children this remedy should always be thought of.

Calcarea fluor.—Cough with expectoration of tiny, yellow, tough lumps of mucus. Cough with tickling and irritation in the throat on lying down, from elongation of the uvula, or dropping at the back of the throat.

Calcarea phos.—Cough with expectoration of albuminous matter, not watery. In cough of consumptives as an intercurrent remedy. Suffocative cough in children, better lying down.

Calcarea sulph.—Cough with sanious, watery sputa.

Natrum mur.—Cough with excess of watery secretions. In consumption with watery sputa, tasting salty, winter cough. Stitches in liver with cough. Dry, short cough, day and night, from irritation in pit of stomach.

Natrum sulph.—Cough with a sensation of all-goneness in the chest. Muco-pus, thick, ropy and yellowish-green expectoration; must press upon chest to relieve soreness and weakness.

Silicea.—Cough provoked by cold drinks. Soreness and weakness of chest relieved by warm, moist air. Laryngeal, morning cough with tough expectoration. Dyspnœa on stooping or lying on back. Expectoration of profuse, yellowish-green pus of greasy taste and offensive odor. Suffocative night-cough. (Lilienthal.)

CLINICAL CASES.

Dr. J. A. Biegler reports in the *Trans. I. H. A.*, 1888, a case of subacute laryngitis cured by *Kali phos.*[30]. The prescription was given "as a forlorn hope," because the case came late under treatment, with weakness, pale, bluish face, etc. Speech slow, becoming inarticulate, creeping paralysis, and because Grauvogl says: "We know that the oxidation processes, the changes of gases in the respiration, and other chemical transformations in the blood, are brought about by the presence of *Kali phos.*"

Dr. F. W. Southworth reports two cases of spasmodic cough, promptly relieved by *Magnes. phos.* 4x and 6x respectively, the leading indications being its spasmodic character, worse on lying down and at night, and on breathing cold air; better on sitting up; tightness across the chest. The second case had spurting of urine when coughing.

Dr. Fisher was consulted by a lady (*enciente*) who was suffering from a cough which caused great inconvenience, as with every cough there was emission of urine. *Ferrum phos.* cured her very speedily. A short time ago the lady, under similar circumstances, was again troubled with a cough. *Ferrum phos.* this time also cured her as speedily. (From Schüssler.)

CROUP.

Kali mur.—Is the principal remedy for the membranous exudation, alternating with *Ferrum phos.* The chief remedy in false croup.

Ferrum phos.—This remedy should be alternated with *Kali mur.,* breathing short, oppressed and hurried.

Calcarea phos.—Useful if the foregoing fail to act. "Suffocative attacks on lifting up the child from the cradle. After nursing, after crying, or being raised from the cradle, breathing ceases, the head turns backward, the face is blue, there is fighting with hands and feet; after the attack great laxation." (Bradford.)

Kali phos.—If treatment is delayed till the last stage, syncope; for nervous prostration, pale, livid countenance; in alternation with *Kali mur.*

Magnesia phos.—Spasmodic closure of the windpipe. Sudden shrill voice; suffocative cough.

Calcarea sulph.—Useful after the exudation stage when, after the hard membrane has been softened, there exists a tough mucus in the throat causing much discomfort. It will change the croupous to a catarrhal cough, and when given in season will sometimes prevent exudation.

CLINICAL CASES.

D. R., a boy, æt. 7, who took spurious croup when there was a sharp, keen, northeast wind, having had, a few years before, a very severe attack of true croup; this past autumn had again an attack, with fever, and a loud, barking cough. *Acon.* and *Hepar sulphur.,* which have been recommended by so many authors against spurious croup, produced no change whatever, so that I prepared myself, in the case of this boy, for a continuance of the affection, as usual, for several days. The nights especially were very restless, with much coughing, rough and hard, so that his relatives were very anxious. There were dry heat and great oppression present. I exchanged my *Hepar sulph.* for *Kali mur.*, and gave every two hours a full dose. After a few doses the cough became loose, lost completely the barking sound, and the whole of the following night my little patient slept quietly, so that on the following morning he awoke, able to get up, quite lively and well. (Schüssler.)

In croup, do not be afraid of high potencies; they often do much better than the low. (E. H. H.)

DELIRIUM.

Ferrum phos.—When there is present high fever.

Natrum mur.—Delirium occurring at any time, with starting of the body, wandering delirium with muttering; frothy tongue. Delirium tremens. Chief remedy; if it does no good give *Kali phos.*

Kali phos.—Delirium tremens; the horrors of drunkards, fear, sleeplessness, restlessness and suspiciousness, rambling talk, endeavors to grasp or avoid imaginary objects and images. Give alternately with *Natrum mur.*, as this remedy restores the normal consistency of the brain substance which is disturbed in this disease.

CLINICAL CASE.

I was consulted by the relatives of a man suffering from delirium tremens. I ordered *Natrum mur.* A complete cure followed speedily. *Natrum mur.* is the principal remedy, as delirium tremens is caused by a disturbance of the balance of the molecules of the *Natrum mur.* and molecules of water in some portion of the brain. (Schüssler.)

DENTITION.

Ferrum phos.—Teething troubles with feverishness, flushed face, sparkling eyes, dilated pupils, and extreme restlessness and irritability. The febrile conditions are acute but not so turbulent as *Aconite.* Raue says: "It is especially useful when the respiratory tract becomes involved; indicated by rapid breathing, hard dry cough, hoarseness and restlessness."

Magnesia phos.—Convulsions in teething without fever, in alternation with *Ferrum phos.* "In convulsive cases, where *Bellad.* seems indicated, but does no good, spasmodic colic, loose bowels, this is a magnificent remedy." (J. C. Morgan, M. D.)

Calcarea phos.—The chief remedy in teething disorders. If they appear too late it should be given to hasten development. It is the remedy for troublesome ailments during dentition. Especially useful in flabby, emaciated children with open posterior fontanelles. Child does not learn to walk or forgets to walk and loses flesh. Has a sputtering, pus-like diarrhœa and vomiting.

Natrum mur.—Where there is much dribbling or flow of saliva.

Silicea.—Especially suitable for children with large heads, open sutures, much sweat about head, large abdomen, fine skin, oversensitiveness, imperfectly nourished, due to malassimilation.

Calcarea fluor.—This remedy also greatly facilitates dentition. Vomiting during dentition. Malnutrition of the bones, especially of the teeth. "Spasms, commencing by holding breath, incessant crying and momentary loss of consciousness." (Dr. J. W. Ward.)

CLINICAL CASES.

Case of vomiting of food and drink during dentition, undigested diarrhœa, curdled milk, with green specks in it, much offensive flatus. During sleep head wets pillow, head small. *Calcarea phos.*[2] cured. (Raue, *Record,* 1873.)

DENTITION.—Child, 18 months old; hot skin, cheeks highly flushed, sparkling eyes, pupils dilated, and extreme restlessness and irritability. *Ferr. phos.* 6x trit., in water every hour. The first dose had a decided quieting effect, the child going to sleep shortly after taking it and the cheeks becoming much less flushed. A few repetitions of the remedy entirely removed all the dental irritation. (Wilde.)

I have had many cases of that troublesome affection with children that I have easily cured with *Magnes. phos.* For the benefit of young practitioners, I will add that I generally prevent the recurrence of that trouble by treating the mother in the following manner: As soon as I see one of my regular patients having reached the fifth or sixth month of pregnancy, every morning and evening I order the pregnant woman to take a dose of *Calc. phos.* 3x trit. The results that I have obtained are: first, to prevent the usual decay of the mother's teeth; and, second, to see her offspring cutting teeth sooner and without any trouble. (E. A. de Cailhol, M. D.)

DIABETES MELLITUS.

Natrum mur.—Polyuria; unquenchable thirst; emaciation, loss of sleep and appetite; great debility and despondency. Aggravation on alternate days; hammering headache.

Natrum sulph.—This is the chief remedy. Schussler gives as a special reason for its use **deficiency of the pancreatic secretion.**

Kali mur.—Excessive and sugary urine. Great weakness and somnolence.

Kali phos.—The symptoms for which this remedy must be given intercurrently are nervous prostration, weakness, sleeplessness and voracious hunger; it establishes normal function of the medulla oblongata and pneumogastric nerve, which latter acts on the digestion or stomach and on the lungs.

Ferrum phos.—Diabetes, when there is a quickened pulse or when there exists pain, heat or congestion in any part of the system, as an intercurrent remedy.

Calcarea phos.—Polyuria, with weakness, much thirst, dry mouth and tongue; flabby, sunken abdomen; craves bacon and salt. **Glycosuria when lungs are implicated.**

Calcarea sulph.—Schüssler says that this may possibly be a remedy useful for this disease; also *Kali sulph.*

CLINICAL CASES.

A writer explains the biochemic treatment of diabetes as follows:

Lactic acid is composed of *Carbonic acid* and water, and must be split up on its way to the lungs. This is done by the catalytic action of *Sodium phosphate* in the blood. Any deficiency of *Sodium phosphate* will cause a disturbance in the water in the system by allowing an excess of *Lactic acid* to accumulate. Nature in her effort to eliminate the water produces the symptoms called diabetes.

But while a lack of *Sodium phosphate* is the principal cause of diabetes, the chief remedy is *Sodium phosphate;* because it regulates the supply of water in the blood. *Sodium phosphate* also gives off oxygen, so necessary for the process of the decomposition of sugar, and thereby prevents its reaching the kidneys as sugar, and also thins, to its normal consistency, bile that has become inspissated from a lack of *Sodium phosphate.*

If a case of diabetes has advanced to any considerable degree, the kidneys will have become inflamed by the *Lactic acid* and sugar that passes through them. This injury to the tissue of the kidney calls upon the red corpuscles of the blood for *Iron phosphate,* which will, in most cases, cause a deficiency in that inorganic salt. Nature, in her efforts to supply iron, will probably draw on the nerve fluid, *Potassium phosphate* will be too rapidly consumed, and the patient suffers from nervous prostration.

The treatment, therefore, for diabetes mellitus is: the *Phosphates of sodium, iron* and *potassium,* and the *Sulphate of sodium.* For the great functional disturbance of nerve centers caused by the demand made on the blood for the *Potassium phosphate,* producing sleeplessness and voracious hunger, *Potassium phosphate* is the infallible remedy. It establishes normal functional action of the medulla oblongata and pneumogastric nerve, which latter acts on stomach and lungs. For the great thirst, emaciation, and despondency, give *Sodium chloride.* It equally distributes the water in the system and quickly restores the normal condition.

The phosphates may be combined where two or more are indicated, but the *Sodium sulphate* and *Sodium chloride* should be given in separate solutions. Where there is great emaciation or poor appetite *Calcium phosphate* should be given, a small dose after each meal.

In my opinion, diet cuts but little figure in the treatment of diabetes, except as to the amount of food taken. The main object is have the food digest. Diabetic patients should never overeat; better eat six times daily than overeat once.

Of course, diet of fat meats or greasy food cannot be beneficial, for the very important fact that it overworks the liver, causes a deficiency and consequent thickening of bile and mucus, and sometimes a crystallization of cholesterin in gall duct, which gives rise to symptoms called hepatic colic, jaundice or bilious headache.

Dr. W. J. Hawkes, of Los Angeles, reports the following interesting case in the *Pacific Coast Journal of Homœopathy,* October, 1913:

Miss Barr, music teacher, daughter of Dr. James Barr, 1400 West 36th Place (I give name and address with permission), consulted me July 22, 1911. Diabetes in aggravated form was her ailment. She was emaciated so that she weighed less than eighty pounds, and was so weak she could walk but a short distance. The emaciation of her neck was remarkable. Her appetite was enormous—was continually hungry. Her thirst was as great as her appetite; said she drank gallons of water every day, and was always thirsty. Mouth and lips dry and pasty. Large quantity of sugar in urine.

The emaciation, though eating and drinking so enormously, first suggested *Natrum muriaticum.* Questioning from that keynote developed as clear a picture of the remedy as one could desire—worse on alternate days in the forenoon, typical headache; desire for salt, etc. I gave her a few powders of the 30th potency, and asked for a report in a week. I also instructed her to measure the urine passed during twenty-four hours for several different days in the meantime. One week later, July 29th, she reported not much change in the symptoms, and that she was passing *seven and one-half quarts of urine in twenty-four hours!* I was, of course, skeptical, and believed a mistake in measurement had been made, so I asked her father to do the measuring. He confirmed her report—she passed *seven and one-half quarts in twenty-four hours!* She reported weekly during July, August and September. There was steady and marked improvement over each previous week. She reported once during November, not at all in October, once in December, once each in January, February and March, April, June and September, 1912.

She has been to all external appearances perfectly well during the past six months; says she feels as well as she ever did, and she certainly looked the part when she last called, September 18th last. She now passes about three pints of urine in twenty-four hours. The only evidence that she is not well is one and one-half grains sugar to the ounce in the urine, and she has not fully regained her normal or usual weight. She has regained about ten pounds.

When I first prescribed for this patient I had never heard of this remedy having been prescribed for diabetes.

Dr. E. B. Rankin reports a case of diabetes insipidus improving under *Natrum phos.* 6x, in thirst, appetite and general strength, also in quantity of urine. However, no permanent result was obtained in this case.—*Southern Journal of Homœopathy,* April, 1886.

Schüssler notices two cures of this disease, communicated to him from Scotland, and one in which an Italian doctor employed successfully *Natrum sulph.* in diabetes. The details are wanting.

I have had occasion to treat many cases of that affection that I consider of a nervous origin. The treatment that has always succeeded with me has invariably been *Natrum sulph.* and *Magnesia phos.* 6x trit.; the length of treatment has been from forty-eight hours to a week; one dose of each of these salts in alternation every hour. (E. A. de Cailhol, M. D.)

Mrs. M., aged 42, consulting me, declared that she passed nearly four gallons of urine in twenty-four hours; its specific gravity was 1.040. I learned from her that the disease originated from a nervous shock (conjugal onanismus). I cured that disease in three months with *Natr. sulph., Natr. phos., Kali phos.* and *Magnes. phos.,* given according to the symptoms that I had to fight against. Having seen her three years after, the cure was perfect and no sign of relapse. (E. A. de Cailhol, M. D.)

DIARRHŒA.

Ferrum phos.—Diarrhœa from a relaxed state of the villi, or absorbents of the intestines not taking up the usual amount of moisture. Stools of undigested food, brought on by a chill beginning with fever. Prolapsus recti. "Pain non-intermittent. Diarrhœa copious, watery, sudden, painful, often accompanied by vomiting." (Guilbert.) Diarrhœa in children, stools watery, mucous, green and frequent; child rolls its head and groans; face pinched, eyes half opened; urine scanty, pulse and respiration quickened, starting in sleep. Stool undigested; the skin is hot and dry, and there is thirst. Dentition. The child flushes on light exercise.

Kali mur.—Diarrhœa after fatty food, pastry, etc. Evacuations light colored, pale yellow, ochre or clay-colored stools. Diarrhœa in typhoid fever; stools like pale yellow ochre. White or slimy stools, with the characteristic white coating of the tongue. **Stools bloody or slimy.**

Kali phos.—Foul diarrhœa, often accompanied by other diseases, to heal the conditions causing putrid evacuations. Diarrhœa of strong odor, occasioned by fright and other similar causes. Diarrhœa with depression and exhaustion of the nerves, with or without pain. Evacuations like rice water. Prolapsus recti. Tympanites. Stools putrid, like rice water, bloody, carrion-like odor. Noisy, offensive flatus. Profuse, painless and imperative stool while eating, followed by unsatisfied urging. Rectum burns and feels sore; prolapsed.

Natrum mur.—Diarrhœa with watery, slimy, frothy stools. Transparent, glairy slime, excessive use of salt. *"Natrum mur.* is chiefly used for chronic diarrhœa of children. The emaciation of the neck, the greasy appearance of the face, and the peculiar desires and aversions furnish the leading indications."* (Bell & Laird.) Slimy coating of tongue with minute bubbles of saliva on tip.

Natrum phos.—Itching, sore and raw anus. Stools white or green from deficient bile. **Diarrhœa caused by excess of acidity;** stools sour smelling, green, with yellow, creamy coating of tongue. Vomiting of sour fluid, curdy masses. Summer diarrhœa connected with a lack of digestive power, in which the stools are either clay-colored or habitually greenish. Colic is frequently present. Also, where there is habitual constipation with occasional attacks of diarrhœa, in young children. "Jelly-like masses of mucus, painful straining, coagulated casein, scanty and frequent." (Guilbert.) Diarrhœa from bad habits in feeding.

Natrum sulph.—Diarrhœa; stools watery, dark, bilious, or of green bile. The stool is not painful except for some colic and rumbling before it. Worse from eating. "This is one of the most frequently indicated remedies in cases of chronic diarrhœa, where the loose, gushing morning stool is the leading symptom. The flatulent symptoms are very characteristic, but not necessarily present. Aggravation in damp weather. Green diarrhœa in scarlatina. Wart-like eruptions on arms and between thighs. Chronic hereditary looseness of bowels in old women." (Bell & Laird.) Chronic diarrhœa coming on some time after rising and moving about.

Kali sulph.—Diarrhœa yellow, slimy or watery, purulent stools. Yellow coating of tongue, especially at root. Symptoms of cholera, cramps, etc. Black, thin, offensive stools.

Calcarea sulph.—Diarrhœa purulent, mixed with blood, with clay-colored tongue. In typhus; from maple sugar and change of weather.

Calcarea phos.—Diarrhœa in teething children, as an intercurrent or alternate remedy. Intercurrently in consumption of the bowels. One of our most valuable remedies for the diarrhœa of scrofulous and rachitic children. Green, slimy, undigested diarrhœa. Stool is hot, watery, profuse, offensive, noisy and sputtering.

Magnesia phos.—Stools watery, expelled with force, with griping pains in the bowels, flatulent colic relieved by drawing up limbs, or hot applications. Vomiting and cramp in calves of legs. Pain at intervals.

Silicea.—Infantile diarrhœa, cadaverous-smelling, after vaccination, with much sour perspiration on head, and hard, hot, distended abdomen.

CLINICAL CASES.

Chronic diarrhœa in old maid, æt. 75, of years' standing, cured by *Ferrum phos.* (W. P. W.)

Morning diarrhœa on rising; sudden urging, gushing, accompanied with flatulence. The stool splatters all over the vessel. *Natrum sulph.* cm. cured. (C. Lippe.)

An old man was attacked by a severe vomiting and diarrhœa, accompanied by exceedingly painful cramp in the calves. Evacuations had the appearance of rice-water. I undertook the treatment about six hours after the beginning of the attack, and one dose of *Kali phos.* effected a cure. The speedy cure of this case of choleraic diarrhœa would justify the belief that *Kali phos.* is a specific against cholera. (Schüssler.)

Dr. Goullon relates a case of chronic diarrhœa of two years' standing. Stools of mushy consistence, coated tongue, cured with *Calcarea sulph.—Allg. Hom. Zeit.*

Among the first cases in which I tried these remedies was a negro child, about two months old. The following are about the symptoms presented: Painful diarrhœa, constant rolling of the head, eyes turned up, tongue brownish-yellow, no desire to nurse for some time. The mother said it had been sick for a week, and she had been giving it different things; but as it got worse, she called me. I told her I was afraid there was little chance for its recovery, but I would do what I could for it. Prescribed *Magnesia phos.* and *Calcarea phos.* in alternation, every fifteen minutes. This was about nine or ten o'clock A. M. I returned about three o'clock P. M. to see if it were still alive, and to my astonishment found it better. It had ceased rolling its head, eyes were natural, and nursed once or twice, and was sleeping. Ordered the medicine to be continued at longer intervals. The next morning it was considerably better. At this visit I found the tongue covered with a thick *white* coating, and the mouth sore. I now prescribed *Kali mur.*, the remedy for this condition, in place of the *Calcarea phos.*, to be alternated with the *Magnesia phos.* every hour. The next day the tongue was clear, and after leaving a few more powders, to be continued for a day or two longer, the case was dismissed. (E. H. H.)

Dr. T. F. Allen cured a case of chronic diarrhœa in an old lady, with morning aggravation on beginning to move, with *Natrum sulph.* 7x. (N. A. J. H.)

DIPHTHERIA.

Ferrum phos.—At the commencement and for the fever.

Kali mur.—This is the sole remedy in most cases, in alternation with *Ferrum phos.*, which latter will lessen the fever, and is always indicated at the commencement. *Kali mur.* stands in the same biological relation to the albuminoid substances (*i. e.*, the fibrin) as does the phosphate of lime to the albumen. When an intense irritation has attacked those cells which form the seat of the disease in diphtheria, or relatively the *Kali mur.* molecules which are contained in them, there arises a disturbance of the proper balance of the molecules of this salt and consequent loss of some molecules, perhaps only a small number. At the same time a portion of the albuminoid substances (the organic basis of the cells) is set free and appears on the surface of the mucous membrane, where it is recognized as the diphtheritic exudation. So long as the disturbance of the proper balance in the motion of *Kali mur.* molecules lasts, the exudation will derive supplies and continue to go on. For the purpose of curing diphtheria by means of the biochemic method, new molecules of this salt must be applied to the respective tissues of which *Kali mur.* molecules have become inharmonious in their function, and for this reason the remedy must be given in molecular form. Dose, 10 to 15 grains of 3d or 6th trituration in a tumbler of water, a dose every two hours, or a powder the size of a pea, dry on the tongue.

Calcarea fluor.—When the affection has gone to the windpipe through mismanagement, give this remedy and *Calcarea phos.* alternately.

Calcarea phos.—Diphtheritic exudation spreading to the trachea. Such a complication is very rare when the Tissue Remedies are used exclusively. A white speck or patch remains after the main exudation has come off.

Kali phos.—In the well-marked, malignant, gangrenous condition, patient exhausted, prostrate. Also for the after-effects of diphtheria, such as weakness of sight, nasal speech or paralysis in any part of the body, squinting, etc. The **putrid character** is well marked, as seen by the putrid-smelling odor from mouth.

Natrum mur.—Diphtheria, if the face be **puffy and pale** with heavy **drowsiness**; watery stools, flow of saliva or vomiting of watery fluid. **Dryness of the tongue,** stertorous breathing, etc. The use of *Natrum mur.* must be discontinued with the disappearance of these symptoms.

Natrum phos.—Diphtheritic throat, falsely so called (not true), when the tonsils are covered with a yellow, creamy coating, and the back part of the roof of the mouth looks creamy-yellow; the coating of the tongue is moist, creamy or gold colored.

Natrum sulph.—In diphtheria as an intercurrent remedy where there is vomiting of green matter or water, and the peculiar welling-up of mucus from the stomach.

NOTE.—Under no circumstances should other remedies, such as lime water, carbolic acid, iced water, etc., be used along with these remedies, because they may interfere with the proper action of these salts. (Schüssler.)

CLINICAL CASES.

Fully developed case of diphtheria with the characteristic glandular enlargement, tonsils, uvula and entire soft palate were covered with a thick, diphtheritic exudation. Deglutition was attended with great pain and accompanied with the utmost effort, and there was exceeding prostration. *Kali mur.*⁶ every two hours. The following day there was a marked improvement, and in four days every vestige of the throat trouble had disappeared, and the child recovered rapidly under *Calcarea phos.* (W. H. Pratt, M. D., *North American Journal of Homœopathy,* May, 1883.)

Last summer I had a case of diphtheria that was a little out of the usual order. I saw the case on Saturday, July 21. It looked like a simple ulcerated sore throat, and I prescribed *Calc. sulph.* and told the mother that if she was not better in the afternoon to let me know. When I got home, about four o'clock, she and her father were at my office. I found her quite feverish and her speech considerably muffled. I examined her throat carefully and found a distinct grayish patch on each tonsil. I now prescribed *Ferrum phos.* and *Kali mur.* in alternation. About nine o'clock I called and found that she was evidently not relieved in any way whatever. She now complained of something continually coming into her throat. I thought perhaps it was waterbrash and gave a few doses of *Natrum phos.* but to no effect. Continued the first remedies through the night. The next morning much worse. The membrane had spread considerably and the tonsils were much enlarged. The rising of mucus in the throat continued. Saw her three times on Sunday. Gave her lower potencies. Left her at night on 3x. Monday morning the mother met me with tears in her eyes and wanted to know if I had not better call another physician. Found her very ill indeed. It flashed upon me that the constant welling-up of mucus in the throat is a symptom of *Natrum sulph.* I consequently gave it alone in the 200 (B. & T.) potency, and in a few hours there was a decided change for the better. In a few days she was well. (E. H. H.)

In fourteen cases of diphtheria the biochemic measures left nothing better to be desired, *Kali mur.* rapidly making a change, the whitish-gray exudation being diminished, shrivelling and coming away with the gargle and mouth-wash made with *Kali mur.,* also occasional doses of *Ferrum phos.* The treatment worked splendidly. In three cases the patients labored under prostration from the first, and *Kali phos.* had to be given intercurrently; in two cases *Natrum mur.* alternately with *Kali mur.,* the chief remedy. In the latter cases there existed considerable running of saliva, heavy drowsiness and watery stools. No secondary affection resulted, such as frequently arise under ordinary treatment, as paralysis, defective vision, or neuralgia. (M. D. W.)

Case from the practice of Schüssler: In a village a few miles from the town of Oldenberg, a child was taken ill with diphtheria, which at an early stage was complicated by an affection of the larynx. The child was treated by the ordinary method and died. Almost at the same time a child of another family in the village was attacked by diphtheria with the same complication. The father of the latter child came to me. I prescribed *Kali mur.* for the disease in the first instance, and *Calcarea phos.* for the affection of the larynx, to be taken alternately. I requested the father to inform me without fail of the result, which he promised to do. Two days after I received a letter from him in which he informed me that the child had completely recovered.

In diphtheria (maligna), where every known remedy failed, *Kali phos.* and *Kali mur.* with, sometimes without, *Natrum mur.* effected subsidence of malignity, and hastened the cure.

In paralysis after diphtheria, I know of no better remedy than *Kali phos.* (Dr. F. from Schüssler.)

The following cases are of interest, as showing the action of *Ferrum phos.* in diphtheria:

1. Young lady with sore throat, tonsils swollen moderately and quite red, a little feverish. *Ferrum phos.*[30] every three hours for a day and a half, then paused, being better. Became worse and sent for me. Diphtheritic membrane covered the right tonsil. *Ferrum phos.*[30] as before. The next day the membrane was nearly all gone, swelling and redness were better. Continued prescription every four hours. The following day only a slight vestige of the membrane remained. Medicine given less often, and the next day was perfectly well.

2. Boy, æt. 5, febrile state, glistening, flushed eyes, red cheeks, tonsils red and swollen, especially the right, on which was a tuft-like exudation about its centre and about one-quarter inch in diameter, hanging down, the upper attachment looking blackish next to the tonsils; foetid breath. *Ferrum phos.*[30] The next day the tonsil was clear, but a similar exudation appeared on the posterior wall of the pharynx; continued the same remedy every four hours; the following day he was well. (J. C. Morgan, M. D., *Hahnemannian Monthly*, vol. vii.)

DIZZINESS.

When it occurs in nervous subjects who, without having any active symptoms of dyspepsia, do not well assimilate the nutritive portion of the food. *Calcarea phos.* ix, given after meals, will be found useful. (C. R. Fleury.)

DROPSICAL AFFECTIONS.

Kali mur.—Dropsy arising from heart, liver or kidney affections, when the prominent characteristic symptoms of this remedy are present. Dropsy from obstruction of bile ducts and enlargement of the liver. There is generally a white-coated tongue. Dropsy from weakness of the heart (in alternation with *Kali phos.*). Dropsy, with palpitation. Dropsy in which the liquid drawn off is whitish, or white mucus is deposited in the urine. Persistent white coating on the tongue. Hydrocele.

Natrum sulph.—Simple dropsy invading the areolar tissues of the body. Preputial œdema or scrotal œdema. Œdema of internal as well as external parts.

Natrum mur.—Dropsy and dropsical swellings of any of the subcutaneous areolar tissues of the body. Anasarca. Preputial or scrotal œdema.

Ferrum phos.—Dropsy from loss of blood or draining of the system, alternately with *Calcarea phos.*

Calcarea phos.—Dropsy from non-assimilation. Anæmia or loss of blood or vital fluids. Hydrops genu.

Calcarea fluor.—Dropsy caused by heart disease, dilatation of any of the cavities. Hydrocele of long standing.

Kali sulph.—Post-scarlatinal dropsy.

CLINICAL CASES.

Scarlatinal dropsy in a child, æt. 4; *Digital., Apis, Arsen.* and *Apoc.* failed. Quantity of urine voided in twenty-four hours was very scanty, and during the past forty-eight hours had ceased entirely. The patient was fearfully anasarcous. Reclining position was impossible. *Natrum mur.*[6] every two hours. In twenty-four hours the child voided two quarts of urine and a speedy recovery followed. (W. M. Pratt, M. D.)

Dr. Goullon, Jr., who used *Kali mur.* with much success in a swelling of the feet and lower extremities, adds the following particular indications for its use: The remedy in question appears indicated in chronic persistent swelling of the feet and lower limbs, when the swelling is soft at first, afterwards becoming hard to the touch, without pain or redness. It is, however, itchy; and at one stage may be termed snowy-white and shining. Lastly, the swelling becomes less perceptible in the morning than in the evening, but may acquire such dimensions as to cause great tension, with a feeling as if it would burst.

A little girl, æt. 9, had recovered from diphtheria and scarlatina rather easily, and was allowed to be in the convalescent room. Suddenly she began to swell without any apparent cause. Her face became puffy; the feet also œdematous to above the ankle. Urine scarcely decreased, containing no albumen. No pain over the kidneys on pressure. Pulse somewhat feverish, but appetite, sleep and stools still natural. i gave three different medicines—amongst these, *Aconite*—without success. Dropsy (anasarca et ascites) was increasing rapidly; urine scanty; only very small quantities occasionally, being slightly turbid and containing much albumen. Whether any epithelial sheathings were present was not ascertained. Kidneys were now more sensitive to pressure. Occasionally delirious. *Natrum mur.* alone cured this case in about a fortnight. (Dr. Cohn, from Schüssler.)

DYSENTERY.

Kali mur.—Intense pain in the abdomen, cutting as from knives, calls to stool every few minutes, with tenesmus, extorting cries, purging with slimy, sanious stools. In most cases this remedy with *Ferrum phos.* cures.

Ferrum phos.—If affection begins with violent fever, this, with the foregoing remedy, usually suffices for a cure. If pain is dependent on inflammation making no intervals and increased by pressure. Never useful if tenesmus is present.

Kali phos.—When the stool consists of blood only, and the patient becomes delirious, abdomen swollen, or when stools have a putrid odor. Putrid, very offensive stools, and great dryness of the tongue. Prolapsus recti. Tenesmus after stools.

Magnesia phos.—Crampy pains eased by bending double, by warmth, friction or pressure. Tenesmus and tormina, with constant desire to pass water and go to stool. Pains in rectum with every stool as from a prolonged spasm of muscles.

Calcarea sulph.—Stools purulent sanious (mixed with blood), especially in cases that persist after *Kali mur.*

Natrum sulph.—If bilious symptoms are present.

CLINICAL CASES.

Dr. E. H. Holbrook reports a case of dysentery which was greatly relieved by *Calcarea sulph.* cm. Turning into a bilious diarrhœa, *Natrum sulph.* cured.

Lady complaining of extreme tenesmus and tormina, and constant desire to pass water and go to stool. Every time this pain came on, must rise and bend forward, and the only relief obtained was from hot water. *Magnes. phos.* 2c. every fifteen minutes cured third dose. (Dr. Reed.)

In treating a case of dysentery lately I was at my wits' end to control the terrible pain in defæcation. *Merc. cor.* suited the case well, and the stools were growing less frequent, but the pain was increasing, being so severe as to cause fainting. Something had to be done if I held my case. The pain in the rectum and abdomen was *very severe,* more in rectum than abdomen. The tenesmus was like a prolonged spasm of the muscles employed in defæcation. I exhibited "Schüssler's" *Magnes. phos.* in hot water. A hypodermic of morphia could hardly have acted quicker. The pain was *almost entirely* relieved by the first dose. The whole condition changed for the better, and I discharged my case the next day. In all my experience I never had a more prompt or pleasing result. *Magnes. phos.* is a grand antispasmodic, and fully as reliable as our more frequently used remedies. I was led to think of it for my case of dysentery by a statement made to me by Dr. E. E. Snyder, of Binghamton, N. Y. He gave it with equally as prompt results in spasmodic tenesmus vesicæ occurring in a case of cystitis resulting from gonorrhœa. It certainly did me great service. (H. K. Leonard, M. D.)

DYSMENORRHŒA.

See also Menstruation, and Women, Diseases of.

Calcarea phos.—When during puberty the patient has not been careful, with consequent dysmenorrhœa. Nymphomania. Labor-like pains before and during catamenia, with violent backache, vertigo, sexual excitement and throbbing headache.

Ferrum phos.—Pain at the monthly periods, with flushed face and quick pulse, with vomiting of undigested food, sometimes acid taste. To be taken also as a preventive before the periods if these symptoms are recurrent. Excessive congestion at the monthly periods, blood bright red, the vagina dry and sensitive.

Kali phos.—Great pain at the time of menses in pale, lachrymose, irritable, sensitive females.

Magnesia phos.—The chief remedy in ordinary cases of menstrual colic, painful menstruation or pain preceding the flow. Warmth is soothing; neuralgic, cramping pains, worse by motion. **Membranous dysmenorrhœa.** It suits well also a nervous form of dysmenorrhœa.

Natrum mur.—Menses scanty and dark, preceded by frontal headaches; often subject to fever-blisters on lips, and during summer to urticarious eruptions. Sore burning in vagina and cutting-burning in the womb. Great melancholy. Also, too profuse and too early, with bursting headache, and frequent shivering.

Natrum sulph.—With colic, menses acrid. Pinching in abdomen, early in the morning. Violent epistaxis. Vulvitis. Trembling or twitching of the hands and languor of feet.

Silicea.—With great coldness. Icy coldness of the whole body from the commencement of the flow. Vagina sensitive.

CLINICAL CASES.

Miss N., aged 19, troubled with pains before and during the first day or so of the flow, which would confine her to bed. Plethoric, robust and perfectly well in every other way. Several ten grain powders of *Ferrum phos.*, to be given in hot water every half hour until the pain was relieved, which occurred after the third powder, and then to continue the powders in water every other night before retiring during the next interval with a hot saline sitz bath at least once a week at night. The menses came all right and have been coming ever since with no return of pain and perfect regularity.—F. D. Bittinger, M. D., Dayton, O.

J. T. Kent reports a case of dysmenorrhœa of years' standing cured by *Calcarea phos.* in two months.—*Homœopathic Physician,* 1884.

Dr. R. D. Belding (*N. Y. St. Trans.*) reports a case of dysmenorrhœa, of years' standing, characterized by pain and soreness in left hypochondrium going through to right scapula, worse lying on left side, with headache and diarrhœa. Patient feels best in cool, dry weather, every summer has urticarious eruptions. Dreams of robbers, has frequent cold sores on upper lip. *Natrum mur.*[200] cured.

Dr. D. B. Whittier (in *Hahnemannian Monthly,* July, 1887) reports several cases of dysmenorrhœa cured with *Kali phos.* and *Magnesia phos.*

Dr. A. P. Davis relates a case of dysmenorrhœa with severe pains in uterus, back and lower limbs; heat applied to abdomen did not relieve; a large dose of *Magnes. phos.* 6x lessened the pain in one-half hour; another dose brought on a free flow. The pain usually lasted several hours previous to flowing. The remedy was given as a preventive during several subsequent months with good effect, and the patient finally cured. Dr. Davis regards *Magnes. phos.* superior to *Cimicifuga* in neuralgia of the uterus and in the relief of menstrual pains, and as very useful in uterine engorgement, and gives a case of menorrhagia cured with the 6x.

Kali phos. in Dysmenorrhœa.—Dr. D. B. Whittier reports the cure of a dysmenorrhœa of fifteen years' standing (in a highly neurotic and hysterical woman) by a course of *Kali phos.* continuing over six months after allopathic medicines, and apparently indicated homœopathic medicines had failed. Some of the symptoms were: the mammæ were so painful that the touch of her clothing was unbearable. The menstrual pains were cramplike, with severe bearing down in the hypogastrium, and most severe after the flow commenced. When the suffering was most intense a sharp, shooting pain would extend from the hypogastrium to the epigastrium, followed by a sensation as if something were flowing up to the stomach, and immediately succeeded by a vomiting of bile or frothy, acid substances, sometimes streaked with blood. The vomiting would relieve the painful distress of the stomach, when the uterine pains would be increased and sometimes continue for twenty-four hours. A headache, at first general, soon settled over the left eye. When the headache was severe the pains elsewhere were lessened, and *vice versa*. The first menstrual period following the administration of the *Kali phos.* was comparatively comfortable. —*Hom. Journal of Obstetrics,* November.

Dysmenorrhœa that had lasted for some time in which at each menstrual period a membrane was discharged, varying in size from one to two inches long. The pains came on after the flow began, in the abdomen low down, and were relieved by lying curled up in bed with a hot water bag on the abdomen. The pains would last for a day—dull, aching—and next day, or day after a membrane would be passed. I gave her after one of her menstrual periods *Magnes. phos.* cm., one dose dry. The next menstruation was easier somewhat, but not much. *Magnes. phos.* in water for two days, night and morning, and the next menstrual period was painless, though she passed the membrane as before. After that the menses were perfectly painless. (Dr. Campbell, in *Proceedings of Hahnemannian Association,* 1889.)

I had a patient with very severe shooting neuralgic pains during the menstrual period. The pains were in the stomach and lasted the first day or two. Commenced in the back and came directly around and centered in the pit of the stomach. They were relieved by heat and pressure. *Magnes. phos.* 10m., one dose, and she had no more pain. (J. T. Kent, M. D.)

A most instructive case of membranous dysmenorrhœa cured with *Magnesia phos.* 4x was recently reported in the *"Homœopathic World."* It was a case of several years' standing and the cure was complete.

EAR, DISEASES OF.

Ferrum phos.—Inflammatory earache from cold, with burning, throbbing pain. Sensitive to noise. Congestive stage of otitis. Earache, with sharp, stitching pain. Noises in the ears, arising through blood-pressure from relaxed conditions of the vessels not returning the blood properly. Inflammatory conditions, radiating pains, sensitiveness, especially in affections of the ear in anæmic subjects. A clinical symptom is: "Noticeable pulsation in the ear; every impulse of the heart is felt here, beating in the ear and head; the pulse can be counted." (Houghton.) Chronic, non-suppurative catarrh of the middle ear, where the membrana tympani is thickened, and there is probably anchylosis of the small bones.

The following are also indications for its use: "1. A marked tendency for the inflammatory process to be diffused instead of circumscribed. 2. Dark, beefy redness of the parts. 3. A muco-purulent discharge and a tendency to hæmorrhage. 4. The complete establishment of the discharge is not followed by the relief of the pain. 5. The paroxysmal character of the pain." (Wanstall, *American Institute Transactions,* 1886, p. 389.) Also, the absence of exudation, the radiating pains and sensitiveness, and the general anæmic and debilitated condition of the patient. Deafness from inflammatory action, or suppuration, when there are cutting pains, tension, throbbing or heat, tinnitus aurium from excessive flow of blood to the part. Inflammation of the drum, especially when the membrane is dry, and its vessels engorged. Diffuse inflammation of the external auditory canal and acute affections of middle ear. (H. C. F.) Catarrhal affections of Eustachian tubes. "For earache after exposure to cold or wet I have no better remedy." (R. S. Copeland.)

Kali mur.—Earache, with white or gray-furred tongue and swelling of the glands, swelling of the throat. Eustachian tubes swell, cracking noise in the ear when swallowing. Deafness from swelling of the Eustachian tubes. It is also the principal remedy for deafness from swelling of the external ear. Deafness with swelling of the glands or cracking noises on blowing the nose, tongue white. Chronic dermatitis. Moist exfoliation of the epithelial layer of the tympanum. In ulcerations, where pus is whitish; granular conditions of meatus and of membrana tympani; excessive granulations. "One of the most effective remedies we have ever used for chronic catarrhal inflammation of the middle ear, especially the form designated 'proliferous.' Stuffy sensation, subjective sounds, deafness, naso-pharyngeal obstruction, granular pharyngitis, closed Eustachian tubes, retracted membrana tympani, etc., walls of external meatus atrophied. Seems to affect more decidedly the right Eustachian tube. In chronic suppuration it reduces proliferation, checks granulation and hastens repair." (H. C. Houghton.)

"*Kali mur.* is chiefly suited to the second or later stages of catarrhal states of the naso-pharynx and Eustachian tube which, by continuity of the mucous membrane, extend to the cavity of the middle ear itself. The condition of the pharynx, as seen by simple inspection, is that of a *thickened mucous membrane,* with inflammation present in subacute or chronic form and usually centering around the follicles, giving a coarsely granular appearance to the surface. It is not so much an intensely red membrane as one pale in appearance which indicates its use, as if the more active hypertrophic condition were passing over into a less active or passive atrophic state. The presence of small spots of whitish exudation would be a further indication for its selection, and also the condition of the tongue if coated white or gray. The accompanying nasal condition is characterized by swelling of the lining membrane, obstruction, and thick, yellow discharge, or later on by thick, whitish mucus. Its use is said to lessen susceptibility to these catarrhal states.

"This same condition extending up into the Eustachian tube gives rise to such thickening of the lining membrane that the tube, for a time, is partially and sometimes wholly occluded. The aural symptoms resulting from this condition of the tube are well understood, consisting of deafness of varying degree, subjective noises in corresponding degree, and those sometimes startling and disagreeable snappings in the ear which arise from the sudden partial opening of the tube during deglutition, whereby the air is allowed to rush forcibly through the tube into the tympanic cavity, relieving thus the partial vacuum which always ensues when the tympanum becomes a closed cavity, and rarification of the contained air takes place. Of course, if specular examination be made at such times, more or less retraction of the tympanic membrane will be visible. In this condition of the tube the remedy applies less to those states which are recent and acute than to their later effects, or to the less active forms of inflammation from the outset, and its action is said to be greater upon the Eustachian tube of the right side than upon that of the left.

"In the tympanic cavity itself the process of slow proliferation, with interstitial thickening and consequent slowly progressing deafness, with or without subjective noises, and without pain, seems to constitute the indication for this remedy. It is also especially useful at the termination of more active and painful attacks, to clean up the remains of inflammation and prevent, as far as possible, its evil effect in inducing thickenings in the tympanic mucous membrane and permanent changes in the delicate structures contained within the tympanic cavity. In suppurative disease of the ear this remedy is less frequently required than for the catarrhal process, but in cases where granulation is excessive it is sometimes employed to check the exuberance of their growth and favor resolution, while its usefulness at the termination of suppurative attacks in the middle ear has been found very great in modifying those tendencies to adhesions which constitute one of their chief dangers.

"Finally, in the external ear the use of this remedy has been hitherto comparatively infrequent, its indications being chiefly a dry and scaly proliferation of the epidermis of the external meatus, with tendency to atrophy of the walls. A swollen condition of the glands about the ear, the angle of the jaw, and the neck would further indicate its selection.

"My own experience with *Kali mur.* has been largely confined to chronic catarrhal conditions of the middle ear, and after keeping a careful record of its action in nearly two hundred of these cases, in private practice, I am convinced that it is one of the most useful agents we possess in their treatment. It will even aid us efficiently in holding in check many of those inveterate cases of years' standing which go persistently from bad to worse upon the slightest provocation, and which no man living can hope to cure. Its most satisfactory results are obtained in those cases which may have been gradually progressing for months, or even for two or three years, but which have not yet given rise to those permanent tissue changes which are sure to follow in the later course of the disease." (Prof. H. P. Bellows, M. D.) Otitis externa, with thickening and narrowing of the meatus and thin, flaky discharge from ear.

"*Kali mur.* favors the opening of the Eustachian tube. After its use inflation becomes easy." (R. S. C.)

Natrum mur.—Deafness from swelling of the tympanic cavity, with watery conditions. Roaring in the ears, tongue covered with bubbles, saliva profuse, etc. Catarrh of tympanic cavity and Eustachian tube, purulent discharge from ears. Itching and burning in the ear. Stitches in the ear.

Kali phos.—Dulness of hearing with noises in the head. Deafness from want of nerve perception, noises in the head with weakness and confusion. Itching in the auditory canal; hearing supersensitive, cannot bear any noise. Weakness, general exhaustion of the nerves or nervous system. "Ulceration of the membrana tympani, suppuration of the middle ear, pus being watery, dirty, brownish and **very foetid.** Ulceration angry, bleeding easily, showing little tendency to granulate or secrete laudable pus. It is especially valuable in old people. Atrophic conditions in old people, tissues dry up, become scaly, showing lack of vitality." (Houghton.) If the humming and buzzing in ears are not removed by *Kali phos.*, though indicated, follow with *Magnes. phos.*

Calcarea sulph.—Discharge of matter from the ear, sometimes mixed with blood. Deafness with middle ear suppurations, swelling of gland, etc. Sensitive swelling behind ear, with tendency to suppuration.

Calcarea phos.—Cold feeling of outer ears. The bones around the ear ache and hurt. Earache with rheumatic complaints, associated with swollen glands in scrofulous children. Chronic otorrhœas in children associated with painful dentition. (H. C. F.) Perforation of tympanum with deafness and otorrhœa. (Cooper.)

Magnesia phos.—Deafness or dulness of hearing from diseases of the auditory nerve-fibres. It supplements *Kali mur.* Proliferous disease of the middle ear. (Dr. Rounds.) Otalgia, purely nervous in character.

Kali sulph.—Earache with secretion of thick, yellow, or

greenish fluid after inflammation. Sharp, cutting pain under the ears. Stitches, tensive and piercing pain below the mastoid process. Discharge of watery matter or yellow pus. Throat deafness with catarrh, causing swelling of Eustachian lining and middle ear, with yellow, watery discharge and yellow coating on the tongue. Deafness worse in a heated room. Stinking otorrhœa. Polypoid excrescence closes meatus. In suppurative inflammation of the middle ear when the discharge is thick. (H. C. F.)

Silicea.—Dulness of hearing with swelling and catarrh of the Eustachian tubes and of the cavity of the tympanum. External ear inflamed, swelling of the external meatus. Mastoid disease (see clinical case below). Oversensitive to noise. Foul otorrhœa. Ears open at times with loud report. Suppurative otitis when discharge is thin, ichorous, and offensive and attended with bone destruction.

Natrum phos.—Ears sore, outer part covered with soft, thin, cream-like scabbing, deposit on tongue yellow. One ear red, hot, frequently itchy, accompanied by gastric derangement and acidity. Discharge of pus from ears.

Natrum sulph.—Earache as if something were forcing its way out. Worse in damp weather. Ringing in ears as of bells.

Calcarea fluor.—Mastoid disease when the periosteum is affected rather than the bone itself. (Houghton.) Calcareous deposits on the tympani and tinnitus.

CLINICAL CASES.

Boy, with history of catarrhal disease of the ear of seven years' standing, suffers at times pain, and has often tinnitus; at present suffering with a subacute attack of catarrhal inflammation of middle ear with slight pain. *Ferrum phos.* relieved this; the next time he was seen there still remained closure of the Eustachian tube; the mucous membrane of the pharynx was pale. *Kali mur.* entirely removed this, and normal hearing returned.

A boy, æt. 15, had an ear trouble of twelve years' standing, and suffered from suppuration of the middle ear, resulting from scarlet fever. At present both ears are inflamed; no pain, but has subjective noises, hearing greatly diminished, pus fills the meatus, Eustachian tube is dilatable, right membrana tympani is granular and left perforated pharynx thick. *Calcarea sulph.* commenced at once and continued to improve; the granular appearance of the right membrana tympani disappeared, and the improvement was phenomenal.

Chronic suppurative inflammation of the middle ear from scarlet fever, both ears suppurating, both canals filled with pus of a dark color and fœtid in character. *Kali phos.* entirely cured. (Houghton, *Clinical Otology.*)

CALCAREOUS DEPOSITS AND TINNITIS AURIUM.—Case of man, aged 43, complained of crawling sensation all over skin, roaring in ear, worse night, cold feet, ankles and wrists; calcareous deposits on membrana tympani of right ear, largest about size of a pin. *Calc. fluor.*[200] cured in four months. Deposits and roaring remained cured as proved by examination less than a year afterward. (Dr. Royal E. S. Hayes.)

Prof. Houghton, in his excellent treatise on *Clinical Otology,* presents many remarkable cases illustrative of the action of these remedies. The above cases were selected as those in which no other remedies or means were employed. Numerous cases of the beneficial action of *Ferrum phos., Kali mur.* and *Calcarea sulph.* in aural practice can be found in this work.

Acute inflammation of the middle ear commenced by a full feeling in the ear and dull hearing. Pain occurred on performing Valsalva's procedure. This condition, which grew rapidly worse, continued for forty-eight hours, when the physician was called and found the following conditions: The pain was paroxysmal, there was a sensation of a plug in the ear, membrana tympani injected and bulged, but no evidence of exudation in the tympanic cavity. Posterior wall of meatus auditorius bright red in color, ear very sensitive to manipulation. *Ferrum phos.* 6x, every hour. Improvement was immediate. Remedy discontinued in forty-eight hours.

Dr. H. W. Champlin reports several cases of otitis media treated successfully with *Ferrum phos.* He says it is effectual in potencies from 3x to 6x, and insists that it should be given alone. Prescribe no other medicinal agent with it.

Mrs. ——, æt. 45, February 16, 1887. About three years ago began to be troubled with pain and noises in the left ear, aggravated greatly at the time of the menses, the pain severe and neuralgic in character, extending over the left side of the head. The noises seem to get their character from some pronounced sound which is heard, and this persists sometimes for hours. For the last six months there has been no further pain on left side, but deafness is constant. The right side is now beginning to become deaf, but with no pain and no noises. This has been going on upon the right side for several months. General health excellent, with the exception of redness, fulness and desire to rub and pull the skin about the neck, for a few days after the menses, with marked swelling of the glands of the neck at the same time. This has been noticed only during the time that the ears have been troublesome. The fork is heard best on the left side by bone conduction, and best on the right side by air conduction. Meatus tympani dry and depressed. Eustachian tube on the left almost occluded, on the right more free. Frequent burning of the auricle on the left side. *Kali mur.* 6x cured. (H. P. Bellows, M. D., in *N. E. Med. Gaz.,* November, 1889.)

A weak, cachectic woman suffered for three or four days from earache and pain in the right side of the head. The ear has been discharging for three days, but no mitigation of the pain, which is very severe and radiating from the ear, membrana tympani beefy red, swollen and perforated, discharge profuse and muco-purulent, meatus red, swollen and inflamed. *Ferrum phos.* 2x in water, every hour. In three days was better in every way, discharge and pain less. A week later all inflammatory symptoms had disappeared.

Dr. Wanstall reports three other cases cured by the use of *Ferrum phos.*, from the 2x to the 12x trituration, with results the most gratifying, controlling the high fever, delirium and pain accompanying the acute middle ear inflammation.—*Transactions American Institute of Homœopathy,* 1886, p. 398.

Case of a young girl, light complexion, scrofulous, with brown, offensive secretions from the right ear. Polypoid growth or excrescence closes the meatus near the opening. For eight weeks she had been entirely deaf in this ear, the deafness having gradually increased for four months. *Kali sulph.*[12] given. In two weeks the offensiveness had entirely disappeared. On examination find polypus shrivelled to a small, hard, black mass. The hearing has entirely returned, with a slight whizzing noise. Every third day two doses were taken. This case was entirely cured. (W. P. Wesselhœft, M. D. From Hg.)

OTITIS EXTERNA.—Dr. Stanley Wilde reports a case of otitis externa with subsequent otorrhœa and deafness, the latter resisting several remedies as *Merc. sol., Hydrastis* and *Sulphur.* The case presented a thickening and narrowing of the meatus, with a thin flaky discharge therefrom, watch hearing 4 in. *Kali mur.* 3x stopped the discharge and the hearing became normal. Dr. Wilde has used this remedy with good effect in Eustachian deafness in children from chronic enlargement of the tonsils.—*Hom. Review.*

Dr. Goullon reports a case of an old gentleman who suffered greatly with a buzzing in ears, which was made much worse in the noisy street. The patient had repeated attacks of inflammatory rheumatism, and the tinnitus was probably of rheumatic origin. Mentally much depressed. Difficult hearing. After a few days' use of *Kali phos.*[6] all symptoms, including the mental condition and difficult hearing, permanently disappeared.—*Pop. Hom. Zeitung.*

A gentleman wrote me the symptoms of otitis of a little child, æt. 4 months, who had a discharge from one ear of an ichorous, thin, offensive character, producing an eruption wherever the pus came in contact with the integument. I at once sent *Kali phos.* 6x, ordering it given every six hours. In three months the running had all ceased and the hearing was perfect. I frequently use the *Silicea* in alternation with the *Kali phos.*, when the connective tissue is involved. (A. P. Davis, M. D.)

Another case of "otitis catarrhalis internus" came into my office to see me, after spending over $600 with the "regulars." This case was the most remarkable that I ever witnessed or treated. The man was a tall, slim, sanguine, nervous specimen of the genus *homo,* rude, illiterate, backwoods, gawky looking, seedy, cross between the ourang-outang, monkey, and Chinaman, but possessed of sensation, motion and reflection, proving to my mind that he was a man for "a' that" and "a' that." Well, I went through the examination sufficiently scrutinizingly to ascertain the exact pathological condition of the trouble I had to meet. There was an enormous protuberance involving the whole mastoid region, the skin red and glistening, soft, pappy, showing signs of an induration and broken-down connective tissue, and the whole mass filled with pus, and emitting an odor that was as sickening as carrion. I at once plunged a knife into the mastoid process, out of which ran about a half pint of blood and pus. After cleansing the tumor with Eucalyptus I bound up the wound, leaving in it a drainage-tube. I treated the wound every day, putting him under the influence of *Silicea,* a dose every two hours. Under the treatment I had the satisfaction of seeing him improve from day to day, and in four weeks the whole trouble ceased. He had no relapse, but the cure advanced steadily until he was well. This case was pronounced hopeless by several allopaths. (A. P. Davis, M. D.)

Wm. McKee, æt. 27, suffers from deafness, due to chronic non-suppurative catarrh of the middle ear. While a lad, and on to manhood, went out a great deal at night to dances and parties, where he would dance and romp until in a great heat and profuse sweat, when he would go out of doors and remove his coat. In this way he would contract a cold, and one cold after another, until he found himself a sufferer from chronic catarrh of the nose and throat, the discharge being continual and very annoying. At this time (about six years ago) he noticed a noise commencing in his ears, and it gradually increased until he became aware of the fact that his hearing was damaged. He then commenced treatment, and not getting immediate relief from his first doctor he changed, and soon changed again, in this way going to several doctors, a few of them old-school specialists, and then gave up discouraged, and let the disease run its course unhindered. When he came to me (last March) he said he had been unable to hear anything but confused noises, even when the loudest tones were used to accost him, for five years. He is of medium height, rather slender, with inclination to red hair; has blue eyes, a fair complexion, and has a slightly anæmic appearance. He describes the noise in his ears as dull and rumbling, if he pays no particular heed to it; but if he concentrates his thoughts on it, he can imagine that it resembles almost any kind of a noise. One thing I wish to mention which was quite prominent, and quickly disappeared under the remedy—viz., he would be awakened in the night by a loud bombing noise and afterward be unable to sleep "for the racket in his ears." There were a number of nervous symptoms in the case that led me to show him to Dr. Bartlett. 1. Slight melancholia, would go off alone and brood over his troubles for hours. 2. He would stagger while he walked. I found his tendopatella reflex much decreased and on standing with his eyes closed he would fall over in my arms, couldn't manage at best to take three steps forward with eyes closed without falling. I have kept him pretty steadily on *Ferrum phos.,* and the improvement is remarkable. He can hear every word of the longest sentence by slightly raising the voice when accosting him at several feet away. The noises are greatly lessened, he sleeps well, and the nervous symptoms are fast disappearing. I have continually inflated the middle ear by Politzer method, once a week. (Dr. F. W. Messerve.)

MASTOID PERIOSTITIS—SILICEA.—Dr. A. T. Sherman of Minnesota, reports a case of a man who had suffered for six days with pain in mastoid region. On examination found the membrana tympani highly injected, tuning-fork was heard indifferently on each side when pressed against parietal bones; hearing impaired on the affected side. Temperature 100. Very weak, nervous; complete muscular paralysis of right side of face. The condition of the sense of hearing precluded brain disease. There was no difficulty in swallowing, or other evidence of paralysis of the muscles of the fauces, which placed the trouble beyond the origin of the petrosal nerve. There was no disturbance of taste or of the salivary glands, which placed the trouble beyond the origin of the chorda tympani. He diagnosed mastoid periostitis with pressure on the seventh nerve immediately on its exit from the duct of Fallopius. On protruding his tongue it was drawn somewhat toward the affected side. While contemplating incision, patient mentioned that on the previous morning he had found relief and some sleep by *placing the head in a warm poultice of Indian meal.* Gave *Silicea*^{200}, a dose every three hours. In forty-eight hours all pain had ceased and temperature normal. *Relief from moist warmth* was the guiding symptom to the remedy.

MENIERE'S DISEASE.—Dr. Fellows reports in the *"Clinique"* two cases of this disease greatly and speedily relieved by *Silicea* 3x and 6x, given several times daily.

Mrs. ———, æt. 34. March 30, 1886. For several years has been troubled with deafness from time to time, upon the right side, accompanied by tinnitus of ringing and pulsating character, and with occasional pain. Mt. slightly depressed and thickened upon the right side. Nose catarrhal in slight degree.

H. D. R. w. $= 22'' = 29''$ *Cath.*^{2} *Calc. phos.* 2x N. and M.

To spray the nostrils with weak, warm solution of common salt.

April 7. H. D. R. w. $= 21'' = 31''$ *Cath.*^{2} *Kali mur.* 6x N. and M.
April 14. H. D. R. w. $= 22'' = 52''$ *Cath.*^{3} *Kali mur.* 6x N. and M.
April 21. H. D. R. w. $= 36'' = 6$ ft. *Cath.*^{3}

Tinnitus has ceased. *Kali mur.* 6x N.

April 27. H. D. R. w. $= 46'' = 7$ ft. *Cath.*^{3}

No further tinnitus. *Kali mur.* 6x alt. N.

It is now three years since this case was discharged, and at the expiration of two years I heard that there had been no recurrence of any trouble whatever. As another year has passed without news from the patient, the improvement doubtless remains permanent. It is needless to say that the spraying with salt solution in this case was not sufficiently potent to detract from the cure, while the catheter could have been but an aid only, especially when the permanence of the relief is considered.

In closing my remarks upon the use of *Kali mur.* in these aural diseases, I will simply state that my experience agrees with the observation of others that it follows particularly well after *Ferrum phos.* or *Merc. dulcis,* and is itself sometimes followed especially well by *Calcarea sulph.* (H. P. Bellows, M. D., in *N. E. Med. Gaz.,* Nov., 1889.)

SILICEA IN SUPPURATIVE OTITIS.—Dr. Bellows records a case of distressing and frequently recurring frontal headache, which seemed traceable to chronic middle ear suppuration. The tympanum was perforated. *Silicea* 3 taken for some months dried up the discharge, healed the tympanum, and made the hearing normal, while the headaches soon disappeared.—*N. E. Med. Gazette,* Feb. 1893.

ENURESIS.

See Urinary Disorders.

EPILEPSY.

Kali mur.—The specific or the chief remedy in this disease, especially when it occurs with or after the suppression of eruptions.

"*Kali muriaticum* is one of the tissue remedies too easily overlooked. Its delicate affinity for the nerve centres makes it a slow acting remedy. Inasmuch as the physician too frequently seeks palliation in epilepsy, it is not generally employed long enough. Without doubt it preserves the fibrin factor and prevents a tissue metamorphosis. This, he believes, should be the therapeutic aim in treating this disease. It is simple enough to relieve a fit, for it is in itself self-limiting. The real object is to overcome the morbid degeneration. The protoplasmic fibres are surely strengthened by *Kali mur.,* and such a condition tends to preserve the brain integrity. When the brain-cells are properly nourished, they can withstand the irritation of the sensory fibrillæ which surround them. This being done, we have made the first advance toward the removal of the cause of the disease. While he does not make the claim of any specific, and while he admits the difficulty in curing this terrible disease, the writer's record book gives much substantiation of the above statement."— *The Clinique,* June 15, 1897.

Kali phos.—Epilepsy or epileptic fits with shrunken countenance, coldness and palpitation after the fit.

Magnesia phos.—Epileptic fits, sometimes the result of vicious habits, which must be restrained.

Ferrum phos.—Epileptic fits with rush of blood to head.

Natrum phos.—Is frequently useful as an alternating remedy, and for intestinal irritation (worms, etc.).

Natrum sulph.—Traumatic epilepsy. Head injuries resulting in spasms.

Silicea.—Nocturnal epilepsy, especially about the time of the new moon; feeling of coldness before the attack, spasms spread from the solar plexus upward. Exalted susceptibility to nervous stimuli, with exhausted condition of the nerves.

CLINICAL CASES.

Mrs. ——, widow, æt. 30, ever since death of husband, six years ago, epileptic attacks at night while sleeping; groans, bites her tongue, bloody foaming, bowels very constipated, no uterine trouble. *Silicea*²⁰⁰ greatly lessened the frequency of the attacks. (Hoyne.)

KALI MUR. IN EPILEPSY.—Dr. C. C. F. Wachendorf reports the case of a man, æt. 45 years, who had an eruption in September, 1888, which disappeared until August, 1889. In November, 1889, the eruption was suppressed, and he began to have irregular attacks of "fainting fits." He would grow pale, a warm feeling following; then spasm, with pain in the cerebellum, and burning in the region of the stomach. Attacks nearly always preceded by fright or fear. *Nux, Bufo* and *Arsenicum* were each tried in turn, but failed. Then *Kali mur.* 6x was prescribed on the indication, *"Epilepsy from suppressed eruptions."* After the sixth day he had no attack. He still takes occasional doses of the medicine to keep up its action.

A case of ten years' standing resulting from injury to the head was cured by *Natrum sulph.*²⁰⁰. Dr A. L. Blackwood, 1889.

A lady, æt. 32, married, one child 6 years old, has had spasms since the birth of the child, every few days, and very severe during the menses, twenty-four hours at a time, and from a few moments to an hour apart, these continuing three to six days, then every two to four days, in the interim of menses. The woman was short build, heavy set, short neck, round full abdomen, red flushed face, sanguinobilious temperament and of rather mild disposition. Headache all the time in temples and back of head, as well as constant heat on top of head; also severe pain in the lumbar region and across sacrum, numb feeling in lower limbs and cold, clammy perspiration over the whole body. Physicians had pronounced her case "epilepsy," caused by uterine trouble. Without regard to diagnosis,

14

or former treatment by allopathic medication, I at once gave her *Calcarea phos.* and *Kali phos.*, three doses each per day, and during menses *Magnes. phos.* every two hours during the first two days of the menses. In two months from the first time I saw her, she was apparently well in every way, and became pregnant again, and by the use of the *Calcarea phos.* had no further trouble. (A. P. Davis, M. D.)

A boy of 13 had suffered since the age of 6 from trembling of the limbs, and was gradually passing into a state of epilepsy. He received, on the 8th of October, 1888, *Kali chlor.*, six powders. Since the 10th of December he has had no return of it. (*Monatsblätter.*)

A girl, 23 years old, who had suffered since her seventeenth year from epilepsy, received, after having two violent attacks, on the 11th of June, 1885, six powders of *Kali phos.*". On the 11th of April, 1887, she wrote: "Since the 15th of June, 1885, I have not had an attack." (*Monatsblätter.*)

ERYSIPELAS.

Ferrum phos.—Rose and erysipelatous inflammations of the skin, for the fever and pain and severe symptoms of inflammation.

Kali mur.—Vesicular erysipelas; the chief remedy. Erysipelas bullosum.

Kali sulph.—Blistering variety, to facilitate the falling off of scabs.

Natrum phos.—Erysipelas; smooth, red, shiny, tingling or painful swelling of the skin. Infiltrated inflammation of the skin.

Natrum sulph.—For the smooth form, red, shiny, and coming in blotches, skin much swollen, with or without vomiting of bile. Œdematous puffy inflammation of the skin.

CLINICAL CASES.

FERRUM PHOSPHORICUM.—A case is reported by an Indian native practitioner in the *Homœopathic World* recently, which well displays the activity of this remedy. The case was one apparently of phlegmonous erysipelas of the left thigh in a boy of 6. It had been going on for some six weeks, and was little influenced by the *Mercurius iodatus, Hepar sulphuris* and *Silicea* at first prescribed. *Ferr. phos.* 6x wrought an immediate change for the better, and effected a rapid cure.

Mrs. Forbes, a widow, was lying very ill with erysipelas; high fever and quite prostrate. The members of her family thought her dying, as she had become delirious. Her head and face so swollen that her eyes were literally closed, suffering intense pain. *Natrum sulph.* and *Ferrum phos.*, alternately, a dose every hour and oftener, were given. After the second dose of the former she ejected a great quantity of bile. The severe symptoms subsided. This was on Saturday night. The medicine was continued. *Ferrum phos.* now only intercurrently, as the pulse had become less frequent. To the astonishment of all her friends, on Wednesday morning she was so well that she went out to her work as usual.

Statistics show a death-rate of 2,000 per annum from this disease. In a similar case of erysipelas in a lady, æt. 87, these two remedies and a few doses of *Kali phos.* cured her, when the usual treatment, painting with iodine, brandy, etc., had no effect in arresting the disease. (M. D. W. From Schüssler.)

EXOPHTHALMIC GOITRE.

Natrum mur.—Palpitation, heart's pulsations shake the body; short-breathed on least exertion.

CLINICAL CASES.

In two cases, ladies with swelling on each side of the neck; voice changed, eccentric dilatation of the heart, with systolic bellows sound. Cured by *Natrum mur.*²⁴ in a few months. (Dr. Hofrichter.)

EYE, DISEASES OF.

Ferrum phos.—Inflammation of any part of the eyes without secretion of mucus or pus. Pain in the eyeball, made worse by moving the eyes. Burning sensation in the eyes. They appear inflamed and red. Retinitis. Great redness with severe pain, without mucus or matter. "Conjunctiva congested, and with a sensation as if grains of sand were under the eyelids, vision dim, letters blur while reading, even though the refraction be normal, or if any error exists and is corrected by lenses, or where there is an insufficiency of the internal recti muscles so far as can be determined. Photophobia worse from artificial lights." (H. F. Ivins, M. D.)

Dr. Robert Cooper reports as having observed three times that a stye appeared on the lower lid of the right eye in patients who were taking this remedy for debility. *"Ferrum phos.* is especially adapted to conjunctivitis with great relaxation of that membrane, and surpasses *Aconite* in the majority of acute superficial inflammations of the eye. In retinitis, with great engorgement of the retinal vessels. It has been found of great service." (H. C. French, M. D.)

Kali mur.—Affections of the eye with discharge of white mucus or yellow-greenish matter (also *Kali sulph.*). Feeling of sand in the eyes. Yellow, purulent scabs on the lids, specks of matter. Blisters on cornea. Inflammation of the iris. Superficial flat ulcer arising from a vesicle. Retinitis. Parenchymatous keratitis. Of great use even in the early stage. "In diffuse interstitial keratitis in which the cornea is flecked over a large extent of its surface with light deposits, we have found it of great value. Indeed, we believe it will prove to possess a specific influence over many of the pathological changes in that organ. In chronic abscess of the cornea it has been found to do good." (H. C. French, M. D.)

In the *North American Journal of Homœopathy,* Sept., 1885, p. 14, Dr. Geo. S. Norton writes of the use of this remedy in ulceration of the cornea. He has found it useful in ulcers of a clearly asthenic type, inflammations of a low degree, tedious cases, redness of the conjunctiva is not excessive. Photophobia, pain and lachrymation are very moderate or absent entirely. Any part of the cornea may be the seat of the ulcer, but it is liable to begin at the periphery and spread to the centre. The base of the ulcer is dirty-white or yellow, often vascular, and surrounding inflammation is very marked, discharge moderate and of white mucus; sometimes there is purulent infiltration extending between the layers of the cornea (onyx) or into the anterior chamber (hypopyon), but even then it is asthenic. Sometimes the disease appears more like an abscess, breaking down later into an ulcer. The tongue will usually have a thin, white coating. (See Clinical Cases.) **Cataract** after *Calc. fluor.* Dr. Norton communicates to us the following: *Kali mur.* is especially adapted to the non-vascular variety of parenchymatous inflammation of the cornea (*Aurum mur., Cannabis* and *Merc.*, active and vascular variety); there may be some photophobia and lachrymation, but never excessive as under *Calc. phos.* The pains are not distinctive, but are always moderate. Redness is present, but is never expressive, bright-red or fiery. Trachoma.

Kali phos.—Eyesight weak from an exhausted condition of the system, after diphtheria. Sensation of sand or sticks in the eyes. Soreness of eyeballs and edges of lids. Burning in eyes as if full of smoke. Eyes twitch, become blurred, black spots before eyes. Photophobia. Excited, staring appearance of the eyes, a symptom of nervous disturbances during the course of a disease; drooping of the eyelids, strabismus not spasmodic, squinting after diphtheria. Muscular and accommodative asthenopia and inco-ordination of the ocular muscles, especially from defective innervation. (H. C. F.)

Kali sulph.—Eyelids covered with yellow crusts, discharge from eyes yellow or greenish matter, yellow, purulent slime or yellow, watery secretions. Cataract, dimness of crystalline lens (*Natr. mur.*). Ophthalmia neonatorum, thin yellow or sanious discharge with closely adherent membrane on the palpebral conjunctiva. It is useful where other remedies fail. We have found *Kali sulph.* a valuable agent in abscess of the cornea, and superior to *Kali mur.* in cases of pus in the anterior chamber (hypopyon), two or three cases of which under this remedy (3x) alone have cleared up with gratifying promptness. (H. C. French, M. D.)

Magnesia phos.—Drooping of the eyelid, affections of the eyes with sensitiveness to light, or contracted pupils, vision affected, sees sparks, colors before the eyes, twitching of eyelids, spasmodic squinting, dulness of vision from weakness of optic nerve, strabismus. Diplopia, supraorbital neuralgia, relieved by warmth. Hyperæsthesia of the retina with flashes of light and black specks before eyes, with general nervous excitability. (H. C. F.) Retinitis pigmentosa. (R. S. C.) Ciliary neuralgia has been frequently cured with this remedy.

Natrum mur.—Asthenopia, muscular; the most important remedy. Blister on cornea, discharge of clear mucus from eyes or flow of tears with obstruction of tear-ducts, neuralgic pains periodically returning with flow of tears. Eyes water, secretion causes scalding of skin or eruption of small vesicles; granulated eyelids without secretion of tears. Tarsi much thickened and red. White spots on the cornea. The eye may also be syringed with a solution of this remedy externally, daily. The molecules of the salt which remain on the spot cause by their hygroscopic nature a gradual moistening and absorption of the spot. Ciliary neuralgia. Incipient cataract. Iritis. *Natr. mur.* is most suitable where the humors of the eyeball are increased in quantity, thus causing internal pressure. "Is of possible value in glaucoma." (R. S. C.)

Natrum phos.—Discharge of golden-yellow, creamy matter. Conjunctivitis with discharge of yellow, creamy matter. Hypopyon. Lids glued together in the morning; note conditions of the tongue, palate, presence of acid risings, etc. Burning lachrymation, eyes bloodshot. Dim sight, as if a veil were before the eyes. Scrofulous ophthalmia; squinting caused by intestinal irritation, worms, etc. Ophthalmia in newborn infants; also externally as a wash. "Ophthalmia, profuse, creamy, sticky secretion and dim vision, especially in old women; also when accompanied by diarrhœa." (Duffield.) Sees sparks before eyes. Boring pains in the eyes of rheumatic origin.

Natrum sulph.—Pain over eyes. Granular conjunctivitis. Photophobia in scrofulous ophthalmia. "No remedy, *Graphites* possibly excepted, has such terrible sensitiveness to light in chronic ophthalmias." (H. C. Allen.) Yellowness of the conjunctivæ. Large, blister-like granulations with burning lachrymation, burning of edges of lids. Hypopyon.

Silicea.—Stye on the eyelids, also use as a lotion to remove and hasten the discharge painlessly. If much inflammation, *Ferrum phos.* Deep-seated abscess of cornea. Hypopyon. Photophobia, sudden paroxysms of nyctalopia. Amblyopia and cataract after checked foot-sweat. Boils and cystic tumors around eyelids. Opaque cornea. Ciliary neuralgia over right eye. Kernels and indurations of the lids. Scrofulous ophthalmia.

Calcarea phos.—Spasmodic affections of the eyelids, if

Magnes. phos. fails. Parenchymatous keratitis in scrofulous diathesis. Useful in checking cataract. Dry inflammation of the eyes during dentition. Photophobia. Corneal opacity. No use where the palpebral conjunctiva is much involved. Congenital amblyopia in children of a rachitic constitution and scrofulous diathesis, with general characteristics of the drug. Useful in non-vascular form of diffuse keratitis with more marked photophobia than under *Kali mur.* and accompanied by well known scrofulous cachexia. Cataract appearing with lupus, cancer or tuberculosis, gout, etc.

Calcarea sulph.—Deep ulcers on cornea, ophthalmia, pus thick and yellow. Inflammation of the eyes with discharge of thick, yellow matter. Deep-seated abscess of the cornea (*Silicea*). Hypopyon, to absorb the effusion of pus in the eye (after *Silicea*). Retinitis. Sensation of foreign body; has to tie up, after injuries. Pus in anterior chamber. Phlyctenular keratitis and conjunctivitis, cervical glands enlarged. Inflamed canthi. "Has in my hands reduced purulent discharge in ophthalmia neonatorum." (H. C. F.)

Calcarea fluor.—Flickering and sparks before the eyes, spots on the cornea, conjunctivitis, cataract. Indurations in the lids. Enlarged meibomian glands.

This remedy has been found of use in cases of partial blindness. Dimness of vision from overstraining the eyes. "I have prescribed *Calcarea fluor.* recently in my clinic in a number of cases. In one case of senile cataract where it was used there certainly was great improvement in sight." (R. S. Copeland.)

CLINICAL CASES.

The following cases were furnished by Dr. T. M. Stewart, of Cincinnati:

1. Weak child, 2 years of age, thin skull. fontanelles open, soft cataract of left eye. *Calcarea fluorica* 6x; in three months' examination bowed anterior fontanelle closed, and child much improved in general health. No change in cataract.

2. The following troublesome symptoms not entirely relieved by wearing proper correcting glasses for compound hyperopic astigmatism were completely cured: The glasses were prescribed in June and patient reported

in November following. Complained of some itching and burning, blurring of sight occasionally, floating specks before eyes, light aggravates all symptoms. *Kali phos.* 6x cured.

3. Epiphora from refractive error not entirely relieved from wearing corrective glasses. *Calcarea fluor.* 6x entirely relieved the following symptoms: Itching of mucous surface of lids, eyes water and sensation of air blowing on eyes after use of glasses.

Parenchymatous keratitis, inflammation of right cornea extending over the whole of its surface, of three months' duration; patient could only count fingers; some pain, slight photophobia and redness, pupil dilates slowly under *Atrop.,* but quickly contracts again. *Aurum mur., Cinnabar.,* with instillations of *Atrop.,* did no good. *Kali mur.* 6x cured. Cases of chorio-retinitis cured by *Kali mur.*—Allen & Norton, *Ophthalmic Therapeutics,* p. 106.

In the *Homœopatische Monatsblätter* for 1882, p. 95, is a report of thirteen cases of cataract *cured*—eleven with *Calcarea fluor.* Improvement showed itself within eight days. The other two cases required *Kali mur.* after *Calcarea fluor.*

The following cases from *N. A. J. H.,* September, 1885, p. 15, reported by George S. Norton, M. D., show the beautiful action of *Kali mur.* in ulceration of the cornea.

Case of ulcer of the cornea large in size, steadily increasing in extent, vascular base, moderate redness, no pain, slight photophobia, profuse lachrymation, nose sore, corners ulcerated. *Kali mur.*⁶. Improvement set in at once, and ulcer commenced to heal; within five days the vascularity disappeared, and in ten days the eye was perfectly well.

Case of ulcer of the cornea with elevated edges and vascular base, resulting from phlyctenular keratitis; in spite of all treatment it had steadily increased; cornea hazy around ulcer. *Kali mur.*⁶. The ulcer began at once to heal and in two weeks all inflammatory symptoms had disappeared.

Ulcer of the cornea from the same cause as the above, also a rapidly increasing purulent infiltration between the corneal layers. Photophobia well marked; moderate redness and no pain. Several remedies were administered with no benefit. *Kali mur.*³ was prescribed, and a rapid cure followed.

Child with ulcer near centre of cornea, which was deep; infiltration considerable. Pus in the anterior chamber; moderately red, no pain. *Atrop.,* instillation. Hypopyon disappeared, and in twenty-four hours a rapid recovery followed under *Kali mur.*³.

Mrs. B. L., from C——, came to me on account of a swelling on right eye which appeared suddenly. A specialist had advised operation; the palpebral aperture, which was opened with difficulty, was filled with a yellowish-green, projecting mass. The conjunctiva was infiltrated and sight was lost. *Kali sulph.*⁶ removed the swelling and inflammatory symptoms completely and permanently in one and one-half days. (Quesse.)

Mrs. M. N., aged 46, was sent to me for treatment on May 9, 1892, by Dr. Boericke, with keratitis, involving the lower nasal third of the left cornea. The inflammation had existed since the previous Christmas, and had been subjected to rigorous allopathic treatment, with no improvement. The entire bulbar and palpebral conjunctiva was intensely inflamed. The corneal surface was vascular, with a decided ring of leucocytes round the border of the cornea, limited to the diseased area. There was a dense, irregular white opacity reaching down into the interstitial elements, occupying the centre of the affected territory, and covering an area of about one-eighth of an inch square. The clouded territory reached to the axis of vision. She could with difficulty discern large objects on the temporal side, but had no central vision. On May 9th she was put on *Kali mur.* 3x, every three hours. There was a marked improvement during the first twenty-four hours, and an astringent which had been given for the conjunctivitis was reduced in power and frequency, and finally discontinued. After the seventh day the *Kali mur.* was given in the 6x, every four hours, and was so continued up to the day of discharge. On the 23d vision was 5/20. The larger part of the cloudy area had cleared up, and the leucoma had almost disappeared, and it is safe to predict a complete restoration of vision in a few weeks under *Kali mur.* (H. C. French.)

Child, æt. 8, with opacity of both corneæ, with fresh ulceration and some infiltration, no redness. The ulceration healed, and the infiltration speedily cleared up under *Kali mur.*[6].

An ulcer at outer edge of cornea slightly excavated, with vessels running to it, improved under this remedy rapidly.

It may be that *Kali mur.* will be found useful in cases of clear ulceration and absence of infiltration. It is worth a trial.

A girl had, on the lower edge of the left cornea, a little blister, from which a bundle of small veins ran. Feeling of sand in the eye. Edges of eyelids are scabby. *Kali mur.*[12]. internally and externally, every six hours for three days, cured the cornea in ten days, and in three weeks the scurfiness of the eyelids, which she had had for two years, had nearly disappeared. (W. P. Wesselhœft, M. D. From Hg.)

Dr. Koch writes: An old woman came to me æt. 72. She had worn a green shade over her eyes to my recollection, since my younger days, when, as a student, I spent my holidays at Simbach with my grandparents. This person complained of a constant burning sensation in her eyes, causing a continued flow of smarting tears. This commenced at eight o'clock in the morning and lasted till sunset. During the night it was better. She had much thirst, but little appetite. Externally the conjunctiva palpebrarum was in a chronic state of inflammation. On each side of the nose there were excoriation and eczema of the skin caused by the flow of acrid tears. The punctæ lachrymosa were dilated; but the tear-ducts were unobstructed. I hesitated whether I should give *Natrum mur.* or *Arsenic.;* but Dr. Schüssler's special mention of *Natrum mur.* in regard to these excessive lachrymal secretions determined my choice, and I gave *Natrum mur.* in water, one teaspoonful three times a day. In three weeks the symptoms all greatly subsided, and shortly after entirely disappeared. (From Schüssler.)

I have hitherto only given *Natrum phos.* in scrofulous subjects, and only then when my old remedies, *Calcarea carb.*, etc., failed. One case was particularly striking on account of its being cured so rapidly. In May last a little girl, æt. 8, was brought to me, who suffered from severe conjunctivitis, with great dread of light. She had been treated for some time by an ordinary practitioner, but without effect. I ascertained that her eye affection dated from the time she had had measles, some years previous. *Calcarea carb.* and other medicines proved ineffectual. The enlargements of the glands of the neck, and the creamy secretion of the eyelids, led me to try *Natrum phos.*, of which I administered a dose three times daily. A week later on, and the child was brought to me, her eyes bright and perfectly cured. (From Schüssler.)

Louis G——, æt. 19, came to my office, July 3d, 1886, by advice of his physician, Dr. Nichols, of Hoboken, N. J. The young man was of good physique and apparently perfectly healthy. He stated that his right eye had been "bloodshot" for a week, and that the vision had been steadily failing for five days. Examination of the eye showed moderate photophobia, lachrymation, conjunctival redness and ciliary injection. The cornea was very hazy, appearing like ground glass throughout its whole extent, but was not vascular; the surface was clear. The vision was reduced to counting fingers six inches from the eye. The history of the case, though not clear, pointed toward a strumous rather than a syphilitic origin. *Atrop.* was instilled, and *Kali mur.* was given internally. Under this treatment alone he steadily and rapidly improved until he was discharged, August 19th, with vision 15/40. On December 27th he was again seen, when the vision in the right eye was found to be perfect (15/15). But the disease was making its appearance in the left eye, as evidenced by moderate inflammatory symptoms and cornea hazy at the outer edge L. V. 15/30. The same treatment was prescribed which had been so successfully employed before, but for two weeks the cornea gradually grew more opaque, the redness increased, the pain became more marked as if there were something in the eye, the photophobia and lachrymation became excessive, and the vision decreased to counting fingers at six inches. *Rhus tox.* 6x was then alternated with *Kali mur.* 6x when the sthenic type of the disease soon changed, and the inflammatory symptoms rapidly abated, after which, under *Kali mur.* alone, the improvement continued so long that in eight weeks his vision was 15/40, and later became perfect.

Dr. Koch informed us that a farm servant came to him, and said he could not see. Some time before this, a piece of wood had struck him in the eye. He had been treated for it; had had purgatives, leeches and cold water applications, and now his sight was quite gone. The particulars of the case were these: The bulbus was infiltrated with vascular engorgement. The conjunctiva was swollen, and the eyelid also in an irritated and inflamed condition. The cornea was dim, with a smoky appearance of the anterior chamber (*i. e.*, between the cornea and iris), and some matter could be seen floating quite distinctly. I found no foreign body. The subjective results were severe burning pain in the eye, as if from a foreign body, and a continuous flow of tears. The man had to keep his eye tied up.

His appetite was good, and pulse normal. As to the therapeutic treatment, I had evidently to deal with two different affections—hypopyon (matter in the eye), and conjunctiva. First of all I gave *Ferrum phos.*, a dose every two hours, and in a week the burning pain and watering of the eye were less. One week after this the man complained that his sight had not improved. Now I had the task of absorption of the matter before me, as well as the clearing of the cornea. To meet the first condition I gave *Hepar sulph.*, but after a fortnight I could recognize no special progress. I felt rather in a fix with the case, as absorption would not take place. Remembering an expression of Dr. Quagleo, that he considered Schüssler's *Calcarea sulph.* a still more powerful medicine, I gave some *Calcarea sulph.* to be taken in water in three doses. Scarcely a week after, the man came to me, greatly delighted, saying he could see gleams of light in the right eye. Positively, I found the cornea less cloudy, and could observe that some of the matter had been absorbed. I now gave him only a dose night and morning. In three weeks absorption was complete, and dimness of the cornea quite removed, and his sight restored. Besides all this, all the inflammation of the conjunctiva was also cured. (From Schüssler.)

A woman, æt. 56, from Simbach, who always wore blue spectacles, came to see me, as she had become blind in the right eye. The cause and consequent suffering were as follows: Three years ago, one noon-day in the winter, she was walking from Arnstorf to Simbach. The whole of the meadows were covered with snow, on which the sun was shining brightly, causing a strong refraction. Suddenly she felt a severe pain in the right eye, and immediately discovered that she had lost the sight of it. She took some snow and held it over her eye, which she thought did her some good. On reaching home she sent for the doctor, who put a leech to the right temple and gave her a strong purgative. She had to keep her bed for three weeks. The pain subsided, but her sight did not return. Some time after, she traveled all the way to Passau, to consult Dr. E., the oculist. He gave her a laxative and some ointment, to be rubbed all around the eye (*Ungt. hydrarg.*). As the ointment affected the gum and loosened the teeth, she stopped using it, her sight being no better. Later on, when she heard that Prof. Rothmund had operated on the pastor of Landau for cataract, she went to see him. "If this medicine won't help you, you will remain blind for life," were the Professor's words. His prescription was *Potassium iodide*. After having had the prescription made up three times, and using it steadily, she felt no improvement, and was quite inconsolable. With her right eye she saw nothing; all seemed smoke and mist; and the other eye was becoming weaker and weaker from month to month. External examination showed the conjunctiva intact, as also the cornea, iris, etc. All pointed to internal disease of the inner medium of the eye. I could see but little of the retina, as there was a kind of mist over it, which seemed to spread from the vitreous humor over the background of the eye. I introduced the rays of light in different directions, and by this means I was better able to obtain sight of the retina. It appeared dim and misty, the veins were clearly seen, forming a dark network. In some places there were indistinctly defined spots, some larger than others, appearing to me like the residue of extravasated blood. The arteries were scarcely visible, and seemed to me pale and more contracted than in the normal condition. The necessary therapeutic treatment clearly indicated to me was to produce abortion of the exuded substance, this being the cause of the dulness of sight. According to Professor Rothmund's opinion, inflammation of the retina always arises in the connective tissue, and as this exuded substance appears of a coagulated nature which no doubt is fibrinous, and, as is well known, can be hypertrophied, and is capable of fatty degeneration, I found that of the remedies I could think of the most suitable seemed to be *Kali mur.* I now gave the woman eight powders, each containing two centigrammes; the powder to be dissolved in half a wineglassful of water, a tablespoonful to be taken night and morning. A fortnight after, the patient came back, saying, "I don't think I am any worse. Please give me some more of those powders." She received a dozen, with the same directions. One morning she called quite early, and told me in great glee that on rising that morning she could see the window-sash quite distinctly. I tested her sight from different distances, and found that she had really improved. "I can see pretty well through the mist," she said. *Kali mur.* was continued in small doses, and in four months her sight was restored. (From Schüssler.)

Girl, æt. 16, recurring keratitis. Left eye much inflamed, photophobia, slight haziness of the cornea, and traversed with red vessels; zonular redness. *Calcarea phos.* 3x completely restored the patient. I have never found it of any use where the palpebral conjunctiva was much engorged. (R. T. Cooper.)

Bookkeeper, æt. 28. Overstrained eyes. "Feel like chilblains," must wipe them often and pull at the lashes. Is emmetropic, though can read No. 15 at fifteen feet with difficulty from blurring of the letters, not improved by glasses. A candle held twelve inches seems double, and the left image is seen with the right eye, hence he has asthenopia from paresis of the internal recti muscles. *Natrum mur.*[200] cured. (T. F. Allen.)

The late Dr. Kafka records a case of incessant lachrymation of the right eye, caused by exposure to a strong north wind, and dependent on hyperæmic obstruction of the lachrymal passages. *Natrum mur.*[6] cured in four weeks, and was equally efficacious when, on later occasions the trouble returned.—*Hom. Recorder*, Jan., '93.

Dr. M. E. Douglass relates a case of sudden blindness occurring in connection with the albuminuria of pregnancy, and refers to another in which *Kali phos.* 6x produced a recovery.—*Am. Med. Mo.*, Aug., 1889.

The Sight Restored in a Case of Choroido-Retinitis by Kali mur., Natrum phos., Calc. phosph. and Kali phos.—By C. Stirling Saunder, L. R. C. P., Lond.

Master ——, aged 14, had for some time been suffering from nervous debility and a high-strung nervous constitution. His most marked defect, however, was his eyesight which, notwithstanding the trial of glasses of various strengths and tints, became weaker and weaker, until at last it was discovered that he could hardly see clearly at all. He was taken to several oculists, and the last one (a noted London specialist) pronounced the *sight of one eye gone* and that the other would follow in due course, owing to the disease known as *choroido-retinitis* (or effusion from blood vessels into the choroid and retina), obliterating the sight. The writer took this boy in hand last autumn, only promising to try and save the sight of the better eye. He was kept from school, and diligently took a course of the above-mentioned remedies. As his sight seemed to have wonderfully improved in about two months' time, he was again taken to the oculist above-mentioned who was quite astounded at the change which had taken place in the discs of his eyes, having found complete absorption of the exudation in the bad eye, with a return of the lost sight, which enabled him to resume his studies at school.

FEVER, SIMPLE.
See also Special Fevers.

Ferrum phos.—Catarrhal fever with quickened pulse. Feverishness in all stages, all inflammatory fevers, rheumatic, etc., the chief remedy. "The most beneficial results have been obtained from its use in the prevention of traumatic fever." Synochal fevers. Chill every day at I P. M. Dry heat of palms, face, throat and chest.

Kali mur.—With constipation and a thick white fur on the tongue. Catarrhal fever, great chilliness, the least cold air chills him through, has to sit close to the fire to keep warm and still is chilly. Better covered up in bed. (*Holbrook.*)

Kali sulph.—When the blood heat rises in the evening it assists in producing perspiration, and warm coverings should frequently be applied and this remedy given very frequently. Also fevers from blood-poisoning.

Natrum mur.—Hay fever with watery discharge from the eyes and nose.

Kali phos.—Nervous fevers, high temperature, quick and irregular pulse, nervous excitement or great weakness and depression. In fevers of low type, dry mouth, sordes on the teeth and delirium, this remedy has produced the grandest results. (Meadow.)

CLINICAL CASES.

M. L., a gentleman, æt. 38, took a chill while in a state of perspiration. He suffered in consequence from tearing pains in the limbs, noises in the ears, with dulness of hearing and frontal headache. These pains were accompanied by fever, and although he had night-sweats, they brought no relief. The appetite was poor and the tongue covered with a white coating. I gave a small quantity of *Kali mur.* in water every two hours. A rapid general improvement set in but pain and numbness in the feet were still present. Also the habitual perspiration of the feet was still absent. At this stage the patient received *Silicea,* two doses daily for a week. Perspiration of feet was re-established, and on the reappearance of this the rest of the ailments left him, and health was quite restored. (From Schüssler.)

Dr. G. H. Martin reports a case of high fever (104°), general exhaustion, lameness in muscles, headache and diminished appetite, in which he prescribed *Ferrum phos.* 12x, which did no good, the patient declaring the following day that his symptoms were worse. *Ferrum phos.* 6x, which was then prescribed, caused an immediate improvement.

FISTULA IN ANO.

Calcarea phos.—*Calcarea phos.* 1x and *Silicea* 3x, a dose three times a day, alternated every week, is the treatment recommended by Dr. C. R. Fleury.

Calcarea sulph.—Painful abscesses about the anus in cases of fistula. Pus-like discharge from bowels.

GALL-STONES.

Calcarea phos.—To prevent the re-formation of new stones.
Magnesia phos.—Spasms from gall-stones.
Natrum sulph.—Cannot bear tight clothing around waist.

CLINICAL CASES.

CASE 1.—Woman, married, grown children, aged 37. Headache followed by vomiting of bile for several years. Face purple. Heat ameliorates the pain. Pain begins in right eye, spreads over the forehead with a dragging feeling in back of head. Pain in sacrum extends to thighs, aggravated on right side. Nervous, easily startled, apprehensive. Intensely fastidious. Had gall-stone colic three months ago. Cold feet. Headache at menstrual period for sixteen years. Menstrual flow thick, clotted, dark, lasts one day. Stool, light color when sick, darker when in better health. Must restrain herself or she will commit suicide. Slow pulse at times. Tired all the time. Condemned to an operation by the surgeon for gall-stone. Fissured tongue. *Natrum sulphuricum* cured; the gall stones disappeared.

CASE 2.—Man actively engaged in business, weight 180 pounds, aged 40. Pain in region of gall bladder. Gall-stone colic. Came on after indigestion. Dull aching in that region. Must walk about the room, not ameliorated in any position. Only once has stool become light colored. Pain in region of kidneys also through pelvic region and legs with a cloudy condition of the urine; dribbling of few drops of urine after urination. Dull heavy pain in right side behind the lower ribs, continuous pain; pain extends up right side as far as nipple; stabbing pains in breast. Pain in duodenum aggravated after eating. *Natrum sulph.* cured. The patient is in perfect health. (Dr. Kent, in his Materia Medica.)

Dr. Julia C. Loos reports a striking case of impacted gall bladder in the *Homœopathician,* May, 1912, for which *Natrum sulph.* 50m was prescribed on the following symptoms: Recurrent biliary colic; gall bladder fills one-third abdomen, six days. Adhesions. Desires cold; changing position; aggravation night, eleven to six. Local aggravation motion, painless side; amelioration thigh flexed, warmth. Urine flocculent sediment. Temperature normal, pulse hundred eight. Urging stool only flatus relieves. Tongue dry, fissured coating. Thirst moderate. Fullness drinking. Thigh sharp pains. Perfect cure followed within three days.

GASTRIC DERANGEMENTS
Compare Vomiting.

Ferrum phos.—In the chilly stage of gastric fever. Acute gastritis with much pain, swelling, tenderness at the pit of the stomach, especially if vomiting of food occurs. Dyspepsia with flushed, hot face, epigastrium tender to touch. Indigestion with beating or throbbing pain, heat, redness or flushing of the face, or vomiting of undigested food, the tongue being clean. Indigestion from relaxed condition of the muscular walls of the stomach blood vessels, with burning tenderness, flushed face and pain after taking food. Flatulence, belching with taste of food eaten. Stomachache from cold in children, if pressure aggravates the pain. Stomachache from chill with loose evacuations, caused by insufficient absorption of moisture, from a relaxed condition of the villi. Loss of appetite, disgust for milk, after eating, nausea and vomiting of food; the vomited matters are very sour; can not take acids, herrings, meat or coffee and cakes. Sometimes vomits mornings before breakfast; headache, hammering in the forehead and temples so that she fears apoplexy. Copious menstruation every week, with aching in the abdomen and sacrum. Sleep restless, awful dreams. Does not feel rested in the morning. Cannot bear tight clothing. Thirst for cold water. Desire for some stimulant, brandy, ale, etc. Greasy eructations.

Kali mur.—Gastric or bilious derangement, with gray,

white-coated or mapped tongue. Dyspepsia; pain or heavy feeling in the right side under the shoulder, especially if fatty food disagrees or eyes look large and projecting. Flatulence, with sluggishness of the liver and gray or white-coated tongue. Gastritis, if caused by taking too hot drinks; give this remedy at once. Second stage of gastritis. Indigestion with white tongue, caused by taking rich or fatty food. Bitter taste. Sick feeling after taking fat; vomiting of opaque mucus. Stomachache with constipation.

Kali phos.—Excessive hungry feeling or nausea soon after taking food. A nervous disturbance, depression or weakness; "gone feeling." Flatulence with distress about the heart or simply on left side of stomach, weary pain in left side, weakness of heart. Gastritis if it comes too late under treatment, with asthenic conditions. Indigestion with great nervous depression. Stomachache from fright or excitement. Ulcer or cancer of the stomach. Very thirsty; empty gnawing sensation in stomach relieved by eating. Belching of gas tasting bitter and sour. Constant pain at epigastrium in small spot. The *Kali phos.* patient is more neurasthenic than the *Anacardium* patient; relapses under *Anacardium* are due to dietetic errors, under *Kali phos.* to excitement or worry. (Laird.)

Kali sulph.—Chronic catarrh of the stomach, where there is a yellow-coated tongue. Indigestion with characteristic tongue. Dyspepsia, with **sensation of pressure as of a load and fulness at the pit of the stomach, with yellow-coated tongue.** Sensation of faintness at the pit of the stomach. Indigestion with pain, water gathers in the mouth (after *Natrum mur.* and *Kali mur.*), pain in the stomach just above the angle of the crest of the ilium in a line toward the umbilicus, deep within, beside the right hip. Colicky pains in stomach when *Magnesia phos.* does not give relief.

Magnesia phos.—Pains at the pit of the stomach, nipping, griping, with short belching of wind giving no relief, tongue clean. Cramp in the stomach as if a band were tightly laced or drawn around the body. Flatulence with pain, belching gives no relief. Indigestion with spasmodic, crampy pain, clean tongue. Painful constriction of the muscles of the coat of the stomach, together with hot applications. Convulsive hiccough. Marked disposition to regurgitation immediately after eating. "In gastralgia, magic in effect, often stopping a cramping condition of the stomach when all other remedies have failed. Colic of horses." (Duffield.) Patient craves sugar.

Natrum mur.—Indigestion with pain and water gathering in the mouth, with vomiting of clear, frothy water, or stringy saliva. Stomachache with much saliva gathering in the mouth; waterbrash, watery fluid coming up in throat, not acid, often accompanied with constipation. Offensive breath. Ravenous hunger. Loss of desire for smoking. Violent thirst. Aversion to bread. Sour taste. Feeling of great weakness and sinking at the pit of the stomach. Red spots on pit of the stomach.

Natrum phos.—Acidity, sour risings, excess of lactic acid. Loss of appetite, indigestion felt slightly. On rising in the morning the tongue has a thin, moist coating, a creamy deposit at the back. Flatulence with sour risings. **Gastric derangements with symptoms of acidity.** Gastric ulceration, pain and indigestion, sour taste in the mouth. Indigestion and severe pain after food, or coming on two hours after, with acid-sour risings. Stomachache when worms are present, accompanied by acid risings. Ulceration of the stomach, pain in one spot after food and sometimes sour rising, loss of appetite, face red and blotched, yet not feverish. Heartburn and acidity, vomiting of dark fluid like coffee-grounds. Waterbrash. Gastric troubles after eating fat food. *Natrum phos.* causes the fat to become emulsified.

Natrum sulph.—Biliousness, excess of bile, bitter taste in the mouth, vomiting of bitter fluid, greenish-brown or greenish-gray tongue, or greenish diarrhœa, dark, bilious stools, headache, giddiness and lassitude. Gastric derangements with bitter taste in the morning. Sour eructations, heartburn, copious formation of gas and aggravation from farinaceous food. Flatulence becomes incarcerated in sigmoid flexure and

15

ascending colon, producing violent colic which is relieved by kneading and borborygmus, stitching pains in the liver. (Laird, *N. A. J. H.,* Feb., 1888.) Cannot bear tight clothing around waist.

Calcarea phos.—A course of this remedy is useful in gastric fever as an intercurrent. Pain after eating even the smallest quantity of food. Heartburn, soreness of stomach on pressure, **great craving for bacon, ham, salted and smoked meats.** Bitter taste in morning, with headache. Dyspepsia, with hunger, flatulence and pain in stomach, temporarily relieved by eating and raising wind. "Almost an infallible remedy for excessive accumulation of gas in the stomach." (Foster.) *Calc. phos.* ix, in water, given half an hour after food, is efficacious in non-assimilation of food. Dyspepsia with much distress temporarily relieved by eating.

Calcarea fluor.—Vomiting of undigested food; hiccough from hawking of mucus, weakening and recurring during the day.

Calcarea sulph.—Desire for fruit, tea, claret and green sour vegetables. Great thirst and appetite. Nausea with vertigo. While eating roof of mouth sore, burning in the stomach.

Silicea.—Indurations of the pylorus. Chronic dyspepsia, with acid eructations, with heartburn and chilliness. Disgust for meat and warm food. Extreme hunger. Intolerance of alcoholic stimulants.

CLINICAL CASES.

Mrs. B., aged 58, anæmic, and of nervous temperament has been suffering for over ten years with severe attacks of neuralgia of the stomach. The attacks would last from four to ten hours, and would consist of a series of paroxysms, each of which would last five or ten minutes, with a corresponding interval of rest between.

Her suffering was simply terrible. Up to the time I saw her nothing had been given her but palliative treatment, principally hypodermics of morphine.

When I saw her first she had been suffering for an hour. I at once gave five grains of *Mag. phos.* 3x, in hot water, and repeated the dose every fifteen minutes. After the third dose the pain abated. That attack was conquered. I then prescribed the same remedy in ten-grain doses, after each meal, and after three mild attacks she has had no further trouble for over three years. (B. A. Sonders, M. D., Winterset, O.)

Sudden attacks of deathly sickness at the stomach, coming on at no particular time, even in sleep, and lasting one-half or one hour, appetite poor. *Ferrum phos.* cured, and appetite became ravenous. (Raue, *Rev. Hom. Lit.*, 1875.)

KALI SULPH. IN CATARRH OF THE STOMACH.—Mr. M———, aged 38 years, had been suffering with his stomach for several days. He had a yellow coated tongue and much fulness and pressure at the pit of the stomach. He could not remember when he did not have pain in the stomach more or less. Hot drinks made him worse, and he never was thirsty. His skin was generally dry and often hot and rough, and abdomen was cold to touch. He had some bronchial irritation. If he got chilled he would have colicky pains in his stomach which would extend into the bowels.

At times he would have bloating of the abdomen. *Kali sulph.* 3x was given with some directions about his living, and in a few weeks he was well. Not being used to this form of medicine he was greatly surprised when he was relieved. (O. A. Palmer, M. D.)

An officer suffered for a long time from pains in the abdomen, together with pressure and fulness in the stomach and constipation. The tongue was coated with a yellow slime. He had been treated for three weeks by an allopath without any result whatever. The bowels were so constipated that he could only have a passage by taking a strong purgative. *Kali sulph.* 6x, three powders in water, dose every two hours. The result was surprising. The next morning the patient had a natural stool, and the abdominal distress was nearly all gone. In two weeks he was entirely cured, having taken only two powders.—*Pop. Zeit.*, Dec., 1885.

A young man with chronic dyspepsia. After trying several remedies without effect, I discovered in the mouth a thin, yellow, creamy coating on the soft palate. This induced me to give the patient *Natrum phos.*, which cured him in a short space of time. (C. Hg.)

The following is a resumé from a case in *A. H. Z.*, '82, p. 51: Woman suffered for five years from dyspepsia. After eating, nausea, vomiting of food; the vomit is so sour that it sets teeth on edge; cannot bear sour things. Vomiting appears in the morning and after eating, accompanied by cephalalgia. Hammering in the forehead and temples so violent that she fears apoplexy. Menstruates every three weeks with profuse flow. Troubled sleep, disturbed by anxious dreams. Feels tired in the morning, and feels so tight in her clothes that she must loosen them. *Ferrum phos.*[8] three times a day, a dose before meals, cured the case. Many symptoms pointed to *Natrum phos.*, but the totality of the symptoms favored *Ferrum phos.*

Notes from letter to Schüssler by a doctor in Paderborn (*A. H. Z.*, 1882, p. 102): I recently had a case exactly like the preceding, healed in ten days by *Ferrum phos.*[10], after I had treated him five weeks in vain with *Natrum phos.*

A young man complained of an unnatural appetite. He had to eat almost every hour, feeling such an intense craving for food, yet he felt exhausted and languid. There were no secondary symptoms present. The tongue was clean, the urine was not increased, evacuations normal. *Kali phos.* cured the patient in the course of two days. (From Schüssler.)

Farmer B. consulted me for a singular affection. All acid food caused an attack beginning with a strong chill, followed by fever and profuse weakening sweats. *Natrum mur.⁶.* After fourteen days he informed me that the attacks had entirely ceased, and the partaking of acid foods did not cause him the least discomfort. (Dr. Quesse.)

A landed proprietor, æt. 44, wrote to me a few weeks ago: "The medicine I have taken very steadily, and for a long time attended strictly to my diet. In spite of this, my trouble is no better; I may almost say it has become worse. The conditions are these: 1. I feel almost constantly a taste as of bile. 2. My tongue is covered with a curdy, bitter coating. 3. During the day, especially after food, I suffer from eructations of gases, which have either a bitter taste or are tasteless. 4. My complexion is rather yellow. 5. The appetite very slight; no thirst. My favorite beverage, beer, is distasteful to me. 6. I incline to shiver, and am somewhat faint. 7. My head is but little involved, but feel a constant pressure over one eye. 8. Stools are normal, but scanty, on account of spare diet. The whole condition discloses that I have bile in the stomach." Thus far the patient's own report. To this I may add that the patient in question had already taken by my orders *Nux vom.* and *Pulsat.* He had used the waters of Marienbad the previous summer on the recommendation of another medical man. I sent him now *Natrum sulph.,* with the request to take daily three doses of this powder. The gentleman came six or seven days later to my consulting rooms to thank me for the valuable medicine. "The powder," he said, "has really worked wonders. All my ailments have disappeared as if by magic, and I feel at last perfectly well." (From Schüssler.)

Dr. Mossa, Bamberg, reports: Toward the end of last year I received a letter with the following details, and asking me to forward some medicine: "My boy, a child, æt. 7, hitherto healthy and strong, has been suffering from pains in the stomach for some weeks. Latterly he has vomited all his food, sometimes immediately after taking it, and at other times not till during the night. The child has now become very emaciated. Last week he was frequently feverish. This has, however, not returned since taking the medicine our doctor here has given him. The boy complains of much exhaustion." To form a scientific diagnosis of the case on such information was clearly impossible. But, as it was not convenient for me personally to examine the case, I had to do my best with the details furnished. The nature of the abdominal pains pointed to swelling and enlargement of the organs of the viscera, liver, spleen, etc.; also the feverish attacks, probably subdued by quinine, and the vomiting of food, all coincided with my surmise. As to the selection of the medicine, I hesitated considerably, and then decided to give *Ferrum phos.,* twelve powders, one night and morning. The report some time after was very favorable. The fever had not returned; the vomiting of food and pains in the stomach had quite ceased soon after taking the medicine. The little fellow was so much stronger that he attended school again. (From Schüssler.)

W. Watson, æt. 40. Ulceration of stomach, vomited all his food, and latterly the egesta had the appearance of coffee-grounds. He had suffered from vomiting and indigestion more or less for fourteen years, had seen many doctors, and taken much medicine without avail. I advised him to take *Ferrum phos.* and *Natrum phos.* , in usual quantities, a table-spoonful every two hours alternately for a fortnight. On his second visit he was free from vomiting, had little pain, and felt greatly better. He continued another ten days with the same remedies, and returned quite well. On making special inquiry if he had nothing troubling him, he said: "No, the only thing I sometimes trouble myself about is thinking, after taking any kind of food, whether it will trouble me, but it never does." His cure has proved permanent, as it is now nearly two years since, and he is keeping well. (M. D. W. From Schüssler.)

Patient with troublesome burning in the stomach after eating and continuing until next meal time; pain develops one or two hours after meals; tongue light-gray, no bad taste, no tenderness, bowels regular, stools normal, no thirst, the burning was so troublesome as to keep him awake at night. *Natrum phos.* cured. (*Med. Era.*)

Child with indigestion after typhoid fever. Everything soured on his stomach, breath sour, vomited curdled milk, and sour-smelling fluids, green stool, alternating with constipation, was troubled with colic, white-coated tongue and white around mouth, fretful, cross and restless. *Natrum phos.* cured. (*Med. Era.*)

An old man, some 60 years of age, came to see me; he had "dyspepsia," the doctors said. Emaciated, pale, swarthy, no appetite, restless, bowels inactive, stools sometimes light-colored and at times costive, tongue thickly coated with a brownish-yellow tinge, bitter taste, conjunctiva bluish-white, skin wrinkled and bowels retracted and shrunken, shrivelled, and a pain in the stomach of a burning character after eating; and from the general character of the case, assimilation was greatly at fault. The man had been, and was at the time, taking *Argentum* in pill form, from a "regular," three doses a day, and had been for a year or more; all to no purpose except to hasten the emaciation. After surveying the situation and taking all conditions, I at once put him on *Natrum sulph.* 6x, three doses a day before meals, and *Kali phos.* 6x, as a nerve remedy. These two remedies perfectly cured the "dyspepsia" and all the other troubles, so that in about three weeks he was a well man, the *Natrum sulph.* correcting all the liver and stomach trouble and the *Kali phos.* building up the nerve forces. (A. P. Davis, M. D.)

NERVOUS DYSPEPSIA.—Nausea soon after eating, accompanied by marked drowsiness. Eructations putrid, both to taste and smell. Eructations relieved by nausea. Gnawing pains with fulness in afternoon. These are excellent indications for *Kali phos.* (Dr. Royal.)

GLANDULAR AFFECTIONS.

Kali mur.—This is the chief remedy in glandular swellings, infiltration of the follicular glands of the throat. Glands of the neck are swollen (also apply externally). Scrofulous enlargement of glands, enlarged abdominal glands sometimes with diarrhœa.

Natrum mur.—Chronic inflammation of the salivary glands, with corresponding symptoms, excess of saliva, etc. Chronic swelling of lymphatic glands. Swelling of sebaceous glands.

Natrum sulph.—Sycotic glandular swellings.

Magnesia phos.—Goitre.

Silicea.—In suppurating glands to shorten process, also for scrofula, induration and swelling of glands, with or without inflammation.

Calcarea phos.—Chronic enlargement of the glands, as an intercurrent. Scrofulous enlargement of the cervical glands. Bronchocele, goitre. Incipient tabes mesenterica with fœtid diarrhœa.

Calcarea sulph.—Lymphatic glands discharging pus (compare abscess). Ulceration of the glands.

Calcarea fluor.—Glandular swellings, if very hard. Stony hardness of the glands. Chronic adenitis. Induration in capsular ligaments of joints. Knots and kernels in the female breast. Ganglium tendinosum. Nodulated enlargement of the mammary gland with severe neuralgic-like pains and discharge of a thin, serous fluid.

Ferrum phos.—Acute stage of adenitis. Dr. B. Schmitz cured a case of ranula or sub-lingual swelling which had resisted all medication with *Ferrum phos.*, first centesimal trituration.

Natrum phos.—Goitre. An important remedy in all glandular swellings.

CLINICAL CASES.

NATRUM MURIATICUM DURING EXOPHTHALMIC GOITRE.—Female, aged about 37. The case presented the usual eye, heart and thyroid conditions, but the most persistent and annoying symptoms were dryness of mucous membranes with thirst; lack of control of urine and absolute loss of sexual feeling. *Natrum mur.* 6x was prescribed almost continuously for a year with the result that the eyes went back to normal, the heart beat slowed down, the thyroid enlargement and nervousness became lessened, urinary control was re-established, and the sexual feeling returned, while the patient gained in weight from 134 to 167 pounds. (George S. Ogden, M. D.)

CASE 2.—A Colonial merchant who came to England in despair, none of his friends at the Cape ever expected to see him again. After being under various eminent (allopathic) specialists he was advised to come to me, and in six months' time I sent him back cured by means of *Natr. mur.* 200 and nothing else, but a little *Kali phos.* 6x latterly in alternation. He is still a living wonder to his friends at home and in the Colony, as he not only had the excessively protruding eyeballs, but also terrific palpitation of the heart and nervous exhaustion. (Dr. C. S. Saunders.)

Natrum phos. 3x relieved pressure in thirteen cases of goitre by taking a dose three times a day; pressure was relieved in from three to five days. In some instances a cure was effected. It is well to continue the medicine from four to six weeks. (J. S. Skeels, M. D., *Hahnemannian Monthly,* 1880.)

A swelling under the chin the size of a pigeon's egg was considerably reduced by *Kali mur.*, but still there was induration (hardness) with an uneven surface. *Calcarea fluor.*, taken for a few days, caused it to disappear altogether. Shortly after its disappearance the patient had slight conjunctivitis with swelling, which *Kali mur.* soon cured. (Dr. K. From Schüssler.)

Grauvogl, in his *Text-book,* gives a remarkable result from six weeks' use of *Natrum sulph.* in a case of chronic swelling of the cervical glands, so extensive as to practically obliterate the neck. All known treatment at the universities failed; but *Natrum sulph.* 3x, every two hours, produced rapid improvement in the swelling and general health of the patient.

CALCAREA PHOSPHORICA IN ADENOID GROWTHS.—Dr. G. H. Martin related at the meeting of the California State Hom. Medical Society a case of a boy, 12 years of age, who had an adenoid growth which caused nasal catarrh and deafness of one ear to such a degree that he could not hear the watch when pressed close to the ear. "By the administration of *Calcarea phosphorica,*" he said, "for four months the patient can now hear the watch at six feet, and the catarrh has almost entirely disappeared."—*Pacific Coast Journ. of Hom.*

CALCAREA FLUORICA IN LONG-LASTING AND INDOLENT GLANDULAR ENLARGEMENTS OF THE CERVICAL LYMPHATICS.—Dr. Sybel speaks very highly of the fluoride of lime in the treatment of indolent and long-lasting glandular enlargements of the cervical lymphatics, and especially where the hardness of the gland is pronounced. He thinks that similar results might be obtained in enlarged bronchial and mesenteric glands.

Success was obtained in a number of cases; the three following are presented as typical examples of its action:

1. An unmarried woman, of twenty-five years, had had for many years a

group of enlarged glands, which, situated under the right side of the lower jaw, decidedly disfigured her face. Beyond a small gland at the margin of the group, which showed a tendency to suppurate, the whole mass was hard, showed no inclination to inflame, and was not sensitive to pressure. The small and suppurating gland healed, with a discharge of a caseous mass, under *Hepar sulph.* and *Silicea,* yet the general enlargement remained unaltered. *Calcarea fluorica* 5x was then given once a day. In three weeks the patient claimed a slight diminution, and as this gradually became more pronounced the remedy was continued so that in six to eight weeks the conglomerate mass resolved itself into isolated glands, which finally remained of the size of hazel nuts. The patient thought all further treatment unnecessary and immediately married. The time of treatment lasted from April 25th to the end of November—a relatively short time for such an inveterate affection.

2. A robust young man of twenty years presented in the right submaxillary region, immediately under the jawbone, a conglomerate of several hard lymphatic glands, which, by their size, had a very deforming effect upon his entire face; one at the edge, of the size of a hazel nut, was apparently about to suppurate. The remainder were hard and painless; they had been noticed since childhood, though they had attained their present size only four or five years ago. *Silicea* and *Kali chloratum* controlled the suppuration, and *Calcarea fluorica* in alternation with the *Chlorate of potash* were continued, one of each powder daily. The diminution in size of the glands was continuously noticeable, and at the end of sixteen months they had wholly disappeared.

3. An unmarried woman of fifty years had carried for years an indurated gland in the right submaxillary region of the size of a small hen's egg, but which was neither red nor painful. She had tried all sorts of external remedies without success. *Calcarea fluorica* 5x, one powder morning and evening, and later, only one a day, caused the enlargement to disappear in six weeks; a relatively short time for a glandular enlargement which had persisted for eight years.

4. In a child of five years, who for the past two had had numerous and indurated glandular enlargements in the submaxillary region, the same drug in the fifth decimal trituration dissipated them in a few weeks.—*Berliner Zeitschrift.*

GONORRHŒA.

Natrum phos.—This, according to Schüssler's last (25th) edition, is the principal remedy for gonorrhœa.

Ferrum phos.—Inflammatory stage of gonorrhœa. (N. B. —Avoid pressing along the urethra to bring out pus, as it is very injurious, and retards a cure.) Even walking, going up-stairs, etc., is a great impediment to the cure.

Kali mur.—This is the chief remedy in gonorrhœa. It is,

in fact, a specific for cases in which swelling exists, whether from subcutaneous or interstitial exudation. Gleet combined with eczema, latent or visible, or a disposition to glandular swellings. Figwarts.

Kali phos.—Gonorrhœa with discharge of blood. Balanitis and balano-posthitis.

Silicea.—Gonorrhœa cases of long standing, with thick, fœtid pus. Constant feeling of chilliness, even during exercise. Balanitis.

The following from the pen of the late Dr. T. S. Hoyne has a direct bearing on the subject, and, therefore, we give it in full:

Silicea.—This remedy is frequently condemned by homœopathic physicians, or at least is often adjudged of little value in the treatment of chronic affections. I have jotted down a few cases which may prove of interest.

Mr. A., a street car driver about 48 years of age, with sandy hair and beard, and of rather slight build, came to me with gleet which had been constantly with him for a period of over ten years; he had during this time tried all sorts of remedies with only temporary benefit. Injections of various compositions had controlled it for a brief period, but the discharge invariably reappeared after the stoppage of the injection or even during its continuance. Dilatation of the urethra helped him only for a few days.

The usual routine of remedies, with slight benefit or aggravation as the case might be, was persisted in until the patient became discouraged and did nothing for two or three years.

I obtained the following symptoms at my first and only interview with him: There was a slight discharge of a thin watery character from the urethra every morning, also a slight discharge of prostatic fluid while straining at stool; there was some itching and a few moist spots about the scrotum; bowels constipated nearly all the time, the stool consisting of hard lumps evacuated only by great straining; only at the rarest intervals did he have a loose stool; some burning in the anus after stool. Whereas the patient had formerly been always in good spirits he was now inclined to be very irritable from the slightest cause, and was frequently despondent. The sexual desire was very weak, and after coition he felt as if bruised. He said that he took cold easily, and was then liable to a nightly cough.

Upon the strength of these symptoms he received *Sil.* 200, and I never saw the patient again. A number of months afterward another driver on the same car line called upon me for some of the medicine that cured Mr. A.

Mr. B., a bright young clerk aged about 30, came to consult me about his gleet which was the result of a badly treated gonorrhœa. He had been through the regular course of treatment pursued by allopaths and some homœopathists. He told me that the gonorrhœal discharge had been suppressed several times by injections, the last time being followed by a right sharp attack of orchitis, which had laid him up for a number of days. He then tried a homœopathic physician who gave him a number of remedies without decided benefit, and then resorted to mild injections which were worse than useless for they converted the remnants of the gonorrhœa into a gleet, which had remained unaffected by all sorts of treatment.

I found that the discharge was thin and offensive, very slight in quantity. He had rather frequent emissions, the discharge sometimes being tinged with blood. The urine was turbid and deposited a yellowish sand at times. He could not hold his urine as long as formerly and had to rise once or twice at night to void it. He also had a cold, offensive perspiration of the feet and usually a general perspiration of the whole body every morning. He said that he felt tired all of the time and was disinclined to do any work that he could possibly avoid. He was, like the former patient, very sensitive to the cold air and took cold easily; his sleep was restless and filled with frightful dreams. In the morning on rising he experienced a slight dizziness.

December 10, *Sil.* 200 was prescribed. On the 17th he

reported that the medicine made him worse at first, increasing the discharge and making him urinate oftener than before. *Sac. lac.* was given for two weeks, but the symptoms remained the same day after day.

December 31, *Sil.* c. m. was given, which was also followed by a marked aggravation of all the symptoms. *Sac. lac.* was prescribed for three weeks, but there was no apparent change in his symptoms for the better.

January 25, I gave him *Sil.* 12, which aggravated the symptoms for a few days and then they gradually disappeared. The patient has had no return of the trouble.

Kali sulph.—Gonorrhœa with a slimy yellow or greenish discharge. Gleet. Old gonorrhœas.

Natrum mur.—Chronic gonorrhœa. Transparent, watery discharge, slimy. This remedy and *Calcarea phos.* should be given in alternation for gleet. **Gonorrhœa, with scalding, is** a characteristic of this remedy; in old gonorrhœa, with one last persistent drop. Urethra painfully sore to pressure. After injections of nitrate of silver.

Calcarea phos.—Chronic gonorrhœa with anæmia. Hydrocele.

Calcarea sulph.—Gonorrhœa with sanious, purulent discharge.

Natrum sulph.—Chronic gonorrhœa with yellowish, greenish discharge, which keeps up, of thick consistency. Very little pain. In gonorrhœa, use the third decimal every hour or two, four drops in a little water. (Grauvogl.) Enlarged prostate. Figwarts.

CLINICAL CASES.

In the *Pop. Zeit., Berlin. Verein Hom. Aerzte*, April, 1886. *Ferrum phos.* is recommended in fresh cases of gonorrhœa followed by *Kali mur.* and *Kali sulph.*

A man, æt. 70, suffered for three years from discharge from the urethra; secretion small in quantity; clear mucus; on urinating, violent burning-sticking pains. *Kali sulph., Kali mur.* and *Natrum mur.* did no good. *Magnesia phos.*[6] cured the case in four weeks. The character of the pains was the prominent indication. (Schüssler, *Allg. Hom. Zeit.*, 1875.)

Mr. K., æt. 32, had had gleet for five years; discharge of a thick, yellow consistency, with little or no pain. Cured with two prescriptions of *Natrum sulph.* (J. A. Harrison, M. D.)

HÆMORRHAGE.

Ferrum phos.—Bleeding from wounds externally and internally, in conjunction with surgical aid. Epistaxis of bright red blood, whether from injury or otherwise; this generally suffices, especially in children. Hæmorrhage of bright red blood, rapidly coagulating. Vomiting of bright red blood. Tendency to nosebleed in rapidly growing children.

Kali mur.—When the blood is dark, black, clotted or tough. Vomiting of blood dark, clotted and viscid. Nosebleed in the afternoon.

Calcarea sulph.—Epistaxis. Nasal secretions tinged with blood.

Kali phos.—Epistaxis in weak, delicate constitutions from debility, weakness or old age, predisposition to bleeding of the gums, nose, etc. Loss of blood if dark, blackish, thin, like coffee-grounds, not coagulating. Blood putrid, causing symptoms of decomposition. Septic hæmorrhage.

Natrum mur.—Hæmorrhage, blood pale, thin, red, watery, not coagulating. Epistaxis on stooping, when coughing, with soreness of limbs.

Calcarea fluor.—Hæmoptysis; bright red blood; short hacking cough from over-exertion.

Natrum sulph.—"I have known this remedy in several cases to produce violent epistaxis when wrongly given. In a recent case the 200th potency produced nosebleed, vomiting and purging after every dose taken." (E. H. H.)

CLINICAL CASES.

About twelve years ago I began treating a girl, four years of age, for frequent epistaxis, later for hæmorrhage of the tongue and gums, and alarming nosebleed which could only be controlled by plugging the posterior nares. During the year I plugged the nose several times, applied styptics to mouth and tongue, gave as best I could the indicated remedies: *Ham., Bell., Nit. acid, Ipecac, China,* etc. I classed her as a bleeder, and had the gravest apprehension for her when she should arrive at maturity and menstruation be established. After treating her for about a year for frequent alarming hæmorrhages I gave her *Ferr. phos.* 3x trit., three grains three times a day, and continued its use quite regularly for six months. No attacks occurred while taking the remedy. She remained strong and well, maturing at 14 years of age with normal flow. Had teeth extracted without hæmorrhage, and when she left the city one year ago, was in good health and menstruating normally.

In December, '95, Mrs. B——, aged 65, applied for treatment, presenting ecchymosed spots on legs and thighs, varicose condition of veins and œdema of feet and legs. She received *Ferr. phos.* 3x, every three hours, and improvement was prompt, and at the end of two weeks recovery complete. No return of trouble at present date.

Baby B——, aged two years, returned after a five weeks' sojourn at the seashore, where he was taken in a seemingly hopeless condition from marasmus, and presented the following symptoms: Extreme emaciation and prostration, anæmic, sweating head, legs and feet swollen, ecchymosed spots on legs, effusion of blood about the gums, offensive and at times bloody diarrhœa and cold extremeties. The swelling of legs had the appearance of œdema, not pitting on pressure, however, and the slightest movement caused crying from pain. The epiphyses were not enlarged, and, therefore, I considered the swelling and pain to be caused by effusion of blood in the deeper tissues, constituting, to my mind, a case of scurvy. This child began to improve immediately after taking *Ferr. phos.* 3x, and *Sil.* Occasionally orange juice and grape juice were added to his diet, and he made a steady and uninterrupted recovery.

Miss B——, a teacher in public school, summoned me hastily one day last August. I found her bleeding from the nose and uterus with purpuric spots on the thighs and legs. The bleeding ceased after the third dose of *Ferr. phos.* 3x. I learned that for some years she had had one attack yearly, and prevailed upon her to take one dose a day of the remedy, which she has done to the present time. The purpura disappeared in about ten days and has not returned; she tells me her general health is better than it has been for many years. I wait anxiously to see if the purpura comes next year. No change was made in her diet. (C. E. Gorham, M. D., Albany.)

Hæmoptysis which had continued in spite of remedies was arrested by *Calc. fluor.* (M. J. Bleim.)

Dr. E. B. Rankin, in the *Southern Journal of Homœopathy,* reports a case of hæmorrhage of the bowels, of dark, black blood, viscid and profuse, cured by *Kali mur.* 6x.

Lady, æt. 72, large and corpulent, dark eyes and hair, subject to attacks of apoplectiform cerebral congestion, was found in apoplectic state, with cold extremities, clammy sweat on forehead and face; head hot and livid; unconscious; slow stertorous breathing. *Ferrum phos.*, teaspoonful every half hour; consciousness returned in two hours. Was up the next day. The same remedy has been used in subsequent attacks with the same results. Patient states that never before had she been relieved as soon and effectually. (F. A. Rockwith, M. D., *American Journal Homœopathic Materia Medica,* 1875.)

Dwight H., æt. 12, has been subject to nosebleed for past few years. During this time he became very anæmic. Has taken different remedies from the family physician without permanently arresting the trouble. I was called to see him after a very severe attack and found him much prostrated and blanched from loss of blood. Gave him at once *China off.* 1x, in water, for a few hours, till I could send him some powders of *Ferrum phos.*, which he took in solution for some weeks, a few doses each day, with result of permanently arresting the hæmorrhage. (C. T. M.)

Dr. E. G. Jones reports a case of severe nosebleed from sudden chilling at the menstrual period with arrest of menstruation magically cured by *Ferrum phos.* 3x.

HÆMORRHOIDS.

NOTE.—In the treatment of hæmorrhoids, attention must be paid to disturbances in the function of the liver, the digestive organs, etc., which are, as a rule, present and stand in close connection with the former; otherwise a radical cure of hæmorrhoids cannot be insured.

Ferrum phos.—Inflamed piles, bleeding piles, blood bright red, fluid, but with a tendency to form a thick, soft mass. Before induration.

Kali mur.—Bleeding piles when the blood is dark and thick; fibrinous, clotted.

Kali phos.—Hæmorrhoids, sore, painful and itching.

Calcarea fluor.—Internal or blind piles, frequently with pain in the back, generally far down in the sacrum. Note appearance of tongue, etc., which will indicate the alternating remedy. Piles with pressure of blood to the head. Internal blind piles with constipation, confined state of the bowels. Bleeding piles, alternate with such remedies as are indicated by the color of the blood, etc. Tumors, relaxed elastic fibres. Bleeding hæmorrhoids, bright red blood following a short hacking or hemming cough from over-exertion.

Kali sulph.—Internal and external piles may require this remedy in alternation with *Calcarea fluor.;* the chief remedy when the tongue has a yellow, slimy coating, or discharges or secretions of the characteristic type are present.

Calcarea phos.—Chronic hæmorrhoids in anæmic or weakly patients. Intercurrently with *Calcarea fluor.*

Magnesia phos.—Cutting, darting pains, very acute, often like lightning, so sharp and quick. In external piles, also as a tepid lotion.

Natrum mur.—With smarting, beating and protrusion of the rectum, burning at anus, herpes about anus, stools hard, difficult and crumbling; stitches in rectum and in urethra after micturition.

Silicea.—Intensely painful hæmorrhoids, protruded, become incarcerated and suppurate. Much itching, and pain running into rectum and testicles. Fistula in ano. (*Calcarea phos.*)

CLINICAL CASES.

A young man of 28 had been troubled with hæmorrhoids for some years. Bleeding piles, accompanied by chronic constipation. Much straining at stool, great pressure of blood to head and flushes of heat, tongue mapped or covered with grayish white coating. *Calc. fluor.* 3x and *Kali mur.* 6x completely cured.

HAY FEVER.

Magnesia phos.—Dr. T. C. Fanning recommended this remedy as the best one we possess to prevent a threatening attack of hay fever from maturing, or to relax the same when it has already set in. If the weather has been sultry, and the patient stuffy during the day, oppressed with short, anxious breathing, the spasm during the night will come unless this remedy be given every hour during the day and through the evening in hot water.

Natrum mur.—Hay fever from suppressed intermittents; craving for salt; least exposure to sun brings on violent coryza with sensation of itching in nasal and lachrymal passages.

Silicea.—Itching and tingling in nose and posteriorly at orifice of Eustachian tubes, with violent sneezing and excoriating discharge. Hoarseness, roughness and dryness, with a tickling cough, worse by cold drinks, by speaking and when lying down at night.

HEADACHE.

Ferrum phos.—Headache from cold, sun-heat, a bruising, pressing or stitching pain, pains worse on stooping and moving. Headache from gouty predisposition (alternately with *Natrum sulph.*). Headache with vomiting of undigested food. Congestive, with pressing pain, and sore to the touch. Pressing a cold object against the spot seems to relieve the pain. If furred tongue be present, this is an additional indication. Headaches of children require this remedy. Headache with a throbbing sensation; worse right side. Headache with red face and suffused redness of the eyes. Blind sick headache, with vomiting of food as taken, undigested. Dull right-sided headache from vertex to right supraorbital region. Rush of blood to head. Headaches made worse by shaking the head, stooping, and indeed every motion of the body. Congestive headaches, especially when at the menstrual period. Top of head sensitive to cold air, noise, jar, cannot bear to have hair touched. Headaches following injuries to head, has cured after failure of *Arnica*.

Kali mur.—Headache with vomiting, hawking up of milk-white mucus. Sick headache with white-coated tongue, or vomiting of white phlegm, arising from sluggish liver, tongue furred, gray or white at base, want of appetite.

Kali phos.—Headache, nervous, sensitive to noise, irritability, confusion, relieved by gentle motion. Headache of students and those worn out by fatigue, when no gastric symptoms are felt. The tongue is sometimes found to be coated brownish-yellow like mustard, associated often with foul breath. Pains and weight at the back of the head and across the eyes, **better while eating,** with feeling of weariness and exhaustion (after *Ferrum phos.*). Nervous headache, with inability for thought, loss of strength, irritability, sleeplessness, or despondency. Headache with weariness, yawning and stretching, prostrate feeling, hysterical headaches. Headache with a weary, empty feeling, "goneness" at the pit of the stomach; also if the headache be the precursor of an attack connected with bilious vomiting. Neuralgic headache, humming in the ears, feeling of inability to remain up, yet better under cheerful excitement. Neuralgic headache with nervous symptoms, better during eating, depression. Noises in head on falling asleep. Menstrual headaches with hunger. Severe pain in left mastoid; worse by motion and in open air.

Kali sulph.—Headache which grows worse in a heated room and in the evening, and is better in cool, open air.

Magnesia phos.—Excruciating headaches with tendency to spasmodic symptoms. Neuralgic or rheumatic headaches, shooting or stinging pains, shifting pain, intermittent or paroxysmal in character. Headaches from optical defects, especially useful in tired, exhausted neurotic patients. Nervous headaches with sparks before the eyes; diplopia. Headache worse in occiput, and **constant while attending school and** after mental labor.

Natrum mur.—Dull, heavy headache, with profusion of tears and drowsiness, sleep not refreshing. Headaches with constipation from torpor and dryness of a portion of the internal mucous membrane, when the tongue is clean or covered with clear, watery mucus, has frothy edges, much saliva. Frontal sinus inflammation. Headache with vomiting of transparent phlegm or water, stringy mucus coughed up. "Is applicable to cachectic persons and to those who have lost animal fluids. It is adapted to chronic and to sick headache; to headaches before, during and after the menses; 'to cephalalgia of school girls who apply themselves too closely to their lessons;' to headache commencing in the morning after waking, lasting till noon, or going off with the sun; to catarrhal headache and to migrane." (King.) Hemicrania, loss of consciousness and twitching of limbs. Von der Goltz believes that this is the remedy for syphilitic headaches and reports cures therewith.

Natrum sulph.—Sick-headache with bilious diarrhœa or vomiting of bile, bitter taste in the mouth. Colicky pain, with giddiness, greenish-gray coated tongue. The attacks occur during the menses, periodically, every spring, and are frequently sudden in their onsets. The characteristics are: congestion of blood to head, with fulness; heat in vertex, sensation of pressure in and through the head; mind depressed and melancholy; vertigo and dulness; vomiting, aggravated by motion and reading, ameliorated by quiet. Occipital head-

16

ache. Violent pains at base of brain, as if crushed in a vise or as if something were gnawing there. Beating pain in both temples when walking. Indescribable pain on top of head, as if it would split. Pulsating headache. Headache begins in the morning on waking, increases till noon and subsides about bed time. Cannot tolerate noise. Has to go to bed in a darkened room. Nausea and vomiting. Several cases of chronic headache with these symptoms are reported by Dr. A. M. Duffield, of Huntsville, Ala., as having been cured by this remedy in the 200th potency.

Silicea.—Headaches with concurrent appearance of small lumps or nodules, size of a pea, on the scalp. Congestive, gastric, nervous and rheumatic headaches. Headaches from excessive mental exertion, from overheating, from nervous exhaustion. Scrofulous diathesis. Rachitic, anæmic conditions, caries. Nervous, irritable persons with dry skin, profuse saliva, diarrhœa, night-sweats. Weakly persons, fine skin, pale face, light complexions, lax muscles. Persons who are oversensitive, imperfectly nourished, not from want of food but from imperfect assimilation.

Natrum phos.—Headache on the crown of the head on awaking in the morning; creamy appearance of back part of the palate; yellow moist tongue. Headache, severe pain as if the skull were too full. Frontal or occipital, with nausea or sour, slimy vomiting. Very severe headache, with intense pressure and heat on top of head as if it would open (if *Ferrum phos.* does not suffice). Sickening headaches, ejection of sour froth. Headache after taking wine or milk.

Calcarea phos.—Headache with a cold feeling in the head, and the head feels cold to the touch (*Ferrum phos.*). Pains worse with heat or cold. Headaches of children and school girls, who are nervous, restless, etc. "Suitable for gastric and rheumatic headaches. It is characterized by vertigo when walking or on motion. Fulness and pressure on the head, worse from pressure of the hat. Useful in peevish and fretful children, and in those whose fontanelles remain open too long. Difficulty in performing mental operations. Ill humor and want of disposition to do anything. Forgetfulness; dulness with every headache." (King.)

Calcarea sulph.—Headache with vertigo and nausea, and feeling as if eyes were sunken. Pain around whole head, worse forehead.

CLINICAL CASES.

Patient who, among other symptoms, had some visual disturbances, and when the headache was worse and vision most disturbed he had a sense of fear, especially at night, and an eruption about the ankles which began with itching. I gave him *Nat. phos.* 6x and that was the end of his sufferings. (Chas. Mohr, M. D.)

A very interesting case came under my treatment. A lady, fifty-five years old, had such excruciating headache that she was partially insane; she claimed her brain was ruptured and running out of her eyes. A yellow-gray curd was exuding from her eyes. She had been suffering for some days. I gave her *Kali phos.* 3x, which acted like a charm. In two hours the dose was repeated, and the result was perfect relief. Some four weeks later she had another attack, but not so bad. I gave her *Kali phos.* 6x, and wishing to watch the case, I called in two hours. She said: "That was not the same medicine you gave me before; the action is barely perceptible." I then gave 3x, and in two hours she was well. Now, I have always been in favor of high potencies, but this experience seems to indicate that *quantity* comes in as a factor; if so, it should be noted that one dose of 3x is equal to one thousand of 6x. (Selected.)

1. Severe headache, general soreness of the vertex, soreness of scalp, cannot bear to have her hair touched, great nervousness at night. *Ferrum phos.* 6x gave speedy relief.

2. Frontal headache, relieved by nosebleed which followed. *Ferrum phos.* 6x cured.

3. Patient could not see; seemed as if blood rushed into the eyes. *Ferrum phos.* 6x cured.

4. Dull pain on top of head during menses cured as by magic by a few doses of *Ferrum phos.* (Raue, *Rev. Hom. Lit.*, 1875.)

5. Headache beginning every night at ten o'clock with chill or congestive symptoms. *Magnesia phos.*, 10x dil., cured. (Translated by S. L.)

Case of young lady with excruciating nervous headache, with great sensitiveness to noise during the second day of menstruation. *Kali phos.*" produced, immediately after taking it, a great increase of the menstrual flow with sudden relief of the headache. (W. P. Wesselhœft, M. D. From Hg.)

M. K., æt 16, has suffered for years from periodically returning headaches. The pain is concentrated in the right temple and of a boring nature, as if a screw were being driven in—as the patient expresses herself. Preceding this pain there is a burning sensation at the pit of the stomach, bitter taste in the mouth and lassitude. These symptoms are only felt at night, or in the morning. When the attack comes on, the patient is quite unable to attend to any ordinary duties. Generally vomiting of bile follows, and then improvement sets in. *Natrum sulph.* daily, the size of a bean, dissolved in water, and taken repeatedly, cured the young lady entirely. (From Schüssler.)

Young lady, æt. 16, suffered for years from periodical attacks of sick headache, characterized by boring pain in right temple, preceded by burning in stomach, bitter taste, languor. Pain comes on at night or in morning, followed by vomiting of bile, with subsequent relief. *Natrum sulph.*[6], daily doses, cured permanently.

HEART, AFFECTIONS OF.

Ferrum phos.—First stage of all inflammatory affections of the heart. Endocarditis, carditis, pericarditis, dilatation of heart or of blood vessels (in alternation with *Calcarea fluor.,* the chief remedy). Palpitation of the heart.

Calcarea phos.—Non-closure of foramen ovale. Palpitation with anxiety, followed by trembling weakness. Weak heart action. Sharp pain around heart during inspiration.

Kali mur.—For that condition of the blood that favors embolus, which acts as a plug. In pericarditis as a second remedy and it may complete the cure. Palpitation from excessive flow of blood to the heart in hypertrophic conditions.

Kali phos.—Functional complaints of the heart, intermittent with palpitation after rheumatic fever with exhaustion. Intermittent action of the heart with morbid nervous sensitiveness, effects of violent emotions, grief or care, weakness of the heart, palpitation from direct excitement, on ascending stairs, with shortness of breath. Palpitation with nervousness, anxiety, melancholia, sleeplessness and restlessness. Fainting from fright and fatigue, from weak action of the heart. Palpitation from slightest mental emotion or walking up stairs.

Kali sulph.—Pulse quick with slow, throbbing, boring pain over crest of ilium, disinclination to speak, pallid face. Heart disease causing dropsy also (*Kali mur.*). Palpitation from effects of heat.

Magnesia phos.—Sudden palpitation, when a purely spasmodic affection.   Shooting, darting pains in region of heart.

Natrum mur.—Palpitation with anæmic conditions, watery blood, dropsical swellings, etc.   Palpitation with anxiety, sadness, etc.   Rapid, intermittent pulse with morning headache. Hydræmia and scurvy.   Fluttering motion of the heart, sense of constriction.

Calcarea fluor.—Dilatation, enlargement of blood vessels; chief remedy to restore contractility to the elastic fibres. Dilatation of the heart with enlargement of the organ.   Weak action of the heart.

HICCOUGH.

Magnesia phos.—Idiopathic or reflex after morphine and other remedies failed.   Hiccough very obstinate, causing long lasting soreness.

Natrum mur.—Hiccough after abuse and in consequence of quinine.

CLINICAL CASES.

Dr. Burnett, in his work on *Natrum mur.,* relates a case of singultus of ten years' standing brought about by abuse of quinine and renewed after every dose, cured permanently by *Natrum mur.*

Obstinate case of singultus in a patient suffering from typhoid fever, almost continued, so violent in character that the patient was sore for three days. Other remedies were tried without effect; prescribed *Magnesia phos.* The result was remarkable: within an hour the difficulty was modified, and the next day he was very much improved and speedily yielded to the continued use of the remedy. (John Fearn, M. D., *California Med. Journal,* August, 1887.)

HIP DISEASE.

Calcarea phos.—In the third stage this remedy may stop the further destruction of bone and the suppuration and promote new organization.

Calcarea sulph.—Discharge of pus, etc.

Ferrum phos.—Pain, throbbing, heat and inflammation of soft parts.

Kali mur.—Second stage, when swelling of abscess has commenced.

Natrum sulph.—Affections of the left hip joint in sycotic patients with hydrogenoid constitutions, worse from dampness.

Silicea.—To prevent or control suppuration and heal the parts. "In the third stage, to limit suppuration and the destruction of bone, and to promote new organizations; stinging, itching, burning pains in small spots, sore pain in the hip-joints, in scrofulous and rachitic children." (Arndt.)

Natrum phos.—Hip disease in scrofulous subjects.

HOARSENESS.

Ferrum phos.—Painful hoarseness of singers or speakers from over-exertion of the voice, from draughts, colds and wet. Hoarseness coming on in the evening.

Kali mur.—Hoarseness, loss of voice from cold. In obstinate cases follow with *Calcarea sulph.*

Kali phos.—Hoarseness with exhausted feeling from over-exertion of the voice, and with nervous depression, or if rheumatic affection.

Kali sulph.—Hoarseness from cold, also from over-exertion of vocal organs.

Silicea.—Hoarseness with irritating cough.

Calcarea sulph.—Obstinate hoarseness.

HYDROCELE.

Calcarea fluor.—Dropsy and induration of the testicles and scrotum.

Calcarea phos.—Hydrocele as intercurrent.

Silicea.—Both recent and chronic forms.

CLINICAL CASES.

Silicea[600] cured two cases of hydrocele, one left-sided in a babe four days old, the other right-sided in a child, æt. 4. (Dr. Guernsey.)

A man suffered from a herpetic eruption, for the cure of which *Silicea* was taken. But at the same time a sacro-hydrocele of large dimensions, which he had carried about for years, was reduced to a minimum.—*American Journal of Homœopathic Materia Medica,* vol. ii, p. 205.

HYDROCEPHALUS.
See also Meningitis.

Calcarea phos.—This is the first remedy to be thought of in this disease. Fontanelles, especially the posterior one, wide open. Chronic hydrocephalus; very large head. Bones of skull thin and friable. Screaming and grasping the head with the hands. Head totters. Eyeballs protruding. Ears and nose cold.

HYSTERIA.

Kali phos.—Hysteria in females, nervous attacks from sudden or intense emotions, or from smothering passion in the highly nervous and excitable; also a feeling as of a ball rising in the throat. Hysterical fits of laughter and crying. Hysterical yawning. Hysterical spasms, with unconsciousness and low muttering delirium.

Natrum mur.—Delaying or decreasing menses. Somnambulism. Great sadness, fears, much mucus in urine. All symptoms relieved as soon as she gets into a perspiration. (Lilienthal.) Hysterical spasms and debility.

CLINICAL CASES.

Miss R., æt. 16, menstruated once when thirteen years old, and not since. Was a remarkably healthy and well-nourished girl, until three months before she consulted me, when she began to decline. She lost flesh, became pale, languid and weak, and suffered much with her stomach. When I was called to see her she was not able to retain her food, and it would be vomited as soon as taken; complained of great pain in the stomach immediately after eating, even the lightest food; on several occasions the pain caused severe hysterical convulsions. The tongue was but slightly coated white; bowels constipated; abdomen tympanitic and very sensitive to the slightest pressure; *no fever,* but much thirst; water, like food, was ejected as soon as swallowed. At first I thought that I had a case of nervous dyspepsia to deal with, but finally concluded I had a case of true hysteria, as she was so extremely nervous and hyperæsthetic all over, and much given to tears when any one was around. I also found that she had the convulsions whenever her plans were thwarted in any way, and upon my threatening to put her in cold water if she had another she stopped them. *Ferrum phos.* 12x relieved the stomach trouble in one week, and *Kali phos.* 12x relieved all of the other symptoms in two weeks or more, and my patient was soon as strong and healthy as before her illness. Menstruation returned two months after, and she has been all right since. (George H. Martin, M. D., S. F.)

Miss B., æt. 50, tall, slender and dark, had been suffering many years from an excessively nervous condition, and would become hysterical upon the slightest provocation. She also suffered much from spasmodic retention of urine, and often had to use the catheter. One day she came to me, saying that the end of the catheter had been broken off while she was using it, and the end was still in the bladder. I dilated the urethra with my fore-finger, and soon recovered it, the bladder at the time being well filled with urine. She would not take an anæsthetic, although I advised it, as the pain was intense. That evening, six hours after the removal of the catheter, she sent for me, saying that she was in great pain and very ill. When I saw her I found her very nervous and suffering much from pain in the bladder and abdomen, with a great desire to urinate. The abdomen was enormously distended and very sensitive. There was no fever. I gave *Belladonna* 3x and returned next morning. Symptoms all worse, but still no fever. At-tempted to drain urine, but could not introduce the soft rubber catheter, as the spasm of the urethra was so great. Two hours later returned with silver catheter; introduced it, but only got a few drops of urine. Thinking there might be some uterine trouble, I determined to examine and find out. As she was so sensitive, I gave her a little *Chloroform*. She had not taken but a few inhalations when the tympanitis disappeared. I examined uterus and bladder, and found nothing abnormal, so concluded she was suffering from hysteria. Gave *Magnesia phos.* 12x, which very shortly relieved bladder symptoms, and *Kali phos.* 12x cured the case in about ten days. She has had no more return of the trouble since, and the other symptoms of hysteria were also much modified. (Geo. H. Martin, M. D., S. F.)

INFLAMMATIONS IN GENERAL.

Ferrum phos.—In the hyperæmic stage, indifferent as to the organ involved and regardless of cause. **Always before exudation has set in.**

Kali mur.—In the second stage, recent cell-proliferation and opaque, white discharge.

Kali sulph.—Riper yellow, fatty, degenerated secretion.

Calcarea sulph.—In the third stage, that of resolution, with purulent, profuse secretion.

Silicea.—Lower form, suits also the lower nerve-irritability. (J. C. Morgan.)

INFLUENZA.
La Grippe.

Natrum sulph.—This is the remedy for influenza, since the disease is caused by an excess of water in the cellular tissues. In the sequelæ of this disease brought on by treat-ment with other remedies *Natrum sulph.* is curative. Numer-ous cases have been reported as cured with this remedy.

Kali phos.—Nervous weakness and prostration following an attack of La Grippe. Tired in the morning, twitching of various muscles and neuralgic pains.

Magnesia phos.—Neuralgias following La Grippe, spasmodic in character, periodical and relieved by warmth.

INTERMITTENT FEVER.

Natrum sulph.—Intermittent fever in all its stages requires this remedy chiefly (3x trit.). Hydrogenoid constitution, worse in damp weather. Tertian form. The applicability of *Natrum sulph.* is shown by the following physiologico-chemical considerations. In ague patients the quantity of water in the blood-corpuscles and in the blood serum is increased, and consequently the amount of oxygen taken up by the blood is diminished. *Natrum sulph.* promotes the removal of excess of water from the organism. When by its action the proportion of water in the corpuscles has been reduced to the normal condition, the corpuscles are again able to take up the full amount of oxygen and distribute it to the tissues. As the tissues are in this way brought back from their pathological to their normal physiological condition, they are enabled to remove from the organism the cause of the ague—be it marsh-gas (miasms), or bacteria (fungi). Dry mountain air, which is rich in oxygen, can cure ague spontaneously, because the organism takes up a large amount of oxygen and disposes of much water by evaporation. Ague patients must abstain from milk diet, buttermilk, eggs, fat and fish. "Intermittent fever, bilious, bloody stools; greenish or bronze colored coating on back of tongue, a very constant symptom; conjunctiva yellow." (Duffield.)

Natrum phos.—Intermittent fever with vomiting of acid, sour masses.

Magnesia phos.—Intermittent fever with cramps in the calves. Chills run up and down the back at 7 P. M., also severe chill at 9 A. M. Great prostration. Ague with violent cramps and blueness of extremities.

Kali mur.—Intermittent fever when the fur at the back of the tongue is of a grayish-white or white appearance. (In alternation with *Natrum sulph.*)

Kali phos.—Intermittent fever with debilitating, profuse perspiration. Quartan form.

Ferrum phos.—Intermittent fever with vomiting of food.

Calcarea phos.—Chronic intermittent fever of children, as an intercurrent remedy.

Natrum mur.—Chill about 10 or 11 o'clock A. M. Great thirst throughout all stages. Violent headache relieved by perspiration. Fever-blisters around lips. If hydroa be present in first onset of the fever, even if not present later, after the abuse of quinine. In nursing children, hydroa on the lips and later the ulcers which succeed them, with forenoon attacks, are guiding. (H. C. Allen.) Masked intermittents appearing as neuralgia of head and face.

Kali sulph.—Intermittent fever with yellow, slimy coated tongue.

CLINICAL CASES.

Mr. L., chills and fever for three months. Had quinine and other remedies. Paroxysms every other day at II A. M., with severe pain in limbs and small of back; chill lasts nearly two hours, with no thirst during chill. Fever all the afternoon, with bursting headache and intense thirst for large quantities of cold water. Little or no perspiration, eats and sleeps well, and next day resumes his occupation. *Natrum mur.* 30 trit., every four hours, during the apyrexia. Next chill light and no return. (H. C. Allen.)

Dr. Sherbino, of Dallas, Texas, reports two cases of ague cured with *Magnesia phos.* 12x. The indications were: Before chill, pain in the neck, stiffness, pain down the spine; during chill, cramps in lower limbs, ameliorated by some one taking hold of the foot or feet and drawing on them or extending them [which will relieve any cramp in extremities.—Eds.]; thirst before and during chill, none during heat, or sweat relieves; cramps and vomiting at same time during chill. (S. J. H.)

KIDNEY, AFFECTIONS OF.

Ferrum phos.—In Bright's disease, when feverishness is present. Inflammatory stage of nephritis; all inflammatory pain is relieved by this remedy. "Urine has a profuse mucous sediment; blood is red and charged with blood corpuscles." (Arndt.)   Congestive attacks in cases of chronic Bright's disease. Here it will do more than *Aconite*. It seems to be hyperæmia rather than active congestion. Uræmic vomiting.

Natrum mur.—Tension and heat in renal region. Brickdust sediment; hæmaturia. Dr. Menninger claims that this drug will produce a decrease in the amount of albumen, and an increase in the amount of urea, and a very marked increase in the quantity of chlorides eliminated. In Bright's disease he recommends it as an adjunct to all recognized modes of treatment.

Kali mur.—Inflammatory diseases of the kidneys, for the swelling. Croupous nephritis. Cardiac asthma with sensation as if the heart and lungs were constricted. Nephritis parenchymatosa with much albumen in urine. Dirty, yellow sediment.

Kali phos.—For the great functional disturbance of nerve-centres, in alternation with *Calcarea phos.* for the albumen. Œdema pulmonum, intermittent action of heart.

Calcarea phos.—Albuminous urine calls for use of this remedy in alternation with *Kali phos.* Bright's disease.

Calcarea sulph.—Zwingenberg cured a case of nephritis scarlatinosa with this remedy.

Kali sulph.—Diseases of the kidneys after scarlet fever, albuminous urine.

Natrum phos.—Gravel in the kidneys.

Natrum sulph.—Aids in the throwing off of gravel by increasing the secretion of urine.

CLINICAL CASES.

I have had two cases of Bright's disease following scarlatina. Tube casts were present. Albumen, general anasarca. Heart weakness. Retinitis albuminurica. There seemed to be extensive destruction of tissue, and as the cases also presented a profuse desquamation, I gave them *Calcarea sulph.* 6x, which speedily brought about a cure. (C. E. Fisher, M. D.)

G. S., an old man of 77, consulted me for what he called a "laziness of his kidneys." Urine was, in fact, very scanty and loaded with albumen. The case seemed, at first sight, to be a hopeless one; he was also forgetful and quite nervous. I gave him *Calcarea phos.* 6x tr., a dose every two hours in alternation with *Kali phos.* After six weeks' treatment, urine was normal, his memory was somewhat restored, and since six months he has not complained. As to diet, I only recommended to him to eat asparagus just as much as he could at his meals, and continue the use of the aforementioned medicines. (E. A. deCailhol, M. D.)

LABOR, PREGNANCY, ETC.

Ferrum phos.—"I am in the habit of giving this remedy after parturition with marked relief of after-pains, and preventive of the fever of lactation." (W. M. Pratt, M. D., *North American Journal Homœopathy,* May, 1883.) Mastitis, first stage. Metritis, first stage. Morning sickness, vomiting of undigested food. Rigid os, with flushed face, restless, anxious and impatient. Morning sickness with vomiting of food.

Kali phos.—Feeble and ineffectual labor-pains, spurious labor-pains. Tedious labor from constitutional weakness; this remedy gives vigor and helps materially. Labor-pains weak and irregular. Rigid os, with thick, doughy lips, patient restless, tearful and nervous. "For three years I have employed *Kali phos.*[4] in doses the size of a bean, dry on the tongue, every ten or fifteen minutes, as a remedy to excite labor-pains. It has never failed me, and I seldom have to give the third dose. My practice is extensive; have had over ninety cases in six years. *Magnesia phos.,* in spasmodic pains and eclampsia, has done well for me. I give generally after birth *Ferrum phos.,* a dose daily, to avoid inflammation." (Dr. Rozas, *Pop. Zeit.,* April, 1887.) After pains usually the best remedy. If given steadily several weeks before labor, confinement is less painful.

Kali mur.—Chief remedy in puerperal fever. Mastitis to control the swelling before matter has formed. Vomiting of white phlegm.

Magnesia phos.—Spasmodic labor pains with cramp in the legs, excessive expulsive efforts. Puerperal convulsions. Rigid os, thin lips. Pains weak and short.

Calcarea phos.—Burning pains, hardness and soreness in mammæ, they feel enlarged. Spoiled milk of mother, salty and bluish, child will not take it. Decline after puerpera, or during pregnancy. Prolapsus in debilitated persons. Especially suited to rheumatic patients. Menstruation during lactation. Soreness in sacro-iliac synchondroses. Weariness in all limbs during pregnancy.

Calcarea sulph.—Mastitis, when matter is discharging after prolonged nursing. *Silicea.*

Calcarea fluor.—After-pains if too weak, contractions feeble. Hard knots in the breast. Hæmorrhages. This remedy strengthens the elastic tissue of the gravid uterus, making parturition easy. (S. J. Hogan, M. D.)

Natrum mur.—Morning sickness, vomiting of frothy, watery phlegm, milk watery and bluish.

Natrum phos.—Morning sickness with vomiting of sour masses. This remedy if given early in mastitis will prevent suppuration.

Natrum sulph.—Lessens the secretion of milk.

Silicea.—Suppuration of mammæ, chronic fistulous openings. Hard lumps in breast. Child refuses milk, or vomits as soon as taken. Nipples crack and ulcerate.

CLINICAL CASES.

"The better acquainted I become with this system the more pleased I am with it. In labor, when the pains are too weak and irregular, I have seen nothing act more promptly and effectually than *Kali phos.* For spasmodic, crampy pains, *Magnesia phos.* is a gem. After a delivery, I give *Ferrum phos.*, where I used to give *Acon.* and *Act. rac.*, to be followed or accompanied by whatever may be indicated. I also use as a wash 3x to the vulva and abdomen, and for syringing the vagina morning and night. The parts heal quickly under this treatment, and with the use of other remedies, as indicated, the patient makes a good recovery."—*Eclectic Medical Journal,* E. H. Holbrook, M. D.

A Portuguese house servant, mother of three healthy children, had not been well from the beginning of her fourth pregnancy. About six weeks before full time she was threatened with a miscarriage. Had passed water and blood; the pains were severer and well directed; the os was dilating, and I felt so positive that labor was unavoidable that I advised her to keep about her duties, and gave her *Kali phosphoricum* 6x to help her along. To my great surprise the pain ceased, and she went on to full term. I then delivered her of a scrawny, undersized child which lived three days. (T. C. Wiggins, M. D.)

LEUCORRHŒA.

See also Women, Diseases of.

Kali mur.—Discharge of milky-white, non-irritating mucus, mild, profuse. Excellent in long-standing cases.

Kali phos.—Leucorrhœa, scalding and acrid, yellowish, blistering, orange colored.

Kali sulph.—Leucorrhœa, discharge of yellow, greenish, slimy or watery secretions.

Natrum mur.—Leucorrhœa, a watery, scalding, irritating discharge, smarting after or between the periods. Greenish, after walking, in the morning, with headache, colic, itching of vulva, and bearing-down pressure. After topical application of nitrate of silver.

Natrum phos.—Leucorrhœa, discharge creamy or honey-colored, or acid and watery, discharges from the uterus sour-smelling, acrid.

Natrum sulph.—Leucorrhœa, acrid, corrosive, inflames part.

Calcarea phos.—Leucorrhœa, as a constitutional tonic and intercurrent with the chief remedy; a discharge of albuminous mucus. Leucorrhœa worse after menses, looks like white of egg, with feeling of weakness in sexual organs, worse after stool and urination. Parts pulsate with voluptuous feelings. Patient takes cold readily.

Silicea.—Leucorrhœa instead of the menses, preceded by colicky pains, also during micturition and following obstinate constipation. Deficiency of animal heat. Especially for over-sensitive, weakly women, whose constitutions are imperfectly nourished owing to deficient or imperfect assimilation.

CLINICAL CASE.

M. M., a young lady, æt. 17, consulted me on account of an obstinate acrid leucorrhœa. I tried the whole series of remedies indicated for such cases. All were without effect, so that I could not but wonder at the patience and perseverance of the patient, whom I saw once a week. In this case Schüssler again helped me out of the dilemma. *Kali mur.* effected a quick and permanent cure. (Dr. S., from Schüssler.)

LIVER, AFFECTIONS OF.

See also Gastric Derangements.

Ferrum phos.—Inflammatory stage of hepatitis.

Kali mur.—Jaundice, if the disease has been caused by a chill resulting in a catarrh of the duodenum; white-coated tongue, stools light-colored, sluggish action of the liver, sometimes pain in the right side, light-yellow color of the evacuations denoting want of bile, accompanied by white or grayish-furred tongue and constipation.

Kali phos.—If nervous system be depressed.

Natrum phos.—In lowest potencies for **sclerosis** of the liver and the hepatic form of diabetes, **especially when there is a succession of boils.**

Natrum sulph.—Irritable liver, bilious attack, too much bile, if after excessive study or mental work (also *Kali phos.*). Vomiting of bitter matter or bile. Jaundice arising from vexation, with bilious, green evacuations or greenish-brown coated tongue, or sallow skin; yellow eyeballs. Congestion of liver, with soreness and sharp, sticking pains. Chief remedy. Bursting pains in the region of the gall bladder compelling patient to bend double; bitter taste and much slime in mouth.

Natrum mur.—Jaundice with drowsiness and any of the symptoms present peculiar to this group of ailments. Pain in region of liver.

Calcarea sulph.—Pain in region of liver, in right side of pelvis, followed by weakness, nausea and pain in stomach.

Kali sulph.—Jaundice from gastric catarrh. Purging.

Silicea.—Abscess of liver. Throbbing and ulcerative pain in hepatic region.

CLINICAL CASE.

Last summer my second daughter returned from a visit to New Jersey with an immense wart on her hand. In a few days she was taken quite ill with fever, which I took to be of a bilious nature; gave *Natrum sulph.* She became deeply jaundiced and grew worse while taking this remedy. I then changed to *Kali mur.* and she began to improve immediately and was well in a few days. After she had taken a few doses of the *Kali mur.* the jaundice began to abate and the wart fell off. (E. H. H.)

MARASMUS.

See Atrophy.

MECHANICAL INJURIES.

Ferrum phos.—This is the first remedy in bruises and in fractures to meet the accompanying injuries to the soft parts. The first remedy in cuts, falls or blows, fresh wounds and sprains. It prevents pain, congestion, swelling or feverishness. Can also be used externally. Strains of ligaments or tendons. Tenalgia crepitans. Dr. Sara J. Allen, of Charlotte, Mich., reports gratifying results in the use of *Ferrum phos.* 6x in injuries prescribed according to the above indications.

Kali mur.—Swelling of contused parts, cuts with swelling, the second remedy in sprains, exuberant granulations, proud flesh. "To remove the ecchymosis remaining after a bruise I have found *Kali mur.* incorporated with cocoa butter efficacious." (E. H. H.)

Calcarea sulph.—Bruises, cuts, wounds, etc., when neglected and suppuration sets in, wound discharges pus.

Calcarea fluor.—Bruises of the bones, shins, etc.

Silicea.—Neglected cases of injuries, festering and threatening suppuration. Wounds when discharging thick, yellow matter; also deep-seated suppuration. This should be given first, then *Calcarea sulph.*

Natrum sulph.—Injuries to the skull and effects therefrom. Mental troubles from a jar or knock on the head. (Kent.)

CLINICAL CASES.

Young man hurled from a truck in the fire department. He struck his head. Following this for five or six months he had fits. Was very irritable, wanted to die. His fits drove him to distraction. Never knew when they were coming on. They were epileptiform in character. Had constant pain in the head; much photophobia. *Natrum sulph.* was given, and the first dose cured him. He has never had any pain about the head since, has had no more mental trouble and no more fits. (Prof. J. T. Kent, *Medical Advance,* Sept., 1886.)

In September, last autumn, I was in the Highlands. The dairymaid of a farmer there spoke to me, saying she had hurt her thumb while sharpening a scythe. The case proved to be this: The whole thumb of the left hand was swollen, and of a bluish-red color, and very painful when touched, much inflamed, and there was a small wound at the extensor side at the joint above the nail. On pressure there was a whitish-yellow discharge, mixed with white shreds. Both phalanges were easily displaced, and a peculiar noise was heard, which I had observed before in similar cases. This fact made me decide on giving *Calcarea fluor.* The medical man in the village, whom the farmer had consulted, said amputation was the only thing that could be done for the case. She took *Calcarea fluor.;* and some time after, the farmer had occasion to see me, when he informed me that the servant's thumb was quite well. (From Schüssler.)

FERRUM PHOS. IN SORENESS AND TENDERNESS.—If biochemistry had only developed this remedy it would have given mankind the greatest blessing in the Materia Medica. I use it more than any other remedy and get good results.

I had used it in a very satisfactory way in the following case:

Mrs. D., aged 42, never had been a strong person, and wanted "tonics" all the time from her former physicians. She took cold very easily and had much soreness in her throat and chest. She had frequent headache, which was worse in the temples. The pain in her head was generally throbbing and beating. Head always sore to the touch. She had more or less pain in her eyes, which were always worse on motion. She said they were tender. Her face was flushed and burning, and her tongue was clean and red. She said she had dyspepsia for years, with a tenderness in her stomach and bowels. Her sexual organs were tender and sore.

Her flesh was always sore and tender. The soreness and tenderness of all the parts called my attention to the remedy. I gave her instructions in a general way in regard to diet, baths and exercise, also full directions about the care of her bowels. *Ferrum phos.* 3x, two tablets every two hours, were given, and her recovery was remarkable. Within four months she had no soreness and tenderness, and could truthfully say she was enjoying better health than she ever expected to do.

I always think of this remedy in cases that have either tenderness, irritation, congestion, fever or inflammation of any part or parts. It can be relied upon in all injuries of the soft tissues, as I have proven to myself many times in my surgical work. (O. A. Palmer, M. D.)

"SILICEA IN NEGLECTED INJURY."—Mr. G., aged 40 years, injured his limb below the knees about eighteen years ago, which caused the limb to become inflamed and suppurate in two or three places. He carried the limb in this condition, being better and worse, until I saw him four months ago, when I commenced to treat him. His symptoms were always worse at night, when he would have pain shooting up and down the leg, especially if the room would get cool. Warm applications would relieve the pain.

The ulcers discharged freely thick yellow pus. He had one or two fistulous abscesses of long standing that were surrounded by a dark bluish border. His general health was very much impaired, and I found him very low just after he had had a severe chill of one hour. He was badly afflicted with chronic dyspepsia and acid eructations, with an occasional attack of heartburn and chilliness. I soon found that *Silicea* was the only remedy that would govern the pain and give comfortable sleep at night, and also improve his general condition. His improvement has been very satisfactory, and it is certainly a great victory for the remedy, as everything in the medicine line had been used without any material benefit. (O. A. Palmer, M. D.)

Miss J———, aged 24, had injured her coccyx by falling astride a boulder while walking in the bed of a dried-up stream. May 22, 1893, she complained of much distress in the occiput and had severe pain in the spine if she became fatigued, which occurred after slight exertion about the house, or after a short walk. An hour of shopping would lay her aside for days. Had to move her head forward, but if it were kept forward she had a sense of faintness. She took nothing but *Kali phosphoricum* 6x till June 16th, when I gave her *Pulsatilla*, because her period was delayed. This being unusual, I looked to see if the remedy might be responsible, and found that it produced a "retention or delay of the monthly flow." I directed that *Kali phosphoricum* should be continued after the period was over, taking two doses daily instead of four as formerly.

There had been a steady and marked improvement during these three weeks. She then went to Chicago and did as prolonged and faithful work at the fair as any of her party who were supposed to be well. After this she was quiet in the country until October, and she returned in very good condition. On resuming her old life the same symptoms returned after a time, and again she came under my care. *Kali phosphoricum* always benefited her, but it was not until after galvanism had been applied directly to the seat of the injury, and she had had rest for another summer, that she found herself quite restored.

I do not cite this case to prove that *Kali phosphoricum* will make sound an injured coccyx; only to show its power to relieve many disturbing symptoms arising from so profound a disturbance to the nervous system. (T. C. Wiggins, M. D.)

MEASLES.

Ferrum phos.—Measles in all stages, especially in the initiatory and prodromic, also for the symptoms of inflammatory affections of the chest, eyes or nose, or ears.

Kali mur.—For the hoarse cough, for all the glandular swellings and the furred tongue, with white or gray deposit, it is the second remedy. For the after-effects of measles. Diarrhœa, whitish or light-colored, loose stools, white tongue. Deafness from swelling in the throat. etc.

Kali sulph.—Suppressed rash, rash suddenly recedes with harsh and dry skin. This remedy will assist the returning of the rash.

Natrum mur.—Measles, if there be an excessive secretion of tears or of saliva, as an intercurrent remedy.

CLINICAL CASES.

Dr. Köck, of Munich, reports: In thirty-five cases of measles which came under my treatment, coryza and bronchial catarrh were very slight in the premonitory stage. Conjunctivitis and intolerance of light along with it were the more prominent symptoms. Within a few days after, the rash appeared, lasting five or six days, and then disappeared. But either during the blush of the rash or the fading of it, painful swelling of one or both glands below the ear set in. The children again became feverish, and were crying and moaning, both day and night. The remedy which I now chose was *Ferrum phos.*, and, according to the violence of the fever, I ordered a spoonful of the solution every hour or two. I gave it at the premonitory stage, and when I saw that it proved very satisfactory, I looked for no other remedy. For the glandular swelling, external redness and painfulness, I used the same medicine, and my cases ended very satisfactorily. (From Schüssler.)

MENINGITIS.

Ferrum phos.—First stage of meningitis, high fever, quick pulse, delirium, etc.

Kali mur.—The second remedy, when effusion takes place.

Calcarea phos.—The chief remedy in hydrocephalus, acute and chronic. Hydrocephaloid conditions, open fontanelles, flat, depressed, etc. Prevents hydrocephalus in families predisposed thereto. Give a powder of the second trituration morning and evening. When already developed, alternate with *Argent. nit.*[6] (Grauvogl.)

Natrum sulph.—Violent head-pains, especially at base of brain and back of neck. Crushing pain, as if base of brain were crushed in a vise, or something gnawing there. After injuries to the head.

·CLINICAL CASE.

Mr. D., from Er., suffered from meningitis, and a prognosis of the attending allopath was designated as at least doubtful, and nothing was prescribed. The case was especially severe, since in his family there was a history of hereditary brain disease, and his nearest male relative had died of it. At the time I was called the patient had been nearly two days in a frightful delirium, that had increased almost to madness. Consciousness had disappeared; temperature over 40°. I ordered *Ferrum phos.* and *Kali phos.*°. After a week I found the patient free from fever, still somewhat weak, but subjectively fully recovered. To hasten the convalescence I gave *Calc. phos.*, and eight days later the patient was able to be out and at his calling. (Dr. Quesse.)

MENTAL STATES.

Ferrum phos.—Consequences of anger. Indifference to ordinary matters, loss of courage and hope, trifles annoy.

Kali phos.—Brain-fag from overwork, with loss of appetite, stupor, depressed spirits, irritability, or great impotence, loss of memory or sleeplessness. Crossness and irritability in children; ill temper often arising from nervous disturbances. Fear, fretfulness in children, crying and screaming. Somnambulism. Very nervous, starts at the slightest sound, talks while asleep, wants to be carried while awake from room to room. Wakes easily. Rambling talk while awake. Despondency about business and pecuniary affairs. Indisposition to mix with people. Low spirits, feeling of faintness. Dread of noise. Oversensitiveness to noise. Dulness, want of energy, timidity. Hallucinations, homesickness. Morbid activity of memory, haunted by visions of the past and longing after them. **Hypochondriasis, melancholy,** ill-humored from nervous exhaustion. Mental illusions (an abnormal condition of the gray nervous matter), false impressions and fancies. Lassitude, depressed state, want of energy. Madness, loss of correct reasoning faculty requires this remedy. Mania in its various stages and degrees. Melancholy accompanying exhausting drains affecting the nerve-centres of the spinal cord. **Loss of memory.** Melancholia from overstrain of the mind. In **paresis** it will brighten and stay for a time the incurable disease. Night terrors in children; they awake screaming and in fright. Restlessness and irritability. Too keen sensitiveness. Sighing and depression, with inclination to look at the dark side of everything. Sighing and moaning in sleep. Shyness, excessive blushing from emotional sensitiveness, lack of controlling force c ˙ the nerves of the coats of the vessels. Starts on being tʊ ˌed, or at sudden noises;

whining disposition, makes "mountains out of mole-hills." After effects of grief. It is an invaluable remedy in the convalescing stages of all forms of mental disease.

"When insanity is caused from masturbation, and the patient is not idiotic in his actions, but is restless and morose and at times quarrelsome, even though it be very aggravated but not of too long standing, it yields more readily to *Kali phos.* than any other remedy we have used." (W. E. Taylor, Supt. Western Asylum for the Insane.)

Natrum sulph.—Suicidal tendency, must exercise great restraint. **Mental troubles arising from falls and injuries to head.** Music unbearable. Makes him melancholic.

Magnesia phos.—Illusions of senses. Very forgetful. Dulness and inability to think clearly. Indisposed to any mental effort.

Natrum mur.—Great sadness, apprehension for the future, like to dwell on unpleasant occurrences, consolation only makes matters worse. Hypochondriasis, accompanied with dryness and irritable conditions of mucous membranes, and constipation with hard stool. Sadness with palpitation, avoids company, being too easily vexed.

Natrum phos.—Nervous, irritable, vexed at trifles. Anxious and apprehensive. Imagines that pieces of furniture are persons; that he hears footsteps in the next room.

Silicea.—Imagines he is in two places at the same time. Monomania about pins. Longing for home and relatives, pensive, obstinate, irascible. Prostration and nervous weakness, restlessness and heavy dreams accompany symptoms, which are also aggravated about the time of full moon, in change of weather and during a storm.

Calcarea fluor.—Great depression, with groundless fear of financial ruin. Indecision.

CLINICAL CASES.

IDIOCY—In January, 1891, a lady came to consult me about the mental condition of her youngest boy. Her boy, C. S., was then 26 years old, 5 feet 8 inches tall and although pretty strong physically, appetite good, etc., he was a perfect *idiot*, unable to answer any questions except by yes or no, and even these answers were stupid. His appearance and his manner of acting was that of a child only a few years old. I remarked that all his teeth were decayed, and that one side of his head, the left, was a great deal smaller than the right. He was very nervous in his demeanor, unable to remain quiet on the chair for five minutes, and when these spells of nervousness reached the paroxysm, he generally tore off all his clothing and flung it in every direction about the room, until he was completely naked. However, he seemed to have some fear or respect for his old mother, the only one, indeed, able to handle him. He was not addicted to masturbation, but absolutely nothing seemed to interest him.

From time to time for several years, this boy had been treated by several physicians of the old school, but without any success. This patient was the seventh child of the family; all the others were healthy, as also were the father and mother. I inquired if during the pregnancy of the mother with this child she had been subject to any accident or fright. She answered no; on the contrary, she had always had a quiet and happy life.

I prescribed for this patient: *Magnesia phos., Calcarea phos.*, both in the 3x tr., in 5-grain doses to be taken in alternation every hour during the day, the boy usually sleeping very quietly at night; I recommended that the patient be brought to me every week; of course, I did not promise a cure, but warned the mother to be patient with the poor boy, for the treatment would be a long and tedious one.

After a month of the above treatment, the mother reported that the bad nervous spells of tearing the clothing were stopped; the boy was more quiet, following her all over the house, and seeming to take interest in her household work.

Two months after the beginning of the treatment, his intelligence seemed to develop in some respect; he helped the mother sweeping the rooms and washing the dishes without breaking them, getting interested in many different other things, particularly in looking at images or photos, and pointing correctly that such and such were pictures of his brothers and sisters, etc. After the fourth month of treatment, I advised the mother to let him go with his brothers, who were carpenters, and see whether he could make himself useful for them in their work. So he did; he commenced by helping them in carrying boards and sometimes planing them when necessary; week after week he became more and more interested in their work.

Finally, after eight months' treatment, always under *Magnesia phos.* and *Calcarea phos.*, he was able to do eight hours of common carpenter work for his brothers, and to make $2 a day, without experiencing any dislike, fatigue or laziness. He is still working steady, of course, like a man of poor intellect, but he is no more a burden as before to the great satisfaction of his poor old mother.

The improvement of that idiot has been permanent until now. (Dr. E. A. de Cailhol, Los Angeles, Cal.)

MENTAL DISORDERS.—Lady, 26 years of age, insane but not violent, melancholia due to domestic troubles; weak mind, depressed spirits, cross, fretful, constantly looking on the dark side of life; hallucinations of hearing. Emaciated, sleepless by night, gloomy by day. Great dread, cries much of the time, only takes food by persuasion. Many seemingly indicated remedies were given with no effect; a better history was taken, *Kali phos.* prescribed. In a few short days she became much brighter, played on the piano and sang, and each day improved, both mentally and physically, until she seemed perfectly well and was sent home. (W. E. Taylor, Supt. Western Asylum for Insane.)

Patient, æt. 89, suffering from deep hypochondriasis, melancholia, tediousness of life, fear of death, mistrust, downhearted and morose. After the failure of the ordinary homœopathic remedies he was entirely restored by *Kali phos.*[6].

Another case of religious melancholia, of three weeks' standing, in a woman, was entirely cured by *Kali phos.*[6] in one week. (Dr. Arnberg, *Allg. Hom Zeit.*, 1881.) Detailed description below.

Miss M., the daughter of the late Dr. M., has been suffering since her eighteenth year from occasional attacks of aberration of the mind. But as years passed on, these attacks of insanity became worse and more frequent, until it was deemed advisable by her brother to make arrangements with the doctor of the lunatic asylum in the district to have her removed there. As a last recourse, a friend called to see if new remedies could be of any service in such a hopeless case. Having assured him that *Kali phos.* would do her good, they gave it very steadily, four doses daily for weeks. This was four years ago. The result was most satisfactory. After taking it she never had another attack, and is completely cured; able to superintend home duties, receive callers and make calls, which she had not been able to do for years, on account of feeling so nervous and shy during the intervals of the attacks. Several cases of a similar nature have been treated with equal success—two of these puerperal mania. (M. D. W. From Schussler.)

The following is a case of a lady, æt. 44: "I saw," writes Dr. A., of Arnsberg, on the 7th of February, "a lady suffering from mental derangement. Religious melancholy was at the root, although before this occurrence she had not inclined to religious excitement. She now declared she was lost forever—lamented, cried, wrung her hands and tore her clothes, or pieces of paper which were laid about to prevent her tearing her garments. She did not know those around her, and was unable to sleep. Her eyes had an unconscious stare, and frequently it required two persons to hold her down. Only by holding her nose and by force, a little food or medicine could be put down her throat. I prescribed *Kali phos.*, as her condition, though one of excitement, was originally one of depression, to which *Kali phos.* is suited. Dr. Schüssler says in his book: "A functional disturbance of the molecules of this salt causes in the brain mental depression, showing itself in irritability, terror, weeping, nervousness, etc., as well as softening of the brain." She took *Kali phos.* with excellent results. A former experience gained by this remedy led me to select it.

"On that occasion it was in the case of an old man, æt. 80. He suffered from mental derangement which showed itself in the form of intense hypochondriasis and melancholia. He was tired of life, but had a fear of death. For weeks he had been treated to no purpose with many remedies apparently called for, as *Nux vom., Aurum, Bromide of potassium* in allopathic doses. But he was rapidly cured by the continuous use of *Kali phos.* Even after eight hours from the commencement of the treatment, a certain feeling of calmness was experienced, and that night he had a quiet sleep. I had, therefore, no reason to regret the treatment I selected, as the improvement continued steadily, so that on the 25th of February I discontinued my professional visits.

"I have seen my previous patient frequently, busily engaged in her home with her usual cheerfulness, and she speaks quite calmly of her past illness." (From Schüssler.)

Dr. Alice I. Ross reports a case of mental derangement in a man past fifty. Had not slept for nights. Thought himself friendless and penniless. *Kali phos.* brought about gradual improvement in sleep, appetite, etc., until he fully recovered, a normal, strong and healthy man.—(*Iowa Hom. Journal,* Oct., '13.)

MENSTRUATION.

See also Dysmenorrhœa, and Women, Diseases of.

Ferrum phos.—Pain at the monthly periods with flushed face and quick pulse, with vomiting of undigested food, sometimes acid taste, excessive congestion, blood bright-red. This remedy must be taken as a preventive before the periods if these symptoms are recurrent. Menses every three weeks with pressure in abdomen and small of the back and pain on top of head. Bearing-down sensation and constant dull ovarian pains.

Kali mur.—The monthly periods are too late or suppressed, checked, white tongue, etc. Too early menses, excessive discharge, dark, clotted or tough, black like tar. If periods last too long, too frequent.

Kali phos.—Retention or delay of the monthly flow, with depression of spirits, lassitude and general nervous debility. Menstrual colic or great pain at the times of the periods in pale, lachrymose, irritable, sensitive females, menses too late in some, too scanty in similar conditions, too profuse discharge, deep-red or blackish-red, thin and not coagulating, sometimes with strong odor. Too late and too scanty, irregular, and of offensive odor, with a feeling of weight and fulness in the abdomen, yellow-coated tongue. Menses premature and too profuse in nervous subjects. Dull headache with menses, very tired and sleepy, backaches, intense sexual desire after menses.

Magnesia phos.—The chief remedy in ordinary cases of menstrual colic. Painful menstruation or pain preceding the flow, vaginismus. External parts swollen. Pains severe, intermittent, worse on right side, **relief from heat. Menses too early, flow dark and fibrous, stringy.** Menstrual troubles at the change of life. Flashes of heat with dizziness.

Natrum mur.—Thin discharge, watery or pale; thin watery blood. "In young girls, if the menses do not appear, or when very scanty and at long intervals. Pain in the stomach, nausea, vomiting of food, weakness and faint feeling, desire for sour things, aversion to meat, bread and cooked food. 12th to 30th are the most useful potencies." (Sulzer.) Very gloomy during menstruation, with headache every morning. Menses too profuse and too early, with disturbed sleep, dreams of robbers, etc. Headache and pain in small of back on rising, better by lying on something hard.

Calcarea phos.—Menses too early in young girls, too late in adults. Menstruation during lactation. Insatiable sexual desire before, with great weakness and sinking sensation after menses; patient wants constantly to sit down, hates to get up and move about. Rheumatic pains. After disappointments, cold at every change of weather, with aching pains in the joints. For flabby, shrunken, emaciated patients.

Natrum sulph.—Menses acrid, corrosive, discharge makes thighs sore, preceded by violent, intermittent epistaxis, with colic, pinching in abdomen and burning of the palate, as if raw and sore. Sexual organs inflamed, sore, swollen and covered with vesicles. Menses flow freely while walking.

Silicea.—Menses smell strong, always icy cold during menses with constipation, stools partly recede. Backache with paralytic sensations. Protracted menses during lactation. Menses early but scanty; but rarely profuse.

Calcarea fluor.—Excessive with bearing-down pains, flooding.

Natrum phos.—Menses too early and pale, accompanied by an afternoon headache over eyes, with tendency to sigh, and pain in knees as if cords were shortened, also sore wrists, chilliness and restless sleep.

Kali sulph.—Menses too late and too scanty, with a feeling of weight and fulness in the abdomen, and headache and yellow-coated tongue. Metrorrhagia.

Calcarea sulph.—Menses too late, long-standing, with headache, twitchings and great weakness.

CLINICAL CASES.

Metrorrhagia of six weeks' standing in the case of a fat and robust woman of brown complexion. This person, who was a washerwoman at Grenille, and whom I saw only three or four times at my office, attributed her sickness to her constantly standing in cold water. *Silicea* arrested the hæmorrhage almost immediately, and effected such an improvement in one week that I scarcely knew her again the second week. She did not take any other medicine. (A. Teste.)

Miss S., æt. 22, brunette, short, plump, round body, large, active brain, intellectual, was since puberty troubled every month with dysmenorrhœa, beginning several hours previous, and during the first day of flow, with severe pains in the uterus, back and lower limbs, and these so severe that they seemed unbearable and hysteria seemed threatening. In one of these attacks I was sent for. Found the patient in bed; the feet had been bathed in hot water and hot cloths applied for hours to the lower abdomen; pains no better. I immediately gave her a large dose of *Magnes. phos.* 6x. In less than half an hour the pains lessened; I repeated the dose; in a few moments the patient was easy, the flow began, and went on the usual time. Next month I advised patient to begin the day before period and take three doses, and on the day period was to come on take a dose every two hours. No pains this month. This process was repeated the third month; no more trouble; patient is now well, and no return of pain for over three years. (*Med. Advance,* Dec., 1889.)

DYSMENORRHŒA.—At each menstrual period a membrane, varying in size from one to two inches in length, was discharged. Her symptoms were, after the flow began, severe, sharp, shooting pains low down in the abdomen, > by lying curled up in bed with a hot water-bag on the abdomen. When the severe pains were > a dull aching for a day or two followed, and the next or the following day a membrane passed. With this exception was in very good health. After one of her periods I gave her *Magnesia phos.* c.m. in water, a dose night and morning, for two days. The next menstrual period was nearly free from pain, and the succeeding ones were painless, but the usual membrane was passed. Before this she had always stayed in bed without any relief. Painless menstruation went on for six or eight months, when she got her feet wet just before her menses, and received

Magnes. phos. c.m. It relieved her, and she has had no trouble since. (S. A. Kimball.)

"Married lady, having one child, had every month menorrhagia; twice the flow was so excessive as to cause fears of death. Upon examination found the uterus low down and swollen; the whole vagina filled with indurated uterus; orifice of os tender, red, stretched open about half an inch; inside filled up; outside congested. I began treatment with *Magnes. phos.* 6x, three to four doses a day. No hæmorrhage next month. No pain, and in three months the organ was reduced to its normal size, and dismissed patient cured." (*Med. Advance*, Dec. 1889.)

MORPHINE HABIT.

Natrum phos.—M. J. Luys reports the case of a physician who had been accustomed to take about seven grains of morphine daily. Small doses of *Natrum phosphoricum* were given subcutaneously (with glycerine and water), and as they were gradually increased, the morphine was progressively diminished. In two months the morphine was discontinued entirely, and then the doses were progressively diminished, and finally stopped altogether in two weeks more. There remained no desire for the morphine.

Kali phos.—Young lady, aged 20, intelligent, handsome, moving in the upper circles of society, nevertheless a confirmed *morphine fiend*. Two general practitioners of prominence and a specialist had attempted to cure her but failed utterly, due, as I afterwards learned, to the extreme prostration of the nervous system, amounting to almost total collapse.

I began the treatment with fear and trembling. I followed the mode adopted by our most noted and successful practitioners. But my patient was, apparently, destined to die. I had used one after another all the nerve tonics I could find in any school of medicine. I was defeated and felt thoroughly discouraged.

On my way to the patient's home, after I had resolved to relinquish the treatment, I happened to think of *Kali phos.* I returned to my office, got a supply of it, and started her taking a dose every fifteen minutes. At the same time I stopped all other heart and nerve "tonics." The change was wonderful. I could push the anti-morphine treatment and could sustain the nerve force. The sharp, intense headache, sleeplessness, wild, staring eyes, brown, dry tongue, and that horrible sinking, "all gone" sensation rapidly yielded to the cell-salt, and she made a good recovery. She is now, four years later, a remarkably vigorous, healthy and happy woman, without the least desire for the opiate, and has, as she expressed it, "a perfect terror of morphine."

I ascribe all the credit of the cure to *Kali phos.* (I used the 3x potency), for the other treatment could not have been completed had it not been for the cell-salt. (B. A. Sonders, M. D., Winterset, Ohio.)

MOUTH, DISEASES OF.

Ferrum phos.—Gums sore, red, hot and inflamed. Redness, dryness or heat of the mucous membrane of the mouth.

Kali mur.—Aphthæ, thrush, white ulcers in the mouths of little children or nursing mothers. Canker, ulcers of the mouth. Gumboils, soft swelling before matters form, excoriation of the mouth. Great fœtor from the mouth. The mouth is red and swollen, thick, watery secretions. Gums puffed, white or yellow in color. Gums bleed easily. Mucous patches. Syphilitic ulceration of gums. True gangrene of the mouth.

Kali phos.—Cancrum oris, with mortification of the cheek, with ashy-gray ulcers, fœtid breath. Stomatitis, gums bleed easily when there exists a red line or seam on the edges; water-canker, gangrenous canker. Hydroa, sore crusts and pimples on lips. Gums spongy and receding. Saliva profuse, thick and salty. Inflammation of the tongue when excessive dryness occurs or exhaustion sets in. Edges of tongue red and sore.

Natrum mur.—Thrush with flow of saliva, salivation. Blisters like pearls around mouth. Lips swollen; eruptions on chin. Gumboil with throbbing and boring pains.

Kali sulph.—Dryness and desquamation of the lower lip, it peels off in flakes.

Calcarea phos.—Gums painful and inflamed in teething children. Pale appearance of the gums, sign of anæmia Upper lip swollen and painful.

Calcarea fluor.—Gumboil, hard swellings on the jaws or gums. Indurations. Cold sores at corners of mouth.

Natrum phos.—This remedy has few equals for ulceration of the buccal mucous membrane. "Canker sores" of the lips and cheeks yield to this remedy in the 3x or 6x attenuation where *Borax, Antim., Baptisia, Kali chlor.,* etc., have failed to cure. (*S. J. of H.*)

Calcarea sulph.—Inside of lips sore, raw sores on lips. Gums bleed on brushing teeth.

CLINICAL CASE.

At a meeting of medical men at Schaffhausen, Professor Dr. Rapp said: "In my opinion the greatest merits of Dr. Schüssler's method lie in the introduction of *Kali phos.* and *Magnes. phos.* In ordinary stomatitis, with swelling of the gums, deposit on the teeth and foul breath, *Kali phos.* has given very satisfactory proofs of its value."

MUCOUS MEMBRANES.
See also Catarrhal Affections.

The color and consistency of the secretion must decide the choice of the remedy. **Secretion** albuminous: *Calc. phos.;* causing soreness and chafing: *Natrum mur., Natrum phos.;* clear, transparent: *Natrum mur.;* fibrinous: *Kali mur., Magnes. phos.;* golden-colored: *Natrum phos.;* greenish: *Kali sulph.;* offensive-smelling: *Kali phos.;* purulent: *Calc. sulph., Silicea;* slimy: *Kali sulph.;* yellowish, lumpy: *Calc. fluor.*

MUMPS.

Ferrum phos.—Initiatory stage with the febrile symptoms.

Kali mur.—Swelling of the parotid gland with pain on swallowing. This remedy alone will cure most cases unless there is fever.

Natrum mur.—With much saliva or swelling of the testicles occurring as a metastasis with mumps.

CLINICAL CASES.

I have treated, during the past year, at least a dozen cases of mumps, and I have never had such satisfactory results with other remedies. One case had violent fever, even to delirium, great deal of swelling, pain, etc. The fever was entirely reduced within five or six hours, and the swelling and all the other symptoms were entirely relieved, within three or four days, by the alternate use of *Ferrum phos.* and *Kali mur.* Two cases in one family, with similar conditions, were in a like manner treated with the same results. (S. Powell Burdick, M. D.)

NEURALGIA.

Kali mur.—Lancinating, nightly pains from small of back to feet, worse from warmth of bed. Must rise and sit in chair for relief.

Ferrum phos.—Congestive or inflammatory, from chill or cold, with pain as if a nail were being driven in. Blinding pain, one-sided, in the head, temples, or over eye, or in the jaw-bone. If this does not suffice, give *Calcarea sulph.,* and note the tongue symptoms. Neuralgia accompanied by flushed face, burning or diffused heat, feeling of weight and pressure. Faceache with febrile symptoms. Tic douloureux. Neuralgia along inner orbit and nose. Neuralgia of the mammary glands. Right-sided pain and morning aggravation seem to be special indications.

Kali phos.—Neuralgic pain in any organ, depression, failing of strength, feeling of inability to rise, or to remain up, yet the pain is felt less when standing or walking about. Neuralgia with ill humor, sensitiveness to light and noise, improved or not even felt during pleasant excitement. This remedy is required to tone up the gray nervous substance. Neuralgic pains in the nervous substance threatening paralysis, with a feeling of lameness or numbness. Pains better with gentle motion, worse on rising; pains felt most when quiet or alone. Neuralgic pains and humming in the ears, failure of strength, paroxysms of neuralgic pains with subsequent exhaustion. Neuralgia of the sciatic nerve (see Sciatica). Faceache. Right-sided neuralgias relieved by cold applications. Stitches from upper teeth to ear.

Magnesia phos.—Intercostal neuralgia of a drawing, constrictive kind. Spasms from cold without fever. Neuralgia in the head, pains darting and very intense. Neuralgic pains in any part of the body, when the phenomena of sensation are too acute; pain excruciating or spasmodic, pains in the ends of nerve-fibres. Pains aggravated by mastication or any motion. Pains coming on periodically, being very acute, darting, or shooting along the course of the nerve. Neuralgia from exposure to a strong north wind. Spasmodic pains and affections of almost any kind. Neuralgia every night, well during the day. Typical facial neuralgias. A contra-indication for the use of the remedy is amelioration by cold. **Warm applications relieve, and especially dry warmth.** This remedy is right-sided.

Natrum mur.—Neuralgic nerve-pains recurring at certain times, with flow of saliva or involuntary tears. Darting, shooting along the nerve-fibre with these accompaniments. Orbital neuralgia with lachrymation. Irritation of the fifth pair of nerves, also the facial nerve. Faceache with constipation, worse in the morning, from reading, writing and talking, in school girls.

Natrum phos.—Facial neuralgia, shooting, stitching pains, soreness of right lower jaw.

Natrum sulph.—Attacks of neuralgia from being in damp dwellings, cellars, etc. Tongue thick, yellow, brown coated. Dr. J. T. O'Connor, of New York, reports a cure with this remedy.

Calcarea phos.—Neuralgic pains deep-seated in the bones. Shocks like electric sparks. Neuralgia commencing at night, recurring periodically. Pains worse at night and in bad weather. Tics. Neuralgia ani, worse after stool, long-lasting. Pains with **sensation of crawling, coldness and numbness.**

Calcarea sulph.—This remedy occupies a ground between the very acute pains of *Magnesia phos.* and the paralyzing ones of *Kali phos.* (more in aged persons, if there be a want of regenerative force for the nervous tissue).

Silicea.—Pain mostly in teeth. Lumbo-abdominal neuralgia. Better from wrapping up warmly. Obstinate neuralgia caused by dissipation, hard work and close confinement.

CLINICAL CASES.

Dr. Parenteau in the Société Francaise d'Homœopathie at the last meeting read a paper as follows:

In 1887, in discussing *Ferrum phosphoricum* in this society, Dr. Nimier assured us that this remedy finds an application in supra-orbital neuralgia of the right side with a morning aggravation.

At that time I had a young patient of 15 years, an anæmic girl with imperfect menstruation, who, for three months, caused me despair of curing, owing to the tenacity of her affection, which resisted all remedies prescribed.

I, therefore, resolved to give her *Ferrum phosphoricum* in the 6x potency, and I had the surprise and satisfaction to note that scarcely two days after the administration of the first dose a certain amelioration was produced. Naturally I continued the remedy, and at the end of eight days the amelioration was such that the patient thought herself cured. However, I advised her to continue the treatment for a week longer and then report. She did not come until two months afterward, but the cure was absolute and without relapses.

It is unnecessary to state that whenever I found a supra-orbital neuralgia of the right side, I hastened to give this remedy, but several experiments of this kind having been followed by absolute failure, I was about to believe that my first observation was a simple case of spontaneous cure, when recently I had successively two cases of cure which convinced me that the explanation given by Dr. Nimier was absolutely exact.

In the second case observed, it was not a young girl but a young woman of 27 years, modiste, and who for months had had attacks of right-sided supra-orbital neuralgia with morning aggravations or coinciding with the menstrual periods which were very irregular and with uterine hæmorrhages, etc.

After having vainly tried *Nux vomica*, then *Chamomilla, Belladonna, Colocynth, Ignatia*, etc., I tried *Ferrum phosphoricum.*

As in the first case three days had not passed before the patient returned greatly relieved. I continued the remedy in the 6x dilution for eight days, followed by the 12x and the 18x, and at the end of three weeks the cure was complete without relapse.

The third case was similar to the two others, and I believe that I am able to complete the indications furnished by Dr. Nimier.

As he has said *Ferrum phosphoricum* is useful in supra-orbital neuralgias of the right side with morning aggravation, but it exerts its influence especially on the female sex and notably in young persons. The patients suffer from irregularities in menstruation and often have special uterine troubles with tendency to hæmorrhages. From this condition there almost always results persistent cephalalgias and an anæmia, which may be more or less marked, according to the case.

The following from the pen of Dr. C. C. Huff, of Huron, N. D., from vol. i, of the *Minn. Medical Monthly,* No. 9, illustrates the use of one of these remedies in neuralgia:

"Schüssler describes *Magnesia phos.* as the earthy constituent of muscles and nerves. Dalton says the salts of magnesium have been found to be in larger quantity than those of lime in the muscles. Grant this fact, then, and we have *Magnesia phos.* acting as a nerve remedy, and any disturbance of the system causing a molecular change in the nutritive elements of this salt would produce the characteristic pains of this remedy. They are described as being of a shooting character, like lightning, drawing and tearing, inclined to move from place to place; they, moreover, assume a periodicity of recurrence, not, however, having any regard for regularity. We likewise find these pains in headache, generally frontal, in faceache, neuralgia of the stomach and bowels, of the ovaries and often in the limbs. Stomach-pains frequently radiate from the umbilicus, and are relieved by pressure (resembling in this respect *Coloc., Aloes, Caustic., Nux vom., Iris vers.* and *Sulphur*) and warmth, especially dry heat, best applied by means of an inverted hot plate, lined with flannel. In England the farmers use the remedy with prompt results for flatulent colic in horses. The following is my experience with the remedy, and all my results have been from 12x trituration:

"Case 1. Miss S., æt. 24, dark complexion, nervous temperament, clerk. She had been under treatment for facial neuralgia for two weeks previous, the principal remedy being morphia, without relief. On being called to the case, I found the patient much prostrated, the right side of the face and supra-orbital region somewhat swollen, pains very severe, of a crampy, shooting, darting nature. There was also much tenderness over the affected side. The pains were of an intermittent character, and seemed to affect different parts of the head and face on different days. *Magnesia phos.* cured this case in twelve hours.

"Case 2. Miss B., æt. 22, dark complexion, nervous temperament, slight build, has neuralgia, from exposure to a strong north wind, and was under the so-called 'regular' treatment for three days before I was called, and had taken massive doses of *Bromide of potash* and *Chloral hydrate,* with no relief. I found her in bed, almost frantic with pain, flushed face, eyes injected, with a high degree of photophobia; pain was left-sided and involved the supramaxillary portion of the trigeminus. In character the pain was lancinating, crampy, darting and shooting, frequently extorting cries. *Magnesia phos.* was given and resulted in a speedy recovery.

Case 3. Miss S., æt. 20, brunette, tall and slender, nervo-bilious temperament, occupation topographer. She was taken suddenly with acute pain in right side of the face, the pain involving the supra- and infraorbital region, paroxysmal, of a darting, tearing character. *Magnesia phos.* cured promptly.

"The above cases have been taken from my note-book and are illustrative of the action of this remedy in neuralgia of the fifth nerve and its branches. I have also cured one case of neuralgia of the stomach where the characteristic pains were present. I have relieved colic in young children with the same remedy when *Chamom.*, *Nux vom.* and *Coloc.* had failed."

Case of prosopalgia of several weeks' standing, relieved by warm cotton and aggravated by cold. *Magnesia phos.* 12x cured in three weeks.—*Allg. Hom. Zeit.*, vol. 88, p. 46.

Dr. H. C. Allen reports a case of right facial neuralgia with sharp, quick, spasmodic, lightning-like pains, sensitive to touch, relieved by heat and pressure, accompanied by prostration and night-sweats, cured by *Magnesia phos.*[200] after several other remedies had failed to give permanent relief.

Also, another case cured by the same remedy and potency where the pains were intermittent, darting, lightning-like, suddenly appearing and disappearing, relieved by heat and pressure; at the same time an annoying constipation disappeared.

Prompt curative action of *Magnesia phos.* by Dr. Goullon: "On April 13th a patient wrote me that for nine days she had been in bed without medical help, suffering from a maddening pain. Through catching cold she got a severe trouble in the ear and then a prosopalgia on the left side, affecting the lower maxillary bone, also the frontal, and involving the whole left side of the head, back to the nape of the neck. She went to an apothecary for *Bryon.*, but he advised *Bellad.*, which didn't help. Deep within the ear an abscess developed, which broke two days ago, discharging pus and now water, which is quite irritating, for it has produced an eruption wherever it touched. The ear still pains; the prosopalgia remains as before. The pain is maddening, and there is high fever with sleeplessness; she doesn't sleep at night and only one or two hours in the day. She perspires freely, which is unusual with her. Yesterday she had a severe pain in the right hip, resulting from a bath. I was unable to see the patient, as she, at that time, lived at Leipsic, and yet she needed help at once. What should I give her? *Silicea?* The nightly aggravation would suit this remedy, but the abscess in the ear was gone, yet the facial pain remained. *Spigel?* There were indications for it, as I already knew she had a tendency to heart trouble. She had formerly had pains in the articulation of the hand, in the arm and side, most severe at the heart. She described it as if the heart would be twisted out, with a throbbing as if something were unwound. Perhaps it was a rheumatism, located in the face, but even here *Spigel.* would be called for. Then there is *Arnica,* which has lately been extolled as a specific. Further, I had some reliance on *Stannum,* which had cured for me many neuralgias that even the great nerve remedy, *Quinine,* had left untouched. The *embarrass de richesse* still increased. *Chamom.* ought to be given for the unbearable pain. Again there was *Mercur.* on account of the tendency to sweating, and *Arsenic.* on account of sleeplessness.

"Yet in preference to all these remedies I selected Schussler's *Magnesia phos.*, moistened a powder of milk sugar with the 6th dilution and directed it to be dissolved in half a wineglassful of water, a teaspoonful to be taken every three hours. On April 17th, I had the satisfaction of reading the following lines: "My hearty thanks for your kind and quick assistance. I had immediate relief, and I am happy and thankful. The horrible pain is gone from my face; the scalp is still sensitive, and one place which is certainly connected with the ear still pains. The ear itself pains somewhat and runs yet.' "—*Pop. Zeit. f. Hom.*, XVII, 13 and 14.

Right facial neuralgia, jerking, cutting pain, teeth sensitive worse after going to bed. *Merc.* gave no relief. *Magnesia phos.* in water gave prompt relief, and has acted equally well twice since. This remedy given in another case of left-sided neuralgia did no good. It produced, however, profuse sweat, with dread of uncovering. (W. P. Wesselhœft, M. D. From Hg.)

Chas. M., æt. 47, has for a week or two a severe tearing, gnawing pain in region of right scapula, extending into the right upper arm, and down the forearm into the thumb, with numbness, particularly of the thumb, but without loss of motion or use of arm. The pain comes in paroxysms, and is only relieved by hard rubbing and pounding of the flesh, troublesome as well daytimes as nights. Has taken several remedies, principally *Rhus tox.*, and had electricity each day for a week or more, without benefit. After taking *Calcarea phos.*[6] for a few days, the pain and numbness were much relieved, and being continued, the trouble was cured in about three or four weeks. Any return of it would be at once relieved by this remedy.

A similar case in a young lady, æt. 20, was cured by the same remedy, though she had almost complete paralysis of the hand. (C. T. M.)

Neuralgia. Pain supra-and infraorbital, extending to all the front teeth of right side, intermittent, stabbing, nipping, lightning-like and extremely sensitive to touch, relieved by heat and pressure; coming and going suddenly and attended by prostration and night-sweats. *Magnesia phos.*[200] promptly gave relief.—*Med. Advance,* Dec., 1889.

A lady of healthy appearance suffered since several weeks with faceache, radiating over one-half of the face, lasting five or six hours. Warm wadding relieves. Worse when body gets cold. *Magnesia phos.*[12], every three hours, removed the pain in three days.

Lady, æt. 30, suffered since several weeks with pains in face and teeth, right side, changing locality. Appears every two or three hours and rushes about like lightning. *Magnes. phos.*[12], dose every three hours, relieved in two days.

Lady, æt. 42, with a hectic appearance, catamenia scanty, often omitting. Since two years, boring over the right eye, after a few minutes spreading over the whole right side to the lower jaw, driving out of bed. Stool torpid, little appetite. *Magnesia phos.* overcame all complaints in four days. This remedy regulated the catamenia and all subsequent attacks. (A. Plate, M. D.)

Kali phos.[12] cured a case of neuralgia in the right side of the face, proceeding from hollow teeth, *relieved by cold applications.* *Magnesia phos.* given at first did not relieve probably because there was no relief from warmth. Unlike *Phosphor.* or *Kali,* but similar to *Pulsat.* (W. P. Wessel-hœft, M. D.)

Miss Margaret S. suffered from neuralgia, true nerve-fibre pain, darting through her head along the nerves. She had suffered intermittently for three days. Two doses of *Magnesia phos.* cured her completely. (M. D. W. From Schüssler.)

A severe case of neuralgia in the head. The lady had come sixty miles to attend a musical entertainment, and was compelled to go to bed on account of the pain. After suffering for several hours, I was called, and relieved her completely in an hour with *Magnesia phos.* 6x, a dose every ten minutes. (E. H. H.)

Ada D., a healthy robust child, æt. 8. Her only symptom was a severe pain at the lower part of the sacrum, coming on after stool and lasting the entire day, until she goes to bed, when it ceases. The pain is so severe as to prevent her walking or even standing. *Calcarea phos.* gave immediate relief. (R. T. Cooper, M. D.)

Magnesia phos. relieved a case of ciliary neuralgia involving the left eye extending downwards into neck, with lightning-like pains, relieved by pressure and heat. This case presented a symptom similar to *Mezereum,* namely, sensation as though a stream of cold air were blowing on the eye. (G. P. Hale, M. D.)

Mr. S., a small, undersized man, with dark complexion, dark hair, and very dark eyes; a hard worker, and not very well nourished. Presented himself at the office, complaining of a very agonizing pain in his face, on the right side, seemingly involving the malar bone. While waiting for me he had a severe paroxysm, and the suffering of the man was intense. He described it as boring, like an auger, and after that came pains that he could not describe, except that they were like shocks. *Mag. phos.,* 30x, was given, and he went to work the next day and has not been troubled since.

Miss C., a tall, slender woman, inclined to angularity; brown hair, and somewhat sallow; unmarried, and about 35 years old. She has a severe attack of neuralgia in the inferior maxillary of the right side, this being very common with her. The face is swollen and very hard; sensitive to the touch, and very susceptible to the cold air. The pain is sharp, darting, piercing, and changing from one part to another; can get some relief from hot, dry applications. I gave her *Mag. phos.* 30x, and called to see her next day. The pain was all gone, the swelling very much reduced, and a marked improvement was manifest. The treatment was continued, and the external conditions were all removed. She complained of a tooth that gave her some trouble, saying that it was very loose, and when she pressed down on it there was a throbbing sensation, with a sore feeling. The patient was given *Silicea* cm., and this removed all the remaining trouble, and she has since remained free from all neuralgic attacks.

Mrs. Mc., a slender, delicate looking brunette; very dark hair; married; pregnant four months. While suffering from an attack of influenza she had, as a complication, an attack of right-sided neuralgia, located over the eye, and involving the upper eyelid, which would twitch and quiver when the pain was severe; then lightning-like shocks from the supra-orbital region down into the upper lid very frequent. *Mag. phos.* 30x relieved this case in a very short time. (Chas. C. Huff, M. D.)

Cases Illustrating the Action of Magnesia Phosphorica as an Anodyne in Neuralgias.

CASE 1. (January 21, 1895).—Miss G., aged 48, keeps a boarding-house, has had much worry lately. Been subject to attacks of neuralgic pains in spine, but had none for two years. After a slight attack of influenza, severe pains developed in lumbar region, down right sciatic nerve, and up spine. Tenderness on pressure, with a numb sensation in affected parts. The pains shift their position, are better by rest, worse at night. Sometimes they seize her in paroxysms, obliging her to call out. Patient is much distressed and in great anxiety about the pains; her pulse is weak and vitality depressed. She was kept in bed for ten days, and treated with *Rhus, Actæa racemosa, Bryonia* and *Arsenicum,* but without effect. Then *Magnesia phosphorica* 3x trit. was given, gr. v., night and morning, and at any time if the pains were severe. The pains at once abated, and patient observed that this powder had done her good, and that each dose relieved. She was about again in a few days.

CASE 2.—Mrs. X., aged 58, an apparently healthy, vigorous lady till two years ago, when she suffered whilst abroad from vague neuralgic pains about body, which gradually increased until when I saw her in June last they had become very severe, and had greatly reduced her strength. They were much worse at night, affected various nerve tracts, chiefly below the waist. They shifted about; there was tenderness over the affected parts, and finally she got no sleep at night, but walked about weeping and wringing her hands in despair. There was numbness of the toes, and the condition suggested commencing deep-seated spinal mischief. *Arsenicum, Quinine* and *Phosphorus* helped the general condition. But nothing touched the pains until *Magnesia phosphorica* was given. This gave her several good nights' rest, and continued for a time to lull the pains. The patient has now left Bournemouth, and I hear is getting worse. *Magnesia phosphorica* could not have been expected to cure such a condition, but its effect in temporarily relieving the pain and ensuring sleep was unmistakable, both to the patient and her friends.

CASE 3.—Miss F., aged 36, a sufferer from chronic nephritis, which has much improved under treatment. After some mental upset, severe left-sided facial neuralgia set in, radiating from an upper molar, which had given trouble before, from recurrent inflammation of the root. The pain was better by warmth and pressure on the affected side, worse by talking. *Phosphorus* at first removed the pain, but soon lost its effect. *Magnesia phosphorica* was then given, which greatly relieved. Although the pain recurred occasionally for some days, a few doses of this drug always removed it and no other remedy was required.

CASE 4.—Mrs. W., an old lady of 74, in reduced circumstances. She has been under treatment for slight eczema with constipation and stomach pains. These are better. On September 10th, she complained of frantic neuralgia in upper jaw and face. The pain ran down from infraorbital foramen into upper malleolus, and along right molar bone. It was worse at night, relieved by warmth, worse by least cold. The pain was grasping and tickling; had lasted a week. *Magnesia phosphorica* relieved almost at once, and no other remedy was required.

CASE 5.—Mrs B., aged 50. Progressive optic neuritis, from which she is now quite blind. She has been under treatment for two years, and for a time by various remedies the progress of the disease was arrested, and she could read large print until nine months ago. Since then nothing has availed. There has been frequent supra-orbital neuralgia of the right side. The sight of the left eye had been lost before I saw her. This neuralgia was benefited by *Actæa racemosa,* and when very severe by occasional antipyrin powders. In September last the pain returned with great severity. *Magnesia phosphorica* 3x, 5 grains taken in hot water two or three times a day when the pain was worst, gave immediate relief. A fortnight afterwards she reported the pains had quite left, and this powder had removed far more promptly than anything previously prescribed.

ŒDEMA OF THE LUNGS.

Kali phos.—Œdema pulmonum, spasmodic cough, threatening suffocation, for dyspnœa and livid countenance. Acute œdema, frothy, serous masses brought up in excess.

Natrum mur.—Œdema. Excessive accumulation of watery mucus in the lining of the lungs and bronchi, serous, frothy secretions.

ORCHITIS.

Ferrum phos.—Orchitis after suppression of gonorrhœa.

Kali mur.—Primary remedy if from suppressed gonorrhœa.

Calcarea phos.—May be required later.

Calcarea fluor.—Induration and hardening of testicles.

PARALYSIS.

Calcarea phos.—Coldness, numbness, crawling and weakness in lower extremities. Nervous prostration. Bruised feeling in the back after exhausting diseases and from standing in wet.

Kali phos.—Facial paralysis, loss of stimulating power over some muscles. The mouth is distorted, being drawn over to the unparalyzed side. Creeping paralysis in which the progress of the disease is slow; there is tendency to wasting, with loss of sense of touch, etc. Locomotor paralysis, loss of motor or stimulating power. Paralysis of the vocal cords, loss of voice through relaxed or paralyzed conditions of the laryngeal muscles. Atrophic paralysis, in which the vital powers are reduced and stools have a putrid odor. All varieties of paralysis require this, the chief remedy, such as partial, paraplegia, hemiplegia, facial or ptosis. Paralysis that comes on suddenly. Infantile paralysis.

Magnesia phos.—Languid and exhausted, unable to sit up. Complaints from standing in cold water (*Calcarea*). Paralysis agitans, involuntary shaking and trembling of the hands and limbs, or of the head, an affection of the muscles. Muscular paralysis caused by a disturbed or diseased condition of the different nerve-fibres which convey the motor stimulus to the muscles. Paralysis of white nerve-fibres.

Natrum phos.—Weakness of lower limbs from the knees down. Legs give under her when she walks. (Farrington, *Pennsylvania Homœopathic Medical Society, 1875.*)

Silicea.—Paralysis from tabes dorsalis. Trembling in limbs. Debility. Wandering pains. Paralytic weakness of the joints. Progressive sclerosis of the posterior column.

CLINICAL CASES.

A. G.—— had a love affair, and, in order to kill herself, took poison, which left her with paralyzed hands and feet. I gave her six powders of *Calcarea phos.*, and four weeks later she wrote me that she could go around the room by taking hold of the furniture. She received six more powders, which completed her recovery. (*Monatsblätter.*)

Kali phos. with a few doses of *Calcarea phos.* as intercurrent, cured a case of facial paralysis from working in the water.

PHTHISIS PULMONUM.

Calcarea phos.—Incipient phthisis in anæmic patients, profuse sweat, especially about neck and head. To lessen the emaciation, give also cream, koumiss, small doses of cod-liver oil and carbonaceous food. Chronic coughs of consumptives.

Night-sweats of phthisis with cold extremities. In diarrhœa and chronic forms with but little fever. Hoarseness, involuntary sighing, suffocating attacks. Cough with soreness and dryness of throat, dull aching in chest. Alternating or associated with anal fistulæ.

Calcarea sulph.—Sputa purulent; sanious, mixed with blood. In phthisical coughs with greenish yellow expectoration, rattling cough.

Kali phos.—Shortness of breath on the least motion, putrid sputa.

Kali mur.—Expectoration white and thick.

Natrum sulph.—Hydrogenoid constitution. Phthisis mucosa. Cough with muco-purulent sputa. Lower lobe of left lung affected. All-gone feeling in chest.

Natrum mur.—General malaise after the least exertion, sleepy by day, restless at night. Spasmodic periodical cough with rattling in chest and expectoration of bloody sputa, worse in the evening after lying down, congestion to head with hectic flush, chronic coryza with total loss of taste and smell. Patient always worse near the seashore. Accumulation of transparent mucus in the larynx in the morning. Empty swallowing causes cough.

Silicea.—Profuse discharge of fœtid pus—nightly paroxysms of cough with tickling in suprasternal fossa—tuberculous deposits on skin, showing themselves as lumpy tumors. Emaciation, profuse night-sweats. Terribly offensive foot-sweat. Great constipation; the rectum lacks power to expel stools, and hence it recedes after partial evacuation. Patient is always cold, especially feet. Much prostration and loose, rattling cough, with copious expectoration of thick, yellow-greenish pus. This remedy embraces most of the symptoms that belong to the phthisical dyscrasia, consequently it is a remedy of value for the constitutional condition in congenital or hereditary cases. Dr. Holcombe has used the 6000th potency with wonderful curative power in the last stages of phthisis.

Ferrum phos.—Breathing short, oppressed and hurried, accompanied by heat and feverishness. Hoarseness from over-straining the voice. Cough worse in open air. Hæmoptysis profuse, bright-red, frothy; epistaxis. It is the remedy where, in delicate looking subjects, hæmorrhage is the first symptom. Phthisis florida. "If patients take cold, become prostrated and have a blood-streaked expectoration, this remedy, even in the 300th potency, will quickly quiet the pulmonary congestion." (F.)

"Laryngeal phthisis, arytenoid cartilages pyriform, acute dry tickling cough from laryngeal and tracheal irritation, accompanied by slight or even severe bronchial or laryngeal hæmorrhages." (Ivins.)

CLINICAL CASES.

Mr. T., æt. 30, of a sanguine, bilious temperament, rather dark complexion, five feet ten inches high, weight in health 166 lbs., family consumptive, two sisters and a brother having already died, leaving a brother still enjoying tolerable health. Had several hæmoptyses in the summer while in the hay field, and had constantly declined from that time. Saw him the April following; he having passed through the hands of several physicians, and at that time was so low that his physician said he could not live six weeks, and such was my opinion on seeing him. There was a *large cavity* in the *right lung* at the second intercostal space at about three inches to the right of the sternum; there were heavy râles in the left bronchi, with decided indications of breaking down of the parenchymatous structure, and cavernous lesions there, also the sputa was very heavy and largely *purulent;* there was the odor of the *cadaver* already present, musty and offensive enough from septicæmic influences; he had no appetite and sat up hardly longer than to have his bed made; skin had a *cold, clammy* feel, and he was drenched with *night sweats.* Case was marked with absence of *vital warmth*; indeed, so forbidding was the case that I refused his brother when he asked me to visit him again in a week; he lived forty miles away. He was given a dose of *Silicea²⁰⁰*, every *other* night with *Sac. lac.,* and ordered to report by mail in a week. He had been very much harassed with his *night sweats* and *cough,* which was worse *from motion.* The first mail brought me the intelligence that the medicine acted like a charm and wanted more of the same kind; I sent so that he got a dose of *Silicea* twice a week, and so treated him till June, when he paid me a visit. Left lung appeared to be cleared up, night sweats no longer troubled him, appetite was good, he was steadily gaining in flesh and strength. Nevertheless, in the right lung there yet remained traces of the vomica, which now was much smaller and secreting only a small amount of muco-purulent matter; he was furnished additional medicine and went home, and by the middle of July was on his mowing machine. Patient was alive for four years after enjoying fine health, and I do not know but he is to-day; no man could be more surprised than myself at these results. Were we all deceived? Three good physicians of the leading school of medicine agreed about the diagnosis, and I don't think there is left a possible ground for doubt. The case is exceptional, we agree; but is it not full of suggestions? (G. N. B., in *Brigham's Phthisis*.)

The same excellent work, on page 193, contains the record of another case of phthisis, where *Kali mur.* was the remedy.

Case of a lady who had been bedridden for nine months. Mrs. McH. was given up by four doctors as beyond medical treatment. The professor's diagnosis ran thus: Both lungs diseased, especially the right lung. The heart is greatly dilated, especially the right cavity. The lung disease produced by neglected cold. When her case was brought under treatment by biochemic measures, four years ago, she was also suffering from dropsy. At the stage she came under the new treatment, it took sometimes an hour and more before she could find the right position to rest in. She would often rather spend the night on the sofa than venture to go through the fatigue of going to bed. Her cough and expectoration were very bad, breath extremely short and palpitation constant. She did not know what it was to have a good night, and rarely slept. By patiently adhering to Dr. Schüssler's remedies she recovered greatly, her lungs are wonderfully healed up, and her dilatation of heart almost removed. She now lives in comparatively fair health, so that she was able to nurse her husband during a severe illness, where night watching was necessary. To reassure all concerned, a diagnosis was made. Dr. H., a specialist, concurred in the statement that her right lung, of which a large portion is gone, is now fairly healed up, and dilatation of heart has almost entirely disappeared. (From Schüssler.)

Dr. Snader emphasizes the importance of *Silicea* in night sweats. Of sixty-two cases treated, in forty-three the perspiration was stopped, and in thirteen it was lessened. The potencies used were from the 3d to 30th, and Dr. Snader thinks that the higher potencies, as a rule, act best.

PLEURISY.

Ferrum phos.—For the fever, pain, stitch in the side, catch in the breath and short cough. Breathing short, oppressed and hurried.

Kali mur.—The second remedy, when there is plastic exudation. It will complete the cure.

Natrum mur.—When serous exudation has taken place during and after its course.

Calcarea sulph.—Empyema, pus forming in the cavity of

the pleuræ or in the lungs. Dr. O. S. Haines thinks the remedy is especially useful in empyema after thoracentesis, and reports a cure of a case. (*Hahn. Mo.*, 1901.)

Calcarea phos.—Chronic pleurisy, a sore pain, a "hurt with every breath," cough worse at night, little or no fever, pains not sharp. Worse sudden changes of weather.

CLINICAL CASES.

Boy, æt. 5, with right-sided pleuritic stitch, worse when coughing and on deep inspiration. Rheumatic pains in right shoulder joint. General heat of the body, very little thirst. *Bryon.* did no good. *Ferrum phos.*[12], every two hours, relieved entirely on the second day. I noticed an unnatural excitement about the child the day after having taken *Ferr. phos.* He desired to get out of bed and wished to run about, but was too weak and fell over, very talkative and hilarious.

A similar excitement I noticed in a lad æt. 7, to whom I had given *Kali mur.* during a gastric fever with great benefit. (W. P. Wesselhœft, M. D. From Hg.)

Miss G. R., æt. 20. Was called about midnight to see this young lady, who was said to be suffering from a pain in her side. I found her to be suffering from the symptoms common to an acute attack of pleurisy, high fever and severe pain in the left side of the chest. Gave her *Bryon.*[3] in water. Called next morning, found the fever somewhat less, but pain not relieved; continued the *Bryon.*[3] Called at four P. M.; about the same, pain still severe; gave *Ferrum phos.* in solution; called nine P. M.; the fever had abated, and the pain was much less. Called the next morning; no fever and pain nearly gone. She continued to improve, and after a few days was up and about as usual. (C. T. M.)

PNEUMONIA.

Ferrum phos.—Inflammation of the lungs: it is the first and chief remedy. High fever, breathing short, oppressed and hurried. The patient is listless and apathetic, sometimes drowsy. It should be given in the first stage until free perspiration is established and health is restored. It is of no use after exudation has set in, nor in sthenic cases. It is especially useful in pneumonias of the aged. Pneumonia, congestive stage. Expectoration is clear blood. This is considered by Dr. J. C. Guernsey a very dependable symptom. Secondary congestion following pneumonia. The well lung suddenly becomes congested. Spots of local congestion and hepatization appear particularly in the upper lobes. No special restlessness nor pain on motion. It stands midway between *Aconite* and *Gelsemium.* It is especially useful in children. Crepitant rales. Sputa rust-colored. "This remedy and *Veratrum viride* give me better success in the treatment of pneumonia than any remedies I have ever tried." (G. W. Lawrence, M. D.)

Kali mur.—Fibrinous exudation into the lung substance. The tongue is generally white-coated. The mucus is white and viscid. In the second stage with catarrhal affections affecting the nose, throat and ears, as complications of pneumonia. Heart complications and dropsy indicate the remedy further, the dropsy yields, the cough becomes looser and the consolidation passes off.

Magnesia phos.—Spasmodic cough coming in paroxysms without expectoration. Constriction of the chest. Cough worse at night, worse lying down.

Natrum mur.—Inflammation of the lungs, if there be much loose, rattling phlegm, clear, serous and frothy in character and coughed up with difficulty, worse in the morning. Cough with beating headache, involuntary urination and lachrymation. Pneumonias of alcoholics. While the tongue is usually clean it may be dry and shiny.

Natrum phos.—Bilious symptoms in pneumonia. Thick, ropy, green pus-like expectoration. Soreness of chest, better by pressure. Patient holds on to chest while coughing. Aggravation of all symptoms in damp weather.

Kali sulph.—Inflammation of the lungs with wheezing, if yellow, loose, rattling phlegm be coughed up, or watery mucus. **Rattling cough,** especially in children. Suffocative feeling, desire for cool air. The temperature rises from evening until midnight, and then falls. Coarse rales, rattling cough, but difficult expectoration.

Kali phos.—Typhoid pneumonia, nerve prostration, sleeplessness. Weakness, shortness of breath, putrid mucous discharge, hoarseness. Cough from irritation in the trachea. Expectoration thick, yellow, salty, fœtid. Spasmodic cough with expectoration of frothy, serous masses, which are profuse and threaten suffocation.

Silicea.—Chronic, neglected pneumonia, passing over into suppuration; dyspnœa when lying on back. Deep-seated pain in lung. Cough loose, rattling. Sputa profuse, greasy, fœtid, thick, yellow or green. May have hectic fever, profuse night sweats and debility.

Calcarea phos.—Especially in pneumonia of children. Cough with yellow expectoration, worse in the morning. Stitches in the chest and soreness worse from cold.

Calcarea sulph.—Third stage with purulent, sanious sputa. Severe cough in children with malaise.

CLINICAL CASES.

Case of pneumonia of left upper lobe, with well-marked crepitation and profuse expectoration of frothy, pink mucus, yellow, watery diarrhœa, green vomiting. *Laches., Lycop.* and *Phosphor.* did nothing. *Ferrum phos.,* every two hours, produced immediate improvement, although we considered her moribund (she had tuberculosis); the diarrhœa and vomiting were unaffected. (W. C. Goodno, M. D. From Hg.)

Dr. A. L. Fisher quickly relieved a child of lobular pneumonia, with high temperature, with *Ferrum phos. Kali sulph.,* given on account of thick, yellowish expectoration, speedily cured the case.—*Hom. Journal of Obstetrics.*

Archibald Herbert, suffering from chronic bronchitis, had an attack of pneumonia. An iron moulder by trade, he was exposed to great heat; he had laid down on a form in a state of perspiration, took a severe chill, and inflammation in the right lung was the result. His case was a bad one, complicated by bronchial affection, fever high, cough distressing, a pain deep-seated in the right side, expectoration tenacious, rusty-colored. *Ferrum phos.,* in alternation with *Kali mur.,* a dose every half hour, was taken for twenty-four hours, then every hour. For his prostration and sleeplessness a few doses of *Kali phos.* were taken now and then. The improvement every way was very marked in two days. As the color of the sputa changed to yellow, he took *Kali sulph.* instead of *Kali mur.*; and as this condition was remedied, *Natrum mur.* and *Calcarea phos.* completed the cure in a little more than ten days. He returned to work, free from inflammation and bronchitis. (From Schüssler.)

A case presented itself with the following conditions: Extensive extravasation, with solidification, great pain, hard and exhaustive cough, with characteristic expectoration, little or no sleep. After being treated for about ten days with the ordinary remedies, *Acon., Bryon., Phosphor.,* etc., without improvement, and as the case was assuming graver proportions than I have had for years, I placed him upon *Ferrum phos.* and *Kali mur.* in alternation. In twenty-four hours a marked and amazing improvement resulted, which continued to the termination of the disease with rapid convalescence. The case was a grave one, for the reason that he had been laid up three months with a fractured arm, and was in a very reduced condition when the pneumonia appeared. (S. Powell Burdick, M. D.)

PUERPERAL FEVER.

Kali mur.—This remedy alone may suffice for this disease, or, in alternation with *Ferrum phos.*, for the exudation.

Kali phos.—Puerperal mania or fever, when illusions, absurd notions, or violent madness set in. Specific remedy.

Natrum mur.—A useful intercurrent remedy in puerperal convulsions.

CLINICAL CASE.

Case of puerperal fever. Chill, followed by fever. Suppression of the lochia, milk and urine. Hilarious delirium, profuse critical diaphoresis without thirst or much coated tongue, bowels confined and extensive tympanites over abdominal parieties. *Ferrum phos.*[6] hourly a dose. In ten hours all uræmiform symptoms had subsided; patient cheerful and comfortable. Lochia and milk secretion returned, and urine had been voided freely. A good recovery followed. (F. A. Rockwith, M. D., *American Journal Homœopathic Materia Medica*, 1875.)

REYNAUD'S DISEASE.

Ferrum phos.—Dr. H. V. Halbert, of Chicago, relates a case in which, though, at first, amputation of the fingers and toes seemed inevitable, cure set in and progressed under the steady administration of *Ferrum phos.* 6x.

RHEUMATISM.
See also Arthritis.

Ferrum phos.—If this remedy be taken steadily from the onset, it is often the only one required in rheumatic fever. Acute articular rheumatism, which is very painful, is an inflammatory febrile disease in its first stage. Acute rheumatism when any movement sets up the pain or tends to increase it. Articular rheumatism, especially of the shoulder; pains extend to upper part of chest, attacks one joint after another. The first remedy in all acute rheumatic troubles, muscular, acute or subacute. Worse on motion; better by warmth. Soreness in every part of the body, especially the joints, worse on motion. Lumbago, stiff back, etc. Stiff neck from cold. "Pains especially severe at night, preventing sleep. Marked stiffness on first moving after rest." (Arndt.) Aggravation by motion or idea of motion. Hands swollen and painful.

Kali mur.—Second stage of rheumatic fever, when exudation takes place around the joints. This remedy removes swelling by restoring the non-functional cells of the excretory and absorbing structures to normal action. Rheumatic, gouty pains if movement makes them worse and if there be a white or gray-furred tongue. Swelling of the parts. Pains which are only felt during motion or increased by it, if *Ferrum phos.* does not remove them altogether. Chronic rheumatism with swelling, or when all movements cause pain. Gray or white-coated tongue, or white discharges.

Kali phos.—Acute and chronic rheumatism with pains disappearing on moving about, severe in the morning after rest, and on first getting up from a sitting position. Very painful rheumatism, the parts feel stiff on first attempting to rise up; improves slowly, but is increased by all exertion or fatigue. Stiffness, paralytic tendency. Laming pains, better on gentle exercise.

Natrum phos.—In a recent note to Dr. Goullon, Schüssler calls attention to *Natrum phos.* as a remedy for inflammatory rheumatism, having successfully used it in several cases with rapid curative results. While *Ferrum phos.* corresponds to simple uncomplicated cases, there can be no doubt *Natrum phos.* corresponds more nearly to such cases as are characterized by **yellow-coated tongue,** acid symptoms, or where there is a scrofulous basis. Rheumatic pains in the joints, with profuse sour-smelling sweat. Acute gout, chronic gout, chronic articular rheumatism. *Natrum phos.* acts upon the uric acid of the cells and renders it harmless. "Great stiffness and cracking of joints. Aggravated towards evening." (J. W. Ward, M. D.)

Kali sulph.—Rheumatic fever when the articular pains are shifting, wandering or flitting. Rheumatic headaches. Pains in the joints, chronic or acute, that change about. Acute articular rheumatism of a shifting nature, settling in one part and then in another. Chronic rheumatism of the joints, **pains worse in the evening and in warm air,** better in cool air. Pains in the back, nape or limbs. *"Kali sulph.* I have repeatedly tested in wandering rheumatism, and have had very favorable results." (Dr. Schlegelman.) Rheumatic or neuralgic cases, patients complain of soreness from three A. M. until they get up.

Magnesia phos.—Acute rheumatism of the joints, for the violent pains, as an intercurrent remedy. Excruciating, spasmodic pains during rheumatic fever. "The pains are aggravated by the slightest touch and are improved by warmth and hard pressure." (Puhlmann.)

Natrum mur.—After the second remedy (*Kali mur.*), if the symptoms correspond. Symptoms of tongue, etc. Chronic rheumatism of the joints; joints crack.

Natrum sulph.—Rheumatic pains, pains and stiffness in nape and back, pain in joints, especially of toes and fingers and wrists, pain in hip joints **aggravated when rising from a seat or moving in bed.** (Perkins.)

Calcarea phos.—Rheumatism, which is worse at night, aggravated by heat or cold, worse in bad weather (also *Ferrum phos.*), worse from change of weather. **Rheumatism of the joints with cold or numb feeling,** creeping feeling in parts affected. Sensation of ants crawling on the affected parts. Numbness, lameness. **Every cold brings on rheumatic pains in the joints.** Pains in sutures. Stiffness of neck from exposure to dampness; aching and soreness in limbs. Pains in sacro-iliac synchondroses, worse with every change of weather.

CLINICAL CASES.

Mrs. R., aged 22 years, had suffered for years with debility and indigestion. She was very much subject to colds and rheumatic pains which wandered and shifted around over the body. She was generally worse in the evening in a warm room, but better in the open cool air. She suffered much with neuralgia of the face, which was intermittent and shifting, but better in cool air.

Tongue generally coated a little yellow. She had a great many skin boils which usually came after a rheumatic spell. *Kali sulph.* was so very satisfactory that she keeps it in the house all the time for use if any of the old symptoms return. (O. A. Palmer, M. D.)

KALI MUR.—This is a great remedy, and all its indications should be mastered. The following case well illustrates its ability:

Mr. M., aged 78 years, had been sick for four or five years, and the most of his suffering was in his digestive organs. He had a poor appetite and a white coat on his tongue, most of the time. Eyes were large and protruding. Could not eat fatty or greasy food without increasing his trouble. He had flatulence and stomachache, with constipation and diarrhœa, alternating every three or four weeks.

He has suffered with chronic rheumatism for years, and many of his joints were more or less swollen, all the time, and worse when moved. He was badly troubled with indigestion, and vomited every few days, which gave him relief for awhile. In his prime he was a strong man, and now he is nothing but a grumbling wreck. After giving him general directions in regard to his foods, baths, etc., I gave him *Kali mur.* 3x, three tablets every two hours, which not only relieved his general catarrhal condition, but relieved him every way, so that within six weeks he could walk around and feel comfortable. He gave me to understand that it was the first medicine that had done him any good. (O. A. Palmer, M. D.)

Dr. Feichtman, of Alsó Lendra, in Hungary, reports fifteen cases of acute articular rheumatism quickly cured by *Ferrum phos.*—*Allg. Hom. Zeit.*

Dr. Schlegelman reports the following cases: L., of Regensburg, a strong, healthy man, æt. 26, had taken cold during a state of perspiration and contracted acute rheumatism of the joints (rheumatic fever). At first the right shoulder was attacked, the patient had violent pains and high fever. *Bryon.,* which seemed decidedly indicated here, had no other effect except that the pain on the next morning had changed its seat, and had appeared in the left knee. In this way he continued for several days, under the use of various medicines. Either the one or the other of several joints was affected. The most distressing pains continued day and night, and evidently the patient was greatly reduced. At last I decided to test Schüssler's medicine. I gave *Kali sulph.* The result was very favorable. The wandering pains ceased changing their location, and the pain confined itself to the right shoulder again, but was far less violent than before. Under the continued use of this medicine, the fever and pains gradually disappeared. Sleep and appetite returned, and no other joints were implicated. Eight days after giving the first dose of *Kali sulph.* the patient was dismissed as convalescent. No relapse occurred. (From Schüssler.)

Dr. Schlegelman writes, January, 1876: "I was attacked with rheumatism the latter part of November, traveling by rail, sitting close to the window of a draughty carriage. My whole right side was affected going, and, on returning, the pains were very severe; especially worse on every movement I made. *Bryon.* eased me temporarily. I only reached home at midnight, and had a very bad night. *Bryon.* was of little use now. I applied the electric current next morning repeatedly, but it was of no avail. I then took a pinch of the *Ferrum phos.,* and, as if by magic, the pains disappeared and did not return." (From Schüssler.)

19

In the year 1875, Dr. Schlegelman reported from Regensburg: "D. A., æt. 20, a delicate lady, who suffered in her childhood a good deal from scrofula, was attacked last winter by a severe pain in the back, in consequence of catching cold. The third to the fifth ribs were very sensitive to pressure. Violent trembling of the right foot, and at the same time of the right arm, set in the moment she attempted to move the arm or extend the hand, and thus made all work impossible. The patient was all the more depressed about this, as in her vocation she had a good deal of writing to do. I gave many remedies, *Pulsat., Rhus tox., Bellad., Nux vom., Platina,* etc., all without effect. I sent the young lady into the country; her condition remained the same. New remedies had no better results. At last I thought I had found her remedy in *Zinc. met.,* as I had heard nothing from her for four weeks. How astonished I was to find my patient, whom I thought cured, entering my consulting room on the 30th of September, trembling worse than ever. On my inquiry why she had not called sooner, she told me somewhat timidly she had gone to Mariabrunn to see a herbalist, and used the cure during the time. The result, as I could plainly see, had not been successful. Consequently she placed herself under my treatment again. I told her I was willing to treat her, and opened Schüssler's Therapy. I chose *Magnesia phos.,* and had no reason to regret my choice, for after the first few doses (three times a day, ten grains) a decided improvement was noticed, of which I heard on the 11th of October, when I saw her again. At this date not even a trace of the trembling could be observed. She had written repeatedly after this, and even then had experienced no trembling whatever. The cure was complete, as up to date she had been doing all kinds of needlework and a great deal of writing, without any recurrence of the affection." (From Schüssler.)

Dr. Brisken was called to a case on the eighth day after seizure. All the joints were swollen, and the patient had not been able to stay in bed a single night. In the morning he received *Kali mur.* with such good results that during the next night he was able to stay in bed, and in twelve days was completely cured. (From Schüssler.)

A gentleman, æt. 70, had acute rheumatism in the shoulder and elbow-joints. He had been cupped, which made it worse. His joints were wrapped in waldwolle (turpentine wool), with no effect. He had not been in bed the last two nights, as on lying down the pains were worse. On the third day he came under Dr. Brisken's treatment. After giving him *Ferrum phos.,* the fever ceased in a few days, after which *Kali mur.* was given. In a short time complete recovery resulted. (From Schüssler.)

Dr. Brisken mentions three cases of rheumatic fever. One case was that of a bookbinder, middle-aged, whom Dr. Brisken had treated three years previously for this malady. On that occasion his recovery took from eight to ten weeks. The patient was again attacked in the joints of the hands and knees, when he received *Ferrum phos.* every hour; and as the fever had abated, *Kali mur.* was given the same way. On the fifth day he was able to return to his work. (From Schüssler.)

Edward B., æt. 12, had been complaining a few days, when pains began in all the principal joints, but mostly in wrists and elbows, attended with redness and swelling, with some fever; there was most pain on moving, and he had to sit quiet to be in any comfort. Gave him *Ferrum phos.*° dissolved in one glass and *Kali mur.*° dissolved in another, to be taken alternately every two hours while fever lasted, then continue *Kali mur.* alone. These remedies soon relieved him, and he was out in a few days. A second attack the next year was cured by the same remedies in a short time. (C. T. M.)

Robert D., æt. 34. This patient lives on the bank of the lake and goes frequently into the water, and often gets wet while fishing and shooting. Has had pains about him for a year or two, at times. They are sometimes in one joint and then in another, seem to shift about, and are becoming very troublesome, hindering him from work, and he desires a remedy if possible. I gave him *Kali sulph.*°, several powders, one to be dissolved in water, a dose four times each day. This remedy, after a few weeks, completely cured his trouble, and he has not complained now since a year or more. (C. T. M.)

May, 1879. J. D., a man æt. 69, had been complaining for several weeks of pains in the limbs, which settled in the right leg, from the hip down to the ankle, but were worse at the joints, being of a shifting nature—intermittent—sometimes shooting and darting like lightning, causing the patient to change his position frequently. Warmth gives him relief. He is unable to leave his bed; is almost in despair, thinking he is dying. *Magnes. phos.*, a dose every three hours. The improvement on taking this remedy was marked and rapid, but whenever he stopped with the medicine he felt worse again. By continuing steadily with *Magnes. phos.* a complete cure was effected. (From Schüssler.)

I was called to attend a girl, æt. 12; she had had, some time ago, an attack of rheumatic fever. I found the little patient, who had been taken ill the previous day, in bed. The joints of both knees were swollen, somewhat red, and very painful. The joints of the vertebræ at the nape of the neck were implicated, and every movement out of the constrained position of the neck and back was very painful. Her friends expected that salicylic acid would be applied, which they had already seen used, but I gave *Ferrum phos.* and *Kali mur.* alternately every three hours. Next day, to the astonishment of the friends, the fever and pains were less, and knees were quite free from pain. Now I ordered *Kali mur.* to be given alone for the swelling, and the next morning on my return I found all the symptoms worse. I repeated the *Ferrum phos.* again, and there was a rapid improvement. But in the same degree as the pains were leaving and the swelling decreased, spasmodic pains in the abdomen set in. There was also an occasional vomiting of bilious matter. As soon as these latter symptoms came on, I ordered the little patient some *Magnes. phos.* dissolved in water, in frequent sips, which removed all these symptoms in twenty-four hours. *Ferrum phos.* and *Kali mur.* were continued in less frequent doses. Six days after my first visit the patient was able to leave the bed, and was quite well. (Dr. Schlegel.)

July 29th, 1879. From the reports of a Medical Congress at Dortmund, by Dr. Stens, Jr.: "I should like to report on a case of rheumatism which was cured by *Ferrum phos.* in a very short time, after having tried several of the most reputed remedies which seemed indicated. A lady, æt. 42 (catamenia normal, though scanty), had been treated by me for the last few years. She suffered from digestive derangement, and sometimes from violent attacks of megrin. This lady awoke one morning with a violent pain in the right upper arm and region of right shoulder, being of a tearing nature. She had walked the previous evening through a damp meadow, getting her feet wet. The pains were worse if she moved her arm quickly, but easier on moving it very gently. She was, therefore, keeping it constantly in motion. The parts affected were painful on being touched. Several nights perspiration had been excessive, and afterward made its appearance every morning between two and three o'clock, when the pains were always worse. The patient also complained of a pain in the right hand and powerlessness, which prevented her from lifting anything heavy. She often felt rather exhausted, and had to lie down. I gave her no less than five remedies which seemed to suggest themselves, but without success. The lady's anæmic condition, and partly Dr. Schüssler's recommendation, made me think of iron. I prescribed his own preparation of *Ferrum phos.*, as much as would cover a sixpence, to be taken night and morning. The result was that, after taking the medicine for six days, the pains, with their accompanying symptoms, did not return, even though soon after this wet weather set in, when she had generally felt her pains to be much worse. (From Schüssler.)

Miss A. W., æt. 10½, was taken with a chill on January 1st, 1884. The next day I found her with very high fever, pulse 120; severe pains in back and limbs; nausea and vomiting; joints, small and large, greatly inflamed; hands, feet and limbs œdematous. Could not bear to be touched or moved. Great sensitiveness in every part of the body and limbs. Pains became very much worse at night, increasing to such an extent that her screams could be heard by the neighbors on each side of the house. Constant cry for cold water; vomiting of food and drink almost as soon as swallowed. Tongue coated yellow, with horrible bitter metallic taste. Great prostration. Hereditary, gouty-rheumatic and dropsical diathesis. Has had for some time back a ravenous appetite, especially for sweet things, which was freely indulged. Treatment. After wasting much of the first week with various remedies with no improvement, I determined to adhere to the system of Schüssler. For the fever, vomiting of food and drink, and the inflammation, I gave *Ferrum phos.* 6x. Pains aggravated at night, *Calcarea phos.* 6x; for rheumatic gout, œdema, dropsy, yellow coated tongue with bitter taste, *Natrum sulph.* 3x, about ten grains in half a goblet of water, a teaspoonful every other hour in alternation with the first two, which were given dry and at the same time. From the commencement of this treatment, decided improvement began, and by the fourteenth day of her sickness she was able to sit up. Previous to her sickness she had become so stout that she could not stoop to button her shoes, and her cloak could scarcely be buttoned around her. Indeed, it was so uncomfortable buttoned that she would go with it open almost all the time. After her recovery she was able to stoop, and her cloak could be lapped several inches.—E. H. Holbrook, M. D., in *Eclectic Medical Journal.*

Dr. Sulzer, of Berlin, reports a case of fever and violent pain in the right shoulder joint, high temperature, full and rapid pulse, thirst and lo.s of appetite. Shoulder red swollen and sensitive to pressure. The pressure of the pillow was unbearable. *Ferrum phos.* 6x cured.—*Allg. Hom. Zeit.*

RICKETS.

Calcarea phos.—In delicate children, caused by soft sponginess of the bone, from want of phosphate of lime molecules. Skull soft and thin, with crackling noise when pressed upon, delayed closure of fontanelles, sallow, earthy complexion, face pimpled, retarded dentition, emaciation, lateral curvature, swollen condyles in both extremities, spina bifida, non-union of broken bones, systematic dyscrasias. Potts' disease, shrunken children, hard lumps on the cranium, diarrhœa during dentition with much flatus, cold tremors, child cannot hold head upright. Its principal indications are the fontanelles which remain wide open, the diarrhœa and the emaciation of the child.

Kali phos.—Atrophy of the bones, with putrid-smelling discharge from the bowels. Indigestion with nervous depression.

Natrum mur.—Particularly useful when the thighs are notably emaciated and the disease is in its early stages, with slight pliability of the bones. (Gilchrist.)

Silicea.—Open fontanelles, head too large and rest of body emaciated, with pale face, abdomen swollen, hot; ankles weak, profuse head sweat and body dry, likes wrapping up warmly, offensive diarrhœa, stools contain undigested food, with great exhaustion, but painless; inflammation, swelling and suppuration of glands and bones, ulceration and necrosis, cellular inflammation, boils. Abscess, etc., with tardy recovery and subsequent induration.

Natrum phos.—This remedy is highly recommended for poorly nourished children who are threatened with rachitis and continually pass clay-colored stools. Dose 10 grains, four times a day. Rachitis with excessive acidity.

CLINICAL CASES.

Dr. Knüppel, of Magdeburg, reports (*Alleg. Hom. Zeit.*, 1882, u 4) cases in which children had formerly been born rachitic, but through the maternal ingestion of *Calcarea phos.*² during last months of pregnancy all subsequent children were born perfectly healthy.

Child, æt. 2 years, with right thigh swollen to three times its natural size from hip-joint to knee, stony hard, having existed for six weeks; yielded promptly to *Calc. fluor.* In this case even touching the limb was followed by the greatest distress, even prolonged crying. (J. W. Ward, M. D.)

SCARLATINA.

Ferrum phos.—Simple cases of scarlet fever. (In alternation with *Kali mur.*)

Kali mur.—Often suffices in mild cases with *Ferrum phos.*, brings rash out and prevents sequelæ. Dr. P. D. Peltier believes this remedy with *Ferrum phos.* excels *Belladonna* in its curative action, and is also as efficacious as a prophylactic. Lymphatic enlargements, etc.

Kali sulph.—Desquamation, skin peels off, it assists desquamation and formation of the new skin, also for the development of the rash. Discharges of foul, offensive ichorous pus from ears, fœtid discharges from all mucous surfaces.

Kali phos.—Post-scarlatinal dropsy.

Natrum mur.—Drowsiness, twitching and vomiting of watery fluids.

Silicea.—Scrofulosis, glands swollen and threaten to suppurate, boils, abscesses, subsequent induration of glands from tardy reconvalescence.

Natrum sulph.—Rash rough and pimply, rising of mucus in the throat.

CLINICAL CASES.

A. S., the child of a post official visiting here, was taken ill with an attack of very slight scarlatina. The rash had disappeared after scarcely twenty-four hours. The throat symptoms, at first threatening to be severe, disappeared in three or four days. On the seventh day almost complete retention of urine set in, as in twenty-four hours only a very small quantity was passed, although the child drank a good deal. The urine contained some albumen, the feet were swollen, the abdomen very much distended. As the child was all this time in high fever, and at night delirious, I advised the parents on my visit on the morning of the eighth day to consult a second physician. Dr. Gerster, who was called in to consult with me, agreed completely with my diagnosis. When I told him that I had not had any results from any of the medicines, such as *Bellad., Canthar.* and *Arsenic.*, we agreed to give *Kali mur.*, every two hours a small powder. In the evening the little one was already better. She had passed a tolerable quantity of urine free from albumen, the pulse steadier, the skin moist. The following night the little girl slept quietly for several hours. In the morning almost free from fever, and could be considered convalescent. We continued the use of *Kali mur.*, and a few days after she was able to return home perfectly well. (From Schüssler.)

Dr. Holbrook reports a case of scarlatina (*Southern Journal of Homœopathy*) treated with *Kali mur.*[200] alone making a good recovery, and, given to the rest of the children in the home, prevented their having it, though with the sick one nearly constantly.

"A few days ago," writes the pastor in W——, "two of my children had the scarlatina, one of them being complicated with diphtheria. The allopathic physician pronounced the latter case hopeless. That which most frightened me was the complete insomnia day and night. The convulsions and typhoid symptoms did not yield to any remedy. I employed several remedies without result. At last, in looking over Schüssler's work, I found that *Natrum mur.* was the remedy indicated. I at once made use of it, but with little confidence. However, the result was striking; after the first dose the child had a peaceful sleep, and slept quietly all night. I continued the remedy, and my child, declared hopeless, was cured in a few days." (*Jour. Pop. de Hom.*)

Several cases of scarlatina this winter did not do well under the usual remedies but were speedily relieved and cured by *Natrum sulph.* The rash instead of being smooth was rough and pimply, and in some cases rising of mucus in the throat. (E. H. H.)

SCIATICA.

Kali phos.—Affection of the sciatic nerve which extends down the back of the thigh to the knee, dragging pain, torpor, stiffness, great restlessness and pain, nervous exhaustion, lack of motor stimulus, moving gently for a time gives relief, neurasthenic type.

Natrum sulph.—Sciatica when symptoms of constitutional gout exist. Pain in hip joint, worse when rising from a seat or moving in bed.

Magnesia phos.—Sciatica with excruciating, spasmodic pains, relieved by heat.

Natrum mur.—Tensive pain in the right hip joint and knee, of a remittent character, **painful contraction of hamstrings,** limb emaciated and painful to touch, pains renewed or increased in a recumbent posture, even in daytime, more toward noon, relieved by heat. Chronic cases after quinine.

Silicea.—Sciatica, chronic cases. Pain worse on motion. Pain in hips. On walking calves feel too short.

Calcarea phos.—Crawling and tingling with the pain. Attacks return in cold weather. Tearing, shooting in hip bone.

CLINICAL CASES.

Mr. B. has been suffering for seven months with sciatica in left leg; the pain was very severe and fast undermining his health; he had been treated by a very skillful physician all this time, and almost every known remedy was tried, until the physician himself gave up the case and said that he could do nothing more. I was called, found patient suffering with a dull, tensive pain, extending the whole length of the sciatic nerve of the left leg, worse on slightest motion; prepared a small powder of *Kali phos.* 6x, in half a glass of water, and gave a teaspoonful every ten minutes for an hour, when the pain was much better; patient then slept until morning. Next night the pain returned; gave same remedy, but with no results. The next night gave *Kali phos.*[12], and very soon the pain was relieved; continued *Kali phos.*[12] every two hours, a small powder dry for a week, and then four times a day for a month; once during that time he had a slight attack, which was soon stopped by putting one of the powders in a half glass of water, and giving a teaspoonful every ten minutes for awhile. A year has passed and there has been no return of the trouble. (G. H. Martin, M. D.)

A lady who had to be brought home from camp-meeting, I found suffering with an intense pain down the sciatic nerve. There were some fever and extreme soreness to the touch or movement. She would cry out with pain from the slightest movement. Tongue was coated greenish-yellow. Gave *Ferrum phos.*[200] and *Natrum sulph.*[200] in water alternately. The next day she could move without much pain, and was able to shift herself from one side of the bed to the other. The third day she was able to sit up, and was soon convalescent. (E. H. H.)

Sciatica cured by *Magnesia phos.* A man who had been washing sheep had sciatica and could not lie down. All the sleep he got was in a chair, and hot applications to the right sciatic nerve alone relieved. *Magnesia phos.* 30x cured him without much trouble. (H. P. Holmes.)

SCROFULA AND TUBERCULOSIS.

[The following is taken from Schüssler's 24th Edition, published in 1897.]

Magnesia phosphorica and **Natrum phosphoricum.**—The possibility of leucocytes undergoing cheesy metamorphosis is due to the fact that they contain albumen and fat. A conglomeration or mass of leucocytes that has not yet undergone cheesy degeneration constitutes scrofula, while tuberculosis is the state after such degeneration. Hence scrofula is the first, tuberculosis the second. Much can be accomplished in almost any stage and in all scrofulous diseases by the use of the phosphates, selected according to their characteristic indications.

In regard to tuberculosis, *Magnesia phosphorica* deserves special attention, and the latest experience endorses it as a remedy for lupus. As long as no cheesy degeneration is present *Natrum phos.* is able to release the imprisoned leucocytes.

A mass of leucocytes undergoing cheesy degeneration furnishes a nutrient soil for bacilli, and hence must be cast off and eliminated as a foreign body by normal cell action. Every healthy cell possesses the property of recognizing and repelling inimical substances. Perfectly healthy cells are not found in the neighborhood of tubercles. Such must be formed through the action of the indicated phosphates, which bring about their new cell formation and also enter into their composition.

Koch's *Tuberculin* cannot effect such results, since it is a substance foreign to the cells and hence is repelled.

The expulsion of a tubercle by means of the normal cell action is the expression of Nature's power of healing. The possibility of such a natural recovery can readily be conceived by any rational man.

NOTE.

[In a former Edition, the 20th, we find the following, which we append as a note to Scrofula and Tuberculosis.]

Tuberculin, from which the tubercular lymph has lately been manufactured, will yet have to undergo many metamorphoses before it is discovered that they who use it are on the wrong track.

"Man dreht sich rechts,
Man dreht sich links,
Doch hängt der Zopf stets hinten."

There are still to be found, here and there, physicians, who, infatuated with the bacteriological fad, seek to cure by means of tuberculin diseased tuberculous conditions.

They point to their successes, but that these rest upon errors, even in the face of their numerous failures, they are unwilling to doubt.

It is not excluded from possibility that bacilli might be found in the sputum of any one suffering from a simple bronchial catarrh, but otherwise perfectly healthy, which had just been inhaled and retained in the thick secretion.

An enthusiastic follower of Koch affected with the bacillus mania will at once upon the discovery of the bacilli in the sputum conclude that tubercles are present in the lung tissue, and, following this erroneous conclusion, will bring at once tuberculin to the field.

After the cure has been accomplished, which is to say, when the catarrh under favorable influence of external conditions has cured itself, the patient, believing himself to have been affected with tuberculosis, willingly pays the expenses of the hunt for the bacilli.

Bacilli which are found on healthy cells will be cast off and eliminated. Bacilli which, as above mentioned, meet on a catarrhal secretion in the air passages will be expectorated with the secretion. Bacilli meeting in a mass of leucocytes, which have undergone cheesy degeneration, adhere and thrive therein, because this mass, being inactive, cannot throw them off. It becomes their breeding place,* and the bacilli act as the *cause* of disease. However, if this nutrient soil, in consequence of rational means, is cut off and eliminated then the bacilli will go the same path, or be left to the same fate as the cheese mites—when consumed.

If the bacilli did not require this mass of cheesy degenerated leucocytes for breeding ground, if they could breed in healthy places, then they would soon undermine the whole organism and tuberculosis, indeed, would not have time to become chronic and the patient would die before both lungs would have been undermined by the bacilli.

It is different with the germs which cause acute infectious diseases, measles, scarlatina, typhus, small-pox, etc. These germs cannot find a pathological ground whereupon to breed, and they are proportionately quickly cast off and eliminated by healthy cell action.

A wise Daniel may yet prepare a remedy from measles or scarlet fever germs which will be just as worthless and perhaps as harmful as tuberculin, and the antihydrophobic virus of the French Pasteur, with which not only does he seek to cure hydrophobia, but even epilepsy.†

Tuberculin may, in some cases, effect favorable changes in certain affections of short or long duration, but no cure, and in many cases aggravations are produced, shortening the patient's life.

Recently in the Berlin Medical Society Dr. Henoch reported his experience in the children's ward of the "Charité." He first alluded to the in-

---

*As no one can with certainty say whether such a pathological condition is present or not in his organism, it is wise to avoid conditions which may lead to such conditions.

†Pasteur, who was a celebrated chemist, but no physician, was ignorant of pathology and therapeutics, and reminds one of the tailor of Louis XIV, who one day handed to that monarch a memorial on the condition of domestic economy and internal politics.

It is self evident that one must be well grounded in physiology, physiological and pathological chemistry, pathology and pathological anatomy in order to discover rational methods of cure. Chemistry alone is not sufficient, it has other problems to solve.

competence of statistics and statistical tables, which prove nothing to the practical physician. Here the experience of individuals only can be decisive. Even also the term improvement signifies nothing, since the very meaning of "improvement" is subjective and involuntary. However, it is different with the marked aggravations as he observed them. The 22 sick children of his division which were treated with Koch's lymph with the utmost care and precaution, not a single case of even a doubtful improvement could be traced, but several cases, on the other hand, were made worse in consequence of new complications brought on by its use.

Improvements or apparent improvements can easily be explained. Tuberculin can, like any other experiment, produce an increase of expectoration, and perhaps a quantity of bacilli will be separated from their soil, and naturally a decrease of expectoration follows the so-called secondary action. If such secondary action lasts for some time then the general health of the patient will improve, and with good appetite and proper care he will gain in weight.

The joy caused by such a favorable turn will last until the secondary action is exhausted and new colonies of bacilli settle in the infected soil.

And this will soon occur, because the nutrient soil of the bacilli cannot be eradicated by tuberculin but still remains present.

The endeavor to eradicate the infected soil by means of tuberculin recalls a proverb of the Poet Haller, who says of mankind:

Unselig Mittelding von Engel und von Vieh,
Du prahlst mit der Vernunft, und du gebrauchst sie nie.

SEPTICÆMIA.

Kali phos.—Septic hæmorrhages of putrid blood. Cured a case of blood poisoning of the foot with infiltration, offensive odor.

SKIN, DISEASES OF.

Ferrum phos.—Inflammation of the skin when there exists either fever, heat, pain, throbbing or redness; pimples, heat and congestion of the skin.

Kali mur.—Acne. Pimples on the face with thick white contents, caused by a disturbed action of the follicular glands. They remain indolent, and they are apparently connected with gastric or genital derangement. Often will prevent suppuration.

Eczema. Crusta lactea, scrufy eruptions on the head and face of little children. Dandruff. This is the principal remedy in alternation with *Ferrum phos.*, arising from vaccination with impure lymph. Eczema resulting from deranged uterine functions, characteristic tongue, dry, flourlike scales on the skin. Albuminoid discharge from the skin with white tongue. Vesicular eczema, albuminoid secretions or contents. It will often act magically in very obstinate forms of chronic eczema.

ERUPTIONS. Acne, pustules, pimples, etc., connected with stomach derangements, white tongue accompanied with deranged menstrual periods, sero-fibrinous secretions.

ERYTHEMA. After *Ferrum phos.* if swelling be present and vesicles or bullæ form.

HERPES ZONA. Shingles, vesicles encircling half of the body like a belt. white tongue.

LUPUS. Useful in stubborn cases with gastro-intestinal symptoms.

WARTS. On the hands, also externally.

SYCOSIS. Primary remedy. Early stage pustules, later dry flour-like scales persistent with glandular involvement.

BUNIONS. Chilblains and lupus, principal remedy.

Kali phos.—ECZEMA. If nervous irritation and oversensitiveness accompany it. Greasy scabs with offensive smell; secretions of the skin, irritating, causing soreness of the parts, itching, with a crawling sensation, gentle friction agreeable, excess causes sore, chafed skin, bloody, watery secretions, excessive, offensive perspirations. Itching of scalp; back of head sore as if hair was pulled. Alopecia areata. Carbuncles.

CHILBLAINS. On toes, hands and ears, tingling and itching pain. Recent, not suppurating. Neurotic subjects.

MALIGNANT PUSTULE. Blisters and blebs all over the body, watery contents, skin withered and wrinkled. Neurotic symptoms and pain exaggerated.

Kali sulph.—Dryness of the skin from suppressed skin diseases. Dread of hot drinks.

ECZEMA. Discharge of yellow, effete matter, eczema suddenly suppressed with other symptoms of this drug.

ERUPTIONS. Suddenly receding through a chill or from other causes. Diseased condition of the nails, interrupted growth, skin scales freely on a sticky base. Sores. on the skin, with yellow, watery secretion on limited portion, with peeling off of skin.

PSORIASIS. Several cases of this affection are reported as having been cured with this remedy. Great desquamation of the epidermis is a keynote indication.

DANDRUFF. Yellowish or white scales on the scalp (also as a wash), falling off of hair, lower lip dry and scaly.

"The internal use of *Kali sulph.*, a dose every four hours, has invariably cured every case of tinea capitis. I rely upon this remedy exclusively, using no wash or greasy ointments whatever." (A. P. Davis.) Effects of ivy poisoning. Burning, itching papular eruptions. Nettlerash.

Magnesia phos.—Barber's itch; herpetic eruptions with white scales. Dandruff, pustules and pimples on scalp. Rash like insect bites, worse about knees, ankle and elbows.

Natrum mur.—ERUPTIONS. With clear, watery contents, small vesicles or blisters with colorless, watery contents, forming into thin scabs or crusts which fall off and readily form again. Pustular eruptions on forehead. Skin of hands, especially about nails, dry and cracked.

ECZEMA. White scales, eruptions with watery contents from eating too much salt.

INTERTRIGO. Soreness of the skin in children with watery symptoms, white scales on the scalp. Intertrigo between thighs and scrotum with acrid discharge and excoriation.

PEMPHIGUS. Fluid from blisters and blebs like water.

RUPIA. Blisters, not pustular eruptions.

SYCOSIS. If watery symptoms correspond.

DANDRUFF. White scales on scalp. Falling of hair from lack of nutrition.

WARTS. In palms of hands or scales, large and sensitive.

URTICARIA. About the joints especially.

HERPES ZOSTER. Second remedy, herpetic eruptions occurring through the course of any disease.

Effects of bites of insects (externally), warts in the palms of the hands. Urticaria and miliary eruptions.

Natrum phos.—Soreness, chafing of the skin in children.

Swelling of the sebaceous glands; eruptions from vaccination. Goitre.

ECZEMA. With symptoms of acidity, secretions creamy, honey-colored, golden-yellow scabs. Crusta lactea about ears of little children.

LUPUS both internally and externally.

ERYTHEMA. Rose-rash (with *Ferrum phos.*), sore patches on the skin, yellow, creamy discharge, hives, itching all over the body, like insect bites.

Natrum sulph.—Chafing of the skin in children with bilious symptoms. Chilblains.

ECZEMA. Vesicles, eruptions containing yellowish, watery secretions. Yellow scales.

PEMPHIGUS. Watery vesicles or blebs all over the body. Debilitated subjects.

WHEALS. Containing a yellow watery secretion. Œdema of the skin.

WARTS. It abstracts water from the base of the warts and causes a shrinking of the same. Warts caused by long exposure to dampness.

Silicea.—Itching exanthema, small pustules filled with lymph, dying quickly. Small wounds suppurate profusely. Phagedænic ulcers, carbuncles. Suppurative process in the skin. Acne, burns by day. Pemphigus, zona, rhagades, rose-colored blotches. Erysipelas with suppuration. Boils come in crops. Malignant pustules. Diseases of the finger nails, brittleness, etc.

Calcarea phos.—Chafed skin, excoriation, itching of the skin.

ECZEMA. Eruption of the skin, with yellow-white scabs and vesicles (albuminous, white of egg contents), anæmia, bloodlessness of the skin. A cachectic eczema worse from changes of weather.

FRECKLES. Lessened by this remedy.

HERPES. Itchings acute or chronic, intercurrently.

LUPUS. If partial manifestations of scrofulosis.

PRURIGO. Pruritus, troublesome itching of the skin, often in old people (4x tr.), alternately with *Kali phos.*

ACNE. In young people during puberty who suffer from headaches after mental application.

PERSPIRATION. Too frequent or excessive, especially if about the head, vesicular blisters with albuminous contents, tubercles on the skin.

Calcarea sulph.—Scald-head of children, if there be purulent discharges or yellow purulent crusts, festers, etc. Pimples, if matter forms on their heads, pustules, nodules, suppurating purulent scabs, suppuration of the skin, sores discharging pus or sanious matter. Herpetic eruptions, all over itching of soles.

CHILBLAINS. Discharging pus.

Calcarea fluor.—Chaps, cracks of the skin, also use externally with vaseline, fissures in the palms of the hands, fissures of the anus, horny skin, suppurations with callous, hard edges. Carbuncles. Brittleness of finger nails. Teeth are also likely to be brittle.

ECZEMA. Due to venous hyperæmia, worse in damp weather, better at night. Squamous eczema with thickening and cracking of the skin. Eczema of anus consequent to hæmorrhoids.

PSORIASIS of extremities, which is uncommonly hyperæmic, deep reddish in tint.

CLINICAL CASES.

Eczema in a child, on cheeks, chin and behind ears, skin swollen and inflamed and underneath it indurations. Pustules developed early, cured in one week by *Kali mur.* 6x, every four hours. (D. B. Whittier, M. D.)

Dr. H. Goullon reports in the *Pop. Zeit. für Hom.*, April, 1885, a case of sycosis cured by *Calcarea sulph.*[6]; the case presented the yellow purulent conditions calling for this remedy.

Dr. S. writes: Mrs. S., æt. 24, of Regensburg, who had been suffering for several years from lichen, had used various well known medicines, which had done her no good. I tried various remedies, and at last cured her. A few months ago she came again, and the lichen was worse than ever. My former remedy had no effect and with several others, *Arsen.*, etc., it was no better. I gave her *Calcarea sulph.*, night and morning, in quantities as large as a bean, and in a fortnight the cure was complete. (From Schüssler.)

Case illustrative of the beneficial action of *Calcarea sulph.* in pemphigus foliaceus.—*Allg. Hom. Zeit.*, 1882, p. 42.

Julia C., æt. 3, eruptions all over the face and on the hands, which are kept covered to prevent scratching; has been afflicted eight months and been under the best allopathic treatment without benefit. Gave her at first *Kali mur.*⁶, in solution. This remedy was continued for some time, but without much benefit, if any. Gave her then *Calcarea phos.*⁶, in solution. This remedy produced a change for the better in a week, and it being continued cured the case in two months. The heat of the following summer seemed to produce a relapse, when the same remedy again cured it, and she remains well. (C. T. M.)

Case of skin disease lasting for years, consisting of a recurring eruption of fine red pimples, and, when very severe, the pimples run together, the surface presenting a red swollen appearance, a strong alkaline fluid oozes out copiously; after this exudation the inflammation subsides, and the cuticle comes off in fine scales. Eruption itches and stings intensely, and although formerly relieved by cold water the irritation has become relieved lately by heat. He has also used *Acetic acid,* except on the face, which allayed the itching and redness. He has taken in the last year Fowler's solution of *Arsenic,* but without relief. The attacks are worse in the fall and spring, and the eruption is mostly on the face, arms and chest. Constipation is present. After using *Kali sulph.* a few days, commenced having boils and had a great many, after which the skin was better than it had been for years, bowels also better.

Psoriasis on left leg and elbow, whitish scales, burned and itched little when scratched. *Arsenicum* and *Arsenicum iodatum* were given without effect. *Kali sulph.* 3x, three times a day, cured patient in four months completely. The guiding symptom was great desquamation of the epidermis. (Oscar Hansen, Copenhagen, 1898.)

In another case, a great deal worse, having lasted twenty-five years, the scaly eruption, mostly on arms, relieved by hot water, entirely disappeared, but returned a year after, when the same remedy in repeated doses of the 30th, finally the 200th, brought relief. (C. Hg.)

*Kali mur.*¹³, given for gleet, the discharge having a milky appearance, produced no visible effects upon the flow, but increased very markedly the dandruff on the head, which fell in small white flakes over the coat-collar, accompanied by itching. (W. P. Wesselhœft, M. D. From Hg.)

Lady, blonde, æt. 20, fair skin ordinarily. Consulted the writer for erythema. For two days cheeks were swollen, fiery-red, and burnt like fire, no itching, eruption or roughness. One dose *Ferrum phos.,* m. m. *(Swan).* In thirty minutes the burning fiery redness was gone, and there was no return, the cure being perfect. (Boardman, *London Homœopathic World,* 1883.)

Case which had suffered from effects of ivy poisoning (*Rhus tox.*) for eight months. Was formerly treated by external remedies, but has repeatedly broken out again with small, hard herpetic vesicles, forming into a thin scab, with itching and some moisture. The eruption appears in the left axilla, about the neck and on the backs of both hands. She has a sensation of faintness at stomach and befogged feeling in head, fearing to lose her reason. Very vivid dreams. *Sulphur, Rhus* and *Sepia* had no beneficial effect. Two doses of *Kali sulph.*[12], taken in water morning and evening for four days, cured the case in four weeks. (W. P. Wesselhœft, M. D. From Hg.)

Case presenting the following symptoms: Bald spot as large as a silver dollar on left side of the head. Hair falls out easily when combing, all over the head, also of beard. Came on after gonorrhœa a year ago, and has probably taken much potash. *Lycop., Natrum mur.*, were of no avail during four or five months. After taking *Kali sulph.*[12], every third day a powder for three weeks, the hair ceased falling, and the bald spot is covered with hair. (W. P. Wesselhœft, M. D. From Hg.)

Th., æt. 15, thick crop of papules on forehead, face and both hands, red looking, *itches and burns in daytime only.* The spots on forehead are much worse when he takes off his hat. Not at all annoyed in the evening when warm, or at night. The entire eruption vanished in less than a fortnight under *Silicea*[200]. (R. A. Cooper.)

SLEEP, DISTURBANCES OF.

Magnesia phos.—Sleeplessness after exhaustion or lack of brain nutrition. (J. C. Morgan.) Insomnia from nervousness and emotions.

Ferrum phos.—Insomnia from hyperæmic conditions. A beautiful hypnotic, but those who usually sleep well are kept awake by it. Restless at night, anxious dreams. Drowsiness in the afternoon.

Kali mur.—Startled at the least noise. Somnolence, restless sleep.

Kali phos.—Sleeplessness after worry, excitement, business troubles, and from nervous causes generally. Sleepless from overexertion. Often accompanied by irritability, great despondency and frequent urination. The true remedy restores normal stimulating power in the gray nervous matter, and consequent contraction of the arteries, which diminish the flow of blood to the brain, and natural healthful sleep results. Sometimes a course of this remedy is needed. Somnambulism of children requires a steady course of this remedy. Yawning, stretching and weariness. Constant dreaming of fire, robbers, of falling, of ghosts, etc. Night terrors of children, awakening from sound sleep, screaming with fright. Lascivious dreams. Twitching of muscles on falling asleep.

Natrum phos.—Drowsy feeling, yet not sleepy.

Kali sulph.—Very vivid dreams.

Natrum mur.—Excessive sleep traced to an excess of moisture in the brain substance. Sleepiness, the natural amount of sleep is unrefreshing. Constant and excessive desire to sleep. Drowsiness, saliva dribbles from the mouth. Sleeplessness with great nervous irritability, associated with coldness of legs. Sleep restless and setting in late—frequent starting during sleep.

Natrum sulph.—Drowsiness often the precursor of jaundice, when there exist a grayish or brownish-green coated tongue and other bilious symptoms. Awakened by asthma.

Calcarea fluor.—Vivid dreams, not unpleasant, but with sense of impending danger, death, of new scenes, places, etc.

Calcarea phos.—Drowsiness in old people, with gloomy thoughts, hard to wake in morning, constant stretching and yawning, children cry out at night.

CLINICAL CASES.

KALI PHOS. IN SLEEPLESSNESS.—Mr. S., aged 51 years, had been sick five weeks with what the doctors called typhoid fever. He had been running down for nearly two years. He had lost nearly all of his strength and flesh and could not sleep, even though he had taken all of the old remedies. When I was called he was badly alarmed and very nervous. During his sickness he had had a great deal of headache and depression of spirits. His tongue was coated a dark brown, and his breath was very offensive. He complained of a "gone sensation" in his stomach. The stools were putrid and foul, with considerable flatulence.

His fever did not run high, and varied about two degrees from morning to night. I gave *Kali phos.* for the sleeplessness and nervousness, and *Ferrum phos.* for the fever. The result was he slept well from the first and wanted to know what he took. I experimented some by not giving it every day, and I found that he could not rest without it. It proved to be the remedy for him. (O. A. Palmer, M. D.)

"Mrs. C. says when she has a severe pain in back of neck and head, and so nervous she could not allow any one to talk to her, could not lie still or sleep, one powder of *Kali phos.* would relieve her in a few minutes, and she would sleep as if she had taken morphia, and would feel sleepy for the entire day and night following the dose." Dr. J. C. Nottingham, who prescribed the *Kali phos.*, believes the symptoms were due to sexual excesses.—*Medical Advance.*

A gentleman, who has suffered from great sleeplessness, depression and occasional tendencies to suicidal mania, writes: I do not know how to thank you for the medicine you gave me; it has done me much good. I have taken the *Kali phos.* and occasional doses of *Kali mur.* very faithfully, and will continue to do so, as it keeps me right. (From Schüssler.)

Mrs. W., æt. 60, much sleeplessness with great nervous irritability and coldness of extremities for three months. She cannot keep them warm in any manner, coldness is subjective, but not objective. *Natrum. mur.* 6th trit. promptly cured the insomnia, "soothed her nerves," and cured the other symptoms. (J. C. Burnett, M. D.)

I have treated many cases of that affection with *Magnes. phos.* 3x tr., where I suspected the cause to be of a nervous origin. Generally a good dose of that medicine in two or three tablespoonfuls of water, teaspoonful doses every four or five minutes, overcame the difficulty after half a dozen teaspoonfuls have been taken. (E. A. de Cailhol, M. D.)

SMALLPOX.

Kali mur.—This is the principal remedy; it controls the formation of pustules. Dr. Saunder, of London, asserts that *Kali mur.* is prophylactic of the disease. He has never known a vaccination to "take" when the remedy has been given either directly before or after it in the 3x potency. In epidemics none of his patients get the disease if *Kali mur.* has been administered as a prophylactic.

Ferrum phos.—If the fever be high, alternately with *Kali mur.*

Kali phos.—Putrid conditions, heavy odor, exhaustion and stupor. Adynamic symptoms indicating blood-decomposition.

Calcarea sulph.—Pustules discharging matter.

Natrum mur.—Salivary flow, confluence of pustules and drowsiness.

Kali sulph.—To promote the formation of healthy skin and the falling off of the crusts.

Natrum phos.—When the pustules become purulent.

SORE THROAT.

Ferrum phos.—Throat dry, red, inflamed, with very much pain (very frequent doses), reduces congestion, heat, fever, pain and throbbing in ulcerated sore throat, sore and inflamed palate, acute stage of laryngitis. Burning of the throat with pain. Sore throats of singers and those who use the voice daily. Tendency to evening hoarseness.

Kali mur.—When swelling of the glands or tonsils sets in, give this and *Ferrum phos.* alternately. Throat ulcerated with whitish or grayish patches or spots, and the characteristic white tongue. Syphilitic sore throat; pain on swallowing. Hawks up offensive, cheesy small lumps. Professor Wertheim, of Vienna, recommended this remedy as a wash and gargle in sore mouths and throats. **Granular pharyngitis.** Adenoid elevations; secretion of mucus which is white and tough; also in posterior nares. Patient hawks and snuffs to get it out. In follicular pharyngitis, with tough, tenacious secretion and cough, temporarily relieved by removal, after great effort, of the clinging sputa. There is dryness, difficult and painful swallowing. We have found it more frequently useful than *Kali bichromicum.* (H. C. French, M. D.)

Kali phos.—Gangrenous sore throat. Throat very dry; desire to swallow all the time. Salty mucus raised from throat.

Natrum mur.—Enlargement of the throat. Goitre, if with watery secretions. Inflammation of the mucous lining of the throat, transparent mucus covering the parts, relaxed uvula. Chronic sore throat with feeling of plug or lump, and great dryness of throat. Constriction and stitches in the throat. Follicular pharyngitis, especially in smokers after nitrate of silver treatment.

Natrum phos.—Tonsils coated with a yellow creamy mucus, raw feeling, moist deposit on the tongue mornings, looking yellow. Secretion as of a lump in the throat, worse swallowing liquid.

Calcarea phos.—Clergyman's sore throat, as intercurrent.

Calcarea sulph.—Suppurating sore throat (see Tonsillitis), ulcerated sore throat, yellow matter, last stage.

Magnesia phos.—In chronic pharyngitis with choking on attempting to eat fast.

Natrum sulph.—Sore throat with feeling of lump on swallowing dry. Ulcerated sore throat. Diphtheria with vomiting and welling up of mucus from the stomach. Palate burns during menses.

Calcarea fluor.—Relaxed condition of the uvula, tickling in the larynx. Exciting cough. Hawking of mucus early in morning. Burning in throat better by warmth. Follicular sore throat with plugs of mucus constantly forming on the tonsils.

CLINICAL CASE.

An actor, Mr. E., consulted me for a severe irritation in the throat that interfered much with speech, and on account of an exceedingly bad breath. This was especially disturbing, as he was obliged to appear in a role, three days later, in which proximity with his fellow actors was necessary. From an examination I concluded that it resulted from a deficiency of *Kali phos.*, and so I ordered this remedy. On the evening of the second day Mr. E. informed me that he was fully recovered; of the foul breath there was not a trace to be perceived. He also stated that he was able to notice an improvement even after the second dose. (Dr Quesse.)

SPASMS, CONVULSIONS, ETC.

Ferrum phos.—Convulsions, with fever in teething children.

Kali phos.—Fits from fright, with pallid or livid countenance. Hysterical spasms with unconsciousness and low muttering delirium.

Magnesia phos.—Cramps in any part of the body, legs, throat, larynx, etc. Writer's cramp. Muscular contraction, twitchings and spasms. Convulsions with stiffness of the corners of the mouth. Spasm of the throat on attempting to swallow, spasmodic stammering. Tonic spasms, violent contractions and rigidity of the muscles during longer or shorter intervals. Tetanus, lockjaw (rub it into the gums). Tetanic spasm, like *Bellad.*, where the latter does no good. (J. C. M.)

Calcarea phos.—Convulsions from teething without fever, if *Magnesia phos.* fails. Fits during development in childhood, in youth or in old age, where the lime salts are at fault. In anæmic, pale patients, in the strumous and scrofulous. Cramps and convulsive movements of all kinds if *Magnesia phos.* fails.

CLINICAL CASES.

Spasms with contractions of the fingers, open eyes, during intervals has a spasmodic cough. *Magnesia phos.*, 9x, cured.—Raue's *Record Homœopathic Literature.*

A. R. V. G., a young lady, æt. 18, had visited, along with her mother, in the past summer (1875), a hydropathic establishment. Without being ill, she had used the baths, even during her catamenia. Immediately after this she took violent spasms or cramps, which set in daily and continued after having returned home. A medical man was consulted, as the disease increased in spite of the different medicines she took. A second doctor was consulted who quite agreed in the diagnosis as well as the treatment adopted by his colleague. Injections of morphium very strong and repeated several times daily were the main remedies applied; but the distressing ailment could not be removed; on the contrary, the cramps increased in violence and frequency. The medical men in attendance finally declared that there was no chance of improvement until the patient would take some steel-baths in the spring. The parents were afraid that their daughter would not live to see the spring, and if she did, that she would not be fit to be removed. They, therefore, telegraphed requesting a visit from me. On the 6th of September last I saw the patient for the first time. I had known her formerly and was astonished to see, instead of the blooming healthy girl she had been, a pale, emaciated figure whom I should not have recognized. During my presence she had an attack, her features were distorted, the eyes turned upward, froth came to the mouth, and then a fearful paroxysm of beating and striking with the hands and feet, such as I had never seen before. This was only the commencement. Suddenly the trunk of her body was contorted in an indescribable manner, the back of the head pressed deeply into the pillows, the feet forced against the foot of the bed, her chest and abdomen became arched like a bridge, drawn up almost half a yard. In this unnatural position she was suspended several seconds. Suddenly the whole body jerked upward with a bound, and the poor sufferer was tossed about for some seconds with her spine contracted. During the whole attack, which lasted several minutes, she was quite unconscious; pinching and slapping had no effect, dashing cold water in the face or applying burnt feathers to the nostrils was ineffectual, the pupils were quite insensible to the light. *Ignat.*, which I ordered, had no effect; *Cupr. met.* acted better, but only temporarily; *Bellad., Ipecac.* and *Pulsat.* (the latter for suppressed catamenia) were of no use. The attacks did not increase, neither did they decrease in the least degree. The morphium injections, too, were continued at the desire of her friends. When at my visit on the 4th of October, the spasms came on again with such violence that the bedstead gave way, I consulted Schüssler's Therapy and ordered *Magnes. phos.* After taking this remedy on the 10th of October, the catamenia appeared, but her condition otherwise was in no way changed. The spasms continued with the same violence. Then, remembering Schüssler's injunction to use *Calcarea phos.* where *Magnes. phos.*, though indicated by the symptoms, proves ineffectual, I gave here *Calcarea phos.*, on the 16th of October, a full dose every two hours. Immediately the spasms became less frequent. On the sixth day there was an attack, weak and of short duration. From this date she had peace till the 6th of November, the day of the return of the catamenia, which was preceded by short slight attack. On the 14th of

December I had a call from the young lady, looking well and blooming, was entirely cured of her attacks, and at the beginning of December she had been quite regular, without experiencing any inconvenience. (From Schüssler.)

A very interesting case came under my treatment, which deserves the attention of the profession. I was called to a lady advanced in years. She had been suffering for nearly five weeks from fearful attacks of convulsive spasms. During the last twenty-four hours she had thirty attacks. The spasms darted through her body like an electric shock, so that she fell to the ground. The attack lasted a few minutes, after which she felt well enough, but rather exhausted. The sufferer did not venture to leave her bed now, afraid of being injured. She had been treated by her first doctor with *Flor. zinci.,* Fowler's solution, and friction, but without success. When I saw the lady, I thought of trying Schüssler's functional remedies. Knowing that *Magnes. phos., Kali phos.* and *Calcarea phos.* are prescribed for allaying spasms, I chose the latter, *Calcarea phos.,* under the circumstances. Next day, to the astonishment of those about her, I found the old lady walking about the room. She met me with a smile, exclaiming, "Ah! Doctor, my spasms are cured." And so it was. She had not another attack. (Dr. Frechtmann. From Schüssler.)

Dr. F., of Alsó, Hungary, reports: I was requested to go into the country to see a man who had been suffering the last three days from spasmodic, convulsive sobbing. He was lying in bed. Subcutaneous injections of morphia, friction with chloroform and sinapisms (mustard poultices) were all of no use. Although the sobbing was mitigated for two or three hours, it returned with more violence than ever. I gave him a powder of *Magnes. phos.* in half a tumblerful of water. After the second tablespoonful the sobbing ceased altogether, to the astonishment of all those present. (From Schüssler.)

Frequent reports of writers' cramp cured with *Magnesia phosphorica* have been published since the former edition of this work was issued.

SPERMATORRHŒA.

Natrum phos.—Emissions every night, sexual desire almost gone. Semen thin, watery, smells like stale urine. In the provers it produced seminal emissions every night; at first there seemed to be erethism with lascivious dreams, but later emissions took place, one or two in a night, without any sensation whatever. These were followed by weakness of the back and trembling of the knees, which felt as if they would give way. (Farrington.)

Kali phos.—Nervousness growing out of excessive sexual excitement, whether indulged or suppressed. Impotency and nocturnal or other discharges with these nervous indications.

(Nottingham.) Intense sexual desire. Painful emissions at night. Prostration and weak vision after coitus.

Natrum mur.—Discharge of prostatic juice. Pollutions, followed by chilliness, lassitude and increased sexual desire. Impotence.

Silicea.—Sexual erethism, with paralytic disease. Persistent sexual thoughts; often nocturnal emissions.

Calcarea fluor.—Constant dribbling of seminal and prostatic fluid, with dwindling of the testicles.

SPINE, DISEASES OF.

Kali mur.—Tabes dorsalis, wasting of the spinal cord.

Kali phos.—Idiopathic softening of the spinal cord with molecular deadening of the nerve centres. "Spinal anæmia from exhausting diseases, such as diphtheria, reflex paraplegia, with laming pains aggravated by rest, but most manifest on beginning to move about." (Arndt.)

Natrum phos.—Spinal anæmia. "Paralytic weakness of the lower extremities, with general prostration, heaviness and sensation of fatigue, especially after a short walk, or ascending steps, legs give way, so as to be unable to progress farther." (Arndt.)

Calcarea phos.—Spinal anæmia. Spinal curvature, spinal weakness. "Cramp-like pain in the neck, pains and aches between the scapulæ, backache and pains in the lumbar region, curvature of spine in the lumbar region, abscess near the lumbar region, tabes mesenterica, rachitis, open fontanelles, flabby, emaciated, shrunken children, disposition to furuncles and ulcers, peevish and fretful children, worse from bodily exertion, worse in the open air." (Arndt.) Inflammation proceeding from disease of the bony structure of spine.

Calcarea fluor.—Spina ventosa. Spinal anæmia.

Silicea.—When the bony structure of the spine is affected, myelitis, coccygodynia, spondylitis. Posterior spinal sclerosis.

CLINICAL CASES.

Thos. T. McNish, M. D., Allegheny, Pa., in *American Homœopathist*, October 15, '97. Two years ago I was consulted by a farmer, sixty years old, spare, of nervous temperament, about a dyspepsia of three years' standing. It was an aggravated and aggravating case, but I am not going to detail it further than to say that I gave *Sepia*, 30th trituration, and this single remedy effected a perfect cure.

The patient then informed me he had another complaint of far older date, which he had not mentioned before because he believed it incurable, but the successful treatment of his dyspepsia gave him hope that the other disorder might be cured. The history of the case was briefly this: Nineteen years before, while digging a well, he strained his back; the effects, however, soon passed off and he believed himself well, when he was suddenly seized with what he called "a cramp" in the lower dorsal and upper lumbar region, which twisted him around until he "faced the rear." The spasm, which was very painful, was repeated several times. After an interval of some weeks he had another attack, and from that time forward they increased in frequency until he had one or more daily. His general health did not seem to suffer.

He received treatment from many physicians (all of the old school) with very slight benefit and at last placed himself in the hands of a specialist who gave him electrical massage once or twice a week. This was continued regularly for four years, during which time the attacks decreased in frequency (but not in intensity), so that they did not recur oftener than once a week, and occasionally the interval was two weeks. (I neglected to say, in the proper place, that the patient was always twisted toward the right side. There was very slight tenderness over the first lumbar vertebra.)

You will readily understand that I was not enamored of this case, and indeed hesitated to undertake it, but the insistence of the patient decided me, and after two weeks' study and reflection I prescribed *Mag. phos.*, 6x trituration, four doses daily. This was continued for one month.

The effect of the medicine was remarkable. From the time of taking the first dose the spasms ceased, and though more than eighteen months have since passed they have never returned.

SPINAL IRRITATION.

Natrum mur.—Easily fatigued, weakness from slightest exertion, restlessness of limbs, pain in back and sensitiveness of spine. Sleepless, restless and weak. Headache on walking. Salty taste and repugnance to food. Vision becomes dim after reading, at times only half of object visible. *Natrum mur.*, in its first effects, stimulates the nervous system, causing muscular contractions very much like those induced by galvanism. It also increases the red corpuscles, glandular secretions, digestion, etc. It is from this stimulating action

that salt is so effective, when applied locally with friction to
weak muscles, etc. Later, however, *Natrum mur.* exhausts
the nerves, diminishes glandular activity, and develops asthenia
and anæmia with emaciation. The skin is dry, harsh and
sallow; mucous membranes are dry, cracked and glazed, with
smarting and rawness, or with scanty, corroding discharges.
Great complaints are made that the mouth is dry, when in
reality the annoyance arises from the stickiness of the secretions; they are not normally fluid. Now, from this atonic effect
of salt, we observe spinal neurasthenia. The small of the back
feels paralyzed, especially in the morning, on rising. Back
feels as if broken. Legs weak, trembling; worse in the morning. Feet heavy as lead. With all this, it may readily occur
that the bladder becomes weak; troublesome, dribbling of urine
after a normal stool. And we may admit this vesical symptom
as a concomitant of spinal weakness, even though the prover
had no such association, because such a combination is quite in
keeping with the genius of the remedy. We may regard both
spinal and cystic atony as a part of a general tendency in salt to
produce exhaustion, hence not a symptom of paralysis, but
rather of neurasthenia.

Silicea.—Spinal irritation alternating with offensive foot-
sweat. Spinal irritation of children depending on worms
(*Natr. phos.*), markedly aggravated at the time of the new
moon. Spinal irritation with stiffness of nape of the neck and
headache. Weak back and paralyzed feeling in lower extremities. Burning in back, constant aching in centre of back.
Coccyx painful. Patient is very sensitive to the least noise,
has rough and yellow finger-nails, icy-cold feet even in bed.
Unhealthy skin, every little injury suppurates. Feels better
from warmth in general.

Kali phos.—Neurasthenia, especially from sexual excess,
characterized by severe spinal irritation.

Calcarea fluor.—Backache simulating spinal irritation, with
weak, dragging, down-bearing pain. Bowels confined.

SPINAL MENINGITIS.

Natrum sulph.—Violent pains in back of neck and head. Drawing back of the neck and spasms of the back, together with mental irritability and delirium. "In the spinal meningitis of to-day, if all the remedies in the Materia Medica were taken away from me and I were to have but one with which to treat that disease, I would take *Natrum sulph.*, because it will modify the attack and save life in the majority of cases. It cuts short the disease surprisingly when it is the truly indicated remedy. The violent determination of blood to the head that we find in the disease, clinically, is readily relieved." (J. T. Kent.)

SUNSTROKE.

Natrum mur.—The pathological conditions of this affection arise from sudden abstraction of moisture in the tissues at the base of the brain; *Natrum mur.* is the chief remedy in these conditions. Engorged venous sinuses with tendency to extravasation; temporary cerebral congestion.

SYPHILIS.

Ferrum phos.—Bubo with heat, throbbing or tenderness.

Kali mur.—Soft chancre, the principal remedy throughout (3x tr.) and also externally as a lotion; chronic stage of syphilis. In bubo for the soft swelling. Mucous patches. Syphilitic ulceration of gums. Dr. C. S. Saunder, of London, asserts that this drug is quite as specific in syphilis as *Mercury*. He has proved this statement many times in practice.

Kali phos.—Phagedænic chancre and bubo.

Kali sulph.—Syphilis with the characteristic symptoms, evening aggravation, etc. Chronic syphilis.

Natrum mur.—Schüssler's last edition gives this remedy as one of the most prominent if not the chief remedy in syphilis. Chronic syphilis, serous exudations.

Natrum sulph.—Condylomata of anus, syphilitic in origin, externally and internally.

Silicea.—Chronic syphilis with suppurations or indurations. Ulcerated cutaneous affections where mercury has been given to excess, nodes in tertiary syphilis; caries and necrosis with discharge of offensive pus.

Calcarea sulph.—In bubo to control suppuration (with *Silicea*). Chronic suppurating stage of syphilis.

Calcarea fluor.—Chancres hard and indurated.

CLINICAL CASE.

Chancroid ulcers surrounded by congested areola, grayish exudation covering surface. Deep excavations, wider at bottom, painful micturition. *Kali mur.*³ every three hours. Improvement soon set in, the pain on urinating disappeared, and the ulcers rapidly healed. (F. A. Rockwith.)

TESTICLES, DISEASES OF.

Ferrum phos.—First stage of orchitis, inflammatory condition, pain, etc.

Kali mur.—Primary remedy if from suppressed gonorrhœa. Hydrocele in little boys.

Calcarea phos.—Orchitis, hydrocele, sometimes after *Natrum mur.*

Calcarea fluor.—Dropsy of the testicles. Indurations of same.

Natrum mur.—Œdema of the scrotum and prepuce (also *Natrum sulph.*). Spermatic cord and testicles painfully sore and painful. Aching in testicles. Violent itching on scrotum. Loss of hair from pubes.

TONGUE.

Calcarea sulph.—Coating, yellow at base, clay-colored. Flabby; taste sour, soapy, acrid. Inflammation of the tongue when suppurating.

Ferrum phos.—Inflammation of the tongue with dark-red swelling. Cancer.

Kali mur.—For the swelling in glossitis. Coating white, dry, grayish-white, slimy.

Kali phos.—Inflammation of the tongue when excessive dryness occurs, or exhaustion. Coating like stale, brownish-liquid mustard, excessively dry in the morning, as if it would cleave to the roof of the mouth. **Brown tongue.** Edges of tongue red and sore. Tongue excessively dry in the morning.

Kali sulph.—Coating yellow, slimy, sometimes with whitish edge. Insipid, pappy taste.

Calcarea phos.—Swollen, stiff, numb, white-furred, pimply. Cancer.

Natrum mur.—Coating slimy, clear and watery, especially when small bubbles of frothy saliva cover the sides and tips. Loss of taste, mapped tongue. Clean, moist tongue. Tongue numb and stiff. Children slow in learning to talk. Sensation of a hair on tongue. Dryness of tongue and mouth, more a sensation.

Natrum phos.—Coating at the base moist, creamy or golden-yellow. Blisters and sensation of hair on tip of tongue. Cancer.

Natrum sulph.—Coating dirty brownish-green or grayish-green. Taste bitter and sour. Slimy tongue, burning blisters on tip. Red tongue.

Silicea.—Induration of the tongue, hardening. Inflammation resulting in suppuration.

Calcarea fluor.—Cracked appearance of the tongue, with or without pain. Induration of the tongue, hardening after inflammation.

Magnesia phos.—Yellow, shiny coating, especially with pain in bowels and pressure in stomach.

NOTE.—The coating of the tongue does not always wholly influence the choice of a remedy in all affections of the tissues. If any one, suffering from a chronic catarrh of the stomach, take also another (acute) disease, the coating of the tongue will not always have that peculiar appearance which will indicate the remedy suited to the acute disease. If any disease, particularly of a chronic nature, shows itself without decisive symptoms, then the coating of the tongue will, in most cases, guide in the choice of an appropriate remedy. (Schüssler.)

TONSILLITIS.

Ferrum phos.—Tonsils red and inflamed, painful on swallowing. This remedy at first alone.

Kali mur.—The second remedy, as soon as there is any swelling of the throat. Throat spotted white or gray. Chronic or acute tonsillitis with much swelling.

Kali phos.—Tonsils large and sore, with white, solid deposit on them, like diphtheritic membrane.

Natrum phos.—Catarrh of the tonsils with a golden-yellow tinged exudation, from an acid condition of the stomach. Chronic swelling of the tonsils.

Calcarea phos.—Chronic swelling of the tonsils, causing pain on opening mouth, deafness and difficulty of swallowing; intercurrent. Husky voice. "In spongy hypertrophy of the tonsils in children, in the 2x trituration we have found a faithful and protracted use of the drug in many cases to produce a marked diminution in the size of the tonsils." (H. C. French, M. D.)

Calcarea sulph.—Tonsillitis, last stage, when matter discharges or abscess forms.

Natrum mur.—Uvulitis; here the mucous cells are the seat of the disease. Hence not *Kali mur.*, but *Natrum mur.*, is the remedy. Chronic enlargement of the tonsils has been cured by the remedy in the 30th potency.

Magnesia phos.—Tonsillitis worse right side. Throat very red and puffy. Patient is chilly and tired, head aches and is flushed.

CLINICAL CASES.

I have used *Natrum mur.* repeatedly, and especially in obstinate cases of salivation, with excellent results. One case in particular was cured with remarkable rapidity by this remedy. A young lady, æt. 20, who suffered from severe inflammation of the tonsils, so that she could scarcely swallow milk or water, had received from me a preparation of mercury. The inflammation of the tonsils was reduced very quickly, but another evil set in—namely, violent salivation. The gums were loosened, bleeding easily and standing back from the teeth, and the teeth were blackened. I thought of curing this affection also with *Mercur.*, with which I had often before succeeded in such cases, but by continuing this remedy the evil was only increased. Now I ascertained from the patient that in the previous summer she had been ill at N., and the doctor had given her a good deal of calomel, which caused fearful and long-continued salivation. She was afraid the evil would again become very tedious, as it had been so bad at N. I now stopped the *Mercury* and ordered *Natrum mur.*, a dose the size of a bean every two hours. The success surpassed my most sanguine expectations. In twenty-four hours the swelling of the glands had distinctly diminished, and in three days a complete cure was effected. (From Schüssler.)

Enlarged tonsils with partial deafness, by R. T. Cooper, M. D. J. D., æt. 5, a thin, delicate-looking boy, very tall for his age, for two years suffered from partial deafness, which has much increased since he came to Southampton, two months since. His mother is frightened, fearing he is becoming incurably deaf. At first he would, or rather could, not allow me, from the excessive pain it occasioned, to examine his throat (he was then suffering from an exacerbation) ; but it was evident, from the external swelling and the history, where the true cause of the dysecoia lay. The tale his mother tells is that he was vaccinated when three years old, that after much constitutional disturbance, eruption subsided, leaving the tonsils in their present swollen condition. Symptoms are worse after coming in from open air and in damp weather. *Calcarea phos.* had an immediate beneficial effect, so that in three days throat could be examined. Both tonsils were swollen and red and formed an almost complete embankment between the mouth and throat. In three weeks hearing was quite restored, and swelling subsided.—*Monthly Homœopathic Review*, September, 1867.

Dr. W. had a severe attack of tonsillitis, involving both tonsils, which were very much enlarged, causing difficult and painful deglutition. Temperature, 102; pulse, 130; patient exceedingly nervous. Gave *Ferrum phos.*, 6x, and *Kali phos.* 6x, in alternation, every fifteen minutes. Saw the patient in six hours and all symptoms were much worse, then gave *Kali mur.* 6x instead of *Kali phos.*, continued *Ferrum.* The next morning found that the patient had passed a hard night. Then gave *Ferrum phos.* 12x and *Kali mur.* 12x. In six hours found the patient very much improved, less pain, less swelling, temperature 100, pulse 100; continued the remedies, and in two days the patient was out, and suppuration did not take place. This was as truly a case of quinsy, which usually goes on to suppuration and runs a seven days' course, in spite of all we can do, as any case I ever saw. The aggravation caused by the remedies given in the 6th potency and the improvement which took place after their administration in the 12x were interesting facts. The patient remarked that he could feel the effects of the last remedies all through the body, quieting and soothing the nervous irritability, immediately after every dose. (G. H. Martin, M. D.)

One evening a gentleman brought to my office his son, aged 8 or 10 years. As he stood before me, I noticed that he labored terribly in breathing, and that his chest was bowed out like a chicken's. I looked into his throat, and found both tonsils inflamed and so much enlarged that there was scarcely space enough between them to insert a slip of writing paper. He was slightly feverish, and the tongue was coated white. I prepared some powders of *Kali mur.*[200] (B. & T.) and ordered them to be given dry every half hour for three hours, and then every hour through the night. The next morning, quite early, I called and to my astonishment found him sitting up in bed quite bright and breathing naturally. His chest had assumed a more normal form, and the tonsils were considerably diminished in size. The same remedy was continued through the next day, and the next morning the little fellow met me in the parlor, comparatively well. (E. H. H.)

TOOTHACHE.

Ferrum phos.—Toothache with hot cheek, inflamed gum, or root of tooth. Worse with hot, better with cold liquids, gums sore, red and inflamed. Great soreness of teeth, feel elongated. Odontalgia.

Kali mur.—Toothache with swelling of the gums and cheeks, to carry off the exuding effete albuminoid substance.

Kali phos.—Toothache of highly nervous, delicate or pale, irritable, emotional persons. Toothache with easily bleeding gums. The gums have a bright red seam or line on them. Teeth feel sore; grinding of teeth; severe pain in decayed or filled teeth.

Kali sulph.—Toothache aggravated in the warm room and in the evening, but is better in the cold open air.

Magnesia phos.—Toothache if hot liquids ease the pain (if cold eases the pain, *Ferrum phos.*). Neuralgic, rheumatic toothache, very intense and shooting, eased by heat. Pains relieved by pressure, but increased by slight movement. Toothache worse after going to bed and from cold washing and cold things generally; in filled teeth. Non-inflammatory toothache.

Natrum mur.—Toothache with involuntary flow of tears, or great flow of saliva.

Silicea.—Toothache when very intense at night, when neither heat nor cold gives relief, and when caused by chilling of the feet. Toothache when the pain is deep-seated in the periosteum or fibrous membrane covering the root of the tooth, and abscess forms. Toothache caused by sudden chill to the feet when damp from perspiration. Looseness of the teeth.

Calcarea phos.—Too rapid decay of the teeth, strumous conditions. Teething ailments during pregnancy. Teeth ache worse at night.

Calcarea fluor.—Toothache if any food touches the tooth. Toothache with looseness of the teeth; enamel of the teeth rough and deficient, unnatural looseness of the teeth. "Where the use of *Calcarea fluor.* has been continued for many weeks, I have observed bad effects on the teeth, suggesting its possible use in caries of the teeth, especially in children." (R. S. Copeland.)

CLINICAL CASES.

Three cases of odontalgia were relieved in a few hours by *Ferr. phos.* 6x. The symptoms were: Elongation of tooth, great soreness of tooth to pressure, continued pain, could not sleep, no swelling of face or gums, not relieved by heat or cold.—N. A. J., 1893, p. 54.

TUMORS.

Kali mur.—Recent cases of cancer of the breast where tenderness is a prominent symptom, the bunches in the breast feel soft, use 3x.—E. G. Jones.

Kali phos.—Cancer, pain, offensive discharge and discoloration. Useful where cancer has been removed and is in the healing process.

Kali sulph.—Epithelioma. Cancer on the skin near a mucous lining, with discharge of thin, yellow, serous, purulent secretions. It cured an epithelioma for Dr. H. S. Phillips, of Toledo, Ohio, situated on the left side of the nose, a horny-like scab with a dark swollen inflamed areola. It had lasted over six months. Several other cases of cure of epithelioma by the remedy are on record.

Natrum mur.—Ranula.

Ferrum phos.—An excellent alternate remedy for excessive pain in cancer. Cancer of tongue has been benefited by it. Nævus.

Calcarea phos.—Cancer in scrofulous constitutions. House-maid's knee. Acute or chronic cysts require this remedy. Bronchocele, goitre, cysts. Bursæ.

Calcarea sulph.—Serous swellings, cystic tumors. Excessive granulations and suppurations.

Calcarea fluor.—Blood-tumors on the heads of newborn infants. Knots, kernels, hardened glands in the female breast. Tumors of the eyelids. Enlarged meibomian glands. Swelling on the jawbone, which is hard. Ganglion, round swelling of encysted tumors, such as are found on the back of the wrist from strain of the elastic fibres. Hard swellings having their seat in the fasciæ, capsular ligaments or on tendons. Indurated lumps in cæcal region. Bony periosteal infiltration.

Silicea.—Enlarged glands. Chronic enlargement of lymphatic glands. Swellings, lumps, tumors, etc., which are indurated, but threaten to suppurate. Scirrhous induration of upper lip and face. Uterine cancer. Icy coldness and fœtid, brownish, purulent, ichorous leucorrhœa.

Natrum phos.—Has proved of use in cancer of tongue. Goitre when there is an acid condition producing it.

CLINICAL CASES.

CALCAREA FLUORICA.—A maiden lady of 60 came to consult me on the 13th of October, 1883, telling me she had a shiny swelling on her left index finger which had been there for about 18 months. The lump was hard and painful, and of about the size of a small split walnut, but rather flatter, patient nervous and depressed. Improvement set in at once and in two and one-half months was entirely well. (J. Compton Burnett.)

CALCAREA PHOSPHORICA.—An infant, a fortnight old, was brought to me. Immediately after birth a swelling was noticed on its head, which had continued to grow larger. It was situated on the left tuberosity of the parietal bone, was about 7 em. in diameter, and its height was about 3 em. It felt doughy, not fluctuating. Careful examination showed that the parietal bone was defective below it. From this the tumor issued. It was evidently a meningocele of moderate size. Prognosis was doubtful. There were no signs of pressure on the brain, and the child, with the exception of double inguinal hernia, was healthy. I prescribed *Calc. phos.* 6th trit. three times a day. After taking this medicine three days the tumor was evidently smaller and in 10 days it was quite gone. The hole in the bone gradually filled up, and at the end of three and a half weeks was completely closed. (Frohling, A. h   :xxxii. 65.)

Sanguineous cyst on the right side c   e occipital bone, with open posterior fontanelle. *Calcarea phos.* 2c. cured.—Raue, *Record Homœopathic Literature*, 1873.

Calcarea fluorica.—A recurrent fibroid in the hollow of the knee was removed once by the knife, but returned and grew to the size of a fist. The leg was drawn up to forty-five degrees, and the knee became immovable. This wonderful remedy was prescribed on the symptoms of the case and hardness of the tumor. The tumor gradually dwindled, the limb became normal and as good as ever. (Dr. T. J. Kent.)

Case of polypus of left nostril cured by *Calcarea phos.*—Beebe, *Trans. American Institute,* 1886.

Dr. Orth relates: Elizabeth F., a widow, æt. 70, consulted me on April 5th, on account of an epithelioma seated on the right cheek, reaching from the lower eyelid to the nostril. It was almost circular, and about the size of a florin. The epithelioma had existed for some years, and was at the stage of forming an ulcer, with hard base, and callous edges. I ordered *Kali sulph.*, a powder every evening, and lint saturated with a lotion made of *Kali sulph.* for external application, to be changed frequently. On May 6th I noticed that the ulcer had visibly diminished, and on May 23d the ulcer had cicatrized to the size of a six-penny piece. A few days later the lady left to return home, and I regret I have not heard from her since. (From Schüssler.)

Dr. Spiethoff, of Lubeck, relates a prompt effect from *Calcar. fluor.*[6] and *Silicea.* The patient was afflicted with a large sarcoma on the superior maxilla, giving the froglike appearance to the face. For eight months, old-school physicians had tried to establish suppuration, but failed, except to produce several fistulous openings, discharging a fœtid, almost clear fluid. Without much hope of producing suppuration, *Silicea*[6] was given. No change occurred for two weeks, except the appearance of two protuberances in the median line of the tumor. *Calc. fluor.*[6] was now given, and the next day a profuse suppuration began, greatly ameliorating the case. The prompt action of the remedies was very striking.

Dr. C. H. Thompson, of Santa Rosa, furnishes us a case of neuralgic node in the mammary gland, resembling scirrhus, entirely cured by *Calcarea fluor.*

William W., a factory worker, came to me on September the 4th. He suffered with epithelioma, which was situated on the right side of the nose, almost immediately below the corner of the eye, and about the size of a two-shilling piece. The eye itself seemed to be sympathetically affected, perhaps through the irritation of the discharge, which might have found its way into the eye from the edge of the eyelid, which, however, was not greatly destroyed. Be that as it may, there were conjunctivitis palpebrarum and bulbi, with dulness of the cornea. The ulcer at the side of the nose had existed for four years. At first there was a slightly red spot, which was a little raised and swollen. Later on it became covered with a horny scab, which after a time fell off and left a little sore. This spread slowly but steadily. The patient had, during the whole time of its existence, consulted a great number of doctors. He had also been treated for two months by a specialist for the eye, after it had become implicated; but all without effect. *Kali sulph.* was now given him, a dose night and morning; and externally a lotion of *Kali sulph.* was used. After only a few days the inflammation disappeared. The ulcer began also to heal under the steady treatment. By the 8th of October the sore had cicatrized so that only a speck was left, when the patient was able to resume work again on the 9th of October. (From Schüssler.)

A hard swelling under the chin, about the size of a pigeon's egg, disappeared completely in about four weeks under the use of *Calcarea fluor.* Both old and new school medicines had failed to cure. (Dr. F. From Schüssler.)

Dr. Fuchs, of Regensburg, reports: In August, 1875, I cured a lady, æt. 40, who had suffered for a considerable time from an effusion in bursa of the knee-cap. Twelve doses of *Calcarea phos.,* two doses per diem, according to Dr. Schüssler, removed this chronic condition of housemaid's knee. (From Schüssler.)

NASAL POLYPI.—Mrs. R. had nasal polypi in both nostrils, large, gray and bleeding easily. *Calcarea phos.*[30], a powder every morning for a week. The third week reported entirely free. The larger ones came away entirely; the smaller ones were absorbed. (J. G. Gilchrist.)

MULTIPLE CHELOID, which appeared after the excision of a tumor, in the scar. It was excised at St. Bartholomew's Hospital, but rapidly returned and increased in size, until the patient, a girl, was put on *Silicea*[8], night and morning. The gradual disappearance of the growth under this treatment was one of the prettiest things I have ever seen in medicine.— John H. Clarke, in *Homœopathic World,* August, 1885.

STRUMOUS DACTYLITIS.—At the London Homœopathic Hospital, Gerard Smith exhibited a child, aged four years, who had injured his index finger two years previously. This set up primarily periostitis and abscess, but without symptoms of necrosis, and on probing no sequestrum was found. The swelling of the finger increased during six months until the bone was almost globular. At the end of this period, under a prolonged course of *Silicea,* the bone became much smaller. At the end of a second six months, an abscess again formed, was opened, and a probe passed into a soft mass. The finger again greatly improved, and became smaller under a course of *Hepar* and *Silicca.* Byres Moir and Epps had both frequently had similar cases of strumous dactylitis, in which complete recovery had taken place under *Silicea, Calcarea* and *Calc. fluor.*

"*Calcarea fluorica* in lumps and chronic hard swellings in the female breasts."

I know whereof I speak when I state that these swellings can be easily handled with this remedy.

Mrs. C., age 52, came to me badly alarmed because a leading surgeon had said that she had a cancer of the breast and must have it cut out immediately. After a careful examination of the breast, and taking her history, I said to her, I believe I could remove the hard lump with medicine. After a few moments' thought she said, "Go to work on it."

I made a 4-oz. solution of the remedy by putting some of the 3x tablets into 4 oz. of soft water, and told her to keep the swelling wet most of the time with it, which she did. Internally I gave her 3 cones of the 3x every three hours, and had her report in one week. The one week's treatment had reduced the lump one-fourth and she now fully believes that she is going to recover, which she *did* in six weeks' treatment.

CASE 2.—A lady friend of the above, 42 years of age, presented herself for treatment for a hard lump that had been growing in her right breast for three or four years. It was painful, and she was unable to use her arm for any length of time without the whole organ becoming sensitive and painful so as to prevent her from sleeping. She was a dyspeptic, and after correcting this trouble she received the same treatment as the above, and fully recovered in three months.

This remedy has never failed me in hard swelling of the jaw caused by toothache or injury, and for chaps and cracks of the lips. I used it in one case of rapid decay of the teeth, where the enamel scaled off, and obtained very good results. (O. A. Palmer, M. D.)

Dr. Mossa reports an interesting case in the Berliner Zeitschrift where *Silicea* 30 produced and cured cystic growths. A carpenter showed a swelling in the left bend of the elbow that had been there for over one year. It was soft but recently had become painful. *Silicea*[30] twice daily stopped the pain after three days, but a ganglion appeared at the back of the left hand, size of a hazel nut. In ten days' further treatment with *Silicea,* both cysts disappeared.

TYPHOID FEVER.

Ferrum phos.—Typhoid or gastric fever when commencing; initiatory stage for chilliness. The patient has a full, flushed face and the lips and mucous membranes are red. The pulse is more rapid, but stronger and less irregular than under *Kali phosphoricum.*

Kali mur.—Typhoid or gastric fevers, for gray or white-coated tongue and looseness of the bowels, with light-yellow, ochre-colored stools or flocculent evacuations, and for abdominal tenderness and swelling.

Kali phos.—Typhoid or malignant symptoms, when affecting the brain, causing stupor during the course of the disease, or with symptoms of putrid blood. Debility, weak action of the heart, sleeplessness, offensive breath, putrid odor of stools, stupor. Sordes on the teeth. An excellent remedy in extreme vitiation of the blood, when the system seems full of typhoid poison and the disease is not located in any single organ. Offensiveness of discharges is a very marked symptom for *Kali phos.* There is restlessness, a mild delirium, a thin whitish-yellow coating of the tongue, face pale, pinched, anxious expression. Sharp cutting pains in different parts of the body during the first few days. The characteristic indications are the weak, rapid irregular pulse with a comparatively low temperature.

Halbert recommends *Kali phos.* in cases where the patient has been a mental rather than a physical worker, where neurasthenic conditions are associated with the fever, and when in the later stages there is lack of recuperative power.

Kali sulph.—Typhoid or gastric fever, with a rise of temperature at night and a fall in the morning.

Natrum mur.—Typhoid or malignant conditions during the course of any fever, such as twitchings with great drowsiness, watery vomiting, sopor, parched tongue, etc.

Calcarea phos.—After typhoid or gastric fevers as the disease declines.

CLINICAL CASES.

Typhoid fever in young gentleman with a very active brain; a prominent symptom was that he became very hysterical, would cry like a child and sob whenever he became nervous. *Ignatia, Hyos., Stram.* and *Coffea,* all failed to relieve. *Kali phos.* cured this symptom, and he received no other remedy throughout the fever. After the patient got up, the remedy seemed to act as a tonic. (Monroe.)

The following from the pen of Dr. A. P. Davis, of Dallas, Texas, appeared in the *Southern Journal of Homœopathy,* and is of interest, since it illustrates the value of these remedies in this disease:

"The most rational course to pursue is to *supply deficiencies,* and to assist nature remove *excesses.* There is depression, perceptible in all cases of typhoid fever; and as this depression is the result of molecular change, the molecules of several elements must receive our special attention. Whether this molecular change can be brought about by the use of *Baptis., Rhus tox., Bryon., Phos. ac., China, Cimicif., Ferrum phos., Natrum mur.* or *Natrum phos.,* or what not, is the question that demands special attention. Some have claimed success by the use of *Baptis. tinct.,* others by *Rhus tox.,* as their sheet anchor, giving incidental treatment as they thought symptoms called for, and some success has followed this method of procedure. It is a conceded fact that the inflammation in the glands of Brunner and Peyer keep up the fever, and the remedy that cures these glands cuts short the disease, and the remedies that I have found to do this most certainly are *Ferrum phos.* and *Kali mur.,* given in alternation every hour during fever, where there is a white or grayish coating on the tongue. The *Ferrum* is the best fever remedy, and the *Kali mur.* the best eliminator in such conditions. If the tongue should become brown, give *Kali phos.*, and especially in those cases where the patient is delirious or nervous, and in the more malignant form of the disease. If the tongue assumes a yellow, shiny coating, then resort to *Magnesia phos.*, and especially when there are pain in the bowels and a sensation of pressure in the stomach. If the tongue has a golden-yellow coating, creamy, moist, give *Natrum phos.* Should the tongue have a dirty brownish-green coating, give *Natrum sulph.* These remedies are especially indicated in this condition of the tongue. Last of all, when the patient begins to convalesce, finish up the treatment with *Calcarea phos.*, as a connective tissue and blood-cell constituent is needed. In all cases where these tissue remedies have been used by me they have proved abundantly sufficient, and will cure, if given as indicated. They supply the inorganic elements that are disturbed or lacking in all diseased states, and if a strict observance is had in their selection, the physician will certainly cure any disease that can be cured at all. I usually give them the 4x to 6x potency, and while many may consider me dogmatic in the use of these remedies, I can see no reason as yet to change off into the intricate mazes of supposed pathogenetic provings of polypharmacy. While I still use many polychrests, I lend a decided preference to the proper use of the Tissue Remedies where indicated."

Miss Nettie W., æt. 23. Was called in consultation, found the patient apparently in last stage of the disease, with the symptoms usual in such cases. As other remedies had been tried and she seemed sinking, I advised *Kali phos.*, in solution. Under the use of this remedy she rallied, and it was continued some days, with the result that she ultimately recovered.

Another similar case was given the same remedy when others seemed of no avail, with the same good result of producing a change for the better within a few hours, followed by recovery. (C. T. M.)

TYPHUS FEVER.

Ferrum phos.—The first stage in alternation with *Kali phos.*

Kali mur.—For constipation, stools light-colored.

Kali phos.—Malignant fever, putrid fever, camp fever, nervous or brain fever, farm fever. The chief remedy for brown tongue, petechiæ, sleeplessness, abnormal brain function, stupor, delirium.

Natrum mur.—Typhus fever when the stupor and sleeplessness are very great.

Natrum phos.—Golden-yellow coating on tongue; creamy, moist.

TYPHLITIS.
(See also Appendicitis.)

Ferrum phos.—Fever, inflammation, high temperature and pulse, also for the pain.

Kali mur.—Swelling and exudation, hardness, etc.

Kali sulph.—To aid the absorption of any secretions and to lessen tendency to inflammatory conditions in abdomen; colicky pains from the excessive secretions which are not carried off and keep filling up around the appendix. (F. D. B.)

Silicea.—Formation of pus, abscess, etc.

Calcarea sulph.—Relieves the pain in right side of pelvis, tends to counteract and cure the ulceration if any in the intestines and prevents disintegration of those tissues, tones up the weakness, removes distention, etc. (F. D. B.) Abscess, yellow, sanious matter.

Natrum sulph.—Flatulent colic, beginning in the region of the right groin, a characteristic symptom. Tenderness and distention with tendency to perforation. Torpidity of bowels and general bilious condition sometimes superinduce or predispose to this trouble. (F. D. Bittinger, M. D.) "Dull pain in right ileo-cæcal region. Shifting flatus. Tenderness to pressure and coated tongue." (J. W. Ward, M. D.) Vomiting, which is persistent.

CLINICAL CASES.

The following case, furnished by Dr. I. E. Nicholson, of Oakland, California, is so beautifully illustrative of the action of these remedies in typhlitis, that it is reprinted in full as furnished by the Doctor:

"I was called on the morning of April 14th, 1887, to attend to Mr. E. K., a young man, æt. 22, with hereditary tendency to phthisis pulmonalis, who resides in Connecticut, and was sojourning in our city for the benefit of his health, and found him suffering with agonizing pain in the right iliac region. He had been attacked suddenly at 2 o'clock A. M. with this pain, and had vomited several times before I saw him. Upon examination I found a tumor in the right iliac fossa, so tender to the touch that he could not bear even the weight of the bed clothing. His bowels had moved twice within a few hours. I learned that he had eaten of a mince pie at dinner the day before, and had passed a quantity of currant seeds in one of his movements. There could be no doubt as to the diagnosis—typhlitis—and that a currant seed was the *casus mali*. His temperature was 103 F., and pulse 120. For several inches around the tumor the belly was as hard as a rock, showing a great amount of infiltration. I at once gave him *Ferrum phos.* and *Kali mur.* (6x trit.) to be taken every half hour in alternation, day and night; poultices of flaxseed were kept constantly applied, as hot as could be borne, to alleviate the pain.. At the end of thirty-six hours his temperature had fallen to 100 F., and pulse to 90. This treatment was continued without intermission, and the inflammatory symptoms steadily improved and the size of the tumor gradually lessened. At the end of a week the temperature and pulse became normal, the tumor had entirely disappeared, the belly was soft and a mere trace of the tenderness remained. He took no other medicines. The result in this case is, I think, phenomenal, since in this class of cases the prognosis is always unfavorable, and the credit of the case can be clearly given to the *Iron* and the *Potash*, the one removing the inflammation, the other causing the absorption of the infiltration, thus bringing about resolution and aborting perityphlitis and the consequent suppuration. Dr. Burdick, of Oakland, and Dr. Brigham, of San Francisco, were both called in consultation, and both agreed with me as to the disease, and both acquiesced in the treatment. We have no medicine which is the peer of *Ferrum phos.* as a fever remedy, whether idiopathic or symptomatic, and none better than *Kali mur.* to cause the absorption of infiltrations."

Calcarea fluor. 3x rapidly absorbed an indurated and sensitive tumor, extending from the cæcum to the lower border of the liver.

ULCERS AND ULCERATIONS.

Ferrum phos.—Ulcerations of glands, to relieve the throbbing pain, soreness, redness, heat and congested condition. Ulcers if there be fever or heat, or redness and congestion.

Kali mur.—Ulcer with fibrinous discharge. Ulceration of the os and cervix uteri, with thick, white, mild secretions; all ulcerations where there is swelling or a dirty-white tongue, or a mealy, flour-like scaly surface, or a fibrinous discharge; proud flesh, exuberant granulations. **Ulceration of cornea.** (See Eye, Diseases of.)

Kali sulph.—Tuberculous ulcers, with a continuous oozing of yellowish pus and lymph, will often yield to this remedy.

Natrum phos.—Ulceration of the stomach or bowels. Syphilitic ulcers, yellow coating having appearance of half-dried cream.

Silicea.—Ulcers of the lower limbs when deep-seated and the periosteum is affected. *Silicea* has ulcers that are spongy, readily bleeding, with torpid, callous edges, fistulous ulcers, secreting a thin, fœtid, ichorous, yellow fluid. Sluggish ulcers, in hard-worked and ill-fed people. Ulceration following abrasion of the skin over the shin-bone. Use also locally, or infusion of hay, which contains *Silicea*. Suppurative processes, massive and repeated doses in scrofulous, glandular swellings with suppuration.

Calcarea phos.—Ulceration of bone substance, as an intercurrent.

Calcarea sulph.—Ulceration of the glands. Ulcers open. Purulent sores which may result from abrasions, pimples, wounds, burns, scalds or bruises. Ulcers of the lower limbs, with a discharge of yellow, sanious matter.

Calcarea fluor.—Ulcerations of bones. Varicose ulcers. Ulcers with elevated hard edges with dark purplish discolorations.

CLINICAL CASES.

A girl came into my office, who had sores on both legs, running a thin, ichorous secretion, red, angry and painful, which had been bothering her for four years, breaking out, then scabbing over, partially healing, then taking on inflammation, so that sleep was disturbed; locomotion produced severe pains, in fact, the sores were seemingly very severe. I at once gave her *Silicea* 6x and *Calcarea phos.* 6x, three doses each per day, bound up the limbs with flannel roller bandage, and in four weeks all the sores were healed up and the patient well, cheerful and happy. (A. P. Davis, M. D.)

A. S., æt. 16, for three years had indolent ulcers on lower half of left leg, which is red, very much swollen. Three fistulous ulcers secreting a thick, yellow pus and which have thrown off many splinters of bone. Pains principally at night. Emaciation, poor appetite. Frequent cough in morning, with thick, yellow expectoration, and considerable weakness in morning. Lungs normal. *Calcarea fluor.* 6x, morning and evening, for eight days, alternating with intervals of four days without medicine. Cured in five months. Externally only glycerine. No enlargement of the limb was noticeable after six months. (Dr. Hansen, *Allg. Med. Zeit.*)

In treating a chronic syphilitic ulcer, I observed a yellow coating on the surface of the ulcer, which had the appearance of half-dried cream. After *Natrum phos.* the coating disappeared within four days and the patient was otherwise much improved. (C. Hg.)

URINARY DISORDERS.

Ferrum phos.—Incontinence of urine, if from weakness of the sphincter muscle. Wetting of the bed, especially in children. Enuresis nocturna, from weakness of the muscles, often seen in women, when every cough causes the urine to spurt. Cystitis, first stage, with pain, heat or feverishness. Suppression of the urine with heat. Excessive secretion of urine. Polyuria simplex. "Irresistible urging to urinate in the daytime, aggravated by standing and accompanied by pain along the urethra and neck of the bladder. Retention of urine with fever in little children, as well as involuntary spurting of urine with every cough." (M. Deschere, M. D.) Some varieties of red wine will cure nocturnal enuresis in children, owing to the iron contained therein. Dose night and morning. Diurnal enuresis depending on irritation of neck of the bladder and end of penis.

Kali mur.—Cystitis, second stage, when swelling has set in (interstitial exudation), and discharge of thick, white mucus. "In this trouble there is no better internal remedy." (Peltier.) The principal remedy in chronic cystitis. Urine dark-colored, deposit of uric acid, where there exist torpor and inactivity of the liver.

Kali phos.—Cystitis in asthenic conditions with prostration. Frequent urination, or passing large quantities of water. Frequent scalding; nervous weakness. Incontinence of urine from nervous debility, bleeding from the urethra. Paralysis, affecting the sphincter muscle, causing inability to retain the urine. Enuresis in *older* children. Urine quite yellow. Itching in urethra. Cutting pain in bladder and urethra.

Kali sulph.—According to Mitchell this remedy was used by Haerman, of Paris, and endorsed by the late T. F. Allen for *oxaluria*.

Magnesia phos.—*Constant urging to urinate whenever the person is standing or walking.* Spasmodic retention of the urine. Gravel. Pain after the use of the catheter, a sensation as if the muscles did not contract. Child passes large quantities of urine.

Natrum phos.—Incontinence of urine in children with acidity. Polyuria. Urine dark-red, with arthritis. Frequent micurition. Diabetes. Atony of the bladder. Gravel. Schüssler in his last edition claims that this is the chief remedy in catarrh of the bladder.

Natrum sulph.—Sandy deposit or sediment in the urine, gravel, lithic deposits, brickdust-like coloring matter in the water, associated with gout. Polyuria simplex, excessive secretion if diabetic. Urine loaded with bile. Wetting of the bed at night, or retention of urine.

Silicea.—Urine loaded with pus and mucus. Red sandy deposit of uric acid. Enuresis from worms and in chorea. Must get up at night to urinate.

Calcarea sulph.—Inflammation of the bladder, in chronic stage, pus forming. Red urine with hectic fever. Nephritis scarlatinosa. (S. Lilienthal.)

Calcarea phos.—Urine copious. Enuresis, wetting the bed in *young* children and in old people, as an intercurrent after *Natrum sulph.* For gravel, calculous, phosphatic deposit. To check the reformation of stone in the bladder, also buttermilk or koumiss as a dietary help. Flocculent sediment in urine.

Natrum mur.—Polyuria, with much emaciation; hæmaturia after scurvy; cutting pain *after* urinating. Cystitis. Involuntary urination when walking, coughing, etc. Incontinence of urine. Cutting in urethra after urinating.

Calcarea fluor.—Copious urine with frequent urging. Urine scanty and high colored, and emits a pungent odor.

CLINICAL CASES.

Dr. S. B. Dickerman, of Abington, Mass., reports a case of enuresis cured with *Ferrum phos.* 200th. The enuresis occurred in the daytime; he seldom wet the bed at night. The guiding symptoms emphasize its use in *diurnal* enuresis.

Case of incontinence of urine due to loss of muscular power, cured by *Ferrum phos.—Transactions American Institute,* 1882, p. 181.

Dr. Schüssler, in a private communication to Dr. Zoeppritz, mentions the case of a lad to whom he had given, without effect, *Ferrum phos.* for enuresis. A pustular eruption near the corners of the mouth appeared for which he prescribed *Natrum mur.*, which cured both the eruption and the enuresis.

Dr. Cornelius, Oldenberg, reports a case of spasmodic retention of the urine. No urine was at first excreted; even the catheter failed to bring any away. *Magnesia phos.* was given, which relieved somewhat; some urine was passed. In five days, no permanent or decided results being obtained from this remedy, Schüssler's advice was followed, and accordingly *Calcarea phos.* was given, which cured in one day. Some two months later another attack came on, which was likewise immediately cured by *Calcarea phos.*, for on the following day the patient was well. *All. Hom. Zeit.*, 1885, p. 70.

Dr. Crüwell reports on incontinence of urine: When I became acquainted with Dr. Schüssler's preparations I was very anxious to test the effects of *Kali phos.*, as Dr. Schüssler recommends this against paralysis and paralytic conditions. Whoever has been occupied with the study of psychology is naturally ready to suspect paralysis everywhere. I acknowledge I may have given *Kali phos.* too frequently, as I was desirous to find out what it could do. For various reasons it led me to give it for incontinency. I gave it three times daily in a little water. In five cases, two of which I treated without good results, *Kali phos.* brought about amazingly rapid improvement. With a young girl, æt. 7, I had until lately to repeat the remedy every time it was given up, as the incontinency always returned when it was discontinued. The most successful case was that of an old gentleman, æt. 60. No doubt in this case there existed a sub-paralytic condition of the sphincter muscle. Some months after treatment he called back to say that he was perfectly cured, but desired to have some of the powders, simply by way of precaution. (From Schussler.)

Lad, æt. 10, after homœopathic treatment had been unsuccessful, suffered with enuresis, urine pale, watery and very profuse. *Ferrum phos.* 6x, a powder in hot water three times daily, cured. (C. W. Hakes, M. D.)

INCONTINENCE OF URINE.—Lady, æt. 35, had had trouble for three years, and could assign no cause thereto; was able to retain the urine at night but not in daytime, when she passed large quantities of water involuntarily. General health good. *Ferrum phos.* 3x, four times a day. A week later she reported that she could now retain the urine much better during the day. The medicine was continued for three weeks longer, when she informed me that the power over the bladder was now complete, and that she was better than she had been for two years. Nine months afterwards the patient came to me again with a return of the malady; and although she was then *enciente, Ferrum phos.* again completely stopped the incontinence. (Wilde.)

Nephritis (chronic). Case of Dr. Cornelius, of Oldenburg, characterized by albuminous urine containing casts, specific gr. 1,016, great debility, palpitation, headache, etc. *Natrum mur.* 6 brought speedy improvement, increase in weight and with the aid of *Calc. phos.* restoration to health.

VACCINATION.

Should any bad results show themselves *Kali mur.* will give entire satisfaction. (Schüssler.) If necessary follow with *Silicea.*

VEINS, DISEASES OF.

Calcarea fluor.—Varicose veins, varicose ulceration of the veins (as a lotion also). Sharp piercing pains, patients can not be on their feet. The chief remedy for varicose veins. Dr. Porter recommends this remedy in varicose veins about the vulva, and in distention of the ovarian and sub-ovarian plexus of veins. Differentiating *Silicea* from *Calcarea fluor.,* he finds that the latter medicine has a greater affinity for muscular tissue, and has relief from cold, while *Silicea* is worse from cold. He quotes several symptoms from Farrington, indicating the fluoride of lime in affections of the lower tissues. Little vesicles form around scars; lacerations of the cervix, with a considerable amount of scar-tissue.

Ferrum phos.—Varicocele with pain in testicles. This is a powerful vein remedy, though its action on the arteries is its prime sphere. It has cured a small aneurism and the great indication for it is **throbbing.** Varicose veins in young persons.

CLINICAL CASES.

Young man, æt. 18, complained of daily pain in left testicle, incapacitating him for work. Examination showed a varicocele, well developed, probably caused by constant heavy lifting. After five weeks' use of *Ferrum phos.,* daily one dose, cured. (Dr. Mayer, Stuttgart.)

A physician of Bogota, S. A., relates a case of varicose ulcers of some standing, both on legs and arms. *Calc. fluor.* 6x was given night and morning. Healed in fifteen days.

VERTIGO.

Ferrum phos.—Giddiness from rush of blood to the head, with flushing, throbbing or pressing pain.

Kali phos.—Dizziness, swimming of the head, when from cerebral or nervous causes, and weakness, not gastric. Vertigo from anæmia. Vertigo, worse rising and looking up.

Kali sulph.—Vertigo, especially on looking up and rising.

Natrum sulph.—Giddiness, with bilious coating on the tongue, or bitter taste in the mouth; gastric derangement; excess of bile. Vertigo with inclination to fall on the right side.

Natrum phos.—Giddiness with gastric derangements, acidity and want of appetite, gold-colored, creamy coating on the tongue.

Magnesia phos.—Vertigo from optical defects.

CLINICAL CASES.

Dr. E. B. Rankin, of Washington, D. C., reports in the *Southern Journal of Homœopathy,* April, 1886, a case of vertigo of several weeks' standing, accompanied by vomiting of acid substances cured by *Natrum phos.* in one week.

I have made but little use, as yet, of Dr. Schüssler's *Kali phos.,* but have, notwithstanding, effected a few very interesting cures.

A woman, æt. 64, came under my treatment, who had been for many years treated without success. She had taken steel baths, a great many steel-pills and drops and quinine. She complained of a severe vertigo, felt mostly on rising from a sitting position, and on looking upward. She was constantly in dread of falling, and did not venture to leave her room. I gave her all the usual remedies without any benefit. At last I gave her, in May, 1875, two doses daily of Dr. Schüssler's *Kali phos.* I had the pleasure of seeing a rapid and decided cure following this. The patient can attend to her domestic duties; she can go out alone, even to distances, and is almost completely cured of her painful sensation of giddiness. (From Schüssler.)

VOMITING.

Silicea.—Child vomits as soon as it nurses. Vomiting in morning with chilliness.

Ferrum phos.—Vomiting of blood, bright-red blood, with tendency to form a gelatinous mass. Vomiting of the food with sour fluids; vomiting of food, the food returning undigested, sooner or later, after taking it.

Kali phos.—Nausea and vomiting of sour, bitter food and of blood.

Kali mur.—Vomiting of blood, dark, clotted, viscid. Vomiting of thick, white phlegm.

Natrum mur.—Vomiting of acid, sour fluid, not food.

Vomiting of curdled masses and acid fluids. Dark substance like coffee-grounds. Vomiting of watery, stringy, transparent mucus.

Natrum phos.—Vomiting of sour, fluid, curdy masses with yellow, creamy coating of tongue.

Natrum sulph.—Bilious vomiting, morning sickness and bitter taste in the mouth. Vomiting of greenish matter. Constant nausea.

Calcarea fluor.—Vomiting of undigested food, if *Ferrum phos.* does not suffice. Vomiting during dentition.

Calcarea phos.—Vomiting after cold water and ice-cream. Infants vomit often and easily and want to nurse all the time. Vomiting with teething troubles.

CLINICAL CASES.

W. J. Martin, M. D., in the *Transactions Penna. Hom. Med. Society,* 1886, reports a case of persistent vomiting, accompanied by pain in the abdomen, cured by *Magnes. phos.* 12 after the ordinary homœopathic remedies had failed.

A young girl about 18 consulted me (so writes a student of medicine) for painless vomiting, which had existed for a long time, and occurred after almost every meal. The color of her face and the visible mucous membranes were pale. Menstruation was scanty and delayed. No other symptoms of importance; pregnancy was not present. I ordered *Ferrum phos.* 6x. After a time I accidentally saw the patient again, and received the pleasing news that the vomiting had entirely disappeared from the commencement of the use of the remedy. (*Monatsblätter.*)

1. F. R., fifty years old. Had suffered for eight months from weight in stomach about an hour after each meal, with nausea, sometimes vomiting and much accumulation of water in the mouth. *Pulsatilla* had been given with little or no result, also *Natrum* and *Nux vomica.* His condition became worse. Vomiting of food set in after each meal some three or four hours. *Ferrum phos.* third every hour. This relieved the condition at once.

2. H., eleven years old. Weakly and of slim build, suffered for a long time from vomiting of food, stitches in the side and palpitation of the heart. Closer examination showed his liver and kidneys to be healthy. *Ferrum phos.* cured in four days.

3. L. S., twenty-four years. Medium height, pale, poorly-nourished aspect, had for several weeks vomiting of food immediately after eating. Patient is weak and sleepy in day-time. *Ferrum phos.* in a few days markedly improved the condition; the vomiting disappeared and the other conditions were beneficially influenced.

4. E. E., forty-two years. Sickly build and delicate; four years ago

had a gastritis and was cured by Homœopathy. Since that time, however, has had a weakness of the digestive organs which troubles him from time to time. Six weeks ago a marked aggravation set in. Feeling of fullness in the epigastrium, many eructations, vomiting, rush of blood to the head and cold feet. Examination showed the region of the stomach to be swollen and sensitive; liver, kidneys, heart, etc., healthy. *Ferrum phos.* 3x, every hour. In three days the patient was all right, vomiting had entirely ceased and the remaining symptoms had lessened markedly.

5. E. B., thirty-five years. Sufferer for several weeks from stomach disorder, with pressure, vomiting of food immediately after each meal; often redness of the face. Vomiting ceased after twelve hours' use of *Ferrum phos.*, and never returned.

6. L. R., thirty years. Scrawny and anæmic; suffered from stomach disorders for years. These for the past eight weeks have been much worse. There is present vomiting of food and patient feels in consequence thereof weak and exhausted. On the twenty-sixth of October she received *Ferrum phos.* Four days later her condition was improved; vomiting occurred less often and the case progressed to complete recovery.

7. F. A. For fourteen days had suffered from vomiting of food after each meal. In twenty-four hours *Ferrum phos.* cured the vomiting, which did not return.

WRITER'S CRAMP.

Natrum phos.—While writing, hand trembles. Crampy pain. Rheumatic pain in joints of fingers. Aching in wrists.

Kali mur.—Hands get stiff while writing.

Magnesia phos.—Is often to be used with benefit.

Calcarea phos.—Cramp-like pain in fingers and wrist.

WHOOPING COUGH.

Ferrum phos.—Whooping cough with vomiting of blood. Inflammatory catarrhal stage.

Kali mur.—If there be white-coated tongue and a thick white expectoration; short, spasmodic cough.

Natrum mur.—When the mucus is frothy, clear and stringy.

Kali phos.—Whooping cough in very nervous, timid sensitive children (intercurrent). Also when exhaustion sets in.

Kali sulph.—Whooping cough, decidedly yellow slimy expectoration.

22

Magnesia phos.—Whooping cough, beginning as a common cold, convulsive fits of nervous cough, ending in a whoop. Give this remedy steadily.

Calcarea phos.—Whooping cough in weakly constitutions, or in teething children, and in obstinate cases with emaciation.

CLINICAL CASES.

My experience in the treatment of whooping-cough, while not extended, has been quite satisfactory to me, especially since adopting the biochemic treatment of Schüssler. Under this treatment the cough may be modified, the paroxysms lessened in severity and frequency, and the duration of the disease very materially shortened.

The treatment is substantially as follows: In the earlier stages of the disease *Ferrum phos.* is given for the febrile symptoms alternated with *Kali mur.* for the fibrinous expectoration. If the disease has reached that stage when the cough has become spasmodic in character, ending in the characteristic whoop of nervous origin, then *Magnesia phos.* is the remedy *par excellence,* and as this stage is usually reached before the doctors' services are sought this remedy will form the basis of treatment in nine-tenths of all cases. Indeed, a vial of this remedy with directions to give a quantity the size of a pea in hot water every four hours regularly, and repeated whenever a paroxysm of coughing comes on quite frequently constitutes the whole treatment.

In severe cases other remedies are used according to indications, the character of the expectoration guiding in the selection of the remedy. *Calcarea phos.* is often used in winding up the treatment as a general restorative, or when the lime salts seem to be deficient.

I usually use the 6x potency of these remedies, though sometimes a lower is demanded. I have never used the higher potencies.

The dose will be equal to that recommended above for *Magnesia phos.* Very often, indeed, generally, I add the required quantity to water in a tumbler, and give a teaspoonful of the solution at a dose. (Dr. B. F. Beane, Eldorado, O.)

Dr. J. T. Frawley, of Cleveland, Ohio, reports a case of whooping-cough, which had developed a high temperature and symptoms showing that pneumonia was developing, cured with *Kali mur.* 3x in hot water, its action was prompt in allaying the acute symptoms.

Child, æt. 18 months, in the last stage of whooping-cough, with blistered lips and mouth; black, thin, offensive stools five times a day; hard and tympanitic abdomen; wasted to a shadow and given up to die by parents and physicians, got completely well from *Kali sulph.* (C. B. Knerr, M. D.)

Case in which *Kali sulph.* was given for whooping-cough, which immediately improved. The second day after taking the medicine he complained of stiff neck. The head is inclined toward the left, and the left shoulder raised. Great pain on moving head from side to side, or backward, but can move it forward without pain. This continued seven days. (W. P. Wesselhœft, M. D.)

MAGNES. PHOS. FOR WHOOPING COUGH.—In the spring of 1881, when there was an epidemic of whooping cough amongst the children here, a little child, æt. 10 months, was given up by the family doctor. I heard this from the father of the child, who was in great grief. He mentioned that the spasms, which occurred about ten times in the course of the day, were so severe that the little face became quite livid blue and swollen. I at once gave *Magnes. phos.* One single powder moderated the spasms so forcibly that they returned only occasionally, and the attacks were quite mild. Five days later I gave some *Kali phos.*, but without beneficial effect, then *Calcarea phos.*, and it had no good effect, as the paroxysms grew only worse for want of *Magnes. phos.* I ordered it to be taken again, and in a very short time the spasms and whoop were gone, and the child recovered rapidly. (From the *Rundschau.*)

WOMEN, DISEASES OF.

See also Leucorrhœa, Dysmenorrhœa and Menstruation.

Ferrum phos.—DYSMENORRHŒA.—Pain at the monthly periods, with flushed face and quick pulse, with vomiting of undigested food, sometimes acid taste.

MENSTRUAL.—Excessive congestion, blood bright-red. This remedy must be taken as a preventive before the periods if these symptoms are recurrent. It prevents menorrhagia in those predisposed thereto.

MORNING SICKNESS.—In pregnancy, with vomiting of food as taken, with or without acid taste, the food returns undigested.

METRITIS.—First stage to remove the fever, pain and congestion.

VAGINITIS.—Inflammation of the vagina, vaginismus, pain in the vagina from coition. Excessive dryness and sensitiveness, spasms of vagina.

Kali mur.—MENSTRUATION.—The monthly periods are too late or suppressed, checked, white tongue, etc. Too early menses. Excessive discharge, dark, clotted or tough, black, like tar. If periods last too long, too frequent.

MORNING SICKNESS.—In pregnancy, also vomiting of white phlegm.

UTERUS.—Ulceration of the os and cervix uteri, with the characteristic discharge of thick, white, mild secretions (glandular or follicular) from the mucous membrane (alkaline). Congestion of the uterus, chronic. Hypertrophy, second stage.

LEUCORRHŒA.—Discharge of milky-white mucus, non-irritating, mild. Puerperal fever, chief remedy.

Kali phos.—AMENORRHŒA.—Retention or delay of the monthly flow, with depression of spirits, lassitude and general nervous debility.

LEUCORRHŒA.—Scalding and acrid. Yellowish, blistering, orange colored.

MENSTRUAL.—Menstrual colic or great pains at the times of the periods in pale, lachrymose, irritable, sensitive females. Menses too late in same, too scanty in similar conditions, too profuse discharge, deep-red or blackish-red, thin and not coagulating, sometimes with strong odor. Uterine hæmorrhage. Pain in left side and ovaries. Intense pain across sacrum.

MISCARRIAGE.—Threatened in nervous subjects.

LABOR.—Weak and deficient pains. Puerperal mania. Child-bed fever.

Kali sulph.—LEUCORRHŒA.—Discharge of yellowish, greenish, slimy or watery secretions.

MENSTRUATION.—Too late and too scanty, with a feeling of weight and fulness in the abdomen; yellow-coated tongue.

Silicea.—Is especially adapted to weakly, oversensitive women, light complexion, lax muscles, scrofulous constitution; for nervous, irritable women with dry skin; night-sweats; for constitutions with imperfect assimilation.

MENSES.—Acrid, smell strong, excoriating, generally too profuse. Leucorrhœal discharge instead of menses. Icy coldness, especially of feet during menses. Nausea during sexual intercourse. Nymphomania. Backache with a sense of paralysis of the limbs. Offensive foot-sweat. All symptoms better from warmth.

LEUCORRHŒA.—Instead of menses. Painful, smarting leucorrhœa during micturition. Prof se discharge of whitish water with itching of parts. Const.pation, stool slips back.

LABOR, ETC.—Suppuration of mammæ. Chronic fistulous openings. Hard lumps in breasts. Child refuses milk or vomits as soon as taken. Nipples crack and ulcerate.

Magnesia phos.—MENSTRUAL COLIC.—The chief remedy in ordinary cases. Painful menstruation or pain preceding the flow. Vaginismus. Pains radiate from spine, relieved by warm clothing and pressure, aggravated by cold. **Membranous dysmenorrhœa.** It is a new development of the virtues of *Magnes. phos.* to find it capable, by its physiological action, of relaxing a contracted uterus. Fifteen grains in hot water produced the effect in five minutes, enabling a retained placenta to be removed.

Natrum mur.—LEUCORRHŒA.—A watery, scalding, irritating discharge, smarting after or between the periods. Slimy, corroding.

MENSTRUATION.—Thin discharge, watery, or pale, thin, watery blood. Too profuse and too early, with splitting headache, great sadness, sweet risings. After local use of nitrate of silver. "In young girls, if the menses do not appear, or when very scanty and at long intervals. Pain in the stomach, nausea, vomiting of food, weakness and faint feeling, desire for sour things, aversion to meat, bread and cooked food. Twelve to thirty are the most useful potencies." (Sulzer.) Pressing towards genitals in morning.

MORNING SICKNESS.—Vomiting of watery, frothy phlegm.

Natrum phos.—LEUCORRHŒA.—Discharge creamy or honey-colored, or acrid and watery. Discharge from the uterus sour-smelling, acid.

MORNING SICKNESS.—With vomiting of sour masses, sterility with acid secretions.

PROLAPSUS UTERI.—With weak, sinking feeling worse after defæcation.

UTERINE REGION.—Weakness and distress in.

UTERINE DISPLACEMENTS.—With rheumatic pains.

Calcarea phos.—LEUCORRHŒA.—As a constitutional tonic and intercurrent with the chief remedy. Discharge of albuminous mucus. "In cases where menstruation is too early, too long-lasting and profuse, often amounting to metrorrhagia, especially in slender and weakly women." (Mossa, *Allg. Hom. Zeit.*, 1883.) Menses too early in young girls, too late in adults, especially rheumatic patients. Throbbing in genitals with voluptuous feelings.

DYSMENORRHŒA.—Labor-like pains before and during catamenia. Uterine spasms after stool or micturition. **Nymphomania** with heat and weight on vertex, worse before menses. **Menses** too early, every two weeks, with voluptuous feelings.

Calcarea fluor.—AFTER-PAINS.—If too weak, contractions feeble.

MISCARRIAGE.—Flooding, to tone up the contractile power of the uterus.

MENORRHAGIA.—Due to venous relaxation.

MENSTRUATION.—Excessive, with bearing-down pains, and flooding.

DISPLACEMENTS.—Displacement of the uterus, dragging down of the uterus, associated with great mental anxiety. Prolapsus of the uterus. Dragging pains in the region of the uterus and in the thighs. Chronic interstitial metritis.

Calcarea sulph.—Menses late, long-lasting with headache, twitchings and great weakness. Pregnancy, vomiting with bitter taste. *Calcarea sulph.* 6 is the best remedy for extravasation of pus within the pelvic tissues unconfined by any pyogenic membrane or when a pus-bag is formed by rupture of an abscess wall without pus finding an outlet into the pelvic viscera. Patient pale and weak. (B. F. Betts, M. D.)

Natrum sulph.—Dysmenorrhœa with colic and chilliness, acrid menses, profuse with vesicular vulvitis. Nosebleed before menses.

CLINICAL CASES.

Dr. V. W. Connor, of Lansing, Mich., reports an interesting case of chronic pelvic cellulitis, where the patient had been bed-ridden for nine years, cured with *Kali mur.* 3x. Improvement began at once and she gained 35 lbs.

E. S. Bailey, M. D., reports a case of menorrhagia cured by *Ferrum phos.* 3x. The case presented a history of profuse menstruation, the flow was depleting, no pain or local tenderness—in fact, no tangible symp-

toms, the condition of anæmia representing the cause in this case.—
Clinique, 1886, p. 374.

Dysmenorrhœa, menses late and scanty; *Kali sulph.*, every four hours,
cured permanently and completely. (W. M. Pratt, M. D., *North American Journal of Homœopathy*, 1883.)

Doctor Phil. Porter reports a cure of papillomatous erosion of the
cervix with *Calc. fluor.* 6x, in which the local symptoms were accompanied by a dyscrasic condition, enlarged cervical glands, emaciation and
weakness. His prescription was based upon the constitutional changes,
the local conditions (the fissured appearance of the cervix), and an
abundantly yellowish leucorrhœa.—*Hahnemannian Monthly.*

Case of dysmenorrhœa with neuroses, presenting recurring neurotic
outbursts, painful and intense. Intense suffering during menses, headache, etc., had had nearly every homœopathic remedy, with no permanent
relief. *Kali phos.* 6x cured. (D. B. Whittier, M. D., *Trans. Mass. State
Hom. Med. Society*, 1886.)

A lady called to see me just after a severe hæmorrhage from the
womb—in fact, every time she menstruated she almost flooded to death.
Upon examination I found the uterus hard and so large that it completely filled the vagina; this had doubtless been coming on for six
years, since the birth of her child, as she complained of an increasing
weight in that region all the time. I at once began to give her *Calcarea
fluor.*, a dose every four hours. This reduced the induration in four to
six weeks to its natural size, and five years have passed and no return
of the trouble. (A. P. Davis, M. D.)

Mrs. W., two weeks pregnant, had been vomiting nearly everything
that she had eaten for these two weeks. Only food was vomited, and
that soon after eating. Gave *Ferrum phos.* 12x four times a day, a
small powder dry. What I wish to say of this case is this: Mrs. W.
has had four children, and with every one had commenced vomiting almost at the moment of conception, and would continue all through
pregnancy. The last four or five months of the time she would have to
remain in bed, being so weak that she could not get about. She commenced the same way this time, but after giving the *Ferrum phos.* a
few days the vomiting was very much controlled, and in a month had
ceased entirely, and she went to term in splendid condition. While we
cannot absolutely say that she would have been the same as at other
times, yet it is natural to suppose that she would have. (G. H. Martin,
M. D.)

Mrs. E., æt. 38, suffered for many years from chronic peritonitis and
ovaritis. She would have subacute attacks, which would last for several
months, confining her to her bed or room; hardly would she be well of
one attack before another would be induced by a cold or some slight
over-exertion. Was nervous and much depressed. One evening was
seized with very severe pain in the uterine and left ovarian regions, extending over the whole abdomen, which was very sensitive to the slightest touch. Pulse, 120; temperature, 104. *Ferrum phos.* 12x and *Kali
phos.* 12x were given in water every fifteen minutes, in alternation for

two hours, when the pains were somewhat less. The remedies were then given every hour for several days, until all pain and sensitiveness had gone. The patient was kept under treatment for two weeks longer, when she was obliged to go away. She gradually grew stronger and better, and now two years have passed, and she has never had the slightest sign of the trouble, which she had had for so many years, and is well and strong. (G. H. Martin, M. D.)

Miss B., æt. 20, had been suffering for the past two years with severe ovaralgia at the menstrual period. She had been under the treatment of several physicians and the only relief that they were able to give her was by the use of *Morphine,* that being only temporary. We called late one night to see her and found her suffering with severe pain in the left ovary, of a dull, dragging character, and but slightly intermittent. Patient, hysterical and very excitable. Gave her *Kali phos.* 6x, in water every ten minutes, for half an hour, when patient went to sleep, not awaking until morning, when she was free from pain. Gave her *Kali phos.* 6x, night and morning, for a month; at the next menstrual period was again called and found her suffering much as before. Gave *Kali phos.* 12x every ten minutes and after two doses was relieved. Gave *Kali phos.* 12x, *once* a day for a month, and now, after eighteen months, has had no more pain, and is feeling better in every way. (G. H. Martin, M. D.)

Lady about 40, anteflexion of uterus with very peculiar nervous condition. Very solicitous about health, weak, exhausted with slight effort. Irritable and easily displeased, which was unnatural to her. Had suffered many annoyances. Hyperæmia of the brain and hyperæsthesia, which condition made her utterly miserable most of the time. *Kali phos.* entirely cured. (Sarah N. Smith, New York.)

WORMS.

Ferrum phos.—Intestinal worms, predisposition to passing undigested food. Thread-worms.

Kali mur.—Small white thread-worms, causing itching at the anus; white tongue, give *Natrum phos.* in alternation.

Calcarea fluor.—Intestinal, long, round, or thread-worms with characteristic symptoms of acidity, or picking of the nose, occasional squinting. Pain in the bowels, restless sleep. Itching of the anus, especially at night in bed, face white about the mouth or nose. Grinding of the teeth in children. Pin-worms. This remedy probably acts by destroying the excess of lactic acid which seems to be necessary for the life of these worms.

CLINICAL CASE.

NATR. PHOS. A WORM REMEDY.—Dr. Schüssler recommends this drug as efficient in verminous affections. Dr. A. C. Kimball, of Barteville Station, Neb., reports a case in his practice with the following results: The patient, a boy aged five years, had spasms and had been treated by several physicians without benefit. After using *Natr. phos.* 3 for six weeks, three times a day, he passed four feet three inches of tapeworm, much to the astonishment of all interested. This is the first recorded case of *Natr. phos.* producing such a result. It is believed that the entire worm was passed, there being no evidence of any remaining. *Natr. phos.* is especially efficient in cases of pinworms.

YELLOW FEVER.

Natrum sulph.—If it assumes the form of a severe bilious remittent fever, and there is excess of bile. Vomit greenish, yellow-brown or black.

Ferrum phos.—For the fever in alternation with the preceding. At the beginning of the attack.

Kali phos.—For collapse and depressed vital forces. Also for deep green, bluish or black vomit and hæmorrhages.

PART IV.
REPERTORY.

Mental States and Affections.

ABERRATIONS, mental: *Kali phos.*
AFTER-EFFECTS OF—
    disappointment: *Calc. phos.*
    grief: *Calc. phos., Kali phos.*
    vexation: *Calc. phos.*
    fright: *Kali phos.*
AGORAPHOBIA: *Kali phos.*
AMELIORATION AFTER SLEEP: *Ferr. phos.*
AMBITIONLESS: *Natr. phos.*
ANGRY, IRRITABLE: *Natr. mur.*
ANXIETY: *Calc. phos., Kali phos., Natr. phos.*
APPREHENSIVENESS: *Natr. phos., Kali phos., Natr. mur.*
ATTENTION, difficult to fix: *Silicea.*
BLUSHING, from emotions: *Kali phos.*
BRAIN-FAG, from overwork: *Kali phos., Silicea, Natr. mur.*
CARRIES THINGS from place to place: *Magnes. phos.*
CONSOLATION, aggravated by: *Natr. mur.*
CROSSNESS, in children: *Kali phos.*
CHANGEABLE MOOD: *Calc. sulph., Kali phos.*
CRETINISM: *Calc. phos.*
CRYING MOOD: *Kali phos.*
DARK FOREBODINGS: *Kali phos.*
DEJECTION OF SPIRITS: *Natr. mur.*
DELIRIUM, in general: *Ferr. phos., Kali phos., Natr. mur*
    tremens: *Ferr. phos., Kali phos., Natr. mur.*
    low muttering: *Kali phos.*
    wandering: *Natr. mur.*
    very talkative, being wide awake: *Natr. mur., Ferr. phos.*
DEPRESSED MOOD: *Calc. fluor., Calc. sulph., Kali phos., Natr. mur.*
DERANGEMENTS, MENTAL: *Kali phos.*

DESPAIRS OF GETTING WELL again: *Natr. sulph.*
DESPONDENCY about business: *Kali phos.*
DIFFICULTY OF THOUGHT: *Silicea.*
DISAPPOINTMENT, after: *Calc. phos.*
DISGUST OF LIFE: *Silicea.*
DISHEARTENED: *Natr. sulph.*
DISINCLINATION TO CONVERSE: *Kali phos.*
   mix with people: *Kali phos.*
DREAD, nervous: *Kali phos.*
   of noises: *Kali phos., Silicea.*
DULNESS: *Kali phos., Magnes. phos., Natr. phos.*
EFFECTS OF, disappointment: *Calc. phos.*
   fright: *Kali phos.*
   grief: *Calc. phos., Kali phos.*
   vexation: *Calc. phos.*
EMOTIONS, sudden hysteria from: *'Kali phos.*
   blushing from: *Kali phos.*
ENERGY, want of: *Kali phos.*
EXCESSIVE SHYNESS: *Kali phos.*
EXCITEMENT, nervous: *Kali phos.*
FALSE IMPRESSIONS: *Kali phos., Natr. phos.*
FANCIES: *Kali phos.*
FEAR OF FALLING: *Kali sulph.*
FEARFULNESS: *Kali sulph.*
FEARS FINANCIAL RUIN: *Calc. fluor.*
FORGETFULNESS: *Calc. phos., Magnes. phos.*
FRETFULNESS: *Calc. phos., Kali phos.*
FRIGHT, effects of: *Kali phos.*
FROLICSOME: *Natr. mur.*
GLOOMY MOODS: *Kali phos., Natr. mur.*
GRASPING FOR IMAGINARY OBJECTS: *Kali phos.*
GREAT IMPATIENCE: *Kali phos.*
GRIEF, after effects of: *Calc. phos., Kali phos.*
HALLUCINATIONS: *Kali phos., Natr. phos.*
HAUNTED by visions of the past: *Kali phos.*
HEARS footsteps on awaking at night: *Natr. phos.*
HOMESICKNESS: *Kali phos.*
HOPELESS about the future: *Natr. phos., Ferr. phos.*
HYPOCHONDRIASIS: *Kali phos., Natr. phos.*

HYSTERIA, from sudden emotions: *Kali phos.*
ILL-HUMOR in children: *Calc. phos., Kali phos.*
ILLUSIONS, of senses: *Kali phos.*
    of sensation: *Magnes. phos.*
IMAGINES furniture to be persons: *Natr. phos.*
    he must starve: *Kali mur.*
IMAGINARY OBJECTS, grasping at: *Kali phos.*
IMPAIRED MEMORY: *Calc. phos.*
IMPATIENCE: *Kali phos.*
INCLINATION TO DANCE and sing: *Natr. mur.*
INDIFFERENCE to everything: *Ferr. phos.*
INDECISION: *Calc. fluor., Kali phos.*
INSANITY: *Ferr. phos., Kali phos., Silicea.*
IRRITABILITY: *Kali phos., Natr. sulph., Natr. phos., Silicea.*
LAMENTING: *Magnes. phos.*
LAUGHTER: *Kali phos.*
LONGS FOR PAST VISIONS: *Kali phos.*
LOOKS ON DARK SIDE of everything: *Kali phos.*
LOSS OF CONSCIOUSNESS, sudden: *Calc. sulph.*
LOSS OF MEMORY: *Kali phos.*
    sudden: *Calc. sulph.*
MANIA: *Ferr. phos., Kali phos.*
    puerperal: *Kali phos.*
MANIACAL MOOD: *Ferr. phos.*
MELANCHOLIA: *Kali phos., Natr. sulph.*
MELANCHOLIC at puberty: *Natr. mur.*
MENTAL ABSTRACTION: *Silicea.*
    DERANGEMENTS: *Kali phos.*
        from injuries to head: *Natr. sulph.*
MEMORY, LOSS OF: *Kali phos., Calc. phos., Magnes. phos.*
MIND, over-trained: *Kali phos., Silicea.*
MOOD, changeable: *Calc. sulph.*
    crying: *Kali phos.*
    depressed, gloomy: *Kali phos., Natr. mur.*
    lamenting: *Magnes. phos.*
    maniacal: *Ferr. phos.*
    hypochondriacal: *Kali phos., Natr. mur.*
    hysterical: *Kali phos.*
MUSIC AGGRAVATES: *Natr. sulph.*

NECESSITY FOR RESTRAINT: *Natr. sulph.*

NERVOUS DREAD: *Kali phos.*

NIGHT TERRORS, in children: *Kali phos.*

NOISE, oversensitiveness to: *Kali phos., Silicea, Kali mur.*

OBJECTS, imaginary, grasping at: *Kali phos.*

OMITS LETTERS OR WORDS IN WRITING: *Kali phos.*

OVERWORK, brain-fag from: *Kali phos.*

PAST VISIONS haunt: *Kali phos.*

PASSIONATE OUTBURSTS: *Natr. mur.*

PEEVISHNESS in children: *Calc. phos.*

PLAYING WITH PINS AND NEEDLES: *Silicea.*

RAMBLING in talk: *Kali phos., Natr. mur.*

SADNESS with beating of heart: *Natr. mur.*

SCREAMING: *Kali phos.*

SENSES, illusions of: *Kali phos., Magnes. phos.*

SENSATION, illusions of: *Magnes. phos.*

SENSITIVENESS: *Kali phos., Silicea.*

SHYNESS, excessive: *Kali phos.*

SIGHING: *Kali phos., Natr. mur.*

SLOW COMPREHENSION: *Calc. phos.*

SOBBING: *Magnes. phos.*

SOMNAMBULISM: *Kali phos.*

SOPOR AND STUPOR in acute diseases: *Natr. mur.*

SOLITUDE, desires: *Calc. phos.*

STARTINGS, nervous: *Kali phos., Kali mur.*

STUPID: *Calc. phos.*

STUPOR: *Kali phos.*

SUDDEN EMOTIONS, causing hysteria: *Kali phos.*

SUICIDAL TENDENCY: *Natr. sulph.*

SUSPICIOUSNESS: *Kali phos.*

TALKS to herself constantly: *Magnes. phos.*

TALK, rambling in: *Kali phos.*

 while asleep: *Kali phos.*

TALKATIVE: *Ferr. phos., Natr. mur.*

TENDENCY TO SUICIDE: *Natr. sulph.*

TERRORS at night in children: *Kali phos.*

THOUGHT, difficulty of: *Silicea.*

TIMIDITY: *Kali phos.*

TIRED OF LIFE: *Silicea.*

TRIFLES seem like mountains: *Ferr. phos.*
    vex: *Natr. phos.*
USES wrong words in writing or speaking: *Kali phos.*
VEXATION, effects of: *Calc. phos., Kali phos.*
VISIONS of past, haunt: *Kali phos.*
WANT OF ENERGY: *Kali phos.*
WANTS TO BE CARRIED: *Kali phos.*
WEEPING, disposition to: *Kali phos.*
WHINING: *Kali phos.*
WILDNESS: *Natr. sulph.*

Head, Sensorium and Scalp.

ANÆMIA, cerebral: *Kali phos.*
BALD SPOTS: *Kali sulph., Calc. phos.*
BETTER under cheerful excitement: *Kali phos.*
BLOOD rushes to the head: *Ferr. phos., Natr. sulph.*
    tumors on scalp: *Calc. fluor.*
BRAIN, concussion of: *Kali phos.*
    feels as if loose: *Natr. sulph.*
    inflammation of, first stage: *Ferr. phos.*
    softening of: *Kali phos.*
    troubles of children: *Magnes. phos.*
    violent pains at base of: *Natr. sulph.*
    water in: *Kali phos.*
BRAIN-FAG: *Calc. phos., Kali phos., Natr. mur., Silicea.*
BRUISING PAIN in head: *Ferr. phos.*
BRUISES of cranial bones: *Calc. fluor.*
BURNING on top of head: *Natr. sulph.*
CEPHALÆTOMA: *Calc. fluor., Silicea.*
CEREBRAL APOPLEXY: *Silicea.*
COLD feeling in the head: *Calc. phos.*
CONCUSSION OF THE BRAIN: *Kali phos.*
    after effects of: *Natr. sulph.*
CONGESTIVE HEADACHES: *Ferr. phos.. Natr. sulph., Silicea, Natr.*
           mur.
CRANIOTABES: *Calc. phos., Calc. sulph.*
CROWN OF HEAD aches: *Natr. phos., Natr. sulph.*
CRUSTS, yellow, on scalp: *Calc. sulph.*
CRUSTA LACTEA: *Kali mur.*
DANDRUFF: *Kali sulph., Magnes. phos., Natr. mur., Kali mur.*

DULL, RIGHT-SIDED HEADACHE: *Ferr. phos.*

EFFECTS OF FALLS or injuries to head: *Natr. sulph.*

ERUPTION on scalp, itching: *Natr. mur.*

   on occiput, offensive: *Silicea.*

   on margin of hair at nape: *Natr. mur.*

EXCRESCENCES on scalp: *Calc. fluor.*

EXCRUCIATING PAINS in head: *Magnes. phos.*

FALLS OR INJURIES, effects of: *Natr. sulph.*

FALLING OUT OF HAIR: *Kali sulph., Natr. mur., Silicea.*

FONTANELLES remain unclosed: *Calc. phos., Silicea.*

FULLNESS of head: *Calc. phos.*

GNAWING at base of brain: *Natr. sulph.*

HAIR, falling out of: *Kali sulph., Natr. mur., Silicea.*

   painful on combing it: *Natr. sulph., Ferr. phos.*

HEAD, back of, sore: *Kali phos.*

   feels cold to touch: *Calc. phos.*

   fulness of: *Calc. phos., Ferr. phos.*

   large bones separated: *Calc. phos.*

   nods forward involuntarily: *Natr. mur.*

   pressure upon: *Calc. phos.*

   pressure and heat on vertex of: *Natr. phos.*

   sweats in children: *Calc. phos., Silicea.*

HEADACHE, accompanied by, appearance of lumps on scalp:
     Silicea.

   dizziness: *Natr. sulph.*

   after and before menses: *Natr. mur.*

     walking: *Natr. mur.*

   bilious diarrhœa: *Natr. sulph.*

   bitter taste in A. M.: *Natr. sulph.*

   bile, vomiting of: *Natr. sulph.*

   colicky pains: *Natr. sulph.*

   constipation: *Natr. mur.*

   cool feeling in head: *Calc. phos., Silicea.*

   despondency: *Kali phos.*

   drowsiness: *Natr. mur.*

   dulness: *Calc. phos.*

   empty feeling in stomach: *Kali phos.*

   excruciating pains: *Magnes. phos.*

   exhaustion: *Kali phos.*

HEADACHE, accompanied by faintish nausea: *Calc. fluor.*
               flatulence: *Calc. phos.*
               forgetfulness: *Calc. phos.*
               fullness of head: *Calc. phos.*
               furred tongue: *Ferr. phos.*
               hawking up of white mucus: *Kali mur.*
                    watery mucus: *Natr. mur.*
               irritability: *Kali phos.*
               much saliva in mouth: *Natr. mur.*
               nausea: *Calc. sulph., Natr. phos.*
                   and chilliness: *Magnes. phos.*
               optical defects: *Magnes. phos.*
               profusion of tears: *Natr. mur.*
               pulsation on top of head: *Natr. sulph.*
               prostrate feeling: *Kali phos.*
               red eyes and face: *Ferr. phos.*
               sensitiveness to noise: *Kali phos.*
               shifting pains: *Kali sulph., Magnes. phos.*
               shooting pains: *Magnes. phos.*
               sleeplessness: *Ferr. phos., Kali phos.*
               soreness to touch: *Ferr. phos.*
               sparks before eyes: *Magnes. phos.*
               stinging pains: *Magnes. phos.*
               stretching: *Kali phos.*
               tendency to spasmodic symptoms: *Magnes. phos.*
               throbbing sensation: *Ferr. phos., Silicea.*
               vertigo: *Ferr. phos., Natr. sulph., Silicea.*
               vomiting: *Kali mur.*
                   of bile: *Natr. sulph.*
                   slimy: *Natr. phos.*
                   sour matter; *Natr. phos.*
                   transparent phlegm: *Calc. phos., Natr. mur.*
                   undigested food: *Ferr. phos.*
                   weariness: *Kali phos.*
                   white mucus: *Kali mur.*
                   yawning: *Kali phos.*
      after menses: *Natr. mur.*
        walking: *Natr. mur.*
    aggravated by change of weather: *Calc. phos.*

23

HEADACHE, aggravated by cold: *Calc. phos.*
     exertion: *Silicea.*
     evening: *Kali sulph.*
     heat: *Calc. phos.*
     light: *Silicea.*
     mental exertion: *Calc. phos., Magnes. phos., Silicea.*
     motion: *Natr. sulph., Ferr. phos.*
     moving head from side to side or backward: *Kali sulph.*
     noise: *Silicea.*
     pressure of hat: *Calc. phos.*
     reading: *Natr. sulph.*
     shaking head: *Ferr. phos.*
     stooping: *Ferr. phos.*
     warm room: *Kali sulph.*
  ameliorated by cheerful excitement: *Kali phos.*
     cold: *Ferr. phos.*
     cool open air: *Kali sulph.*
     eating: *Kali phos.*
     external warmth: *Magnes. phos., Silicea.*
     gentle motion: *Kali phos.*
     nosebleed: *Ferr. phos.*
     quiet: *Natr. sulph.*
     wrapping up head warmly: *Silicea.*
  as of nail driven in over eye: *Ferr. phos.*
  beginning in the evening: *Kali sulph.*
     in morning: *Natr. mur.*
  before and after menses: *Natr. mur.*
  blind: *Ferr. phos.*
  catarrhal: *Natr. mur.*
  chronic: *Calc. phos., Natr. mur., Silicea.*
  cold aggravates: *Calc. phos.*
     ameliorates: *Ferr. phos.*
  commencing in morning: *Natr. mur., Natr. sulph., Natr.
               phos.*
  congestive: *Ferr. phos., Silicea.*
  cool open air relieves: *Kali sulph.*
  dull: *Natr. mur.*
  dull heavy, on top of: *Ferr. phos*
  during dentition: *Calc. phos.*

HEADACHE during eating: *Kali phos.*

    menses: *Natr. mur., Natr. sulph.*

  evening, beginning in: *Kali sulph.*

  from abdominal irritation: *Silicea.*

  from above downward: *Calc. phos.*

    cold: *Ferr. phos.*

    gouty predisposition: *Ferr. phos., Natr. sulph.*

    hunger: *Silicea.*

    injuries to head: *Natr. sulph.*

    loss of animal fluids: *Calc. phos., Natr. mur.*

    mental exertion: *Magnes. phos., Silicea.*

    nervous exertion: *Silicea.*

    overheating: *Silicea.*

    sun heat: *Ferr. phos.*

  frontal: *Natr. phos.*

  gastric: *Calc. phos., Natr. sulph., Silicea.*

  gentle motion relieves: *Kali phos.*

  hammering: *Natr. mur., Ferr. phos.*

  heavy: *Natr. mur.*

  intermittent: *Magnes. phos.*

  lasting until noon: *Natr. mur.*

  menstrual, with hunger: *Kali phos.*

  migraine: *Natr. mur., Silicea.*

  nape and vertex: *Silicea, Magnes. phos.*

  nervous: *Kali phos., Silicea, Magnes. phos.*

  neuralgic: *Kali phos., Magnes. phos.*

  occipital: *Kali phos., Magnes. phos., Natr. phos., Silicea, Natr. sulph.*

  extending to spine: *Magnes. phos.*

  of cachectic persons: *Natr. mur., Silicea.*

    children: *Calc. phos., Ferr. phos.*

    pale, sensitive persons: *Kali phos.*

    scrofulous people: *Silicea.*

    school-girls: *Calc. phos., Natr. mur.*

    students: *Kali phos., Magnes. phos.*

  on crown of head: *Magnes. phos., Natr. mur.*

    during profuse menses: *Ferr. phos.*

  on awaking in morning: *Natr. phos.*

  paroxysmal: *Magnes. phos.*

HEADACHE, quiet relieves: *Natr. sulph.*
   rheumatic: *Calc. phos., Kali sulph., Magnes. phos., Silicea.*
   right-sided: *Ferr. phos.*
   sick: *Calc. phos., Ferr. phos., Kali mur., Natr. mur., Natr.*
          phos., Natr. sulph., Calc. sulph., Kali phos.
   sudden in its onset: *Natr. sulph.*
   vertex: *Ferr. phos., Natr. sulph.*
   worse near sutures: *Calc. phos.*
      right side: *Ferr. phos.*
HEAT in vertex: *Natr. sulph., Natr. phos.*
HEMICRANIA: *Natr. mur.*
HYDROCEPHALUS: *Calc. phos., Kali phos., Natr. mur.*
ITCHING ERUPTION on scalp: *Natr. mur.*
LUMPS on scalp: *Silicea.*
MENINGITIS: *Ferr. phos., Kali mur.*
MENSTRUAL headache with hunger: *Kali phos.*
MIGRAINE: *Natr. mur., Silicea.*
MOTION aggravates: *Ferr. phos., Natr. sulph.*
   ameliorates: *Kali phos.*
MOUTH full of saliva: *Natr. mur.*
MUCUS, watery, coughed up: *Natr. mur.*
NODULES on head: *Silicea.*
NOISE, sensitive to: *Kali phos., Silicea, Kali mur.*
NOISES in head: *Kali phos.*
NOSEBLEED relieves headache: *Ferr. phos.*
OCCIPITAL HEADACHE: *Natr. phos., Silicea, Kali phos., Natr.*
         sulph.
OPEN FONTANELLES: *Calc. phos., Silicea.*
   across eyes: *Kali phos.*
PAIN, aggravated by heat: *Calc. phos.*
     cold: *Calc. phos.*
     moving and stooping: *Ferr. phos.*
     pressure of hat: *Calc. phos.*
   as if a nail were being driven in: *Ferr. phos.*
     skull were too full: *Natr. phos.*
   around head, worse forehead: *Calc. sulph.*
   beating and bruising: *Ferr. phos.*
   occipital: *Kali phos.*
   periodical: *Natr. mur.*

PAIN, pressing: *Calc. phos.*, *Ferr. phos.*

        on top of head: *Natr. phos.*

    shifting, shooting, stinging: *Magnes. phos.*

    stitching: *Ferr. phos.*

RUSH OF BLOOD to head: *Ferr. phos.*

SALIVA profuse, with head symptoms: *Natr. mur.*

SCALD-HEAD for children, yellow secretion: *Calc. sulph.*, *Kali sulph.*, *Kali mur.*

SCALP, copious scaling of: *Kali sulph.*

    dandruff: *Magnes. phos.*, *Natr. mur.*, *Kali mur.*, *Kali sulph.*

    eruptions on: *Ferr. phos.*

    feels rough: *Magnes. phos.*

    itching of: *Calc. phos.*, *Kali phos.*

    itching eruption on margin of hair: *Natr. mur.*

    itching pustules on: *Silicea.*

    Moist eruptions on: *Kali sulph.*

    nodules on: *Silicea.*

    sensitive: *Natr. sulph.*

        to cold and touch: *Ferr. phos.*

    sore: *Calc. phos.*

    sticky eruptions on: *Kali sulph.*

    suppurations of: *Calc. sulph.*, *Silicea.*

    tinea capitis: *Kali sulph.*, *Silicea.*

    ulcers of: *Calc. phos.*

        with callous edges: *Calc. fluor.*

    white scales on: *Kali sulph.*, *Natr. mur.*

SCHOOL-GIRLS, cephalalgia of: *Calc. phos.*, *Natr. mur.*

SCROFULOUS ulcers of scalp: *Calc. phos.*

SENSATION as if head would open: *Natr. mur.*

    of pressure in and through head: *Natr. sulph.*

    throbbing: *Ferr. phos.*

SORENESS of head to touch: *Ferr. phos.*

SPASMODIC symptoms: *Magnes. phos.*

STITCHING PAINS: *Ferr. phos.*

STUDENTS, headaches of: *Kali phos.*

SUN-HEAT, ill effects of: *Ferr. phos.*

SUNSTROKE: *Natr. mur.*

SUPPURATIONS of the scalp: *Calc. phos.*, *Silicea.*

SWEAT OF HEAD in children: *Calc. phos.*, *Silicea.*

TEARING in bones of skull: *Calc. phos.*
TENDENCY to spasmodic symptoms: *Magnes. phos.*
THROBBING in the head: *Ferr. phos.*
TOP OF HEAD sensitive to cold air: *Ferr. phos.*
TRANSPARENT PHLEGM, vomiting of: *Natr. mur., Ferr. phos.*
ULCERS on scalp, scrofulous: *Calc. phos.*
　　with callous edges: *Calc. fluor.*
UNREFRESHING SLEEP with headache: *Kali phos., Natr. mur.*
VERTIGO: *Calc. phos., Ferr. phos., Kali phos., Natr. sulph., Silicea.*
VERTIGO from nervous exhaustion: *Kali phos.*
　　　anæmia: *Kali phos.*
　　in old age: *Calc. phos.*
　　labyrinthine: *Silicea.*
　　on motion and when walking: *Calc. phos.*
　　　looking up: *Kali sulph., Kali phos.*
　　　rising: *Kali sulph., Kali phos.*
　　with deathly nausea: *Calc. phos.*
　　　gastric derangements: *Natr. phos.*
　　　rush of blood to head: *Ferr. phos.*
　　　tendency to fall to left side: *Silicea.*
VOMITING of bile: *Natr. sulph.*
　　sour froth: *Natr. phos.*
　　transparent slime: *Natr. mur.*
　　undigested food: *Ferr. phos.*
WATERY MUCUS coughed or vomited up: *Natr. mur., Ferr. phos.*
WEIGHT at back of head: *Kali phos.*
YELLOW CRUSTS on scalp: *Calc. sulph.*

Eyes.

ABSCESS OF CORNEA: *Calc. sulph., Silicea, Kali mur., Kali sulph.*
AFFECTIONS, spasmodic, of eyelids: *Calc. phos., Magnes. phos.*
AFTER INJURIES to eye: *Calc. sulph.*
AGGLUTINATION of lids: *Natr. phos., Silicea.*
AMAUROSIS: *Calc. phos.*
AMBLYOPIA after suppressed foot-sweat: *Silicea.*
　　diphtheria: *Kali phos.*
ANTERIOR CHAMBER, pus in: *Calc. sulph., Kali mur., Silicea.*
APPEARANCE, staring, excited: *Kali phos.*
ASTHENOPIA, muscular: *Natr. mur., Kali phos., Magnes. phos.*
BLACK SPOTS before eyes: *Kali phos.*

BLEPHARITIS: *Natr. mur., Silicea.*

BLISTERS on cornea: *Natr. mur.*

BLISTER-LIKE GRANULATIONS: *Natr. phos., Natr. sulph.*

BLOODSHOT eyes: *Natr. phos., Ferr. phos., Natr. mur.*

BLURRING of eyes: *Kali phos., Calc. fluor.*

BOILS around lids: *Silicea.*

BURNING of edges of eyelids: *Natr. sulph.*
    sensation in eyes: *Ferr. phos.*

CANNOT USE EYES by gaslight: *Calc. phos.*

CANTHI inflamed: *Calc. sulph.*

CATARACT: *Calc. fluor., Calc. phos., Kali sulph., Kali mur.*
    after suppressed foot-sweat: *Silicea.*
    smoky pus, in anterior chamber: *Calc. sulph.*

CHROMATOPSIA: *Magnes. phos.*

CILIARY NEURALGIA: *Natr. mur.*
    over right eye: *Silicea.*

CONJUNCTIVA reddened or yellow: *Natr. mur., Natr. sulph.*

CONJUNCTIVITIS: *Calc. fluor., Ferr. phos., Kali sulph., Natr.*
            mur., Natr. phos.
    chronic: *Natr. sulph.*
    granular: *Natr. phos.*
    discharge, white mucus: *Natr. mur.*
        greenish: *Natr. sulph.*
        yellow, creamy: *Natr. phos.*
    phlyctenular: *Calc. sulph.*

CONTRACTED pupils: *Magnes. phos.*

CORNEA, abscess of: *Calc. sulph., Silicea, Kali sulph., Kali mur.*
    first stage: *Ferr. phos.*
    blisters on: *Natr. mur., Kali mur.*
    opaque: *Calc. phos., Silicea.*
    spots on: *Calc. fluor., Natr. sulph.*
        white: *Natr. mur.*
    ulcers, deep, on: *Calc. sulph., Calc. phos.*
    scrofulous: *Calc. phos., Natr. mur.*
        superficial, flat: *Kali mur.*
    smoky: *Calc. sulph.*

CRUSTS, yellow, on eyelids: *Kali sulph.*

CYSTIC TUMORS around lids: *Silicea.*

DARK SPOTS before eyes: *Magnes. phos., Kali mur.*

DEEP ABSCESS of cornea: *Calc. sulph., Silicea.*

DIMNESS of crystalline lens: *Kali sulph.*
DIMSIGHTEDNESS: *Natr. mur., Natr. phos., Magnes. phos.*
DIPHTHERIA, strabismus or squinting after: *Kali phos.*
DIPLOPIA: *Magnes. phos., Kali phos.*
DISCHARGE of thick yellow matter: *Calc. sulph.*
    clear mucus: *Natr. mur.*
    white mucus: *Kali mur.*
    green pus: *Natr. sulph.*
    golden-yellow, creamy matter: *Natr. phos.*
DISCHARGE of yellow, greenish matter: *Kali sulph., Kali mur.*
DISEASES of lachrymal apparatus: *Silicea.*
DROOPING of eyelids: *Magnes. phos., Kali phos.*
DULL VISION: *Magnes. phos., Natr. phos.*
EDGES OF EYELIDS burn: *Natr. sulph.*
ERUPTION of small vesicles about eyes: *Natr. mur.*
EXCITED, staring appearance of eyes: *Kali phos.*
EYES, angles, affections: *Silicea.*
    become blurred: *Kali phos.*
    bloodshot: *Natr. phos.*
    burning sensation in: *Ferr. phos., Kali phos.*
    cannot use by gas light: *Calc. phos.*
    feeling of sand in: *Kali mur., Kali phos., Ferr. phos.*
    flickering before: *Calc. fluor.*
    gauze before: *Natr. mur.*
    inflammation of, with acute pain: *Ferr. phos.*
      ·dry: *Calc. phos.*
      discharge of thick, yellow mucus: *Calc. sulph.*
      without secretion: *Ferr. phos.*
    staring appearance of: *Kali phos.*
    pain over: *Natr. phos., Natr. mur., Magnes. phos.*
    red: *Ferr. phos.*
    sees colors before eyes: *Magnes. phos.*
      sparks: *Calc. fluor., Magnes. phos.*
    sensation of foreign body in: *Calc. sulph.*
    sensitive to light: *Magnes. phos.*
    sparks before eyes: *Calc. fluor., Magnes. phos.*
    twitch: *Kali phos.*
EYEBALL, pains in, aggravated by moving lids: *Ferr. phos.*
EYEBALLS ache: *Calc. fluor.*
    pain in, aggravated by motion: *Ferr. phos.*
    soreness of: *Kali phos.*

EYELIDS, boils around: *Silicea.*
  burn: *Natr. mur., Kali phos.*
  cystic tumors around: *Silicea, Ferr. phos.*
  drooping of: *Kali phos., Magnes. phos.*
  edges of, burn: *Natr. sulph.*
  glued together: *Natr. phos., Silicea, Calc. phos., Kali phos., Natr. mur., Calc. fluor.*
  granular: *Natr. mur.*
EYES, itching: *Magnes. phos.*
  smarting of: *Natr. mur.*
  sore: *Kali phos.*
  spasmodic affections of: *Calc. phos., Magnes. phos.*
  specks of matter on: *Kali mur.*
  styes on: *Silicea.*
  twitching of: *Magnes. phos., Calc. sulph.*
  yellow crusts on: *Kali sulph.*
FLAT ULCER on cornea: *Kali mur.*
FLICKERING before eyes: *Calc. fluor.*
FOREIGN BODY, sensation of: *Calc. sulph.*
GAUZE before eyes: *Natr. mur.*
GLAUCOMA: *Natr. mur.*
GLUING TOGETHER of eyelids: *Natr. mur., Silicea.*
GRANULAR conjunctivitis: *Natr. phos., Natr. sulph.*
  eyelids: *Natr. mur.*
GRANULATIONS look like small blisters: *Natr. phos., Natr. sulph.*
GREENISH discharge from eyes: *Kali mur., Kali sulph.*
HEMIOPIA: *Calc. sulph.*
HYPOPYON: *Calc. sulph., Kali mur., Silicea, Kali sulph., Natr. phos.*
INFLAMMATION OF CANTHI: *Calc. sulph.*
  eyes: *Calc. phos., Calc. sulph., Ferr. phos.*
  dry: *Calc. phos.*
  discharge of yellow matter: *Calc. sulph.*
  with acute pain: *Ferr. phos.*
  without secretion: *Ferr. phos.*
IRITIS: *Kali mur., Natr. mur.*
KERATITIS, parenchymatous: *Calc. phos., Kali mur.*
  pustular: *Calc. sulph., Silicea.*
LACHRYMATION: *Magnes. phos., Natr. mur., Natr. sulph.*
  acrid: *Natr. mur.*

LACHRYMATION, burning: *Natr. sulph., Natr. phos.*
  with eruption of small vesicles: *Natr. mur.*
  with neuralgia: *Natr. mur.*
  worse after nitrate of silver: *Natr. mur.*
LACHRYMAL SAC, disease of: *Silicea.*
  duct, stricture of: *Natr. mur.*
LENS, dimness of: *Kali sulph.*
LETTERS RUN TOGETHER when reading: *Natr. mur.*
LIDS.   (See Eyelids.)
LIGHT, sensitive to.   (See Photophobia.)
LOSS OF PERCEPTIVE POWER after exhaustion: *Kali phos.*
  diphtheria: *Kali phos.*
MOVING EYES aggravates pain: *Ferr. phos.*
MUCOUS DISCHARGES, white: *Kali mur.*
  clear: *Natr. mur.*
MUSCÆ VOLITANTES: *Silicea.*
MUSCULAR ASTHENOPIA: *Nat. mur., Magnes. phos., Kali phos.*
NEURALGIA, ciliary: *Natr. mur.*
  over right eye: *Silicea.*
  periodical: *Natr. mur.*
    with lachrymation: *Natr. mur.*
  relieved by warmth: *Magnes. phos.*
  supraorbital: *Magnes. phos., Ferr. phos.*
  worse right side: *Magnes. phos.*
NYSTAGMUS: *Magnes. phos.*
OBSTRUCTION of tear-duct: *Natr. mur.*
ONYX: *Kali mur.*
OPAQUE CORNEA: *Calc. phos., Silicea.*
OPHTHALMIA, discharge creamy: *Natr. phos.*
    thick and yellow: *Calc. sulph.*
  neonatorum: *Kali sulph.*
  scrofulous: *Natr. phos.*
ORBITS, caries of: *Silicea.*
  pressure and soreness in: *Silicea.*
PAIN, as of splinter: *Calc. sulph.*
  in eyes: *Ferr. phos.*
  in eyeball, aggravated by moving them: *Ferr. phos.*
  neuralgia: *Magnes. phos., Natr. mur.*
PARENCHYMATOUS keratitis: *Calc. phos., Kali mur.*
PERCEPTIVE POWER lost: *Kali phos.*

PHOTOPHOBIA: *Calc. sulph., Kali mur., Magnes. phos., Natr. mur., Natr. sulph., Calc. phos.*

PHOTOPSIA: *Magnes. phos., Calc. fluor.*

PTOSIS: *Kali phos., Magnes. phos.*

PUPILS contracted: *Magnes. phos.*

PURULENT DISCHARGE from eyes: *Calc. sulph., Kali sulph.*

PUS IN ANTERIOR CHAMBER. (See Hypopyon.)

PUSTULAR KERATITIS: *Calc. sulph., Silicea.*

REDNESS of eyes: *Ferr. phos., Natr. mur.*

RETINITIS: *Calc. sulph., Ferr. phos., Kali mur.*

SAND, sensation of, in eyes: *Ferr. phos., Kali mur., Kali phos.*

SCALDING of parts about eye: *Natr. mur.*

SCROFULOUS ophthalmia: *Natr. phos.*

    ulcers of cornea: *Natr. mur.*

SENSATION of foreign body in eye: *Calc. sulph., Ferr. phos.*

    sticks in the eye: *Kali phos.*

SENSITIVENESS to light: *Magnes. phos.*

SIGHT, dim: *Natr. phos.*

    weak: *Kali phos.*

SORENESS of eyeballs: *Kali phos.*

SPASMODIC affections of eyelids: *Calc. phos., Magnes. phos.*

SPARKS before eyes: *Calc. fluor., Magnes. phos., Natr. phos.*

SPECKS of matter on eyelids: *Kali mur.*

SPOTS on cornea: *Calc. fluor.*

        white: *Natr. mur.*

        dark: *Magnes. phos.*

SQUINTING, after diphtheria: *Kali phos.*

    spasmodic: *Magnes. phos.*

    from intestinal irritation: *Natr. phos.*

STARING, excited look: *Kali phos.*

STRABISMUS: *Kali phos., Magnes. phos., Natr. phos.*

STYES on eyelids: *Silicea, Ferr. phos.*

SUPERFICIAL FLAT ULCERS: *Kali mur.*

SUPRAORBITAL NEURALGIAS: *Magnes. phos., Natr. mur.*

TARSAL TUMORS: *Silicea.*

TRACHOMA: *Kali mur.*

TWITCHING of eyelids: *Magnes. phos., Calc. phos.*

ULCERS on cornea, deep: *Calc. sulph.*

        scrofulous: *Calc. phos., Natr. mur.*

        superficial, flat: *Kali mur.*

VESICLES, eruption of: *Natr. mur.*
VISION, affected, sees colors: *Magnes. phos.*
    blurred: *Calc. fluor.*
    sparks: *Calc. fluor., Magnes. phos.*
  dull: *Magnes. phos., Natr. mur.*
WARMTH relieves neuralgias: *Magnes. phos.*
WEAKNESS of sight: *Kali phos.*
WHEN READING, letters run together: *Natr. mur.*
WHITE, MUCOUS discharge from eyes: *Kali mur.*
YELLOW conjunctiva: *Natr. sulph.*
    crusts on eyelids: *Kali sulph.*
    discharge from eyes: *Calc. sulph., Kali mur., Kali sulph.*
    golden and creamy: *Natr. phos.*

Ears.

ACHING OF BONES around ear: *Calc. phos.*
ANÆMIC SUBJECTS, ear troubles in: *Ferr. phos.*
ANACHYLOSIS of small bones: *Ferr. phos.*
ATROPHIC ear troubles: *Kali phos.*
    itching in: *Kali phos.*
AUDITORY CANAL, swollen: *Silicea, Kali mur.*
BLOWING NOSE, cracking noises on: *Kali mur.*
BONES around ear ache: *Calc. phos.*
BURNING of ears: *Natr. phos., Natr. mur.*
BUZZING in the ears: *Kali phos., Magnes. phos.*
CALCAREOUS DEPOSITS on tympanic cavity: *Calc. fluor.*
CATARRH of Eustachian tube: *Kali sulph., Natr. mur., Kali mur.*
    tympanic cavity: *Kali sulph., Natr. mur., Kali mur.*
CHRONIC CATARRHAL CONDITIONS of middle ear: *Kali mur.,*
                                        Kali sulph., Natr. mur.
COLD FEELING of outer ears: *Calc. phos.*
COMPLAINTS, rheumatic, of ears: *Calc. phos.*
CONFUSION in ears: *Kali phos.*
CONGESTIVE STAGE of otitis: *Ferr. phos.*
CRACKING NOISES when swallowing: *Kali mur.*
    chewing: *Natr. mur.*
  blowing nose: *Kali mur.*
CUTTING PAINS in ear: *Ferr. phos.*
    under ear: *Kali sulph.*
DAMP WEATHER aggravates earache: *Natr. sulph.*

DARK REDNESS of internal parts: *Ferr. phos.*

DEAFNESS, from inflammatory action: *Ferr. phos.*

    nerve troubles: *Magnes. phos.*

    swelling of Eustachian tubes: *Kali mur., Kali sulph., Silicea.*

        external ear: *Kali mur.*

        glands about ears: *Kali mur.*

        inner ear: *Kali sulph.*

        throat: *Kali sulph.*

        tympanic cavity: *Natr. mur., Silicea.*

    suppuration: *Calc. sulph., Ferr. phos., Silicea, Kali mur., Kali phos.*

    want of perception: *Kali phos.*

    worse in heated room: *Kali sulph.*

DEPOSIT of calcareous matter on tympanum: *Calc. fluor.*

DIFFUSED INFLAMMATION: *Ferr. phos.*

DISCHARGES FROM EAR, bright yellow: *Kali phos.*

    dirty: *Kali phos.*

    fœtid: *Kali phos.*

DISCHARGES FROM EAR, giving no relief to pain: *Ferr. phos.*

    muco-purulent: *Ferr. phos.*

    offensive: *Kali phos.*

    purulent: *Calc. phos., Kali sulph., Natr. mur.*

        mixed with blood: *Calc. sulph., Kali phos.*

    thick, pus-like: *Calc. sulph.*

    watery matter: *Kali sulph.*

DULNESS OF HEARING: *Ferr. phos., Kali phos., Silicea.*

    from nerve troubles: *Magnes. phos.*

EARACHE with burning pain: *Ferr. phos.*

    discharges of yellowish matter: *Kali sulph.*

    nervous conditions: *Magnes. phos.*

    pulsations: *Ferr. phos.*

    sensation of something forcing its way out: *Natr. sulph.*

    sharp, stitching pain: *Ferr. phos.*

    swelling of the glands: *Kali mur., Calc. phos.*

    throbbing pain: *Ferr. phos.*

    white tongue: *Kali mur.*

    worse in damp weather: *Natr. sulph.*

EARS, affections of, in anæmic people: *Ferr. phos.*

    rheumatic people: *Calc. phos.*

    scrofulous children: *Calc. phos.*

EARS, atrophic, troubles of: *Kali phos.*
>   burn: *Natr. phos., Natr. mur.*
>   buzzing in: *Kali phos.*
>   cold feeling of outer: *Calc. phos.*
>   covered with thin scabbing: *Natr. phos.*
>   cracked in: *Kali mur.*
>   excessive flow of blood to ear: *Ferr. phos.*
>   external, inflammation of: *Silicea.*
>   dry and scaly epidermis: *Kali mur.*
>>   tendency to atrophy of walls: *Kali mur.*
>>   swelling: *Kali mur.*
>   heat in: *Ferr. phos.*
>   humming in: *Kali phos.*
>   inflammation of, after bathing: *Silicea.*
>   itching of: *Natr. phos.*
>>   in: *Natr. mur.*
>   middle, suppuration of: *Calc. sulph., Kali phos., Silicea.*
>   noises in: *Ferr. phos., Kali phos., Kali mur., Natr. mur.*
>   one ear red, hot, burning: *Natr. phos.*
>   open with loud report: *Silicea.*
>   pimples around: *Calc. sulph.*
>   pulsation noticed in ear: *Ferr. phos.*
>   ringing in, as if bells: *Natr. sulph.*
>   roaring in: *Natr. mur.*
>   sharp, cutting pain under: *Kali sulph.*
>   snapping in: *Kali mur.*
>   sore, external: *Natr. phos.*
>   stitches in: *Natr. mur., Ferr. phos., Natr. sulph.*
>   stuffy sensation in: *Kali mur.*
>   tension and throbbing in: *Ferr. phos.*

EUSTACHIAN TUBES, catarrh of: *Natr. mur., Kali mur., Kali sulph., Silicea.*
>   closed: *Kali mur.*
>   swell and cause deafness: *Kali mur., Kali sulph., Silicea.*

EXCESSIVE flow of blood to ear: *Ferr. phos.*
>   granulations within ear: *Kali mur.*

EXCRESCENCE, polypoid, closing ear: *Kali sulph.*

EXFOLIATION, moist, of tympanum: *Kali mur.*

EXTERNAL MEATUS swollen: *Silicea, Kali mur.*
>>   walls atrophied: *Kali mur.*

FŒTID or foul discharges from ear: *Kali phos.*

GLANDS about ear swell: *Kali mur.*

GRANULAR conditions of tympanum: *Kali mur.*

   pharyngitis: *Kali mur.*

GRANULATIONS, excessive: *Kali mur.*

HAMMERING in the ears: *Kali phos.*

HEATED ROOM aggravates deafness: *Kali sulph.*

HEARING supersensitive: *Kali phos.*

INFLAMMATION, diffused: *Ferr. phos.*

   of external ear: *Kali mur., Silicea, Ferr. phos.*

      middle ear, proliferous: *Kali mur.*

   with burning, throbbing pain: *Ferr. phos.*

INFLAMMATORY earache from cold: *Ferr. phos.*

ITCHING OF EARS: *Natr. phos., Natr. mur.*

   in auditory canal: *Kali phos., Natr. mur.*

LOW FORMS OF ULCERATION: *Kali phos.*

MASTOID PROCESS, caries of: *Silicea.*

   diseases of: *Silicea.*

   pains below: *Kali sulph.*

   periosteum diseased: *Calc. fluor.*

   swollen, sore: *Ferr. phos.*

MEATUS CLOSED by polypoid excrescence: *Kali sulph.*

   INNER, granular conditions of: *Kali mur.*

MEMBRANA, TYMPANA, calcareous deposits on: *Calc. fluor.*

   dark, beefy-red: *Ferr. phos.*

   granular: *Kali mur.*

   moist: *Kali mur.*

   retracted: *Kali mur.*

   thickened: *Ferr. phos.*

   ulcerated: *Kali phos.*

   inflammation, proliferous of: *Kali mur., Magnes. phos.*

MIDDLE EAR, suppuration of: *Calc. sulph., Kali phos., Silicea.*

   chronic catarrhal conditions: *Kali mur.*

MUCO-PURULENT discharges: *Ferr. phos.*

NASO-PHARYNGEAL obstructions: *Kali mur.*

NERVOUS OTALGIA: *Magnes. phos.*

NOISE, oversensitive to: *Silicea, Ferr. phos., Kali phos.*

NOISES IN EARS: *Ferr. phos., Kali mur., Kali phos.*

   on blowing nose: *Kali mur.*

   on falling asleep: *Kali phos.*

   on swallowing, cracking: *Kali mur., Natr. mur.*

NOTICEABLE PULSATION in the ears: *Ferr. phos.*

ONE EAR RED, hot and itching: *Natr. phos.*

ON FALLING ASLEEP, noises: *Kali phos.*

OTALGIA, inflammatory: *Ferr. phos.*

    nervous: *Magnes. phos.*

OTITIS, congestive stage: *Ferr. phos.*

    suppurative: *Calc. sulph., Kali phos., Silicea.*

OTORRHŒA, foul, offensive: *Kali sulph., Silicea, Kali phos., Calc. phos.*

OUTER EAR covered with thin deposit: *Natr. phos.*

OVERSENSITIVE to noise: *Silicea, Ferr. phos., Kali phos.*

PAIN, burning: *Ferr. phos.*

    cutting under ear : *Kali sulph.*

    paroxysmal, radiating and sharp: *Ferr. phos.*

    stitching: *Ferr. phos., Kali sulph.*

    tensive below mastoid process: *Kali sulph.*

    throbbing: *Ferr. phos.*

PARTS WITHIN ear dark-red: *Ferr. phos.*

PERIOSTEAL AFFECTIONS of mastoid process: *Calc. fluor.*

PIMPLES around ear: *Calc. sulph.*

POLYPOID EXCRESCENCE closing meatus: *Kali sulph.*

PROLIFEROUS INFLAMMATION of middle ear: *Kali mur., Magnes. phos.*

PULSATIONS in ear can be counted: *Ferr. phos.*

PURULENT DISCHARGE from ear: *Natr. mur., Kali phos., Silicea, Calc. sulph.*

    offensive: *Kali phos., Kali sulph., Silicea.*

RADIATING PAINS: *Ferr. phos.*

RETRACTED TYMPANUM: *Kali mur.*

RHEUMATIC EAR COMPLAINTS: *Calc. phos.*

RINGING in ears as of bells: *Natr. sulph.*

ROARING in the ears: *Natr. mur., Silicea.*

SCROFULOUS children, ear complaints in: *Calc. phos.*

SHARP PAINS in ear: *Ferr. phos., Magnes. phos.*

    under ear: *Kali sulph.*

SNAPPING in ear: *Kali mur.*

SORENESS of ears: *Natr. phos.*

STINKING OTORRHŒA: *Kali phos., Silicea, Kali sulph.*

STITCHING PAINS in ears: *Ferr. phos., Natr. mur.*

STUFFY sensation in ears: *Kali mur.*

SUPPURATION of middle ear: *Calc. sulph., Kali phos., Silicea.*

SWALLOWING, cracking noises on: *Kali mur.*

SWELLING of Eustachian tubes: *Kali mur., Silicea.*

    external ear: *Kali mur.*

      meatus: *Silicea.*

    glands about ears: *Kali mur.*

SWELLING of throat: *Kali mur., Kali sulph.*

    tympanic cavity: *Natr. mur., Silicea.*

TENDENCY to hæmorrhage: *Ferr. phos.*

TENSION IN EARS: *Ferr. phos.*

THROBBING PAIN: *Ferr. phos.*

THROAT swells: *Kali mur., Kali sulph.*

TINNITIS AURIUM: *Ferr. phos., Kali phos., Kali mur., Natr. sulph., Natr. mur.*

TISSUES dry up: *Kali phos.*

    become scaly: *Kali sulph., Kali mur., Natr. mur., Calc. phos.*

TYMPANIC MEMBRANE, calcareous deposits on: *Calc. fluor.*

      granular: *Kali mur.*

      moist exfoliation of: *Kali mur.*

      retracted: *Kali mur.*

TYMPANUM, cavity of, catarrh: *Natr. mur., Kali sulph., Kali mur.*

      swollen: *Natr. mur., Silicea.*

      ulcerated: *Kali mur.*

ULCERATIONS, angry: *Ferr. phos., Kali phos.*

    of low form: *Kali phos.*

ULCERATIONS, membrana tympani: *Kali phos.*

    whitish discharge: *Kali mur.*

Nose.

ACRID DISCHARGE from nose: *Silicea.*

ADHERENT CRUSTS, in pharynx: *Kali mur.*

ALBUMINOUS DISCHARGE: *Calc. phos.*

ANÆMIC PATIENTS, colds in: *Calc. phos.*

BONES OF NOSE, caries of: *Silicea.*

    diseased: *Calc. fluor.*

BURNING in nose: *Natr. sulph.*

CARIES of nasal bones: *Silicea.*

CATARRHS: *Ferr. phos., Kali mur.*

    chronic: *Natr. mur., Silicea.*

24

CATARRHS, dry cold: *Kali sulph.*
  naso-pharyngeal: *Natr. phos.*
  old nasal, with loss of smell: *Natr. mur.*
  posterior nares: *Natr. phos.*
  trickling sensation: *Ferr. phos.*
  with general morning aggravation: *Natr. mur.*
CATARRHAL fever: *Ferr. phos., Natr. sulph.*
COLDS cause vesicular eruptions: *Natr. mur.*
  in anæmic subjects: *Calc. phos.*
  in the head: *Ferr. phos., Kali sulph., Natr. mur.*
  predisposition to: *Ferr. phos., Calc. phos.*
  stuffy: *Calc. fluor., Kali mur., Natr. sulph., Kali sulph.*
COLDNESS of point of nose: *Calc. phos.*
CONGESTED NASAL mucous membrane: *Ferr. phos.*
CORYZA, chronic: *Silicea.*
  clear watery: *Natr. mur.*
  dry: *Calc. fluor., Kali mur., Natr. mur.*
  alternating dry and loose: *Magnes. phos., Natr. mur.*
  yellow, slimy: *Kali sulph.*
COUGHING produces nosebleed: *Natr. mur.*
CRUSTS adhere to vault of pharynx: *Kali mur.*
  in nose: *Natr. mur., Silicea.*
      offensive, yellow: *Kali phos.*
DISCHARGES, acrid: *Silicea.*
  albuminous: *Calc. phos.*
  clear: *Natr. mur.*
  corroding: *Silicea.*
  fœtid: *Kali phos., Silicea.*
  greenish: *Calc. fluor., Kali sulph.*
  gushing: *Magnes. phos.*
  lumpy: *Calc. fluor.*
  non-transparent: *Kali mur.*
  offensive: *Calc. fluor., Kali phos., Silicea.*
  one-sided: *Calc. sulph.*
  opaque, white: *Kali mur.*
  purulent: *Calc. sulph., Silicea.*
  slimy: *Kali sulph.*
  taste salty: *Natr. mur.*
  thick: *Calc. fluor., Calc. sulph., Kali mur., Kali sulph., Kali phos.*

DISCHARGES, tinged with blood: *Calc. sulph.*

    viscous: *Kali sulph.*

    watery: *Kali sulph., Natr. mur.*

    white: *Kali mur.*

    yellow: *Calc. fluor., Calc. sulph., Kali sulph., Natr. phos., Kali phos.*

DRY CORYZA: *Calc. fluor., Kali mur., Natr. mur.*

    old catarrhs: *Kali sulph.*

DRYNESS of mucous membrane: *Natr. sulph., Silicea.*

    posterior nares: *Natr. mur.*

DURING MENSES, nosebleed: *Natr. sulph.*

EDGES of nostril sore: *Calc. sulph.*

EPISTAXIS: *Calc. sulph., Ferr. phos., Kali phos., Kali sulph., Natr. phos., Natr. sulph., Natr. mur., Kali mur.*

    bright red blood: *Ferr. phos.*

    during menses: *Natr. sulph.*

    from coughing: *Natr. mur.*

    from stooping: *Natr. mur.*

    in children: *Ferr. phos.*

    predisposition to: *Kali phos.*

ERUPTIONS, vesicular, with colds: *Natr. mur.*

    herpetic, around nose: *Silicea.*

EXCORIATIONS in the nose: *Silicea.*

FIRST STAGE OF COLDS in the head: *Ferr. phos.*

FŒTID DISCHARGE from nose: *Kali phos., Silicea.*

GREENISH DISCHARGE: *Calc. fluor., Kali sulph.*

GROWTHS, osseous: *Calc. fluor.*

HAWKING of mucus from posterior nares: *Kali phos.*

HAY FEVER: *Natr. mur.*

INEFFECTUAL desire to sneeze: *Calc. fluor.*

INFLUENZA: *Natr. mur., Natr. sulph.*

ITCHING of tip of nose: *Silicea, Natr. phos.*

    wings of nose: *Natr. sulph.*

LOSS OF sense of smell: *Magnes. phos., Natr. mur., Silicea.*

MUCOUS MEMBRANE congested: *Ferr. phos.*

    dry: *Silicea.*

    swollen: *Silicea.*

MUCUS TASTES salty: *Natr. mur.*

NASAL BONES, affections of: *Calc. fluor.*

    caries of: *Silicea.*

NASAL BONES, catarrh, thick discharge: *Calc. fluor.*

>   hawks up salty mucus: *Natr. sulph.*

>   polypi, large and pedunculated: *Calc. phos.*

NOSE, cold at point: *Calc. phos.*

>   crusts in: *Natr. mur., Silicea.*

>   dryness and burning in: *Natr. sulph.*

>   excoriations in: *Silicea.*

>   feels numb on one side: *Natr. mur.*

>   itches at point: *Silicea, Natr. phos.*

>>   wings of: *Natr. sulph.*

>   obstructed: *Kali sulph., Natr. sulph.*

>   one side numb: *Natr. mur.*

>   picking at: *Natr. phos.*

>   redness of, with pimples: *Natr. mur.*

>   stuffing up of: *Calc. fluor., Kali mur., Natr. sulph., Kali sulph.*

>   swollen and scabs and scurfs in: *Natr. mur.*

>   ulcerated in scrofulous people: *Calc. phos.*

NOSEBLEED: *Calc. sulph., Ferr. phos., Kali phos., Kali sulph., Natr. phos., Natr. sulph., Natr. mur., Kali mur., Calc. phos.*

>   after blowing thick yellow crusts from nose: *Kali phos.*

>   afternoons: *Kali mur.*

>   bright-red blood: *Ferr. phos.*

>   during menses: *Natr. sulph.*

>   from coughing or stooping: *Natr. mur.*

>   in children: *Ferr. phos.*

>   predisposition to: *Kali phos.*

NOSTRILS, itching of: *Silicea.*

>   soreness of: *Calc. phos., Calc. sulph.*

OBSTRUCTION of nose: *Kali sulph., Kali mur.*

ODOR, offensive, from nose: *Calc. fluor., Kali phos., Natr. phos.*

OSSEOUS growths: *Calc. fluor.*

OZÆNA: *Calc. fluor., Calc. phos., Kali phos., Silicea, Kali sulph.*

>   syphilitica: *Natr. sulph.*

PERIOSTEUM of nasal bones affected: *Silicea.*

PERVERTED SENSE of smell: *Magnes. phos.*

PHARYNX, adherent crusts in: *Kali mur.*

PICKING at nose: *Natr. phos.*

PIMPLES on nose: *Natr. mur.*

POINT OF NOSE cold: *Calc. phos.*

POLYPI, large and pedunculated: *Calc. phos.*
POSTERIOR NARES dry: *Natr. mur.*
  hawking of mucus from: *Kali phos.*
  yellow discharge from: *Kali sulph.*
PREDISPOSITION to catch cold: *Ferr. phos., Silicea.*
PREDISPOSITION to nosebleed: *Kali phos.*
PRICKING IN NARES: *Natr. phos.*
REDNESS of nose: *Natr. mur.*
  at point: *Silicea.*
RUNNING COLDS: *Natr. mur.*
SCABS in nose: *Natr. mur., Kali phos.*
SCROFULOUS children, nasal affections in: *Calc. phos.*
SCURF in nose: *Natr. mur.*
SMARTING: *Magnes. phos.*
  in right nasal passage: *Ferr. phos.*
SMELL lost or perverted: *Kali sulph., Magnes. phos., Natr. mur.,*
    Silicea.
SNEEZING: *Silicea, Ferr. phos., Calc. phos.*
  from slightest exposure: *Kali phos.*
  ineffectual desire for: *Calc. fluor.*
STOOPING produces nosebleed: *Natr. mur.*
STUFFY colds: *Calc. fluor., Kali mur., Natr. sulph.*
SWELLING of mucous membrane: *Silicea.*
SWOLLEN NOSE in scrofulous children: *Calc. phos.*
SYPHILITIC OZÆNA: *Natr. sulph.*
TIP OF NOSE cold: *Calc. phos.*
  red and itches: *Silicea.*
ULCERATED nose in scrofulous children: *Calc. phos.*
ULCERATION of nose, inveterate: *Silicea, Kali phos.*
VESICULAR ERUPTION with colds: *Natr. mur.*
WHITE around nose: *Natr. phos.*
WINGS of nose itch: *Natr. sulph.*

Face.

ACNE: *Calc. sulph., Kali mur., Silicea, Kali sulph.*
AFTER QUININE, neuralgia: *Natr. mur.*
AGGRAVATION of face symptoms at night: *Calc. phos.*
ANÆMIC face: *Calc. phos.*
BLOTCHED face: *Natr. phos.*
BLUISH FACE: *Natr. phos.*
CARIES of lower jaw: *Silicea.*

CHEEKS, swelling of: *Calc. sulph., Kali mur.*

   hard swelling of: *Calc. fluor.*

   hot and sore: *Ferr. phos.*

CHIN, eruptions on: *Natr. mur.*

CHLOROTIC face: *Calc. phos., Ferr. phos.*

COLD SORES on lips, small: *Calc. fluor., Natr. mur.*

COLD applications relieve: *Ferr. phos.*

COMPLEXION.   (See Face.)

CONTORTIONS from loss of power of facial muscles: *Kali phos.*

COUNTENANCE, hippocratic: *Kali phos.*

CRACKING of skin of face: *Silicea.*

CUTTING PAINS in face: *Magnes. phos.*

DIRTY LOOK to face: *Calc. phos.*

EARTHY FACE: *Calc. phos., Silicea, Ferr. phos.*

EPITHELIOMA: *Kali sulph.*

ERUPTIONS, herpetic: *Calc. sulph.*

   sycotic: *Natr. mur., Silicea.*

EYES, sunken, hollow: *Kali phos.*

FACE, anæmic: *Calc. phos., Ferr. phos.*

   blotched and bluish: *Natr. phos.*

   burning: *Kali phos.*

   chlorotic: *Calc. phos., Ferr. phos.*

   covered with vesicles: *Natr. mur., Natr. sulph.*

   cracked: *Silicea.*

   dirty-looking: *Calc. phos.*

   earthy: *Calc. phos., Natr. mur., Ferr. phos., Silicea.*

   features distorted: *Kali sulph., Kali phos.*

   florid: *Natr. phos., Ferr. phos.*

   flushed: *Ferr. phos.*

   full of pimples: *Calc. phos., Silicea, Natr. sulph., Kali phos.*

     if matter forms: *Calc. sulph.*

   greasy: *Calc. phos., Natr. mur.*

   greenish-white: *Calc. phos.*

   herpetic eruptions on: *Calc. sulph.*

   itches: *Natr. mur., Kali phos.*

   jaundiced: *Natr. sulph.*

   leaden: *Natr. mur.*

   livid: *Kali phos.*

   pale: *Kali phos., Silicea, Natr. sulph., Natr. mur., Natr. phos., Calc. phos., Kali sulph., Ferr. phos.*

FACE, pimples on: *Kali phos., Calc. sulph.*
   prominent parts cold: *Calc. phos.*
   pustules on: *Calc. sulph., Kali phos.*
      forehead: *Natr. mur.*
   red: *Natr. phos., Kali phos., Ferr. phos.*
   red, with distorted features: *Kali sulph.*
   sallow: *Kali phos., Natr. mur., Natr. sulph., Calc. phos.,*
        Ferr. phos.
   sickly and sunken: *Kali phos.*
   sweats while eating: *Natr. mur., Kali phos.*
      cold: *Calc. phos.*
   swelling of: *Kali mur.*
   vesicles over: *Natr. sulph.*
   waxy: *Calc. phos.*
   white about nose: *Natr. mur.*
   yellowish: *Calc. phos., Natr. sulph., Kali phos.*
FACEACHE, aggravated when body gets cold: *Magnes. phos.*
      on right side: *Magnes. phos.*
      after going to bed: *Magnes. phos.*
      in heated room: *Kali sulph.*
      in the evening: *Kali sulph.*
      on moving: *Ferr. phos.*
   ameliorated in cool open air: *Kali sulph.*
      cold applications: *Kali phos., Ferr. phos.*
      by warmth: *Magnes. phos., Silicea.*
   from swelling: *Kali mur.*
   in superior maxillary bone: *Calc. phos.*
   right side of lower jaw: *Natr. phos.*
   neuralgic: *Kali mur., Kali phos., Natr. phos.*
   pain in zygoma: *Natr. sulph.*
   with constipation: *Natr. mur.*
      coldness of nape: *Ferr. phos.*
      great exhaustion: *Kali phos.*
      flushing: *Ferr. phos.*
      lumps or nodules on face: *Silicea.*
FALLING out of whiskers: *Natr. mur.*
FOREHEAD, pustular eruption on: *Natr. mur.*
FRECKLES: *Calc. phos.*
GREENISH-LOOKING face: *Calc. phos.*
GREENISH-WHITE face: *Calc. phos.*

HARD-SWELLING on the cheek: *Calc. fluor.*
        jawbone: *Calc. fluor.*
HEATED ROOM aggravates faceache: *Kali sulph.*
HERPETIC eruptions on face: *Calc. sulph., Natr. mur.*
HIPPOCRATIC countenance: *Kali phos.*
HOT CHEEKS: *Ferr. phos.*
INDURATION of cellular tissues of face: *Silicea.*
INFLAMMATORY neuralgia: *Ferr. phos.*
ITCHING of face: *Natr. mur., Kali phos.*
JAUNDICED face: *Natr. sulph.*
JAWBONE, caries of: *Silicea.*
    hard swelling on: *Calc. fluor.*
    necrosis of: *Silicea.*
JERKING PAINS in face: *Magnes. phos.*
LACHRYMATION with neuralgia: *Natr. mur.*
LEADEN face: *Natr. mur.*
LIPS, cold sores on: *Calc. fluor., Natr. mur.*
    hydroa on: *Kali phos., Natr. mur.*
    lower, swollen: *Kali sulph.*
    skin peeling off: *Kali phos., Kali sulph.*
    tumors on: *Silicea.*
    upper, swollen and painful: *Calc. phos.*
    white: *Kali sulph.*
LIVID face: *Kali phos.*
LOSS of power of facial muscles: *Kali phos.*
LUMPS or nodules on face: *Silicea.*
LUPUS: *Silicea, Calc. phos.*
NECROSIS of jawbone: *Silicea.*
NEURALGIA, after quinine: *Natr. mur.*
                       (See also Faceache.)
PAIN aggravated after going to bed: *Magnes. phos.*
    cutting: *Magnes. phos.*
    in cheeks: *Kali mur.*
    in superior maxillary bone: *Calc. phos., Kali phos.*
    jerking: *Magnes. phos.*
    like lightning: *Magnes. phos.*
    pressing: *Ferr. phos.*
    relieved by warmth: *Magnes. phos.*
            cold: *Kali phos.*
    throbbing: *Ferr. phos.*

PALE face: *Kali phos., Kali sulph., Natr. phos., Silicea, Natr. mur., Natr. sulph., Calc. phos.*

PIMPLES AND PUSTULES on face: *Calc. phos., Calc. sulph., Kali mur., Natr. sulph., Natr. mur.*

PROSOPALGIA: *Magnes. phos., Natr. phos.*

RHEUMATISM in face: *Calc. phos.*

RED FACE: *Natr. phos., Ferr. phos., Kali phos.*

SALLOW FACE: *Kali phos., Natr. mur., Natr. sulph., Calc. phos.*

SICKLY FACE: *Kali phos., Calc. phos.*

SKIN of face cracks: *Silicea.*

SORES, cold: *Calc. fluor., Natr. mur.*
    cheeks: *Ferr. phos.*
    herpetic, hard, on lips: *Calc. fluor.*

SPASMODIC neuralgia: *Magnes. phos.*

SUNKEN FACE: *Kali phos.*

SUPPURATION of cheek threatens: *Calc. sulph.*

SUPERIOR MAXILLARY bone, pain in: *Calc. phos.*

SWEATING while eating: *Natr. mur., Kali phos.*

SWEAT, cold, on: *Calc. phos.*

SWELLING of cheeks: *Kali mur.*
      hard: *Calc. fluor.*
      jawbone: *Calc. fluor.*
      parotid gland: *Calc. phos.*
      submaxillary gland: *Calc. phos.*
      upper lip: *Calc. phos.*

SYCOSIS: *Natr. mur., Silicea.*

THROBBING of face: *Ferr. phos.*

TIC DOULOUREUX: *Ferr. phos.*

VESICLES on face: *Natr. mur., Natr. sulph.*

WARMTH relieves faceache: *Magnes. phos.*

WHISKERS fall out: *Natr. mur.*

WHITE about nose: *Natr. phos.*

YELLOWISH face: *Calc. phos., Natr. sulph., Kali phos.*

Mouth.

ACID TASTE: *Natr. phos., Natr. mur., Silicea.*

APHTHÆ: *Kali mur.*
    caused by using borax: *Natr. sulph.*
    with much salivation: *Natr. mur.*

ASHY-GRAY ULCERS in mouth: *Kali phos.*

BITTER TASTE: *Natr. sulph.*, *Kali mur.*

BLISTERS, pearl-like, at corners: *Natr. mur.*

BREATH, fœtid: *Kali phos.*, *Natr. mur.*
 offensive: *Kali phos.*, *Natr. mur.*

BURNING cracks in lips: *Natr. mur.*
 heat in: *Kali sulph.*

CANKER: *Kali phos.*, *Kali mur.*, *Natr. mur.*
 gangrenous: *Kali phos.*, *Silicea.*
 water: *Kali phos.*

CHILDREN, white ulcers in mouth of: *Kali mur.*

COATING, yellow and creamy, on roof: *Natr. phos.*

COLD SORES at corners of mouth: *Calc. fluor.*

CORNERS OF MOUTH, convulsive twitchings of: *Magnes. phos.*
 cold sores at: *Calc. fluor.*
 cracked: *Natr. mur.*
 humid sores at: *Natr. mur.*
 ulcerated: *Silicea.*

DESQUAMATION of lips: *Kali sulph.*

DISGUSTING TASTE: *Calc. phos.*

DROOLING: *Natr. mur.*

DRYNESS of lips: *Kali sulph.*

EPITHELIOMA: *Kali sulph.*

EXCORIATION of mouth: *Kali mur.*

FŒTID BREATH: *Kali phos.*

GANGRENOUS canker: *Kali phos.*, *Silicea.*

GLANDS, salivary, suppurate: *Silicea.*

GUM-BOIL: *Calc. fluor.*, *Silicea*, *Kali mur.*, *Natr. mur.*

GUMS, bleed on brushing teeth: *Calc. sulph.*
 blisters on: *Natr. sulph.*
 hot and inflamed: *Ferr. phos.*
 spongy and receding: *Kali phos.*
 white: *Kali sulph.*

HARD SWELLING of jawbone: *Calc. fluor.*

HOT, inflamed gums: *Ferr. phos.*

HYDROA on lips: *Kali phos.*, *Natr. mur.*

INFLAMMATION of glands, salivary: *Natr.*
 gums: *Ferr. phos.*

INSIDES OF LIPS sore: *Calc. sulph.*

JAWBONE, hard swelling on: *Calc. fluor.*

LIPS, cracks in: *Natr. mur.*

    painful and burning: *Natr. mur.*

    sore inside of: *Calc. sulph.*

    swollen: *Natr. mur.*

LOCKJAW: *Magnes. phos.*

LOWER LIP, desquamation of: *Kali sulph.*

    dryness of: *Kali sulph.*

    swoolen: *Kali sulph.*

MOUTH, blisters around: *Natr. mur.*

    canker of: *Kali mur., Kali phos.*

        gangrenous: *Kali phos., Silicea.*

        water: *Kali phos.*

        cracked: *Natr. mur.*

    corners of, twitch: *Magnes. phos.*

        ulcerated: *Silicea.*

MOUTH, full of slime: *Natr. sulph.*

    heat in: *Kali sulph.*

    pimples and sore crusts around: *Kali phos.*

    rawness and redness of: *Kali mur.*

    roof of, sore to touch: *Natr. sulph.*

    vesicular eruption around: *Natr. sulph.*

    welling up of mucus in: *Natr. sulph.*

        while eating: *Calc. sulph.*

    white ulcers in: *Kali mur.*

    yellow, creamy coating on roof: *Natr. phos.*

MUCOUS MEMBRANE, reddened: *Ferr. phos., Kali mur.*

NOMA: *Kali phos.*

NURSING MOTHERS, ulcers in mouth of: *Kali mur.*

OFFENSIVE BREATH: *Natr. mur., Kali phos., Natr. phos.*

PAINFUL CRACKS in lips: *Natr. mur.*

PERFORATING ULCER of palate: *Silicea.*

RANULA: *Natr. mur.*

RAWNESS of mouth: *Kali mur.*

REDNESS of mucous membrane: *Ferr. phos., Kali mur.*

SALIVARY GLANDS, inflammation of: *Natr. mur.*

    suppuration of: *Silicea.*

SALIVATION: *Natr. mur., Kali phos.*

SORES in commissures: *Natr. mur.*

STOMATITIS: *Kali phos.*

SWELLING, hard, on jawbone: *Calc. fluor.*
THRUSH: *Kali mur., Natr. mur.*
TRISMUS: *Magnes. phos.*
TWITCHINGS of corners: *Magnes. phos.*
ULCERS IN MOUTH, ashy-gray: *Kali phos.*
    in corners: *Silicea.*
    perforating: *Silicea.*
    white: *Kali mur.*
UVULA relaxed: *Natr. mur.*
UVULITIS: *Natr. mur.*
WHITE ULCERS in mouth: *Kali mur.*
YELLOW, CREAMY COATING of roof of mouth: *Natr. phos.*

Tongue and Taste.

ACID taste: *Natr. phos.*
ACRID taste: *Calc. sulph.*
BITTER taste: *Natr. sulph., Kali mur.*
    in morning: *Calc. phos.*
BLISTERS on tip of tongue: *Natr. phos., Natr. sulph., Natr. mur.*
BROWNISH TONGUE: *Kali phos., Natr. sulph.*
BRIGHT RED, with rawness: *Magnes. phos.*
CLAY-COLORED tongue: *Calc. sulph.*
CLEAN TONGUE: *Ferr. phos., Magnes. phos., Natr. mur.*
COATING ON TONGUE, brownish: *Kali phos., Natr. sulph.*
    clay colored: *Calc. sulph.*
    clean and dry: *Magnes. phos.*
    clean and moist: *Natr. phos.*
    creamy: *Natr. phos.*
    cracked: *Calc. fluor.*
    dirty: *Natr. sulph., Kali phos., Kali sulph.*
    frothy: *Natr. mur.*
    golden-yellow: *Natr. phos.*
    grayish-green: *Natr. sulph.*
    grayish: *Kali mur.*
    green: *Natr. sulph.*
    moist: *Natr. mur., Natr. phos.*
    slimy: *Kali sulph., Natr. mur., Natr. sulph., Kali phos., Kali mur.*
    white-furred: *Calc. phos., Kali mur.*
        on edges: *Kali sulph.*

COATING ON TONGUE, yellow: *Kali sulph., Natr. phos.*
> at base: *Calc. sulph.*

COPPERY taste: *Natr. phos.*

CRACKED tongue: *Calc. fluor.*

CREAMY COATING on tongue: *Natr. phos.*

DARK-RED swelling of tongue: *Ferr. phos.*

DIRTY TONGUE: *Natr. sulph., Kali phos., Kali sulph.*

DRY tongue: *Kali mur., Kali phos., Natr. mur.*

EDGES covered with froth: *Natr. mur.*

EDGES red and sore: *Kali phos.*
> white: *Kali sulph.*

FLABBY tongue: *Calc. sulph.*

FROTHY SALIVA on tongue: *Natr. mur.*

FURRED tongue: *Ferr. phos.*

GLOSSITIS: *Ferr. phos.*
> suppuration in: *Calc. sulph.*
> swelling in: *Kali mur.*

GOLDEN-YELLOW coating on tongue: *Natr. phos.*

GRAYISH tongue: *Kali mur., Natr. sulph.*

GREENISH tongue: *Natr. sulph.*

HAIR, sensation of, on tongue: *Silicea, Natr. mur.*
> tip: *Natr. phos.*

INDURATION of tongue: *Calc. fluor., Silicea.*

INFLAMMATION of tongue: *Ferr. phos.*
> with dryness: *Kali phos.*

INFLAMMATION, suppuration: *Calc. sulph.*
> swelling: *Kali mur.*

INSIPID TASTE: *Kali sulph.*

LOSS OF TASTE: *Natr. mur.*

MAPPED TONGUE: *Natr. mur., Kali mur.*

MOIST, creamy coating on tongue: *Natr. phos.*

NUMB TONGUE: *Calc. phos., Natr. mur.*

PAPPY TASTE: *Calc. sulph.*

RED TONGUE: *Ferr. phos., Natr. sulph.*

SALIVA, bubbles of, on tongue: *Natr. mur.*

SENSATION as if tongue would cleave to roof of mouth: *Kali phos.*
> of hair on: *Silicea, Natr. mur.*
> tip: *Natr. phos.*

SLIMY coating on tongue: *Natr. mur.*, *Natr. sulph.*, *Kali sulph.*
SOAPY TASTE: *Calc. sulph.*
SOUR TASTE: *Calc. sulph.*
SPEECH DIFFICULT: *Natr. phos.*
STIFF TONGUE: *Calc. phos.*, *Natr. mur.*
SWELLING, dark-red, of tongue: *Ferr. phos.*
SWOLLEN tongue: *Calc. phos.*, *Kali mur.*
TALK, slow in learning to: *Natr. mur.*
TASTE, acid: *Natr. phos.*

    acids: *Calc. sulph.*
    bitter: *Natr. sulph.*, *Kali mur.*
    bitter in the morning: *Calc. fluor.*, *Calc. phos.*
    coppery: *Natr. phos.*
    disgusting: *Calc. phos.*
    insipid: *Calc. sulph.*, *Kali sulph.*
    loss of: *Natr. mur.*, *Kali sulph.*
    pappy: *Kali sulph.*
    soapy: *Calc. sulph.*
    sour: *Calc. sulph.*, *Natr. mur.*

TIP OF TONGUE, blisters on: *Natr. phos.*, *Natr. sulph.*
    sensation of hair on: *Natr. phos.*, *Silicea*, *Natr. mur.*
    vesicles on: *Natr. mur.*

TONGUE, brownish: *Kali phos.*, *Natr. sulph.*
    clay colored: *Calc. sulph.*
    clean: *Ferr. phos.*, *Magnes. phos.*
    covered with saliva: *Natr. mur.*
    cracked: *Calc. fluor.*
    creamy coating on root: *Natr. phos.*
    dark-red swelling of: *Ferr. phos.*
    dirty: *Natr. sulph.*
    dry: *Kali mur.*, *Kali phos.*, *Natr. mur.*
    edges red and sore: *Kali phos.*
    flabby: *Ferr. phos.*
    furred: *Ferr. phos.*, *Natr. phos.*, *Natr. sulph.*, *Kali sulph.*,
        Kali mur., *Calc. phos.*
    golden-yellow: *Natr. phos.*
    greenish: *Natr. sulph.*
    induration of: *Calc. fluor.*, *Silicea.*
    inflamed: *Ferr. phos.*

TONGUE, inflamed, with dryness: *Kali phos.*

            suppuration: *Calc. sulph.*

            swelling: *Kali mur.*

      mapped: *Natr. mur., Kali mur.*

      moist: *Natr. phos.*

      numb: *Calc. phos., Natr. mur.*

      pimples on: *Calc. phos.*

      red: *Ferr. phos., Magnes. phos., Natr. sulph.*

      saliva, covered with: *Natr. mur.*

      scalded, as if: *Magnes. phos.*

      sensation of hair on: *Silicea, Natr. mur., Natr. phos.*

      slimy: *Kali mur., Natr. mur., Natr. sulph., Kali phos.*

      stiff: *Calc. phos., Natr. mur.*

      swollen: *Calc. phos., Kali mur.*

      ulcers on: *Silicea.*

      vesicles on: *Natr. mur.*

      white: *Calc. phos., Kali mur., Kali sulph.*

          on edges: *Kali sulph.*

      yellow at base: *Calc. sulph.*

ULCERS on tongue: *Silicea.*

VESICLES on tip of tongue: *Natr. mur.*

WHITE COATING on tongue: *Calc. phos., Kali mur.*

      edges: *Kali sulph.*

YELLOW AT BASE: *Calc. sulph.*

Teeth and Gums.

AFTER WARM FOOD, toothache: *Ferr. phos.*

ARTICULATION slow: *Kali phos.*

BLEEDING of gums: *Kali phos., Natr. mur.*

BROWN DEPOSIT on teeth: *Kali phos.*

CHATTERING of teeth, nervous: *Kali phos.*

COMPLAINTS during teething: *Calc. phos.*

CONVULSIONS during teething: *Ferr. phos., Magnes. phos., Calc. phos.*

COOL OPEN air relieves toothache: *Kali sulph.*

CRAMPS during teething: *Magnes. phos.*

DECAY OF TEETH, pain in: *Kali phos.*

DENTITION, complaints during: *Calc. phos.*

      convulsions during: *Magnes. phos.*

      cramps during: *Magnes. phos.*

DENTITION, difficult: *Silicea.*
    delayed: *Silicea.*
    with dribbling of saliva: *Natr. mur.*
        fever: *Ferr. phos.*
DENTAL FISTULÆ: *Silicea.*
DROOLING: *Natr. mur.*
EASILY BLEEDING gums: *Natr. mur., Kali phos.*
ENAMEL OF TEETH deficient: *Calc. fluor.*
    rough: *Calc. fluor.*
FISTULA DENTALIS: *Silicea.*
GRINDING OF TEETH: *Natr. phos., Kali phos.*
GUMS, bleed easily: *Natr. mur., Kali phos., Calc. sulph.*
    blisters on: *Natr. sulph.*
    burn: *Natr. sulph.*
    inflamed: *Calc. phos.*
    pale: *Calc. phos., Kali sulph.*
    painful: *Calc. phos., Kali sulph.*
    predisposition to bleed: *Kali phos.*
    red seam on: *Kali phos.*
    sensitive: *Natr. mur., Silicea.*
        to touch, cold or water: *Magnes. phos.*
    spongy, receding: *Kali phos.*
    ulcerated: *Natr. mur.*
    white: *Kali sulph.*
GUM-BOIL before matter forms: *Kali mur., Natr. mur.*
    with hard swelling: *Calc. fluor.*
        suppuration: *Calc. sulph., Silicea.*
INARTICULATE speech: *Kali phos.*
INFLAMED gums: *Calc. phos.*
LOOSENESS of teeth: *Calc. fluor., Natr. mur., Silicea.*
MALNUTRITION of teeth: *Calc. fluor.*
NERVOUS chattering of teeth: *Kali phos.*
PAINFUL gums: *Calc. phos.*
PALE gums: *Calc. phos.*
RANULA: *Natr. mur.*
RED SEAM on gums: *Kali phos.*
RHEUMATIC toothache: *Calc. sulph.*
SALIVATION with toothache: *Natr. mur.*
SALIVARY GLANDS, inflammation of: *Natr. mur.*

SENSITIVE gums: *Natr. mur.*
    to pressure or touch: *Ferr. phos.*
SORENESS of teeth: *Kali phos.*
SPEECH slow and inarticulate: *Kali phos.*
SMOKING relieves toothache: *Natr. sulph.*
TEETH, ailments of, during pregnancy: *Calc. phos.*
    decay rapidly: *Calc. phos.*
    develop slowly: *Calc. phos.*
    feel sore: *Kali phos., Ferr. phos.*
    grinding of, during sleep: *Natr. phos., Kali phos.*
    loose: *Calc. fluor., Natr. mur., Silicea.*
    malnutrition of: *Calc. fluor.*
    nervous chattering of: *Kali phos.*
    sensitive: *Calc. sulph., Magnes. phos., Kali phos.*
    too long: *Ferr. phos.*
TEETHING. (See Dentition.)
TEETHING ailments during pregnancy: *Calc. phos.*
TOBACCO-SMOKE relieves toothache: *Natr. sulph.*
TOOTHACHE, aggravated at night: *Calc. phos., Silicea.*
    by cold things: *Magnes. phos.*
    by food: *Calc. fluor.*
    in the evening: *Kali sulph.*
    in warmth: *Kali sulph.*
  after going to bed: *Magnes. phos.*
  alternates with frontal headache: *Kali phos.*
  ameliorated by cold: *Ferr. phos.*
    cool air: *Kali sulph., Natr. sulph.*
    hot liquids: *Magnes. phos.*
    tobacco-smoke: *Natr. sulph.*
    water: *Ferr. phos., Natr. sulph.*
  boring pain: *Calc. phos.*
  caused by chilling of feet: *Silicea.*
  changes place rapidly: *Magnes. phos.*
  congestive: *Ferr. phos., Magnes. phos.*
  inflammatory: *Ferr. phos., Magnes. phos.*
  neuralgic: *Magnes. phos.*
  pains, boring: *Calc. phos.*
    tingling: *Calc. phos.*
    shift: *Magnes. phos.*
25

TOOTHACHE, rheumatic: *Calc. sulph.*
    salivation, with: *Natr. mur.*
    shooting: *Magnes. phos.*
    with dental fistula: *Silicea.*
        easily bleeding gums: *Kali phos.*
        involuntary flow of tears: *Natr. mur.*
        looseness of teeth: *Calc. fluor.*
        swollen cheek: *Kali mur., Calc. sulph.*
           hot cheek: *Ferr. phos.*
ULCERATION OF GUMS: *Natr. mur.*

Throat.

ABSCESS of tonsils: *Calc. sulph., Silicea.*
    pharynx: *Ferr. phos.*
ADHERENT CRUSTS in pharynx: *Kali mur.*
BURNING of throat: *Ferr. phos., Calc. phos.*
CHOKING SENSATION in throat: *Magnes. phos.*
CHRONIC SORE THROAT: *Natr. mur.*
    dryness of throat: *Natr. mur.*
CLERGYMAN'S SORE THROAT: *Calc. phos.*
CONGESTION of throat: *Ferr. phos.*
CONSTRICTION of throat, spasmodic: *Magnes. phos.*
CROUP: *Ferr. phos., Kali mur., Calc. fluor., Calc. phos., Kali phos.*
CRUSTS in pharynx: *Kali mur.*
DEAFNESS in tonsillitis: *Calc. phos.*
DEGLUTITION painful: *Ferr. phos., Calc. phos.*
    must swallow: *Magnes. phos.*
DESIRE to swallow, constant: *Kali phos.*
DIPHTHERIA: after-effects of: *Kali phos., Silicea.*
    false: *Natr. phos.*
    first stage: *Ferr. phos.*
    of soft palate: *Calc. sulph.*
    principal remedy: *Kali mur.*
    when it goes to trachea: *Calc. fluor., Calc. phos.*
    with drowsiness: *Natr. mur.*
        green vomiting: *Natr. sulph.*
        puffy, pale face: *Natr. sulph.*
        watery stools: *Natr. mur.*
DROPPING from posterior nares: *Magnes. phos.*
DRY THROAT: *Ferr. phos., Natr. mur., Natr. sulph.*

ENLARGEMENT of throat: *Natr. mur.*

FAUCES inflamed: *Ferr. phos.*
    painful: *Ferr. phos.*
    red: *Ferr. phos.*
    swollen: *Calc. sulph.*

FEELING OF LUMP in throat on swallowing: *Natr. sulph., Natr. phos., Natr. mur.*

FOLLICULAR PHARYNGITIS: *Kali mur., Natr. mur.*

GANGRENOUS SORE THROAT: *Kali phos.*

GLANDS swollen: *Ferr. phos., Natr. mur., Kali mur., Natr. phos., Kali sulph.*
    external, painful: *Calc. phos.*
    submaxillary, swollen: *Natr. mur.*
    suppurate: *Calc. sulph., Silicea.*

GLOTTIS, spasms of: *Magnes. phos.*

GOITRE: *Calc. phos., Calc. fluor., Silicea, Natr. phos.*
    with watery secretions: *Natr. mur.*

HEAT in throat: *Ferr. phos.*

HAWKS up offensive, cheesy lumps: *Kali mur.*
    salty mucus: *Kali phos., Natr. sulph.*

INFLAMMATION of fauces: *Ferr. phos.*
    throat: *Ferr. phos., Natr. phos.*
    tonsil: *Ferr. phos.*

LARYNGISMUS STRIDULUS: *Magnes. phos.*

LUMP, feeling of, when swallowing: *Natr. sulph., Natr. phos.*

MALIGNANT CONDITIONS of throat: *Kali phos.*

MEMBRANOUS EXUDATION in throat: *Kali mur.*

MUCUS, tough, in throat: *Kali sulph.*

MUMPS, with hawking up of salty mucus: *Natr. mur.*
    salivation: *Natr. mur.*
    swelling of parotids: *Kali mur.*

ON SWALLOWING, feeling of lump: *Natr. sulph.*
    liquids, constriction: *Magnes. phos.*
    painful: *Calc. phos., Ferr. phos., Kali mur.*

PAINFUL deglutition: *Calc. phos., Ferr. phos., Kali mur.*
    fauces: *Ferr. phos.*
    throat: *Ferr. phos.*

PALATE inflamed: *Ferr. phos.*
    sensitive: *Natr. sulph.*

PALATE, yellow coating on: *Natr. phos.*
PARALYSIS, post-diphtheritic: *Natr. mur.*
  of vocal cords: *Kali phos.*
  velum pendulum palati: *Silicea.*
    chronic: *Silicea.*
PHARYNGITIS, follicular: *Kali mur., Natr. mur.*
PHARYNGEAL abscess: *Ferr. phos.*
PHARYNX, adherent crusts in: *Kali mur.*
POSTERIOR NARES, dropping from: *Natr. phos., Magnes. phos.*
QUINSY, discharging pus: *Calc. sulph.*
  periodical: *Silicea.*
RED FAUCES: *Ferr. phos.*
RELAXED sore throat: *Calc. phos., Calc. fluor.*
  uvula: *Natr. mur.*
  causes cough: *Calc. fluor.*
SALTY mucus raised from throat: *Kali phos.*
SENSATION OF CHOKING: *Magnes. phos.*
SPEECH, nasal, slow: *Kali phos.*
SPASMS OF GLOTTIS: *Magnes. phos.*
SUFFOCATIVE FEELING in throat: *Magnes. phos.*
SWALLOW, constant desire to: *Kali phos.*
  must: *Magnes. phos.*
SWOLLEN GLANDS: *Ferr. phos., Calc. phos., Kali mur.*
SYPHILITIC SORE THROAT: *Kali mur.*
THROAT, burning in: *Ferr. phos.*
  congested: *Ferr. phos.*
  constriction in: *Magnes. phos., Natr. mur.*
  covered with transparent mucus: *Natr. mur.*
    tough mucus: *Kali sulph.*
  dry: *Ferr. phos., Natr. phos., Natr. sulph., Kali phos.*
  feeling of plug or lump in: *Natr. mur., Natr. sulph., Natr. phos.*
  ball, hysterical, in: *Kali phos.*
  gangrenous: *Kali phos.*
  grayish patches in: *Kali mur.*
  heat in: *Ferr. phos.*
  inflamed: *Ferr. phos., Natr. phos., Natr. sulph.*
  malignant conditions in: *Kali phos.*
  pains: *Calc. phos., Ferr. phos.*

THROAT, red: *Ferr. phos.*
   relaxed: *Calc. phos., Calc. fluor.*
   sensations of lump in: *Natr. phos.*
   sore and stiff: *Magnes. phos.*
   sore, of singers: *Calc. phos., Ferr. phos.*
   spasmodic constriction of: *Magnes. phos.*
   stitches in: *Natr. mur.*
   suppuration of: *Calc. sulph., Silicea.*
   swollen: *Kali mur.*
   throbbing in: *Ferr. phos.*
   tickling in: *Calc. fluor.*
   tough mucus in: *Kali sulph.*
   ulcerated: *Ferr. phos., Kali mur., Natr. sulph., Natr. mur.*
THYROID GLAND enlarged: *Silicea, Calc. phos., Calc. fluor., Natr. mur.*
TONSILS enlarged: *Calc. phos., Kali phos., Natr. mur.*
   inflamed: *Ferr. phos., Kali phos.*
   periodically: *Silicea.*
   with deafness: *Calc. phos.*
   inflamed, with deafness, much swelling: *Kali mur.*
      pain on opening mouth: *Calc. phos.*
      suppuration: *Calc. sulph., Silicea.*
   sore: *Kali phos.*
   white deposit on: *Kali phos.*
   yellow coating on: *Natr. phos.*
ULCERATED THROAT: *Ferr. phos., Kali mur.*
UVULA elongated: *Calc. fluor., Natr. mur.*
   causes cough: *Calc. fluor.*
   relaxed: *Natr. mur., Calc. fluor.*
UVULITIS: *Natr. mur.*
VOICE, loss of: *Kali phos.*
   sudden and shrill: *Magnes. phos.*
YELLOW coating on palate: *Natr. phos.*
   mucus drops from posterior nares: *Natr. phos.*

Gastric Symptoms.

ACIDS, sensitive to: *Magnes. phos.*
ACIDITY: *Natr. phos.*
AFTER EATING, regurgitation of food: *Magnes. phos.*
APPETITE, increased: *Calc. phos., Calc. sulph., Kali phos., Natr. mur., Silicea.*

APPETITE, loss of: *Ferr. phos., Kali mur., Natr. sulph., Natr. mur., Natr. phos., Kali sulph.*

AVERSION, to acids: *Ferr. phos.*

alcohol: *Silicea.*

bread: *Natr. mur.*

coffee: *Ferr. phos., Magnes. phos.*

fat food: *Natr. phos., Kali mur.*

herrings: *Ferr. phos.*

hot drinks: *Kali sulph.*

meat: *Ferr. phos., Silicea.*

milk: *Ferr. phos.*

sour food: *Ferr. phos.*

sweets: *Kali phos.*

warm food: *Silicea, Ferr. phos.*

BAND around body, sensation of: *Magnes. phos.*

BILIOUSNESS: *Natr. sulph.*

with gray tongue: *Kali mur.*

BILIOUS COLIC: *Natr. sulph.*

BREATH offensive: *Kali phos., Natr. mur.*

BURNING heat in stomach: *Kali sulph., Calc. sulph.*

thirst: *Kali sulph.*

CANNOT BEAR TIGHT CLOTHING: *Ferr. phos., Natr. sulph.*

COLICKY PAINS: *Kali sulph.*

CRAVINGS, bitter: *Natr. mur.*

eggs: *Calc. phos.*

pickles: *Calc. phos.*

salt: *Natr. mur.*

sweets: *Silicea.*

DEATHLY SICKNESS at stomach: *Ferr. phos.*

DESIRES ale: *Ferr. phos.*

alcohol: *Ferr. phos.*

bacon: *Calc. phos.*

bitter things: *Natr. mur.*

claret: *Calc. sulph.*

fruit: *Calc. sulph.*

green and sour vegetables: *Calc. sulph.*

ham: *Calc. phos.*

indigestible things: *Calc. phos.*

salted food: *Calc. phos., Natr. mur.*

DESIRES smoked meats: *Calc. sulph., Calc. phos.*
    stimulants: *Ferr. phos.*
    sugar: *Magnes. phos.*
DREAD of hot drinks: *Kali sulph.*
DYSPEPSIA, acid: *Natr. phos., Silicea.*
    chronic: *Silicea.*
    flatulent: *Magnes. phos.*
    heartburn and chilliness: *Silicea.*
    nervous: *Kali phos.*
    pain after taking food: *Ferr. phos., Natr. sulph.*
    spasmodic: *Magnes. phos.*
    with flushed, hot face: *Ferr. phos.*
        pressure as of a load in stomach: *Kali sulph.*
        white, grayish tongue: *Kali mur.*
        much flatulence: *Calc. phos.*
        pain and salivation: *Natr. mur.*
        waterbrash: *Natr. mur.*
EMPTY, GONE FEELING in stomach: *Natr. phos., Kali phos.*
    relieved by eating: *Kali phos.*
EPIGASTRIUM tender to touch: *Ferr. phos.*
    pain in, constant: *Kali phos.*
        after eating: *Calc. phos.*
ERUCTATIONS, bitter: *Kali phos.*
    sour: *Natr. phos., Natr. sulph., Silicea, Kali phos.*
    burning, tasteless: *Magnes. phos.*
    from hot drinks: *Kali mur.*
    gaseous: *Kali phos.*
    greasy: *Ferr. phos.*
EXCESSIVE HUNGER: *Kali phos., Silicea, Calc. phos., Natr. mur.*
FAINTNESS at stomach: *Kali sulph.*
FATTY FOOD causes indigestion: *Kali mur.*
FLATULENCE, brings back taste of food: *Ferr. phos.*
    excessive accumulation of gas in stomach: *Calc. phos.*
    with disturbance about heart: *Kali phos.*
        distension and constipation: *Magnes. phos.*
        pain, no relief from belching: *Magnes. phos.*
        sluggish liver: *Kali mur., Natr. sulph.*
        sour risings: *Natr. phos., Natr. sulph., Calc. phos., Kali
            phos.*
FULNESS, sensation of: *Kali sulph.*

GASTRITIS: *Ferr. phos., Kali mur.*
   chronic: *Kali sulph.*
   from too hot drinks: *Kali mur.*
GASTRALGIA relieved by warmth and bending double: *Magnes.*
          phos.
GASTRIC abrasions: *Natr. phos.*
   fever: *Ferr. phos.*
   ulcerations: *Natr. phos., Kali phos.*
GONE SENSATION at pit of stomach: *Kali phos., Natr. phos.*
HÆMORRHAGE from stomach: *Kali mur., Ferr. phos.*
HEARTBURN after eating: *Natr. mur., Natr. sulph., Silicea,*
          Magnes. phos.
   and flatulence: *Calc. phos.*
HEAT in stomach: *Kali sulph.*
HICCOUGH: *Magnes. phos., Calc. fluor., Natr. mur.*
HUNGER, excessive: *Kali phos., Silicea, Natr. mur.*
. INDURATION of pylorus: *Silicea.*
INDIGESTION. (See Dyspepsia.)
INFANT vomits as soon as it nurses: *Silicea.*
   wants to nurse all the time: *Calc. phos.*
INTOLERANCE of stimulants: *Silicea.*
JAUNDICE after gastritis: *Kali sulph.*
   from vexation: *Natr. sulph.*
   with bitter taste and constipation: *Kali mur.*
   with drowsiness: *Natr. mur.*
LONGING, for salty food: *Natr. mur.* (See Desires.)
LOSS OF APPETITE: *Ferr. phos., Kali mur., Natr. phos., Natr.*
        mur., Kali phos., Natr. sulph.
   desire for smoking: *Natr. mur.*
NAUSEA: *Kali sulph., Natr. phos., Natr. sulph.*
   and vomiting: *Magnes. phos.*
        of sour food or blood: *Kali phos.*
   after fat food: *Kali mur.*
   with vertigo: *Calc. sulph.*
NON-ASSIMILATION of food: *Calc. phos.*
PAIN in abdominal ring: *Natr. mur.*
   right side under shoulder: *Kali mur.*
   after taking food: *Natr. phos., Calc. phos., Ferr. phos.,*
        Natr. sulph.
   at epigastrium, constant: *Kali phos.*

PRESSURE in stomach: *Magnes. phos.*
PYLORUS, induration of: *Silicea.*
REGURGITATION of food after eating: *Magnes. phos.*
    acidity: *Natr. phos.*
STOMACH, beating in: *Ferr. phos.*
    burning heat in: *Kali sulph., Calc. sulph.*
    chronic catarrh of: *Kali sulph.*
    colicky pains in: *Kali sulph., Magnes. sulph.*
    cramps in: *Magnes. phos.*
    deep-seated pain in: *Kali sulph.*
    distended: *Natr. sulph.*
    empty feeling in: *Natr. phos.*
    enlargement: *Magnes. phos., Kali phos.*
    fulness and pressure in: *Kali sulph.*
    gas in, excessive: *Calc. phos.*
    gone feeling in: *Kali sulph., Natr. phos.*
    heart-burn: *Natr. phos.*
    hæmorrhage from: *Kali mur.*
    heavy: *Natr. sulph.*
    painful: *Ferr. phos.*
    pit of, red spots on: *Natr. mur.*
    regurgitation of food from: *Magnes. phos.*
    swollen: *Ferr. phos.*
    tender: *Ferr. phos.*
    ulceration of: *Natr. phos., Kali phos.*
    weakness and sinking at: *Natr. mur.*
    welling of mucus from: *Natr. sulph.*
STOMACHACHE, aggravated by pressure: *Ferr. phos.*
      food: *Calc. phos.*
    due to worms: *Natr. phos.*
    from chill: *Ferr. phos.*
      fright or excitement: *Kali phos.*
    relieved by eating: *Kali phos.*
    with constipation: *Kali mur.*
      flatulence: *Magnes. phos., Natr. sulph.*
      pain and salvation: *Natr. mur.*
THIRST, burning: *Kali sulph., Natr. mur., Calc. sulph.*
    during evening: *Natr. sulph.*
    for cold water: *Ferr. phos., Kali phos.*

THIRSTLESSNESS: *Kali sulph.*

TIGHT CLOTHING about waist unbearable: *Natr. sulph.*

ULCERATION of stomach: *Natr. phos.*

VOMITING, acid: *Natr. mur.*

    after cold water: *Calc. phos.*

        ice cream: *Calc. phos.*

    before breakfast: *Ferr. phos., Silicea.*

    bile: *Natr. sulph.*

    bitter food: *Kali phos.*

    bright-red blood: *Ferr. phos.*

    clotted blood: *Kali mur.*

    coffee-grounds: *Natr. mur., Natr. phos.*

    curdled masses: *Natr. mur., Natr. phos.*

    dark blood: *Kali mur.*

    greenish water: *Natr. sulph., Kali phos.*

    immediately after nursing: *Silicea.*

    infantile: *Calc. phos.*

    morning: *Silicea.*

    sour: *Ferr. phos., Natr. mur., Kali phos., Natr. sulph.*

    stringy mucus: *Natr. mur.*

    thick, white phlegm: *Kali mur.*

    transparent mucus: *Natr. mur.*

    undigested food: *Ferr. phos., Calc. phos., Calc. fluor.*

    viscid blood: *Kali mur.*

    water, saltish, greenish: *Natr. sulph.*

    watery mucus: *Natr. mur.*

WATERBRASH: *Natr. phos., Natr. mur., Kali phos.*

Abdomen and Stool.

ABDOMEN, colic: *Magnes. phos.*

    cramps: *Magnes. phos.*

    feels cold to touch: *Kali sulph*

    flabby: *Calc. phos.*

    gas accumulation: *Natr. sulph.*

    hardness: *Magnes. phos.*

    large in children: *Silicea.*

    pendulous: *Calc. fluor.*

    swollen: *Kali phos., Kali mur., Magnes. phos.*

    sunken: *Calc. phos.*

    tender: *Kali mur.*

ABDOMEN, tense and tympanitic: *Kali sulph.*

AFTER STOOL, torn bleeding and smarting feeling: *Natr. mur.*
 vaccination, diarrhœa: *Silicea, Kali mur.*

ANUS, fissured: *Silicea, Calc. phos., Natr. mur., Calc. fluor.*
 fistula in: *Silicea, Calc. sulph., Calc. phos.*
 herpetic eruption around: *Natr. mur.*
 itching at: *Natr. phos., Calc. phos., Calc. fluor., Natr. sulph.*
 neuralgia of: *Calc. phos.*
 painful abscesses about: *Calc. sulph.*
 prolapsus of: *Calc. sulph., Kali phos., Natr. mur.*
   disposition to: *Ferr. phos.*
 rawness of: *Natr. phos.*
 soreness of: *Natr. phos., Natr. mur.*
 wart-like eruptions on: *Natr. sulph.*

BELCHING GIVES NO RELIEF in colic: *Magnes. phos.*

BOWELS, great torpor of: *Natr. mur.*
 lining membrane of, protrudes: *Kali phos.*
 looseness of, in old women: *Natr. sulph.*
 pain in: *Natr. phos.*
 sulphurous odor of gas from: *Kali sulph.*

BURNING PAIN in rectum: *Natr. mur.*

CHILDREN draw up legs in colic: *Magnes. phos.*
 large abdomen in: *Silicea.*

CHOLERA: *Ferr. phos., Kali phos., Kali sulph.*

CHOLERA INFANTUM: *Calc. phos., Ferr. phos.*

CHOLERAIC CRAMPS: *Magnes. phos.*

COLIC accompanied with belching: *Magnes. phos.*
 ameliorated by rubbing and warmth: *Magnes. phos.*
   bending double: *Kali phos.*
 at every attempt to eat: *Calc. phos.*
 begins in right groin: *Natr. sulph.*
 belching gives no relief in: *Magnes. phos.*
 crampy: *Magnes. phos.*
 flatulent: *Natr. phos., Magnes. phos., Kali sulph., Natr.
   sulph.*
 forcing patient to bend double: *Magnes. phos.*
 from worms: *Natr. phos., Silicea.*
 in hypogastrium: *Kali phos.*
 lead: *Natr. sulph.*

COLIC, of children: *Calc. phos., Magnes. phos., Natr. phos.*
　　pains radiate from umbilicus: *Magnes. phos.*
　　remittent: *Magnes. phos.*
CONGESTION of liver: *Natr. sulph.*
CONSTIPATION, alternating with diarrhœa: *Natr. mur., Natr. phos.*
　　from want of moisture: *Natr. mur.*
　　with spinal affections: *Silicea.*
　　inactivity of bowels: *Natr. mur.*
　　furred tongue: *Kali mur.*
　　habitual: *Kali sulph.*
　　hæmorrhoidal: *Natr. mur.*
　　inability to expel fæces: *Calc. fluor.*
　　infantile: *Magnes. phos.*
　　hard stool in old people: *Calc. phos.*
　　heat in lower bowel: *Ferr. phos.*
　　hectic fever: *Calc. sulph.*
　　obstinate: *Kali sulph., Natr. phos.*
　　producing fissures: *Natr. mur.*
　　stools light-colored: *Kali mur.*
　　　　dark brown: *Kali phos.*
　　with weakness of intestine: *Natr. mur.*
CRAMPS: *Magnes. phos., Kali sulph.*
DIARRHŒA, after maple sugar: *Calc. sulph.*
　　　　fatty food: *Kali mur.*
　　　　wet weather: *Natr. sulph., Calc. phos.*
　　　　vaccination: *Silicea, Kali mur.*
　　aggravated by fruit: *Calc. phos.*
　　alternating with constipation: *Natr. mur.*
　　bilious: *Natr. sulph.*
　　caused by chill: *Ferr. phos.*
　　　　excessive acidity: *Natr. phos.*
　　　　change of weather: *Calc. sulph., Calc. phos.*
　　　　fright: *Kali phos.*
　　　　relaxed intestinal villi: *Ferr. phos.*
　　dark, bilious stools: *Natr. sulph.*
　　excoriating: *Natr. mur.*
　　flatulent fœtid: *Calc. phos., Kali phos.*
　　frothy: *Natr. mur.*
　　foul, putrid color: *Kali phos., Silicea.*

DIARRHŒA, green stools: *Natr. phos.*, *Calc. phos.*, *Natr. sulph.*

infantile: *Silicea*, *Calc. phos.*, *Natr. phos.*

imperative, watery: *Kali phos.*

involuntary: *Natr. mur.*

painless: *Kali phos.*

purulent: *Calc. sulph.*, *Kali sulph.*

rice water: *Kali phos.*

slimy stools: *Calc. phos.*, *Kali mur.*, *Natr. mur.*, *Kali sulph.*, *Calc. sulph.*

sour smelling: *Natr. sulph.*

undigested: *Ferr. phos.*, *Calc. phos.*

watery: *Natr. mur.*, *Ferr. phos.*, *Natr. sulph.*, *Calc. sulph.*, *Magnes. phos.*, *Kali sulph.*, *Calc. phos.*, *Kali phos.*

with cramps in calves: *Magnes. phos.*

white stools: *Natr. phos.*, *Kali mur.*

with depression: *Kali phos.*

    exhaustion: *Kali phos.*, *Calc. phos.*

    jaundice: *Natr. phos.*

yellow, slimy, watery, purulent: *Kali sulph.*

DUODENAL CATARRH: *Kali mur.*

DYSENTERY, febrile stage: *Ferr. phos.*

stools purulent: *Calc. sulph.*

    pure blood: *Kali phos.*

    sanious: *Calc. sulph.*

    slimy: *Kali mur.*

    very painful: *Magnes. phos.*

with purging: *Kali mur.*

    spasmodic retention of urine: *Magnes. phos.*

ENTERALGIA, relieved by bending double: *Magnes. phos.*

    warmth: *Magnes. phos.*

ENTERIC FEVER: *Ferr. phos.*, *Kali mur.*, *Calc. phos.*, *Kali sulph.*, *Kali phos.*

ENTERITIS: *Ferr. phos.*, *Kali phos.*

FISSURE in anus: *Silicea*, *Calc. phos.*, *Natr. mur.*, *Calc. fluor.*

FISTULA IN ANO: *Silicea*, *Calc. sulph.*, *Calc. phos.*

abdomen swollen: *Kali mur.*

cutting pain in abdomen: *Natr. sulph.*

distress about heart: *Kali phos.*

fœtid: *Calc. phos.*

FISTULA IN ANO, incarcerated: *Magnes. phos.*
  odor of sulphur: *Kali sulph.*
  offensive, noisy: *Kali phos., Calc. phos.*
  shifting of: *Silicea.*
FORCIBLE EXPULSION of stool: *Magnes. phos.*
GALL-STONES, to prevent reformation of: *Calc. phos.*
  spasms from: *Magnes. phos.*
GLANDS, inguinal, enlarged: *Silicea.*
HEAT IN LOWER BOWELS: *Natr. sulph.*
HÆMORRHOIDS, beating in: *Natr. mur.*
  bleeding: *Kali mur., Ferr. phos., Calc. fluor.*
  blind: *Kali sulph., Calc. fluor.*
  chronic: *Calc. phos.*
  cutting, like lightning in: *Magnes. phos.*
  external: *Kali sulph.*
  inflamed: *Ferr. phos.*
  intensely painful: *Silicea, Kali phos.*
  internal: *Kali sulph., Calc. fluor.*
  itching: *Kali phos.*
  oozing: *Calc. phos.*
  smarting and stinging: *Natr. mur.*
  stinging: *Natr. mur.*
HEREDITARY LOOSENESS in old women: *Natr. sulph.*
HERNIA, abdominal: *Calc. phos.*
  incarcerated and inflamed: *Ferr. phos.*
HERPES about anus: *Natr. mur.*
INEFFECTUAL urging to stool: *Kali sulph.*
INTESTINAL ULCERS: *Calc. sulph.*
ITCHING IN ANUS aggravated at night: *Natr. phos.*
JAUNDICE after vexation: *Natr. sulph.*
  caused by a chill: *Kali mur.*
      gastric catarrh: *Kali sulph.*
  caused by gastro-duodenal catarrh: *Kali mur., Natr. mur.*
  with diarrhœa: *Natr. phos.*
LARGE ABDOMEN in children: *Silicea.*
  abscess of: *Silicea.*
LIVER, complete torpidity of: *Kali mur.*
  congestion of: *Natr. sulph.*
  irritable: *Natr. sulph.*

LIVER, region of, painful: *Calc. sulph.*
 sclerosis of: *Natr. phos.*
 sharp, stitching pains in: *Natr. sulph.*
 sluggish action of: *Kali mur.*
 soreness to touch of: *Natr. sulph.*
MARASMUS in teething children: *Calc. phos.*
MESENTERIC GLANDS enlarged: *Calc. phos.*
NAVEL, empty feeling about: *Calc. phos.*
NEURALGIA of the anus: *Calc. phos.*
NOISY offensive flatus: *Kali phos., Calc. phos.*
PAIN around navel causes crying: *Calc. phos., Magnes. phos.*
 abdominal ring: *Natr. mur.*
 in lower part of sacrum: *Calc. phos.*
 in liver and spleen: *Natr. mur., Kali phos.*
 in the bowels: *Natr. phos., Magnes. phos.*
 through right groin: *Natr. phos.*
PAINFUL ABSCESS about anus: *Calc. sulph.*
 about region of liver: *Calc. sulph.*
PARETIC CONDITION of rectum: *Kali phos.*
PERITONITIS: *Ferr. phos., Kali mur., Kali sulph.*
PERITYPHLITIS: *Kali mur., Ferr. phos.*
PILES. (See Hæmorrhoids.)
PROCTALGIA: *Natr. mur.*
PROLAPSUS ANI: *Calc. sulph., Kali phos., Natr. mur., Ferr. phos.*
 disposition to: *Ferr. phos.*
RAWNESS of anus: *Natr. phos.*
RECTUM, burns: *Kali phos.*
 pain in, with every stool: *Magnes. phos., Natr. mur.*
 prolapsus of: *Calc. sulph., Kali phos., Natr. mur.*
 stitches in: *Natr. mur.*
SACRUM, pain in, after stool: *Calc. phos.*
SINKING in epigastrium and about navel: *Calc. phos.*
SPLENIC TROUBLES: *Kali phos.*
SPLEEN, pain in: *Natr. mur., Kali phos.*
STITCHES in rectum: *Natr. mur.*
STOOLS, bilious: *Natr. sulph.*
 black: *Kali sulph.*
 bloody: *Kali mur., Calc. sulph., Kali phos., Ferr. phos.*
 cadaverous-smelling: *Silicea.*

STOOLS, clay-colored: *Kali mur.*

    coagulated casein: *Natr. phos.*

    copious: *Ferr. phos., Calc. phos.*

    creamy: *Natr. phos.*

    crumbling: *Natr. mur.*

    dark: *Natr. sulph., Kali phos.*

    difficult to expel: *Natr. mur., Natr. sulph.* (soft.)

          retain: *Natr. phos.*

    dry: *Natr. mur.*

    expelled with force: *Magnes. phos.*

    flocculent: *Kali mur.*

    fœtid and foul: *Kali phos.*

    frequent: *Natr. phos.*

    frothy and glairy: *Natr. mur.*

    green: *Natr. phos., Natr. sulph., Calc. phos.*

    hard: *Natr. mur., Natr. sulph., Calc. phos.*

    hot, sputtering: *Calc. phos.*

    inability to expel: *Calc. fluor.*

    involuntary: *Natr. mur.*

    jelly-like masses: *Natr. phos.*

    knotty: *Natr. sulph.*

    light-colored: *Kali mur.*

    loose, morning: *Natr. mur., Natr. sulph.*

    noisy: *Calc. phos.*

    offensive: *Kali phos., Calc. phos., Silicea, Kali sulph.*

    painful: *Ferr. phos.*

    pale-yellow: *Kali mur.*

    profuse: *Calc. phos.*

    purulent: *Calc. sulph., Calc. phos.*

    putrid odor: *Kali phos.*

    recede when partly expelled: *Silicea.*

    rice-water: *Kali phos.*

    scanty: *Natr. phos.*

    slimy: *Kali mur., Natr. mur., Kali sulph., Calc. sulph., Calc. phos.*

    sour-smelling: *Natr. phos.*

    sputtering: *Calc. phos.*

    streaked with blood: *Natr. sulph., Calc. sulph.*

    sudden: *Ferr. phos., Natr. phos.*

    undigested food: *Ferr. phos., Calc. phos.*

STOOLS, watery: *Ferr. phos., Natr. mur., Natr. sulph., Calc. sulph.,*
        Magnes. phos., Kali sulph., Calc. phos.
  white: *Kali mur., Natr. mur., Natr. phos.*
  while eating: *Kali phos.*
  yellow: *Kali sulph.*
STRAINING AT STOOL: *Natr. phos.*
SUMMER COMPLAINT in teething children: *Calc. phos.*
TABES MESENTERICA: *Calc. phos.*
TENESMUS: *Kali phos.*
TORPIDITY, complete, of liver: *Kali mur.*
TYMPANITES: *Kali sulph., Kali phos., Magnes. phos.*
  in bilious fever: *Natr. sulph.*
TYPHLITIS: *Ferr. phos., Kali mur., Natr. sulph.*
TYPHUS with constipation: *Kali mur.*
UNDIGESTED STOOLS: *Ferr. phos., Calc. phos.*
ULCERS, intestinal: *Calc. sulph.*
WAIST, cannot bear tight clothing around: *Natr. sulph.*
WART-LIKE ERUPTIONS on anus: *Natr. sulph.*
WEAKNESS in epigastrium: *Kali phos.*
WORMS, intestinal: *Natr. phos., Ferr. phos., Calc. phos.*
  long: *Natr. phos.*
  thread: *Natr. phos., Kali mur., Ferr. phos.*

Urinary Symptoms.

ALBUMINURIA: *Kali mur., Kali phos., Kali sulph.*
ATONY of bladder: *Natr. phos.*
BLADDER, catarrh of: *Natr. mur., Kali mur., Calc. sulph.*
  neck of, cutting pain in: *Calc. phos., Kali phos., Ferr. phos*
  paralysis: *Kali phos., Natr. sulph.*
  stone in: *Calc. phos.*
  spasm of: *Magnes. phos.*
BLEEDING FROM URETHRA: *Kali phos.*
BRIGHT'S DISEASE, for albumen: *Calc. phos., Kali phos.*
  febrile disturbance: *Ferr. phos.*
BURNING after urination: *Natr. mur.*
  during urination: *Natr. sulph.*
CALCULOUS PHOSPHATES in urine: *Calc. phos.*
CUTTING after urination: *Natr. mur.*
  pains in urethra and neck of bladder: *Calc. phos.*

26

CYSTITIS, acute cases: *Ferr. phos., Kali mur.*
  chronic: *Kali mur.*
    suppurating: *Calc. sulph.*
  with asthenic conditions: *Kali sulph., Kali phos.*
DIABETES MELLITUS: *Calc. phos., Ferr. phos., Kali mur., Natr. phos., Natr. sulph., Kali phos.*
ENURESIS, diurnal: *Ferr. phos.*
  in children: *Silicea, Calc. phos.*
    old people: *Calc. phos.*
  nocturnal: *Magnes. phos., Kali phos.*
  worm affections: *Natr. phos.*
FREQUENT URGING to urinate: *Calc. phos., Natr. phos., Ferr. phos., Natr. sulph.*
  urination: *Kali phos., Natr. phos.*
GRAVEL: *Calc. phos., Natr. sulph., Magnes. phos., Silicea.*
HÆMATURIA: *Ferr. phos.*
  from scurvy: *Natr. mur.*
INCONTINENCE OF URINE: *Calc. phos.*
  from weakness of sphincter: *Ferr. phos.*
    nervous debility: *Kali phos.*
    paralysis of sphincter: *Kali phos.*
  in children with acidity: *Natr. phos.*
  while walking, coughing, etc.: *Natr. mur., Ferr. phos.*
INCREASED URINE: *Calc. phos., Ferr. phos., Natr. mur., Natr. sulph.*
INTERMITTENT FLOW: *Natr. phos.*
IRRITATION AT NECK OF BLADDER: *Ferr. phos.*
ISCHURIA: *Ferr. phos.*
KIDNEYS, inflammation, effects of: *Kali mur.*
  pains in: *Ferr. phos.*
  suppuration of: *Silicea.*
LITHIC DEPOSITS in urine: *Natr. sulph.*
NEPHRITIS scarlatinosa: *Calc. sulph., Kali sulph.*
  chronic: *Natr. sulph.*
NOCTURNAL ENURESIS: *Magnes. phos., Kali phos.*
PAINS, cutting, in urethra: *Calc. phos., Kali phos.*
  neck of bladder: *Calc. phos., Kali phos.*
PARETIC CONDITION: *Kali phos.*
POLYURIA, simplex: *Natr. mur., Ferr. phos., Natr. sulph., Natr. phos., Calc. phos., Magnes. phos.*

POLYURIA, with waterbrash: *Natr. mur.*
RETENTION of urine: *Magnes. phos.*
SECRETION of urine, excessive: *Ferr. phos., Natr. sulph., Natr. phos.*
SPASMODIC RETENTION of urine: *Magnes. phos., Natr. phos.*
STONE in the bladder: *Calc. phos.*
SUPPRESSION of urine: *Ferr. phos.*
URGING to urinate, frequent: *Ferr. phos., Natr. phos., Calc. phos., Natr. sulph.*
URETHRA, bleeding from: *Kali phos.*
   cutting pains in: *Kali phos.*
   itching in: *Kali phos.*
URINE, albuminous: *Kali sulph., Kali mur.*
   brick dust sediment: *Natr. sulph., Silicea.*
   bloody: *Natr. mur., Kali phos.*
   calculous phosphates in: *Calc. phos.*
   copious: *Calc. fluor., Calc. phos., Natr. mur.*
   dark-colored: *Kali mur., Natr. phos.*
   emits pungent odor: *Calc. fluor.*
   flocculent sediment in: *Calc. phos.*
   gravel in: *Calc. phos., Magnes. phos., Natr. sulph., Silicea.*
   increased: *Calc. phos., Natr. mur.*
   incontinence of: *Natr. mur., Kali phos.*
   involuntary: *Ferr. phos., Natr. mur.*
   loaded with bile: *Natr. sulph.*
     mucus and pus: *Silicea.*
   lithic deposits in: *Natr. sulph.*
   phosphates: *Calc. phos.*
   pus and mucus, with: *Natr. sulph.*
   red and hectic: *Calc. sulph.*
   sandy deposit in: *Natr. sulph.*
   scanty: *Calc. fluor.*
   secretion excessive: *Ferr. phos., Natr. phos., Natr. sulph*
   spasmodically retained: *Magnes. phos.*
   spurts out with every cough: *Ferr. phos., Natr. mur.*
   sugar: *Natr. sulph.*
   urates: *Calc. sulph., Silicea.*
   uric acid, excess of: *Kali mur., Silicea.*
   yellow like saffron: *Kali phos.*
   yellowish green: *Natr. sulph.*

URINATION, scalding on: *Kali phos., Natr. sulph.*

    intermittent, needs straining: *Natr. phos.*

    painful urging: *Magnes. phos.*

VESICAL NEURALGIA: *Magnes. phos.*

WETTING OF BED in children: *Calc. phos., Natr. phos., Ferr. phos.,*
                              Magnes. phos.

Male Sexual Organs.

BALANITIS: *Kali sulph., Kali phos.*

BUBO: *Calc. sulph., Kali mur., Ferr. phos., Kali phos., Silicea.*

CARIES, syphilitic: *Silicea.*

CHANCRE, hard: *Calc. fluor.*

    phagedænic: *Kali phos.*

    soft: *Kali mur.*

CHORDEE: *Magnes. phos., Natr. phos.*

CHRONIC SYPHILIS: *Silicea, Natr. mur., Kali mur.*

COITUS, prostration after: *Kali phos.*

CONDYLOMATA, syphilitic: *Natr. sulph.*

    cutting in bladder and urethra: *Kali phos., Natr. mur.*

DESIRE, sexual, gone: *Natr. phos.*

DISCHARGE of prostatic fluid: *Natr. mur.*

DRAWING in testicles and spermatic cord: *Natr. phos.*

EMISSIONS, nightly: *Natr. phos., Kali phos., Silicea.*

    with chilliness: *Natr. mur.*

    without dreams: *Natr. phos.*

    during stool: *Natr. mur.*

ERECTIONS: Kali phos.

EPIDIDYMITIS: *Ferr. phos.*

ERETHISM, sexual: *Silicea, Natr. phos.*

GENITALS, itching of: *Natr. sulph.*

GLEET: *Natr. mur., Kali sulph., Calc. phos.*

    combines with eczema: *Kali mur.*

GONORRHŒA, after injections of nitrate of silver: *Natr. mur.*

    first remedy: *Natr. phos.*

    chronic: *Natr. mur., Natr. sulph., Kali phos., Calc. phos.,*
        Silicea.

    discharge bloody: *Kali phos., Ferr. phos.*

        creamy, golden-yellow: *Natr. phos.*

        greenish: *Kali sulph., Natr. sulph.*

        purulent and sanious: *Calc. sulph.*

GONORRHŒA, discharge slimy: *Kali sulph., Natr. mur.*
  transparent: *Natr. mur.*
  yellow: *Kali sulph.*
  watery: *Natr. mur.*
 inflammatory stage: *Ferr. phos.*
 interstitial exudation in: *Kali mur.*
 scalding in: *Natr. mur.*
 subcutaneous exudation: *Kali mur.*
 suppressed: *Natr. sulph.*
 swelling in: *Kali mur.*
 with anæmia: *Calc. phos.*
  itching: *Calc. phos.*
HAIR, loss of, from pubes: *Natr. mur.*
HYDROCELE: *Silicea, Calc. fluor., Calc. phos*
IMPOTENCE: *Kali phos., Natr. mur.*
INDURATION of testicles: *Calc. fluor.*
ITCHING of scrotum: *Silicea, Calc. phos., Natr. phos., Natr. mur.,*
  Natr. sulph.
 in urethra: *Kali phos.*
LOSS OF PUBIC HAIR: *Natr. mur.*
MASTURBATION: *Calc. phos.*
NECROSIS, syphilitic: *Silicea.*
NODES in tertiary syphilis: *Silicea.*
ŒDEMA, preputial: *Natr. sulph.*
 scrotal: *Natr. sulph., Natr. mur.*
ORCHITIS: *Calc. phos., Ferr. phos., Kali mur.*
 from suppressed gonorrhœa: *Kali mur., Kali sulph.*
PERSISTENT sexual thought: *Silicea.*
PHAGEDÆNIC CHANCRES: *Kali phos.*
PREPUTIAL ŒDEMA: *Natr. sulph.*
PROSTATE, abscess of: *Calc. sulph.*
 enlarged: *Natr. sulph.*
 inflammation, suppuration: *Silicea.*
SCROTAL ŒDEMA: *Natr. sulph., Natr. mur., Calc. phos.*
SCROTUM, itching of: *Silicea, Natr. phos., Calc. phos., Natr. mur.*
 sweating of: *Silicea.*
SEMEN thin and watery: *Natr. phos.*
SEMINAL EMISSIONS without dreams: *Natr. phos., Ferr. phos.,*
  Silicea.
 with chilliness: *Natr. mur.*

SEXUAL DESIRE gone: *Natr. phos., Kali phos.*
  increased: *Kali phos., Magnes. phos., Natr. phos., Natr. mur.*
SEXUAL erethism: *Silicea, Calc. phos.*
SPERMATORRHŒA: *Calc. sulph., Natr. phos., Kali phos., Natr.
      mur., Silicea.*
SPERMATIC CORD painful; *Natr. mur.*
SUPPURATING PROSTATITIS: *Silicea.*
SWEAT ON SCROTUM: *Silicea.*
SYCOSIS: *Natr. sulph.*
SYPHILIS, chronic: *Silicea, Kali mur., Calc. fluor.*
  evening aggravations in: *Kali sulph.*
  nodes in tertiary: *Silicea.*
  suppurating stage: *Calc. sulph.*
TESTICLES, aching in: *Natr. mur.*
  indurated: *Calc. fluor.*
  swelling of: *Calc. phos., Natr. mur.*
URETHRA sore to pressure: *Natr. mur.*
  cutting in, after urination: *Natr. mur.*
VARICOCELE, pain in testes: *Ferr. phos.*
VOLUPTUOUS FEELINGS in genitals: *Calc. phos.*
WEAK VISION after coitus: *Kali phos.*

Female Organs.

ABORTION: *Kali phos.*
AMENORRHŒA: *Kali mur., Kali phos., Kali sulph., Natr. mur.,
      Calc. phos.*
  from mental shock: *Kali phos.*
    change of climate: *Silicea, Calc. phos.*
    anæmia: *Calc. phos., Natr. mur.*
BACKACHE, with uterine pains: *Calc. phos.*
BEARING-DOWN PAINS: *Calc. fluor., Ferr. phos., Natr. mur.*
BEFORE MENSES, labor-like pains: *Calc. phos.*
  nosebleed: *Natr. sulph.*
  pain: *Magnes. phos., Ferr. phos.*
  sadness: *Natr. mur.*
BREAST, hard knots in: *Calc. fluor.*
BURNING IN UTERUS: *Natr. mur.*
  vagina after urinating: *Natr. mur.*
CHLOROSIS: *Calc. phos., Ferr. phos., Natr. mur.*
CHRONIC CONGESTION of uterus: *Kali mur., Calc. fluor.*

CONGESTION, excessive, at periods: *Ferr. phos.*
CUTTING in the uterus: *Natr. mur.*
DISPLACEMENT of the uterus: *Calc. fluor.*
    with rheumatic pains: *Calc. phos.*
DRAGGING IN UTERINE REGION: *Calc. fluor.*
DRYNESS of the vagina: *Natr. mur., Ferr. phos.*
DURING MENSES, headache: *Natr. mur., Kali phos.*
    labor-like pains: *Calc. phos.*
DYSMENORRHŒA: *Calc. phos., Kali phos., Magnes. phos., Natr. mur., Ferr. phos.*
    as a preventive: *Ferr. phos.*
    membranous: *Magnes. phos.*
    with vomiting of undigested food: *Ferr. phos.*
        frequent urging to urinate: *Ferr. phos.*
        icy coldness: *Silicea.*
ENDOCARDITIS: *Ferr. phos., Kali mur.*
    chronic: *Calc. phos., Calc. sulph.*
EXTERNAL PARTS tingle: *Calc. phos.*
    swollen: *Magnes. phos.*
FLOODING: *Calc. fluor.*
GENITALS inflamed and swollen: *Natr. sulph.*
GLENNARD'S DISEASE: *Calc. fluor., Silicea.*
GREAT DRYNESS OF VAGINA: *Natr. mur., Ferr. phos.*
HARDNESS OF MAMMÆ: *Calc. phos.*
HYPERTROPHY of uterus: *Kali mur.*
HYSTERIA: *Kali phos.*
ICY COLDNESS at commencement of flow: *Silicea.*
ITCHING OF VULVA: *Natr. mur., Silicea.*
LABIA, abscess of: *Silicea.*
LEUCORRHŒA, acid: *Natr. phos.*
    acrid: *Silicea, Kali phos., Natr. sulph.*
    albuminous mucus: *Calc. phos.*
    corroding: *Natr. mur., Natr. sulph.*
    creamy: *Natr. phos., Calc. phos.*
    greenish: *Kali sulph.*
    honey-colored: *Natr. phos.*
    irritating: *Natr. mur.*
    itching: *Silicea, Natr. mur.*
    like white of egg: *Calc. phos.*

LEUCORRHŒA, mild and milky: *Kali mur.*
    orange-colored: *Kali phos.*
    profuse: *Silicea.*
    scalding: *Kali phos., Natr. mur.*
    slimy: *Kali sulph.*
    smarting: *Natr. mur.*
    sour-smelling: *Natr. phos.*
    thick: *Kali mur.*
    watery: *Natr. mur., Natr. phos., Kali sulph.*
    white: *Kali mur.*
    worse mornings: *Calc. phos.*
    yellow: *Kali sulph., Kali phos.*
LOSS OF HAIR from pubes: *Natr. mur.*
MAMMÆ, hardness of: *Calc. fluor., Calc. phos.*
MASTURBATION in children: *Calc. phos.*
MENSES, acrid: *Natr. phos., Natr. sulph.*
    after, headache, *Natr. mur.*
        intense sexual desire: *Kali phos.*
    before, labor-like pains: *Calc. phos.*
        nosebleed: *Natr. sulph.*
        pain: *Magnes. phos., Ferr. phos., Kali mur.*
        sadness: *Natr. mur.*
    black: *Kali mur.*
    blackish-red: *Kali phos.*
    bright red: *Calc. phos., Ferr. phos.*
    checked: *Kali mur.*
    chilliness with: *Natr. sulph., Silicea.*
    clotted: *Kali mur.*
    copious: *Natr. mur.*
    corrosive: *Natr. sulph.*
    dark: *Kali mur., Calc. phos., Magnes. phos.*
    deep red: *Kali phos., Calc. sulph., Kali sulph.*
    delayed, with headache: *Natr. mur.*
    during headache: *Natr. mur.*
    during bearing-down pains: *Calc. fluor., Calc. phos.*
        colic: *Magnes. phos., Kali phos., Natr. sulph., Ferr. phos.*
        lactation: *Calc. phos., Silicea.*
    every two weeks: *Calc. phos.*
        three weeks: *Ferr. phos.*

MENSES, excessive: *Kali mur., Calc. fluor., Natr. sulph., Ferr. sulph., Kali phos.*

    fibrous: *Magnes. phos.*

    irregular: *Kali phos.*

    labor like pains during: *Calc. phos.*

    last too long: *Kali mur., Calc. sulph.*

    not coagulated: *Kali phos.*

    offensive: *Kali phos.*

    pale: *Natr. phos., Natr. mur.*

    preceded by sexual excitement: *Calc. phos.*

    premature: *Kali phos., Calc. phos.*

    retention of: *Kali phos.*

    stringy: *Magnes. phos.*

    strong odor: *Kali phos.*

    suppressed: *Kali mur., Kali phos., Kali sulph., Natr. mur., Calc. phos.*

    thin: *Kali phos., Natr. mur.*

    too early: *Kali mur., Natr. phos., Magnes. phos., Silicea, Calc. phos.*

      frequent: *Kali mur.*

      late: *Kali mur., Kali phos., Kali sulph., Calc. sulph., Calc. phos., Natr. mur.*

      long lasting: *Kali mur., Calc. sulph.*

      profuse: *Kali phos., Natr. sulph., Ferr. phos., Natr. mur., Calc. fluor., Kali mur.*

      scanty: *Kali phos., Kali sulph., Natr. mur., Silicea.*

    tough discharge: *Kali mur.*

    watery: *Natr. mur.*

    with coldness like ice: *Silicea.*

      congestion: *Ferr. phos.*

      colic: *Magnes. phos., Natr. sulph.*

      constipation: *Silicea, Natr. sulph.*

      fœtid foot-sweats: *Silicea.*

      great weakness: *Calc. sulph.*

      headache: *Kali sulph., Calc. sulph., Kali phos.*

      mental depression: *Natr. mur.*

      morning diarrhœa: *Natr. sulph.*

      ovarian pain: *Ferr. phos.*

      rheumatic pains: *Calc. phos.*

MENSES, with terrible sadness: *Natr. mur.*
        shortening of knee-cords: *Natr. phos.*
        swelling of labia: *Magnes. phos.*
        excitement and sleeplessness: *Natr. phos.*
        twitching: *Calc. sulph., Natr. mur.*
        weight or fulness of abdomen: *Kali sulph.*
MENSTRUATION.   (See Menses.)
METRORRHAGIA: *Silicea, Kali sulph.*
METRITIS: *Ferr. phos., Kali mur.*
NAUSEA during and after embrace: *Silicea.*
NYMPHOMANIA: *Silicea, Calc. fluor., Calc. phos.*
OOPHORITIS: *Ferr. phos., Magnes. phos.*
        chronic: *Calc. phos., Kali phos.*
        gonorrhœa: *Natr. phos., Kali mur.*
OVARIAN NEURALGIA better lying on painful side: *Kali sulph.,*
                      Magnes. phos., Natr. sulph.
PAIN across sacrum, intense: *Kali phos.*
        dull and constant: *Ferr. phos.*
PRESSING toward genitals in morning: *Natr. mur.*
PROLAPSUS UTERI: *Calc. fluor., Calc. phos., Kali phos.*
        relieved by sitting: *Natr. mur.*
        with sinking feeling: *Calc. phos., Natr. phos.*
PULSATION of sexual parts: *Calc. phos.*
SENSATION of a ball rising in throat: *Kali phos.*
SENSITIVE VAGINA: *Silicea, Ferr. phos.*
SEROUS CYSTS OF VAGINA: *Silicea.*
STERILITY: *Silicea, Natr. phos.*
THROBBING in genitals: *Calc. phos.*
ULCERATION of os and cervix: *Kali mur., Silicea.*
UTERINE displacements with rheumatic pain: *Natr. phos., Calc.*
                      phos.
UTERUS, weakness and distress in: *Natr. phos.*
VAGINA dry and hot: *Ferr. phos.*
        burning and soreness in, after urinating: *Natr. mur.*
        great dryness: *Natr. mur.*
        inflammation of: *Ferr. phos.*
        sensitive: *Silicea, Ferr. phos.*
VAGINAL PRURITUS in old women: *Kali phos.*
VAGINAL SEROUS CYSTS: *Silicea.*

VAGINISMUS: *Ferr. phos., Magnes. phos.*
VOLUPTUOUS FEELING: *Calc. phos.*
VULVA, itching of: *Natr. mur., Silicea.*
    vesicular inflammation of: *Natr. sulph.*
WEAKNESS IN UTERINE REGION: *Calc. phos., Natr. phos.*

Pregnancy and Labor.

AGALACTIA: *Calc. phos., Natr. mur.*
AFTER-PAINS: *Kali phos., Magnes. phos.*
    weak, due to feeble contractions: *Calc. fluor., Ferr. phos.*
BURNING in mammæ: *Calc. phos.*
CHILDBED FEVER: *Kali phos., Kali mur.*
CONVULSIONS, puerperal: *Magnes. phos.*
CRAMPS in the legs: *Magnes. phos.*
DECLINE after childbirth: *Calc. phos.*
    prolonged nursing: *Calc. phos.*
    during pregnancy: *Calc. phos.*
EXCESSIVE EXPULSIVE EFFORTS: *Magnes. phos.*
FEET, soreness and lameness of: *Silicea.*
FEVER, puerperal: *Kali mur., Kali phos.*
KNOTS, hard, in the breast: *Calc. fluor.*
Loss of hair during childbirth and lactation: *Natr. mur.*
MAMMÆ feel enlarged: *Calc. phos.*
    fistulous ulcers in: *Silicea.*
    hard lumps in: *Calc. fluor., Silicea.*
MANIA, puerperal: *Kali phos.*
MASTITIS: *Silicea, Calc. sulph., Kali mur., Ferr. phos., Calc. fluor.*
    discharge of brown, offensive pus: *Kali phos.*
MISCARRIAGE threatened: *Kali phos., Magnes. phos.*
MORNING SICKNESS, vomiting of food undigested: *Ferr. phos.*
    frothy, watery phlegm: *Natr. mur.*
    vomiting of sour masses: *Natr. phos.*
    white phlegm: *Kali mur.*
MOTHER'S MILK salty and bluish: *Calc. fluor., Calc. phos.*
NIPPLES crack and ulcerate easily: *Silicea.*
PAIN in feet during pregnancy: *Silicea.*
PAINS, false, ineffectual and tedious: *Kali phos.*
    feeble: *Kali phos.*
    spasmodic: *Magnes. phos.*
PHLEGMASIA ALBA DOLENS: *Natr. sulph.*

PUERPERAL convulsions: *Magnes. phos.*

   fever: *Kali mur., Kali phos.*

   mania: *Kali phos.*

SCIRRHUS of mammæ: *Silicea.*

THREATENED MISCARRIAGE: *Kali phos., Magnes. phos.*

ULCERS of mammæ, fistulous: *Silicea.*

VOMITING with bitter taste: *Natr. sulph.*

WEARINESS in all limbs during pregnancy: *Calc. phos.*

Respiratory Organs.

ABSCESS of lungs: *Silicea.*

ASTHMA, awakes at night with attack of: *Natr. sulph.*

   bronchial: *Kali sulph., Kali mur.*

   aggravated in warm season: *Kali sulph.*

   from the least food: *Kali phos.*

ASTHMA, hay: *Kali phos.*

   humid: *Natr. sulph.*

   in children: *Natr. sulph.*

   nervous: *Magnes. phos.*

   when flatulence is troublesome: *Magnes. phos.*

   with gastric derangements: *Kali mur., Natr. sulph.*

      yellow, lumpy expectoration: *Calc. fluor.*

      hectic fever: *Calc. sulph.*

      spasmodic jerking: *Natr. mur.*

      profuse, watery mucus: *Natr. mur.*

   worse change to damp weather: *Natr. sulph.*

BREATHING hurried and oppressed: *Ferr. phos., Calc. fluor.*

   short: *Ferr. phos., Kali phos., Calc. phos., Kali sulph., Natr. mur.*

BRONCHIAL CATARRH: *Kali mur.* (See Expectoration.)

BRONCHITIS: *Ferr. phos., Calc. sulph., Kali mur., Natr. sulph.*

   chronic: *Natr. mur., Silicea.*

   expectoration. yellow: *Kali sulph.*

BURNING SORENESS in chest: *Ferr. phos.*

CATCH IN BREATH: *Ferr. phos.*

CATCHES COLD EASILY: *Ferr. phos., Natr. mur.*

CHEST, constriction of: *Magnes. phos.*

   contraction of: *Calc. phos.*

   pains aggravated by deep breathing: *Natr. phos.*

      by pressure: *Natr. phos.*

CHEST, pains deep-seated : *Silicea.*
>across : *Calc. sulph.*
>darting : *Magnes. phos., Natr. sulph.*
>rattling of mucus in : *Kali sulph., Natr. sulph., Natr. mur., Kali mur.*
>soreness, ameliorated by pressure : *Natr. sulph.*
>sore to touch : *Calc. phos., Kali phos.*
>weakness in : *Silicea.*

COLDNESS of feet with chest troubles : *Calc. phos.*

CONGESTION of lungs : *Ferr. phos.*

COUGH, acute : *Kali mur., Ferr. phos.*
>aggravated in evening : *Kali sulph.*
>>morning : *Natr. sulph.*
>better lying down : *Calc. phos.*
>barking : *Kali mur.*
>causes headache : *Natr. mur.*
>chronic, of consumptives : *Calc. phos., Silicea.*
>convulsive : *Magnes. phos.*
>croupy : *Kali mur.*
>dry : *Ferr. phos., Magnes. phos., Natr. mur.*
>from cold drinks : *Silicea.*
>loose rattling : *Silicea.*
>tickling behind sternum : *Natr. mur.*
>>in larynx : *Calc. fluor.*
>>in trachea : *Ferr. phos., Kali phos., Silicea.*
>>suprasternal fossa : *Silicea.*
>>throat : *Calc. fluor.*
>hacking : *Calc. fluor.*
>hard : *Ferr. phos., Kali sulph.*
>harsh : *Kali mur.*
>hoarse : *Kali sulph.*
>irritating : *Silicea.*
>loose rattling : *Kali sulph., Silicea, Natr. mur.*
>loud and noisy : *Kali mur.*
>nervous : *Magnes. phos.*
>on lying down : *Magnes. phos., Calc. fluor., Silicea.*
>painful : *Ferr. phos.*
>paroxysmal : *Magnes. phos.*
>periodical : *Natr. mur.*

COUGH, short: *Ferr. phos., Kali mur., Natr. mur.*
  spasmodic: *Magnes. phos., Kali mur., Kali phos., Natr. mur., Ferr. phos.*
  suffocative in children, better lying down: *Calc. phos.*
  tickling: *Ferr. phos., Magnes. phos., Calc. fluor.*
  whooping: *Ferr. phos., Magnes. phos., Kali sulph., Kali phos.*
  with bursting headache: *Natr. mur.*
    night sweats: *Silicea.*
    involuntary emission of urine: *Ferr. phos., Natr. mur.*
    sensation of goneness in chest: *Natr. sulph.*
CROUP: *Ferr. phos., Kali mur., Calc. sulph., Calc. fluor., Calc. phos., Natr. mur., Kali phos.*
CROUPY hoarseness: *Kali sulph.*
DYSPNŒA: *Ferr. phos., Natr. mur., Kali sulph., Calc. phos., Kali phos.*
  during damp weather: *Natr. sulph.*
EMACIATION in phthisis: *Calc. phos.*
EMPYEMA: *Calc. sulph., Silicea.*
EPIGLOTTIS feels closed: *Calc. fluor.*
EXPECTORATION absent: *Ferr. phos., Magnes. phos.*
  clear: *Natr. mur.*
  copious: *Silicea, Kali sulph.*
  coughed up with difficulty: *Natr. mur., Calc. phos., Kali mur.*
  clear, transparent: *Natr. mur.*
  creamy: *Natr. phos.*
  fœtid: *Kali phos.*
  frothy: *Natr. mur., Kali phos.*
  granular: *Silicea.*
  grayish-white: *Kali mur.*
  greenish: *Natr. sulph., Kali sulph., Silicea.*
  golden-yellow: *Natr. phos.*
  loose: *Natr. mur., Kali sulph., Silicea.*
  lumpy: *Calc. fluor.*
  milky: *Kali mur.*
  mucous: *Calc. fluor., Calc. phos.*
  offensive: *Silicea.*
  profuse: *Kali sulph., Silicea.*
  purulent: *Natr. sulph., Calc. sulph., Silicea.*
  rattling: *Natr. mur., Silicea.*

EXPECTORATION, ropy: *Natr. sulph.*

   scanty, blood streaked: *Ferr. phos.*

   salty: *Kali phos.*

   sanious: *Calc. sulph.*

   serous: *Natr. mur., Kali phos.*

   slimy: *Kali sulph.*

   sputum slips back: *Kali sulph.*

   sticky: *Kali sulph.*

   thick: *Natr. sulph., Silicea, Kali mur., Kali phos.*

   viscid and whitish: *Kali mur.*

   watery: *Natr. mur., Kali sulph.*

   white: *Calc. phos.*

   yellow, tough, lumpy: *Calc. fluor.*

   yellowish: *Calc. fluor., Kali sulph., Silicea, Calc. phos., Kali phos.*

FISTULA IN ANO, with chest troubles: *Calc. phos., Silicea.*

FREQUENT HAWKING: *Calc. phos.*

GLOTTIS, spasm of: *Calc. phos., Magnes. phos.*

HÆMOPTYSIS after concussion or fall: *Ferr. phos.*

HAY FEVER: *Kali phos., Natr. mur.*

HECTIC FEVER: *Calc. sulph., Silicea, Calc. phos.*

HEAT IN CHEST: *Ferr. phos.*

HOARSENESS: *Kali phos., Natr. mur., Calc. sulph., Silicea, Calc. fluor., Natr. phos., Natr. sulph., Calc. phos.*

   from cold: *Kali sulph., Kali mur., Ferr. phos.*

HOLDS CHEST while coughing: *Natr. sulph.*

HUSKINESS after singing or speaking: *Ferr. phos.*

INTERCOSTAL muscles sore: *Natr. phos.*

INVOLUNTARY urination when coughing: *Ferr. phos., Natr. mur.*

LARYNGITIS: *Ferr. phos., Kali mur., Natr. mur.*

LARYNX, irritated: *Ferr. phos., Calc. fluor.*

   painful: *Ferr. phos.*

   sore: *Ferr. phos.*

LUNGS, congestion of: *Ferr. phos.*

MUCUS slips back and is swallowed: *Kali sulph.*

NIGHT-SWEATS profuse: *Silicea, Calc. phos.*

ŒDEMA of lungs: *Natr. mur., Kali phos.*

OPPRESSION of breathing: *Ferr. phos., Calc. fluor*

PAINS IN CHEST, across: *Calc. sulph.*

PAINS IN CHEST, aggravated by breathing: *Natr. phos.*
 pressure: *Natr. phos.*
 left side, piercing: *Natr. sulph.*
PHTHISIS: *Calc. sulph., Silicea, Ferr. phos., Kali mur., Calc. phos., Natr. phos., Natr. sulph.*
 florida: *Natr. phos., Ferr. phos.*
PLEURISY: *Ferr. phos., Natr. mur., Kali mur.*
PNEUMONIA: *Ferr. phos., Kali mur., Calc. sulph., Kali sulph., Silicea, Natr. mur.*
PROFUSE night sweats: *Calc. phos., Silicea.*
RATTLING of mucus in chest: *Natr. sulph., Kali sulph., Kali mur., Ferr. phos., Natr. mur.*
SHORTNESS of breath: *Ferr. phos., Kali phos., Natr. mur., Kali sulph., Calc. phos.*
 on going up stairs: *Kali phos.*
SIGHING, TENDENCY TO: *Natr. phos., Calc. phos.*
SORENESS OF CHEST, relieved by pressure: *Natr. sulph.*
 to touch: *Calc. phos.*
 intercostal muscles: *Natr. phos.*
 lungs: *Ferr. phos.*
SORE PAIN above sternum: *Calc. phos.*
SPASMODIC closure of windpipe: *Magnes. phos.*
SPASM OF GLOTTIS: *Calc. phos.*
SPEAKING is fatiguing: *Kali sulph.*
STITCHES in sides: *Ferr. phos.*
SUDDEN, SHRILL VOICE: *Magnes. phos.*
SUFFOCATIVE cough in children: *Calc. phos.*
 feeling: *Kali sulph.*
SWEAT, night: *Calc. phos., Silicea.*
 profuse about head and neck: *Calc. phos., Magnes. phos.*
TRACHEA, irritated and sore: *Kali phos.*
TRACHEITIS: *Ferr. phos.*
VOICE, loss of: *Ferr. phos., Kali mur.*
  from paralysis of vocal cords: *Kali phos.*
 sudden, shrill: *Magnes. phos.*
WEARY feeling in pharynx: *Kali sulph.*
WHEEZING RALES: *Kali mur.*
WHOOPING COUGH: *Ferr. phos., Natr. mur., Magnes. phos., Kali sulph., Calc. phos., Kali mur., Kali phos.*

Circulatory Organs.

ACTION of heart intermittent: *Kali phos., Natr. mur.*

ANÆMIC conditions with heart troubles: *Kali phos.*

ANEURISM: *Ferr. phos., Calc. fluor.*

ANGINA PECTORIS: *Magnes. phos., Ferr. phos., Kali phos.*

ARTERITIS: *Ferr. phos.*

BLOOD VESSELS, enlargement of: *Calc. fluor.*

CARDITIS: *Ferr. phos.*

CHRONIC heart disease: *Silicea.*

CIRCULATION sluggish: *Kali phos.*

DILATATION of blood vessels: *Calc. fluor.*

    heart: *Ferr. phos., Calc. fluor.*

DIZZINESS from weak heart action: *Kali phos.*

EMBOLISM: *Kali mur.*

ENDOCARDITIS: *Ferr. phos.*

EXTREMITIES numb: *Natr. mur.*

FAINTNESS from fright or fatigue: *Kali phos.*

HANDS cold: *Natr. mur.*

HEART, constriction about: *Natr. mur.*

    dilatation of: *Ferr. phos., Calc. fluor.*

    fluttering about: *Natr. mur., Natr. phos.*

    hypertrophy: *Natr. mur.*

    pain at base: *Natr. phos.*

        around, during inspiration: *Calc. phos.*

INTERMITTENT ACTION of heart: *Kali phos., Natr. mur*

LYMPHANGITIS: *Ferr. phos.*

NÆVI: *Ferr. phos., Calc. fluor.*

NON-CLOSURE of foramen ovale: *Calc. phos.*

PAINS at base of heart: *Natr. phos.*

    around during inspiration: *Calc. phos.*

PALPITATION after rheumatic fever: *Kali phos.*

      violent motion: *Silicea, Ferr. phos.*

    feels pulse in different parts of body: *Natr. phos.*

    from excessive flow of blood: *Kali mur.*

      mental emotion or going up stairs: *Kali phos.*

    nervous and spasmodic: *Magnes. phos.*

    with anxiety: *Calc. phos., Natr. mur.*

    sleeplessness: *Kali phos.*

PERICARDITIS: *Ferr. phos., Kali mur., Calc. sulph.*

PHLEBITIS: *Ferr. phos.*
PULSE felt all over body: *Natr. mur., Natr. phos.*
    full, round, not rope-like: *Ferr. phos.*
    intermittent: *Natr. mur., Kali phos.*
    irregular: *Kali phos.*
    quick: *Kali sulph., Ferr. phos.*
    rapid: *Natr. mur., Ferr. phos., Silicea.*
    scarcely perceptible: *Kali sulph.*
TELANGIECTASES: *Ferr. phos.*
TREMBLING about heart: *Natr. phos.*
TUMORS, vascular: *Calc. fluor.*
VARICOSE ulcerations: *Calc. fluor.*
    veins: *Ferr. phos., Calc. fluor.*
VASCULAR tumors: *Calc. fluor.*

Back and Extremities.

ACHING OF LIMBS: *Calc. phos.*
    of shoulders: *Calc. phos.*
    between scapulæ: *Kali phos.*
ANÆMIA, spinal: *Kali phos., Natr. phos.*
ANCHYLOSIS of knee: *Silicea.*
ANKLES feel as if dislocated: *Calc. phos.*
    pain: *Natr. mur., Silicea, Ferr. phos.*
    weak: *Natr. phos., Natr. mur., Silicea.*
ARMS FEEL heavy: *Silicea.*
    tired: *Natr. phos.*
ARTHRITIC rheumatism: *Natr. phos.*
    swellings: *Natr. mur.*
BACK, acute boring pain in: *Magnes. phos.*
    asleep: *Calc. phos.*
    carbuncles on: *Calc. sulph., Silicea.*
    cold: *Natr. mur., Calc. phos., Silicea.*
    crick in: *Ferr. phos., Calc. sulph.*
    darting in: *Magnes. phos.*
    neuralgic pains in: *Kali sulph., Magnes. phos.*
    pain in, low down: *Calc. fluor.*
        between scapulæ: *Calc. phos.*
        relieved by motion: *Kali phos.*
    rheumatic pains: *Kali sulph.*
    soreness in: *Natr. sulph.*

BACK, spasms in : *Natr. sulph.*
   weak feeling in : *Natr. phos.*
      lame : *Natr. mur.*
BACKACHE, aggravated in the evening : *Kali sulph.*
   by motion : *Silicea.*
   extending to nape : *Silicea.*
   in the lumbar region in the morning : *Calc. phos.*
      warm room : *Kali sulph.*
   ameliorated by lying on something hard : *Natr. mur.*
      by motion : *Calc. fluor.*
      in open air : *Kali sulph.*
   simulating spinal irritation : *Calc. fluor.*
BLISTERING FESTERS on fingers : *Natr. mur.*
BOWLEGS in children : *Calc. phos.*
BRUISED feeling all over : *Kali phos.*
   pain in back : *Natr. sulph.*
BUNIONS : *Kali mur.*
BURNING OF SOLES : *Calc. sulph.*, *Kali phos.*, *Natr. mur.*
BURSÆ : *Calc. phos.*, *Calc. fluor.*
BUTTOCK asleep : *Calc. phos.*
CALVES, cramps in : *Calc. phos.*, *Magnes. phos.*
   weakness in : *Natr. mur.*
CARBUNCLES on the back : *Calc. sulph.*, *Silicea.*
CARIES of bones of extremities : *Silicea.*
CERVICAL GLANDS enlarged : *Kali mur.*
   indurated : *Calc. fluor.*
CHILBLAINS : *Kali mur.*, *Kali phos.*
CHRONIC SWELLING of legs : *Kali mur.*
COLDNESS in back and extremities : *Natr. mur.*
   of limbs : *Calc. phos.*
CONTRACTION of extensors : *Natr. phos.*
COCCYX HURTS after riding : *Silicea.*
COXALGIA : *Natr. mur.*
CRACKING of joints : *Calc. fluor.*, *Natr. mur.*, *Natr. sulph.*
   tendons : *Kali mur.*, *Ferr. phos.*
CRAMPS in calves : *Calc. phos.*, *Magnes. phos.*
   hands while writing : *Calc. phos.*, *Natr. phos.*, *Magnes. phos.*
   extremities : *Kali sulph.*
CRAWLING AND CREEPING in the limbs : *Calc. phos.*

CRICK in the back: *Ferr. phos., Calc. sulph.*
   neck: *Natr. phos.*
DRAGGING DOWN in back: *Calc. fluor.*
ELBOW-JOINT swollen: *Calc. fluor.*
EMACIATION of neck in children: *Natr. mur., Calc. phos.*
EPIPHESES swollen: *Calc. phos.*
EXCRUCIATING PAINS in joints: *Magnes. phos.*
EXOSTOSES on fingers: *Calc. fluor.*
EXTENSORS, contraction of: *Natr. phos.*
EXTREMITIES numb: *Natr. mur., Calc. phos., Kali phos.*
FEET, burning of: *Kali phos.*
   cold by day, warm at night: *Natr. phos.*
   fall asleep: *Natr. mur.*
   tender, tired: *Silicea.*
   swell: *Kali mur.*
   itching of soles of: *Calc. sulph.*
   languor and œdema of: *Natr. sulph.*
   tender: *Magnes. phos.*
   tonic spasms of: *Silicea.*
FELON: *Calc. sulph., Ferr. phos., Silicea, Natr. sulph.*
FŒTID PERSPIRATION of feet: *Silicea.*
FIDGETY feeling in feet: *Kali phos.*
FINGER-JOINTS enlarged: *Calc. fluor.*
   inflamed: *Natr. phos., Ferr. phos.*
   itching blisters on: *Natr. mur.*
   stiff: *Calc. sulph., Natr. sulph.*
FISTULOUS ULCERS: *Silicea.*
   about the feet: *Calc. phos.*
FUNGOID inflammation of joints: *Kali sulph.*
GANGLION at back of wrist: *Calc. fluor.*
GAIT unsteady: *Natr. phos.*
GLANDS, cervical, enlarged: *Kali mur., Natr. phos.*
   indurated: *Calc. fluor.*
GOITRE: *Calc. fluor., Natr. mur., Calc. phos., Natr. phos.*
GOUT, acute: *Natr. sulph., Ferr. phos., Natr. phos.*
   chronic: *Natr. sulph., Natr. phos.*
   enlargement of joints by: *Calc. fluor.*
   pains in: *Kali mur., Natr. mur., Calc. phos.*
   periodical attacks of: *Natr. mur.*
   rheumatic, aggravated at night: *Calc. phos.*

HAMSTRINGS, sore: *Natr. phos.*
    painful contractions of: *Natr. mur.*
HANDS cold: *Natr. mur.*
    fall asleep: *Calc. phos.*
    get stiff while writing: *Calc. phos., Kali mur., Natr. phos.*
    involuntary shaking of: *Magnes. phos.*
    palms, hot: *Ferr. phos.*
        hard and sore: *Natr. sulph.*
        skin of, dry and cracked: *Natr. sulph.*
    spasms of: *Silicea.*
    swollen and painful: *Ferr. phos.*
    tremble: *Natr. sulph.*
    warts in palms of: *Kali mur., Natr. mur., Natr. sulph.*
HANGNAILS: *Natr. mur.*
HIPS, pains in: *Kali phos., Natr. mur.*
    left, stitches in: *Natr. sulph.*
HIP-JOINT DISEASE: *Calc. sulph., Kali mur., Ferr. phos., Silicea, Calc. phos.*
HOUSEMAID'S KNEE: *Calc. phos., Silicea.*
IDIOPATHIC SOFTENING of spinal cord: *Kali phos.*
INDURATED cervical glands: *Calc. fluor.*
INFLAMMATION of joints: *Ferr. phos., Kali sulph., Magnes. phos., Natr. phos., Kali mur.*
    fungoid: *Kali sulph.*
    knee-joint: *Calc. fluor.*
INGROWING TOE NAILS: *Silicea, Kali mur.*
INVOLUNTARY jerking during sleep: *Natr. mur.*
    shaking of hands: *Magnes. phos.*
ITCHING of legs: *Kali mur., Kali phos.*
    like insect bites: *Natr. phos.*
    palms: *Kali phos.*
    soles: *Calc. sulph., Kali phos.*
    toes: *Natr. sulph.*
JOINTS, chronic rheumatism of: *Natr. mur., Calc. phos.*
    cracking in: *Calc. fluor., Natr. mur., Natr. sulph.*
    fungoid inflammation of: *Kali sulph.*
    gouty enlargements of: *Calc. fluor.*
    sore pain in: *Natr. phos.*
    swelling around: *Kali mur.*

KNEES, chronic synovitis of: *Silicea.*
> herpes in bend of: *Natr. mur.*
> inflamed: *Calc. fluor.*
> pain: *Natr. phos., Ferr. phos., Calc. phos.*
> weakness of: *Natr. mur.*

LAMENESS, from cold: *Ferr. phos.*
> paralytic and rheumatic: *Kali phos.*

LEGS give way while walking: *Natr. phos.*

LIMBS fall asleep: *Natr. mur.*
> feel tired: *Silicea.*
> itch: *Kali mur.*
> jerking of: *Natr. mur.*
> neuralgic pains in: *Magnes. phos., Kali sulph.*
> numbness and coldness of: *Calc. phos.*
> trembling of: *Calc. phos.*

LOCOMOTOR ATAXIA: *Natr. sulph., Silicea.*

LUMBAGO from strains: *Calc. fluor., Calc. phos., Ferr. phos.*

MENINGITIS, spinal: *Natr. sulph.*

MOTION aggravates pains: *Kali mur., Ferr. phos.*
> ameliorates pain: *Kali sulph., Kali phos.*

MUSCULAR WEAKNESS: *Kali phos.*

NAILS, crippled and brittle: *Silicea, Kali sulph.*
> pain at roots of: *Calc. phos.*

NAPE, drawing in: *Natr. sulph.*
> pains in: *Kali sulph., Magnes. phos.*

NECK, emaciated, in children: *Calc. phos., Natr. mur.*
> stiff from cold: *Ferr. phos., Calc. phos., Natr. phos.*

NEURALGIC pains in limbs: *Kali sulph., Magnes. phos.*

NUMBNESS of limbs: *Calc. phos., Kali phos.*

ŒDEMA of feet: *Natr. mur., Natr. sulph.*

OSSEOUS TUMORS: *Calc. fluor.*

OVERSENSITIVENESS of spine: *Natr. mur., Silicea.*

PAINS IN BACK OR EXTREMITIES, aching between scapulæ: *Calc. phos.*
> acute: *Magnes. phos.*
>> aggravated by exertion: *Ferr. phos., Kali mur.*
>> by fatigue: *Kali phos.*
>> motion: *Ferr. phos., Kali mur.*
>> warmth of bed: *Kali mur.*

Pains in the evening: *Kali sulph.*
    warm weather: *Kali sulph.*
    when rising: *Kali phos., Natr. mur.*
    ameliorated by gentle motion: *Kali phos.*
      in open air: *Kali sulph.*
    boring: *Magnes. phos.*
    darting: *Magnes. phos.*
    in shin-bones: *Calc. phos., Natr. phos.*
      coccyx: *Calc. phos., Natr. sulph.*
      knees: *Calc. phos., Natr. phos.*
      sacro-iliac synchondroses: *Calc. phos.*
      roots of finger nails: *Calc. phos.*
      soles of feet: *Kali phos., Natr. phos.*
      wrist: *Natr. phos.*
    lightning-like: *Kali mur., Magnes. phos.*
    low down in back: *Calc. fluor.*
    neuralgic: *Kali sulph., Magnes. phos.*
    periodical: *Kali sulph.*
    rheumatic: *Kali sulph.*
    shifting: *Kali sulph., Magnes. phos., Calc. phos.*
    shoulders: *Silicea, Ferr. phos.*
    spasmodic: *Magnes. phos.*
    suddenly go to heart: *Natr. phos.*
    through feet: *Silicea.*
Palms of hands hot: *Ferr. phos.*
    itch: *Kali phos.*
    raw and sore: *Natr. sulph.*
Paralytic lameness: *Kali phos., Natr. phos.*
    tendency: *Kali phos.*
Paralysis agitans: *Magnes. phos.*
Panaritium: *Calc. sulph., Ferr. phos., Natr. sulph., Silicea.*
Phalanges easily dislocated: *Calc. fluor.*
Pott's disease: *Calc. phos.*
Proud flesh: *Kali mur., Silicea.*
Psoas abscess: *Silicea.*
Rheumatic fever: *Ferr. phos., Kali mur.*
    gouty pains: *Kali mur., Natr. phos.*
    lameness: *Kali phos.*
    stiffness of neck: *Calc. phos.*
Rheumatism, acute: *Calc. phos., Calc. sulph., Ferr. phos., Kali phos., Kali mur.*

RHEUMATISM, aggravated by change of weather: *Calc. phos.*
        exertion: *Kali phos.*
        fatigue: *Kali phos.*
        heat or cold: *Calc. phos.*
        motion: *Ferr. phos.*
        night: *Calc. phos.*
        warmth of bed: *Kali mur.*
        in the morning: *Kali phos.*
    ameliorated by gentle motion: *Kali phos.*
                 warmth: *Ferr. phos.*
    articular: *Ferr. phos., Kali mur., Calc. phos., Natr. phos.*
    chronic: *Calc. phos., Kali mur., Kali phos., Natr. mur., Natr. sulph., Natr. phos., Kali sulph., Silicea, Calc. sulph.*
    felt during motion: *Ferr. phos., Kali mur.*
    flying about: *Calc. phos., Kali sulph.*
    of joints, violent pains: *Kali sulph., Magnes. phos., Calc. phos., Natr. mur.*
    muscular: *Ferr. phos.*
    subacute: *Ferr. phos.*
SACRO-ILIAC SYNCHONDROSIS, pains in: *Calc. phos.*
SCIATICA: *Kali phos., Magnes. phos., Natr. sulph., Calc. sulph., Natr. mur., Ferr. phos.*
SENSATION OF ANTS creeping over parts: *Calc. phos.*
    insect bites: *Natr. phos.*
SHIFTING PAINS in back: *Kali sulph., Magnes. phos.*
SHOOTING through elbows: *Calc. phos.*
SLOW IN LEARNING TO WALK: *Calc. phos.*
SOLES burn: *Calc. sulph., Natr. sulph., Kali phos.*
    drawing in: *Kali phos., Natr. phos.*
    itch: *Calc. sulph., Kali phos.*
SORENESS BETWEEN SHOULDERS: *Silicea.*
    of thighs: *Calc. phos.*
SPINA BIFIDA: *Calc. phos., Ferr. phos., Calc. fluor., Silicea.*
    ventosa: *Calc. fluor.*
SPINAL ANÆMIA: *Kali phos., Natr. phos., Natr. mur.*
    cord, softening of: *Kali phos.*
    curvature: *Calc. phos., Silicea.*
    irritation: *Calc. phos., Silicea.*

SPINAL ANÆMIA, meningitis: *Natr. sulph.*
   oversensitiveness: *Natr. mur., Silicea.*
SPINE sensitive to touch: *Magnes. phos., Natr. mur.*
STIFFNESS OF BODY: *Kali phos., Natr. mur.*
   after rest: *Kali phos.*
   after cold: *Ferr. phos.*
STIFF NECK from cold: *Ferr. phos., Calc. phos.*
STRAINS of ligaments or tendons: *Ferr. phos.*
STUMBLES easily: *Kali phos.*
SWEAT of axillæ or feet offensive: *Silicea.*
SWELLING of legs, chronic: *Kali mur.*
SYNOVITIS, chronic: *Silicea, Calc. fluor., Calc. phos.*
TENALGIA CREPITANS: *Ferr. phos., Kali mur., Natr. phos., Calc.*
               fluor.
THIGHS, inside of, draw: *Natr. phos.*
TIRED feeling in back: *Calc. fluor.*
TOE-NAILS grow in: *Silicea, Kali mur.*
TOES, itching of: *Natr. sulph.*
TONIC SPASMS of hands, feet or toes: *Silicea.*
ULCERS OF EXTREMITIES: *Kali mur.*
   indolent: *Silicea, Calc. phos.*
   syphilitic: *Calc. phos., Silicea.*
URTICARIA about joints: *Natr. mur.*
WARTS in palms: *Kali mur., Natr. sulph., Natr. mur.*
WEAKNESS, general: *Natr. mur., Natr. phos.*
WEARINESS: *Natr. mur.*
WHITLOW: *Calc. sulph., Ferr. phos., Silicea, Natr. sulph*
WOUNDS SUPPURATING: *Calc. sulph., Silicea.*
WRISTS ache: *Natr. phos., Ferr. phos., Calc. phos.*

Nervous Symptoms.

ADYNAMIA: *Kali phos., Natr. mur.*
ALCOHOLISM: *Magnes. phos.*
ANÆMIA, SPINAL: *Kali phos., Natr. mur., Natr. phos.*
ATROPHIC paralysis: *Kali phos.*
BALL, sensation of, in throat: *Kali phos.*
BLADDER, paralysis of: *Kali phos.*
BODILY pains felt too acutely: *Kali phos.*
CHOREA: *Natr. mur., Magnes. phos., Kali sulph.*
CHOREA, from worms: *Silicea.*

CHOREA, with retarded stools: *Natr. sulph.*

CLENCHED FINGERS or fists: *Magnes. phos.*

CONGESTIVE NEURALGIA: *Ferr. phos.*

CONTORTIONS of the limbs: *Magnes. phos.*

CONVULSIONS during development: *Calc. phos.*

    in teething children: *Ferr. phos., Calc. phos*

    with stiffness: *Magnes. phos.*

CONVULSIVE sobbing: *Magnes. phos.*

CRAMPS, writer's or violin player's: *Magnes. phos., Calc. phos.*

CRAWLING SENSATION, as of ants: *Calc. phos.*

CREEPING paralysis: *Kali phos.*

DEBILITY after acute diseases: *Calc. phos.*

    hysterical: *Natr. mur.*

    nervous: *Kali phos.*

DEPRESSION, nervous: *Kali phos.*

EASILY fatigued: *Kali phos., Natr. mur., Ferr. phos.*

EPILEPSY after suppressed eruptions: *Kali mur., Calc. phos.*

    from fright: *Kali phos.*

    from vicious habits: *Magnes. phos.*

    occurring at night: *Silicea.*

    with rush of blood to head: *Ferr. phos.*

EXHAUSTION, nervous: *Kali phos., Magnes. phos.*

    with colic: *Natr. sulph.*

      erethism: *Silicea.*

FACIAL PARALYSIS: *Kali phos.*

FAILURE of strength: *Kali phos.*

FEARS burglars: *Kali phos.*

FIDGETY feeling: *Kali phos.*

FINGERS CLENCHED: *Magnes. phos.*

GAIT UNSTEADY, as if paralyzed: *Natr. phos.*

GLOBUS HYSTERICUS: *Kali phos.*

HANDS TREMBLE when writing: *Natr. sulph., Magnes. phos.*

HEMIPLEGIA: *Kali sulph.*

HICCOUGH: *Natr. mur., Magnes. phos.*

HYSTERIA from sudden emotions: *Kali phos.*

    obstinate: *Silicea.*

    with debility: *Natr. mur.*

INFANTILE PARALYSIS: *Kali phos.*

INFLAMMATORY neuralgia: *Ferr. phos.*
INVOLUNTARY MOVEMENTS: *Magnes. phos.*
LANGUOR: *Calc. sulph., Magnes. phos., Calc. phos.*
LIGHTNING-LIKE pains: *Magnes. phos.*
LOCKJAW: *Magnes. phos.*
LOSS OF MOTOR power: *Kali phos.*
    sense of touch: *Kali phos.*
NERVOUS EXHAUSTION: *Kali phos., Natr. phos.*
        from sexual excess: *Kali phos.*
NERVOUSNESS at night: *Ferr. phos.*
NEURALGIA, congestive: *Ferr. phos.*
    inflammatory: *Ferr. phos.*
    intercostal: *Magnes. phos.*
    like electrical shocks: *Calc. phos., Magnes. phos.*
    occurring at night: *Calc. phos., Magnes. phos.*
    obstinate: *Silicea.*
    of anus: *Calc. phos.*
    recurring: *Natr. mur., Calc. phos.*
    shifting: *Kali phos., Magnes. phos.*
    worse from change of water: *Calc. phos.*
NIGHT TERRORS of children: *Kali phos.*
PARALYSIS agitans: *Magnes. phos.*
    atrophic: *Kali phos.*
    coming on suddenly: *Kali phos.*
    creeping: *Kali phos.*
    facial: *Kali phos.*
    from tabes dorsalis: *Silicea.*
    infantile: *Kali phos.*
    locomotor: *Kali phos.*
    of any part: *Kali phos., Natr. mur.*
        bladder: *Kali phos.*
    rheumatic: *Calc. phos., Ferr. phos., Kali phos.*
PARESIS: *Kali phos.*
RESTLESS, desire to move: *Natr. sulph.*
SCIATICA: *Kali phos., Magnes. phos., Ferr. phos., Natr. sulph.*
SENSATION OF BALL in throat: *Kali phos.*
    and creeping over parts: *Calc. phos.*
    of numbness: *Natr. mur.*
    of trembling: *Kali phos.*

SENSITIVE TO noise and light: *Kali phos., Silicea.*
  cold air: *Silicea.*
SINGULTUS: *Natr. mur., Magnes. phos.*
SHOOTINGS along nerves: *Natr. mur., Magnes. phos.*
SPASMS from slight provocation: *Silicea.*
  of glottis: *Calc. phos., Magnes. phos.*
  spread from solar plexus: *Silicea.*
  tetanic: *Magnes. phos., Calc. phos., Natr. mur.*
SPASMODIC CLOSURE of sphincters: *Silicea.*
SPINAL ANÆMIA: *Kali phos., Natr. mur., Natr. phos.*
  irritation: *Kali phos., Natr. mur., Silicea.*
SQUINTING from worms: *Natr. phos.*
STARTLED at least noise: *Kali mur., Kali phos.*
STAMMERING, spasmodic: *Magnes. phos.*
STIFFNESS: *Kali phos., Magnes. phos.*
TABES DORSALIS: *Kali mur., Silicea.*
TEETH CLENCHED: *Magnes. phos.*
TETANIC spasms: *Magnes. phos.*
THUMBS DRAWN IN: *Magnes. phos.*
TIRED FEELING: *Natr. sulph., Natr. phos., Magnes. phos., Kali phos., Natr. mur.*
TIC DOULOUREUX: *Ferr. phos., Magnes. phos.*
TREMBLING of the body: *Natr. phos., Natr. sulph., Calc. phos., Kali phos.*
  limbs: *Calc. phos., Silicea.*
TWITCHINGS: *Calc. sulph., Magnes. phos., Natr. mur.*
  of hands during sleep: *Natr. sulph., Magnes. phos.*
  facial muscles from worms: *Natr. phos.*
WEAKNESS: *Calc. sulph., Calc. fluor., Kali phos., Calc. phos., Ferr. phos.*
WEARY FEELING: *Natr. sulph., Calc. phos., Kali phos., Natr. mur., Natr. phos., Calc. sulph., Ferr. phos.*
WRITER'S CRAMPS: *Magnes. phos., Calc. phos., Natr. phos.*

Sleep and Dreams.

AWAKES screaming: *Kali phos.*
AWAKENED by flatulent pains: *Natr. sulph.*
CHILDREN CRY OUT during sleep: *Calc. phos.*
CONSTANT stretching and yawning: *Calc. phos., Kali phos.*
DESIRE TO SLEEP constant: *Natr. mur.*
  in morning: *Kali phos.*

DREAMS, anxious: *Natr. mur., Ferr. phos., Natr. sulph.*
   heavy: *Natr. sulph.*
   lascivious: *Kali phos.*
   of convulsions from fright: *Calc. sulph.*
      falling: *Kali phos.*
      fire: *Kali phos.*
      ghosts: *Kali phos.*
      new scenes, places, etc.: *Calc. fluor.*
      robbers: *Natr. mur., Kali phos.*
   sexual: *Natr. phos.*
   with sense of danger: *Calc. fluor., Magnes. phos.*
   vivid: *Kali sulph.*
   with sense of impending danger: *Calc. fluor.*
DROWSINESS: *Natr. sulph., Natr. phos., Magnes. phos.*
   in the afternoon: *Ferr. phos.*
      old people: *Calc. phos.*
DURING SLEEP children cry out: *Calc. phos.*
   jerking of limbs: *Silicea, Magnes. phos.*
EXCESSIVE sleep: *Natr. mur.*
FALLS ASLEEP while sitting: *Natr. phos.*
FEELS TIRED in the morning: *Natr. mur.*
HARD TO AWAKEN in the morning: *Calc. phos.*
INSOMNIA: *Natr. mur.*
   from exhaustion: *Magnes. phos.*
JERKING of limbs during sleep: *Silicea, Natr. mur., Natr. sulph.*
RESTLESS SLEEP: *Natr. phos., Ferr. phos., Natr. sulph., Kali phos.*
SLEEPLESSNESS after worry: *Kali phos.*
      excitement: *Kali phos.*
   from business worry: *Kali phos.*
      exhaustion: *Magnes. phos.*
      hyperæmia: *Ferr. phos.*
      itching: *Natr. phos.*
      orgasm of blood: *Silicea.*
      nervous irritation: *Natr. mur.*
SLEEP, excessive: *Natr. mur.*
   restless: *Natr. phos., Kali mur., Natr. mur.*
   unrefreshing: *Natr. mur.*
SLEEPY during day, wakeful at night: *Calc. sulph.*
SOMNAMBULISM: *Kali phos., Natr. mur.*

SPASMODIC yawning: *Magnes. phos.*
STARTLED at least noise: *Kali mur.*
STARTING during sleep: *Natr. mur., Natr. sulph.*
STRETCHING: *Kali phos., Calc. phos.*
TIRED IN THE MORNING on awaking: *Natr. mur.*
TWITCHING OF MUSCLES on falling asleep: *Kali phos.*
UNREFRESHING SLEEP: *Natr. mur.*
WAKEFUL at night: *Calc. sulph.*
YAWNING, hysterical: *Kali phos.*
    spasmodic: *Magnes. phos., Calc. phos.*

Febrile Symptoms.

AGUE: *Natr. mur.*
BILIOUS FEVER: *Natr. phos., Magnes. phos., Natr. sulph.*
BLISTERS, fever, on lips: *Natr. mur.*
BRAIN FEVER: *Kali phos.*
CAMP FEVER: *Kali phos.*
CATARRHAL FEVER: *Ferr. phos., Kali mur.*
CHILLINESS: *Silicea, Calc. phos., Kali mur.*
    after dinner, at 7 P. M.: *Magnes. phos.*
CHILL from morning till noon: *Natr. mur.*
    every day at 1 P. M.: *Ferr. phos.*
CHILLS run up and down the back: *Magnes. phos.*
COLD SWEAT: *Kali sulph., Calc. phos.*
ENTERIC FEVER: *Kali sulph., Kali mur., Ferr. phos., Kali phos.,*
                  Natr. mur.
FEET ICY COLD: *Natr. phos.*
    burn at night: *Natr. phos., Silicea.*
FEVER, bilious: *Natr. sulph., Natr. phos., Magnes. phos.*
    brain: *Kali phos.*
    camp: *Kali phos.*
    catarrhal: *Ferr. phos., Kali mur.*
    enteric: *Kali sulph., Kali mur., Ferr. phos., Kali phos.,*
                 Natr. mur.
    from blood-poisoning: *Kali sulph.*
    gastric: *Kali sulph., Kali mur., Ferr. phos., Kali phos.*
    hay: *Natr. mur., Kali phos., Silicea.*
    hectic: *Silicea, Calc. sulph.*
    inflammatory: *Ferr. phos.*
    intermittent: *Magnes. phos., Kali mur., Natr. mur.,*

FEVER: *Natr. phos., Ferr. phos., Kali phos., Natr. sulph., Calc. phos., Kali sulph.*

    malignant and putrid: *Kali phos.*

    nervous: *Kali phos.*

    puerperal: *Kali mur.*

    remittent: *Natr. sulph.*

    rheumatic: *Kali mur., Natr. mur., Ferr. phos.*

    scarlet: *Kali sulph., Kali mur., Natr. mur., Ferr. phos., Kali phos.*

    typhoid: *Kali sulph., Kali mur., Natr. mur., Ferr. phos., Kali phos.*

    yellow: *Natr. sulph.*

INTERMITTENT FEVER. (See above.)

    after quinine: *Natr. mur.*

    chronic: *Calc. phos.*

    with acid vomiting: *Natr. phos.*

        cramps: *Magnes. phos.*

        debilitating perspiration: *Kali phos.*

        vomiting of food: *Ferr. phos.*

        yellow slimy-coated tongue: *Kali sulph.*

NIGHT-SWEATS, profuse: *Natr. mur., Calc. phos., Silicea, Natr. sulph., Calc. sulph., Ferr. phos.*

PERSPIRATION about head: *Silicea.*

    cold: *Kali sulph.*

    debilitating: *Kali phos.*

    fœtid: *Kali phos.*

    profuse: *Kali phos.*

    sour and acid: *Natr. phos.*

    while eating: *Kali phos.*

PETECHIÆ: *Kali phos.*

RIGORS: *Ferr. phos.*

SCARLET FEVER: *Kali sulph., Kali mur., Ferr. phos., Natr. mur., Kali phos., Natr. sulph.*

    as preventive: *Kali mur.*

SENSITIVE to cold air: *Silicea.*

SWEAT about head: *Silicea, Calc. phos.*

    colds: *Kali sulph., Natr. sulph., Ferr. phos.*

    debilitating: *Kali phos.*

    fœtid: *Kali phos.*

SWEAT, night, profuse at: *Natr. mur., Calc. phos., Silicea, Calc. sulph.*

  profuse: *Kali phos., Magnes. phos., Calc. phos.*

  sour and weakening: *Natr. phos., Natr. mur.*

  while eating: *Kali phos.*

  without thirst: *Natr. sulph.*

TEMPERATURE RISES during evening: *Kali sulph.*

TYPHUS FEVER: *Calc. sulph., Kali mur., Natr. mur., Ferr. phos.,} Kali phos.*

YELLOW FEVER: *Natr. sulph., Ferr. phos., Kali phos.*

Skin.

ABSCESS: *Kali mur., Silicea, Calc. sulph., Calc. fluor., Ferr. phos., Kali phos.*

  fistulous: *Silicea, Natr. sulph.*

ACNE: *Ferr. phos., Kali mur., Silicea.*

  rosacea: *Calc. phos., Silicea, Natr. phos.*

ALOPECIA AREATA: *Kali phos.*

  senilis: *Silicea.*

ANÆMIC ERUPTIONS: *Calc. phos*

BARBER'S ITCH: *Magnes. phos.*

BEARD FALLS OUT: *Natr. mur.*

BLEBS on skin: *Natr. sulph., Kali phos., Natr. mur.*

BLISTERS on skin: *Kali phos., Natr. mur., Kali mur.*

BOILS: *Magnes. phos., Calc. sulph., Silicea, Ferr. phos., Kali mur.*

  tendency to: *Silicea.*

BUNIONS: *Kali mur.*

BURNS: *Kali mur., Calc. sulph., Natr. sulph.*

BURSITIS: *Calc. phos., Silicea.*

CHAFED SKIN: *Calc. phos., Natr. sulph., Natr. phos., Kali sulph.*

  from rubbing: *Kali phos., Natr. mur.*

CHAPS: *Calc. fluor.*

CHICKEN-POX: *Ferr. phos., Natr. sulph., Kali mur., Silicea.*

CHILBLAINS: *Kali phos., Kali mur., Calc. sulph., Silicea.*

CHRONIC SKIN DISEASES: *Natr. mur.*

COPPERY SPOTS: *Silicea.*

CRACKS on skin: *Calc. fluor.*

  between toes: *Natr. mur.*

CRAWLING SENSATION on skin: *Kali phos.*

CRUSTA LACTEA: *Natr. phos., Kali mur., Calc. sulph., Silicea.*

DANDRUFF: *Natr. mur.*, *Kali sulph.*, *Kali mur.*
DESQUAMATION, to promote: *Kali sulph.*
ECZEMA after vaccination: *Kali mur.*
    eyebrows: *Natr. mur.*
    from eating too much salt: *Natr. mur.*
    in the bends of joints: *Natr. mur.*
    squamosum: *Silicea.*
    suddenly suppressed: *Kali sulph.*
    with fine scales: *Natr. mur.*
        oversensitiveness: *Kali phos.*
        symptoms of acidity: *Natr. phos.*
        vesicles, whitish: *Kali mur.*
        yellow-greenish secretions: *Kali sulph.*
            watery vesicles: *Natr. sulph.*
            white scabs: *Calc. phos.*
EPITHELIAL CANCERS: *Kali sulph.*
ERUPTIONS, anæmic and gouty: *Calc. phos.*
    burning and itching: *Kali sulph.*, *Kali phos.*
    herpetic: *Calc. sulph.*
    miliary: *Natr. mur.*
ERUPTIONS on flexor surfaces: *Natr. mur.*
    scaly: *Kali sulph.*
    scrofulous: *Calc. phos.*, *Silicea.*
    suddenly receding: *Kali sulph.*
    with stomach and menstrual affections: *Kali mur.*
ERYSIPELAS, blistering: *Kali sulph.*
    deep-seated: *Silicea.*
    occasional: *Calc. fluor.*
    phlegmonous: *Silicea.*
    smooth, red, and shining: *Natr. sulph.*, *Ferr. phos.*
    vesicular: *Kali mur.*
ERYTHEMA: *Natr. phos.*, *Kali mur.*
EXCORIATIONS: *Calc. phos.*
EXCRESCENCES, sycotic: *Natr. sulph.*
EXUDATIONS. (See under Tissues.)
FISSURES of anus: *Calc. fluor.*
    skin: *Calc. fluor.*, *Silicea.*
FELONS: *Calc. fluor.*, *Ferr. phos.*, *Natr. sulph.*, *Silicea.*
FRECKLES: *Calc. phos.*

    28*

FUNGUS HÆMATODES: *Natr. mur.*

HAIR falls out: *Kali sulph., Natr. mur.*

HANG-NAILS: *Natr. mur.*

HERPES, acute: *Calc. phos., Natr. mur., Calc. sulph.*

    chronic: *Calc. phos.*

    circinatus: *Natr. mur.*

    in bends of knee: *Natr. mur.*

    in elbow: *Natr. mur.*

    in palms: *Kali sulph.*

    zoster: *Natr. mur., Kali mur., Silicea.*

HIVES: *Natr. phos., Natr. sulph., Ferr. phos., Kali phos.*

INGROWING TOE-NAILS: *Kali mur., Silicea.*

INFLAMMATION of skin: *Ferr. phos.*

INSECT-BITES: *Natr. mur.*

    rashlike, about knees and ankles: *Magnes. phos.*

INTERTRIGO: *Natr. mur., Kali sulph.*

IRRITATING SECRETIONS: *Kali phos.*

ITCHING of skin: *Calc. phos., Kali sulph., Kali phos., Silicea.*

        soles: *Calc. sulph., Kali phos.*

    after violent exertion: *Natr. mur.*

    all over body: *Natr. phos., Magnes. phos.*

    hands and feet: *Kali phos.*

    senile: *Calc. phos.*

    with crawling: *Kali phos.*

    while undressing: *Natr. sulph.*

    violent: *Natr. mur.*

IVY-POISON: *Kali sulph.*

JAUNDICED SKIN: *Natr. sulph., Kali mur.*

LEPRA: *Silicea.*

LUPUS: *Calc. phos., Kali mur.*

MEASLES: *Ferr. phos., Kali mur., Kali sulph., Silicea.*

MILIARY ERUPTIONS: *Natr. mur.*

MOIST SKIN AFFECTIONS: *Natr. sulph.*

NÆVUS: *Ferr. phos.*

    crippled and brittle: *Kali sulph., Silicea.*

NAILS, diseased: *Kali sulph., Silicea.*

    interrupted growth: *Kali sulph.*

NETTLERASH: *Kali sulph.*

NODES: *Silicea.*

ŒDEMATOUS inflammations: *Natr. sulph.*

PALMS fissured: *Calc. fluor.*
    raw and sore: *Natr. sulph.*
    scaly tetter in: *Kali sulph.*

PEMPHIGUS: *Natr. mur., Silicea., Natr. sulph.*
    malignus: *Kali phos.*

PIMPLES on skin: *Ferr. phos., Kali mur., Calc. sulph., Natr.*
                    sulph., Calc. phos.

POISON OAK: *Kali sulph.*

PRURIGO: *Calc. phos.*

PRURITUS: *Calc. phos., Kali phos.*
    vaginal: *Calc. phos.*

PUSTULES: *Calc. sulph., Silicea.*
    malignant: *Kali phos., Silicea.*

RHAGADES: *Calc. fluor., Silicea.*

ROSE-RASH: *Natr. phos.*

RUBBING agreeable: *Kali phos.*

RUPIA: *Natr. mur.*

SCARLET FEVER: *Ferr. phos., Kali sulph., Kali mur., Natr. mur.,*
                    Natr. sulph., Kali phos.

SCROFULOUS eruptions: *Calc. phos., Silicea.*
    ulceration: *Calc. phos.*

SHINGLES: *Natr. mur., Kali mur.*

SKIN, blebs on: *Natr. sulph., Kali phos., Natr. mur.*
    bleeds when scratched: *Calc. sulph.*
    blisters on: *Kali phos., Natr. mur.*
    burning: *Silicea.*
    chafed: *Calc. phos., Natr. phos,. Natr. sulph., Kali sulph.,*
                Kali phos., Natr. mur., Kali mur.
    chaps on: *Calc. fluor.*
    cracks: *Calc. fluor.*
    dirty: *Natr. mur.*
    dry: *Kali sulph., Calc. phos.*
    flaccid, torpid: *Natr. mur.*
    golden-yellow scabs on: *Natr. phos.*
    greasy: *Natr. mur., Kali phos.*
    harsh: *Kali sulph.*
    heals with difficulty: *Silicea.*
    inflamed: *Ferr. phos.*

SKIN itches: *Calc. phos., Natr. sulph., Kali phos., Silicea.*
  papules on: *Silicea.*
  peels of: *Kali sulph.*
  pimples on: *Ferr. phos., Kali mur., Calc. sulph., Natr. sulph., Calc. phos.*
  scabs on: *Calc. phos., Kali phos.*
  scales on: *Natr. sulph., Natr. mur., Kali mur., Kali sulph.*
  sensitive: *Silicea.*
  sore: *Natr. mur.*
  tubercles on: *Calc. phos.*
  vesicles on: *Calc. phos., Natr. sulph.*
  watery vesicles: *Natr. mur.*
  wheals: *Natr. sulph., Natr. mur.*
  wrinkled: *Kali phos., Calc. phos.*
SMALL-POX: *Kali phos., Ferr. phos., Kali mur., Calc. sulph., Kali sulph., Silicea.*
SUPPRESSION of eruptions: *Kali sulph.*
SWELLING OF SKIN: *Natr. sulph.*
SYCOSIS: *Natr. mur., Kali mur.*
  excrescences in: *Natr. sulph.*
TINEA CAPITIS: *Kali sulph.*
TINGLING OF SKIN: *Kali sulph.*
TUBERCLES on skin: *Calc. phos.*
ULCERATIONS, fitulous: *Calc. fluor., Silicea.*
  indolent: *Calc. fluor.*
  inflamed: *Ferr. phos.*
  proud flesh: *Silicea, Kali mur.*
  purulent: *Calc. sulph., Silicea.*
  scrofulous: *Calc. phos.*
URTICARIA: *Natr. mur., Natr. sulph., Natr. phos.*
VAGINAL PRURITUS: *Calc. phos., Kali phos., Natr. sulph.*
WARTS on palms: *Natr. mur., Kali mur., Natr. sulph.*
WATERY secretions: *Natr. sulph., Natr. mur.*
WHEALS: *Natr. sulph., Natr. mur.*
WHITE scabs: *Calc. phos.*
  scales on scalp: *Natr. mur., Kali mur.*
  vesicles: *Calc. phos.*
WHITLOW: *Calc. fluor., Silicea, Natr. sulph., Natr. phos.*
WRINKLED SKIN: *Calc. phos.*

YELLOW scabs: *Calc. phos.*
 vesicles: *Calc. phos., Natr. sulph.*

Tissues.

ABSCESS, about anus: *Calc. sulph.*
 inflammatory: *Ferr. phos.*
 of gums: *Calc. fluor., Silicea, Calc. sulph.*
 phlegmonous inflammation: *Natr. phos., Silicea.*
 chronic: *Calc. phos., Silicea.*
 alcoholism: *Kali phos., Natr. mur.*
  gastric symptoms: *Natr. phos.*
 to prevent pus formation: *Calc. sulph.* (high).
 to promote pus formation: *Silicea* (low).
 pelvic: *Calc. fluor.*
 swelling: *Kali mur.*
 to shorten suppuration: *Calc. sulph.*
 with fistulous openings: *Silicea.*
 adynamic symptoms: *Kali phos.*
ADDISON'S DISEASE: *Natr. mur., Natr. sulph.*
ADYNAMIC conditions: *Natr. mur., Kali phos.*
ANÆMIA: *Calc. fluor., Calc. phos., Ferr. phos., Natr. mur., Kali phos., Kali mur.*
 in infants: *Silicea.*
 spinal: *Natr. phos.*
ANASARCA: *Natr. mur.*
ARTERIO-SCLEROSIS: *Natr. phos., Silicea, Natr. sulph.*
BARLOW'S DISEASE: *Kali phos., Silicea.*
ATROPHY: *Calc. phos., Kali phos.*
BASEDOW'S DISEASE: *Natr. mur.*
BEDSORES: *Kali phos.*
BLOWS, effects of: *Kali mur., Ferr. phos.*
BOILS: *Silicea, Calc. sulph., Kali mur., Ferr. phos.*
 tendency to: *Silicea.*
BONE, bruises on: *Calc. fluor.*
 brittle and thin: *Calc. phos.*
 cephalomætoma: *Calc. fluor., Silicea.*
 exostosis on: *Calc. phos.*
 fractures of: *Calc. phos., Ferr. phos.*
 inflammation of soft parts about: *Ferr. phos.*
 necrosis of: *Silicea.*

BONE, osteophytes: *Ferr. phos.*

rachitis: *Calc. phos.*

rough, uneven: *Calc. fluor.*

suppuration of: *Calc. fluor., Calc. sulph., Silicea.*

to favor deposit of lime in: *Natr. phos., Calc. phos.*

ulceration of: *Silicea, Calc. fluor.*

BREASTS, knots in: *Calc. fluor.*

fistulous sinuses in: *Calc. fluor.*

tumors in: *Calc. fluor.*

BRONCHOCELE: *Calc. phos.*

BRUISES: *Calc. sulph., Kali mur.*

BURNS: *Calc. sulph., Kali mur.*

BURSÆ: *Calc. phos., Calc. fluor., Silicea.*

CACHEXIA, from ague plus Quinine: *Natr. mur.*

CALCULI: *Magnes. phos., Calc. phos., Kali mur.*

CANCER: *Kali phos., Calc. phos., Kali sulph., Calc. fluor., Silicea.*

CARBUNCLES: *Silicea, Calc. fluor., Kali mur., Kali phos.*

CATARRH: *Natr. mur., Kali sulph., Kali mur.*

ozæna: *Magnes. phos., Natr. phos.*

CELLULAR suppuration: *Silicea, Calc. sulph.*

CHLOROTIC conditions: *Natr. mur., Calc. phos.*

CONDYLES swollen: *Calc. phos.*

CROUPOUS exudations: *Kali mur.*

CYSTS: *Calc. phos., Calc. sulph.*

DEBILITY: *Kali phos.*

DIATHESIS, phosphatic: *Calc. phos.*

scrofulous: *Silicea, Calc. phos.*

DISCHARGES. (See Exudations.)

DROPSY: *Silicea, Natr. mur., Calc. phos.*

from heart disease: *Calc. fluor., Kali mur.*

loss of blood: *Ferr. phos., Calc. phos.*

obstruction of bile-ducts: *Kali mur.*

DROPSY from weakness of heart: *Kali mur.*

simple: *Natr. sulph.*

ECCHYMOSES: *Kali mur.*

ELASTIC fibers relaxed: *Calc. fluor.*

EMACIATION: *Calc. phos., Kali phos.*

while living well: *Natr. mur.*

ENCHONDROMA: *Silicea.*

ENCYSTED tumors: *Calc. fluor.*

EPISTAXIS in children: *Ferr. phos.*

EPITHELIOMA: *Kali sulph.*

EXHAUSTION: *Kali phos.*

EXUDATIONS, albuminous: *Calc. phos.*

    causing soreness, excoriating: *Natr. phos., Natr. mur.*

    creamy: *Natr. phos.*

    fibrinous: *Kali mur.*

    hardened: *Calc. fluor.*

    honey-colored: *Natr. phos.*

    irritating: *Kali phos.*

    lymph: *Kali mur.*

    offensive: *Silicea, Kali phos.*

    purulent: *Kali sulph., Calc. sulph.*

    sanious: *Calc. sulph.*

    serous: *Kali sulph., Natr. mur., Calc. phos.*

    watery: *Kali sulph., Natr. mur., Natr. sulph.*

    yellow: *Natr. sulph., Natr. phos., Kali sulph.*

FELONS: *Calc. sulph., Ferr. phos., Silicea, Natr. sulph., Calc.*
        fluor., Kali phos.

FOLLICULAR INFILTRATIONS: *Kali mur.*

FUNGI, easily bleeding: *Silicea.*

GANGLION: *Calc. fluor., Calc. phos.*

GANGRENOUS conditions: *Kali phos.*

GOITRE: *Calc. phos., Natr. mur., Calc. fluor., Natr. phos.*

GOUT: *Natr. mur., Natr. phos., Natr. sulph.*

GLANDS, hardened: *Calc. fluor.*

    inflamed: *Ferr. phos.*

    scrofulous infiltration of: *Kali mur.*

    sebaceous, suppurate: *Silicea.*

    stony hard: *Calc. fluor.*

    suppurating: *Calc. sulph., Silicea.*

    swelling of: *Kali mur., Natr. phos., Silicea.*

    ulceration of: *Ferr. phos., Calc. sulph.*

GRANULATIONS excessive: *Calc. sulph.*

GROWTHS, osseous: *Calc. fluor.*

HAY-FEVER: *Magnes. phos.*

HÆMORRHAGES black: *Kali mur.*

    bright-red: *Ferr. phos.*

HÆMORRHAGES, clotted: *Kali mur., Ferr. phos.*
   dark: *Kali mur.*
   not coagulating: *Kali phos.*
   septic and thin: *Kali phos.*
HYDROGENOID constitution: *Natr. sulph.*
INDURATIONS: *Calc. fluor.*
INFLAMMATIONS, first stage: *Ferr. phos.*
   second stage: *Kali mur.*
   gangrenous: *Silicea, Kali phos.*
   malignant: *Silicea.*
   septic: *Natr. phos.*
   sero-purulent exudations: *Kali sulph.*
   stage of exudations: *Kali mur.*
INJURIES, mechanical: *Ferr. phos.*
   neglected cases of: *Calc. sulph.*
KERNELS and knots in breast: *Calc. fluor.*
LEUCOSYCOSIS: *Natr. phos.*
LEUCÆMIA: *Natr. phos., Calc. phos., Natr. sulph., Kali phos.*
LUPUS: *Kali sulph., Silicea.*
MALIGNANT PUSTULES: *Silicea, Kali phos.*
MARASMUS: *Calc. phos., Natr. phos., Kali phos.*
MORPHINE HABIT: *Natr. phos.*
MORTIFICATION: *Kali phos.*
NECROSIS of bone: *Silicea.*
NODES on shin: *Calc. fluor.*
NOMA: *Kali phos.*
NUTRITION DEFECTIVE: *Calc. phos.*
ŒDEMA: *Natr. sulph.*
OFFENSIVE DISCHARGES: *Silicea, Kali phos.*
ONYCHIA: *Calc. fluor., Silicea.*
OSSEOUS growths: *Calc. fluor.*
OSTITIS: *Ferr. phos.*
OXALURIA: *Kali sulph.*
PANCREATIC DISEASES: *Calc. phos.*
PHOSPHATIC DIATHESIS: *Calc. phos.*
POLYPI: *Calc. phos.*
   soft: *Kali sulph.*
PROUD FLESH: *Kali mur., Silicea, Calc. sulph.*
PUTRID STATES: *Kali phos.*

PYÆMIA: *Natr. sulph., Kali phos.*

RACHITIS: *Silicea, Calc. phos., Kali phos.*

RANULA: *Natr. mur.*

RAYNAUD'S DISEASE: *Ferr. phos., Calc. phos., Natr. mur.*

SCALDS: *Calc. sulph., Kali mur.*

SATURNISMUS: *Natr. sulph. 2x.*

SCROFULOUS: *Natr. phos., Silicea, Calc. phos.*

SCURVY: *Kali mur., Kali phos.*

SECRETIONS, albuminous: *Calc. phos.*
    fœtid, corroding: *Calc. fluor., Silicea, Kali mur.*
    bloody, purulent: *Calc. sulph.*
    bland: *Calc. phos.*
    fibrinous: *Kali mur.*
    greenish: *Kali sulph.*
    honey-colored: *Natr. phos.*
    irritating: *Kali phos., Natr. mur., Natr. sulph.*
    lumpy: *Calc. fluor.*
    offensive: *Kali phos.*
    purulent: *Kali sulph., Calc. sulph.*
    sanious: *Calc. sulph.*
    serous: *Natr. mur.*
    septic: *Kali phos.*
    sticky: *Kali sulph.*
    yellow: *Kali sulph.*
    watery: *Natr. mur., Natr. sulph.*

SEA-SICKNESS: *Kali phos., Natr. phos.*

SEPTICÆMIA: *Kali phos.*

SEROUS swellings: *Calc. sulph.*

SPINA BIFIDA: *Calc. phos., Calc. fluor.*

SPRAINS: *Ferr. phos.*

STRUMOUS conditions: *Kali mur.*

SUPPURATIONS, chief remedy: *Natr. phos.*
    dirty, foul: *Kali phos.*
    of bone: *Calc. fluor.*
        glands: *Silicea.*
    in general: *Calc. sulph., Silicea.*
    with callous edges: *Calc. fluor.*

SYCOSIS: *Natr. sulph.*

SYPHILIS: *Kali mur.*

TELANGIECTASY: *Ferr. phos., Calc. fluor.*
TISSUES unhealthy: *Calc. sulph.*
TUBERCULOSIS: *Natr. phos., Silicea, Calc. phos.*
    swelling of glands: *Kali mur., Natr. phos.*
    hectic and night sweats: *Calc. sulph., Silicea.*
TUMORS, albus: *Silicea, Calc. phos.*
    blood: *Calc. fluor.*
    encysted: *Calc. fluor., Calc. sulph.*
    of breast: *Calc. fluor.*
ULCERATION, indolent: *Calc. fluor.*
    fistulous: *Silicea, Calc. fluor.*
    of bone: *Silicea.*
    purulent: *Silicea.*
    with proud flesh: *Silicea, Calc. sulph., Kali mur.*
VACCINATION, bad effects of: *Kali mur., Silicea.*
VARICES: *Calc. fluor., Natr. mur.*
VARICOSE VEINS in young persons: *Ferr. phos.*
WASTING DISEASES: *Kali phos., Calc. phos.*
WOUNDS SUPPURATING: *Calc. sulph.*

Modalities.

AGGRAVATION, after rest: *Kali phos.*
    washing and working in water: *Calc. sulph., Natr. sulph.*
    night: *Silicea.*
    continued exercise: *Kali phos.*
    exertion: *Kali phos.*
    motion: *Kali mur., Ferr. phos., Calc. phos.*
    noise: *Kali phos.*
    rising from sitting: *Kali phos.*
    morning: *Natr. mur., Natr. sulph.*
    evening: *Kali phos.*
    full moon: *Silicea.*
    thunderstorm: *Natr. phos.*
    from change of weather: *Calc. phos.*
    cold: *Silicea, Calc. phos., Magnes. phos.*
        weather: *Kali mur., Silicea.*
        air: *Kali phos., Magnes. phos.*
    chilling of feet: *Silicea.*
    eating fatty food: *Kali mur.*
        fish: *Natr. sulph.*

AGGRAVATION, fruit (diarrhœa): *Calc. phos.*

  rich food: *Kali mur.*

  salt plants: *Natr. sulph.*

  getting wet: *Calc. phos.*

  insect-bites: *Natr. mur.*

  lying on left side: *Natr. sulph.*

  nitrate of silver: *Natr. mur.*

  pastry: *Kali mur.*

  motion: *Ferr. phos., Kali mur.*

  continuous motion: *Kali phos.*

  quinine: *Natr. mur.*

  sea side: *Natr. mur.*

  sea bathing: *Kali mur.*

  suppressed foot-sweat: *Silicea.*

  touch: *Magnes. phos.*

  water: *Natr. sulph.*

  working and washing in water: *Calc. sulph., Natr. sulph.*

  afternoon: *Natr. mur.* (menses), *Natr. phos.*

  cold weather: *Natr. mur.*

  damp weather: *Calc. fluor., Natr. sulph.*

  evening: *Kali sulph., Natr. phos.*

  heated room: *Kali sulph.*

  morning: *Natr. mur.*

  open air: *Silicea.*

  pains and itchings, 2 to 5 P. M.: *Kali phos.*

  right side: *Magnes. phos.*

  periodical: *Natr. mur., Natr. sulph.*

  when alone: *Kali sulph., Kali phos.*

AMELIORATION, by bending double: *Magnes. phos.*

  change of weather: *Natr. sulph.*

  cold: *Ferr. phos., Calc. fluor.*

  company: *Kali phos.*

  eating: *Kali phos.*

  excitement: *Kali phos.*

  fomentations: *Calc. fluor.*

  friction: *Magnes. phos.*

  gentle motion: *Kali phos.*

  heat: *Silicea, Magnes. phos.*

AMELIORATION, by lying down: *Calc. phos.*

on something hard: *Natr. mur.*

moist warmth: *Silicea.*

pressure: *Magnes. phos.*

rubbing: *Calc. fluor.*

warmth: *Silicea, Magnes. phos.*

wrapping up head: *Silicea.*

in cold open air: *Kali sulph.*

warm, dry weather: *Natr. sulph.*

warm room: *Silicea.*

INDEX.